FRONTIERS of
BILINGUAL EDUCATION

FRONTIERS of BILINGUAL EDUCATION

Bernard Spolsky
University of New Mexico

Robert L. Cooper
The Hebrew University of Jerusalem

Editors

NEWBURY HOUSE PUBLISHERS / ROWLEY / MASSACHUSETTS

Library of Congress Cataloging in Publication Data

Main entry under title:

Frontiers of bilingual education.

    Bibliography: p.
    Education, Bilingual—United States—Addresses,
essays, lectures.   I. Spolsky, Bernard.   II. Cooper,
Robert Leon, 1931-
LC3731.F76   371.9'7   76-56747
ISBN 0-88377-066-0

Cover design by Kathe Harvey

NEWBURY HOUSE PUBLISHERS, Inc.

Language Science
Language Teaching
Language Learning

Rowley, Massachusetts 01969

Printed in the U.S.A.   First printing: May 1977
                              5   4   3

CONTRIBUTORS

I   Bernard Spolsky, The University of New Mexico
II   E. Glyn Lewis, Wales
III   Joshua A. Fishman, Yeshiva University
IV   J. Donald Bowen, University of California, Los Angeles
V   Norman Segalowitz, Concordia University
VI   Charles A. Ferguson, Catherine Houghton, and Marie H. Wells, Stanford University
VII   Vera P. John and Ellen Souberman, The University of New Mexico
VIII   Theodore Andersson, The University of Texas at Austin
IX   William F. Mackey, Laval University
X   Joan Rubin, East-West Center

ACKNOWLEDGMENTS

The original impetus for this volume and its companion, *Case Studies in Bilingual Education,* was an invitation from Professor Thomas A. Sebeok to suggest topics for inclusion in a series of books he was planning to survey current trends in the language sciences. Bilingual education seemed both current and a trend, and so we invited a number of international scholars to contribute to a collection on this topic. Most of the papers had been written and submitted when the original publishers found themselves unable to continue with the planned series. After a search, we found a publisher prepared to handle an undertaking of this size. The editors and contributors are grateful to Mr. Rupert Ingram of Newbury House Publishers for his willingness to accept the challenge.

Other thanks are due. The editors wish to express their appreciation to the contributors for the patience with which they have borne the uncertainties of delay. We would like to thank Judy Benedetti and Maia Cramer for the clerical assistance they gave during the somewhat prolonged process of preparing the volume, and also a number of University of New Mexico graduate students, among them especially John Read, for editorial advice and help.

TABLE OF CONTENTS

	Acknowledgments	vi
I	The Establishment of Language Education Policy in Multilingual Societies—*Bernard Spolsky*	1
II	Bilingualism and Bilingual Education—The Ancient World to the Renaissance—*E. Glyn Lewis*	22
III	The Sociology of Bilingual Education—*Joshua A. Fishman*	94
IV	Linguistic Perspectives on Bilingual Education—*J. Donald Bowen*	106
V	Psychological Perspectives on Bilingual Education—*Norman Segalowitz*	119
VI	Bilingual Education: An International Perspective—*Charles A. Ferguson, Catherine Houghton*, and *Marie H. Wells*	159
VII	Educational Perspectives on Bilingual Education—*Vera P. John* and *Ellen Souberman*	175
VIII	Philosophical Perspectives on Bilingual Education—*Theodore Andersson*	192
IX	The Evaluation of Bilingual Education—*William Francis Mackey*	226
X	Bilingual Education and Language Planning—*Joan Rubin*	282
	References	295

FRONTIERS of
BILINGUAL EDUCATION

The Establishment

of Language Education Policy

in Multilingual Societies

Bernard Spolsky

Bilingual education is not just another fad, a motto emanating from Washington to quiet current uneasiness about the quality of schools. Nor is it simply what its name proclaims, a label for instruction in more than one language. If you observe how enthusiastically the topic is discussed in communities ranging in complexity from Canada with its two official languages and Papua New Guinea with its 700, in size from New York to Santa Clara Pueblo, and in climate from Alaska to the low islands of the Pacific; if you have become aware of the many and varied programs that now exist in so much of the world (see Spolsky and Cooper, *Case Studies in Bilingual Education*, Newbury House, in press); and after you have read the wealth of scholarship in the field surveyed in this present volume, you will agree that bilingual education, or better, language education policy in multilingual societies, has become a central concern of modern education.

To a linguist, such a state of affairs is not too surprising, for linguists are used to the centrality of language in social concerns. Just as language is a key feature of any human society, so one might expect to find it involved in the major issues facing a society. Students of the sociology of language are making clear how closely intertwined are language and society: to separate them leads to barren analysis, and to assume unidirectional influence is equally misleading. The sociolinguistic situation of a society, in all its complexity, reflects, influences, and preserves the structure of that society. Language is the primary means of socialization, and the most sensitive image and effective guardian of the social system (see Fishman and Spolsky, in press).

Formal education systems reflect this fact in their language policies. While the varieties of language acquired by children in the home are legion, schools generally limit themselves to recognizing a limited number of classical or standard languages, or even one variety of a standard language. And the variety chosen by the school is almost inevitably the language of the politically or economically dominant group. Any child not brought up in a home where this is the normal language has the language barrier to overcome before he or she can gain access to the benefits of education (Spolsky 1971). As Bernstein has suggested, the control of the language of school permits the intellectual class whose power depends on their education and skills rather than their material wealth to make sure that their own children inherit this power (Bernstein 1971).

In his arguments, Bernstein is dealing with the subtle distinctions between styles of use of a single language. Even more obvious is the case where there are differences between school and home languages or dialects. For the Navajo child, the barrier is clear: in 1973, only 30% of the Navajo children coming to school had had any experience with English beforehand, but no more than 3% of their teachers could talk to them or their parents in Navajo (Spolsky 1973). The message is clear—*only by learning English can you expect an education*—and its clarity is emphasized by the fact that almost all college-educated Navajos (a small but rapidly increasing number) choose to speak English to their own children.

Bilingual education focuses on this barrier. It asks first, who is to be educated? Are only speakers of the standard language, plus a small elite of highly motivated others to make it through the system? Or should the schools go out of their way to provide a special program to speakers of other languages and dialects? The first wave of bilingual education is concerned with this question: its aim is to open the doors of the school to all children, to provide vernacular education as well as standard language education for all. Essentially, it is transitional and assimilatory in scope: it aims to use the vernacular or the other language or dialect only so long as the child is acquiring the standard language, and its first goal is to permit all children to have access to the benefits of education, to salvage the children of the linguistic minority (Spolsky 1974).

There is a necessary incidental effect of this kind of bilingual education: at the same time that it is providing access for children to education, it provides access for the community to school. And this incidental effect quickly becomes basic and far-reaching in its own implications. Take the Navajo example again. All the time that it is accepted that education for Navajos can be in English only, the school can remain an alien institution. Its teachers are Anglos, coming from outside the Reservation, living for a few years in school compounds and guarded by a language barrier, a high wire fence, and a way of life from the community whose children they are being paid to educate. To provide even transitional bilingual education requires Navajo speaking teachers; a thousand of them with consequent basic effects on the economic, political, and social balance of the Reservation. And it permits access by the community to the school. Once there are Navajo teachers and administrators, Navajo parents can talk to them about the education of their children. When such access is possible, when bilingual education in some shape has opened the school to the local community, and when steps have been taken to deal with the language barrier, a second and perhaps even more basic question can be faced: education for what? The issues involved in the choice of language education policy are much more than just linguistic. The question of what language to use in school can be answered only when one has decided what sort of society the child is being prepared to live in.

TRADITIONAL EMPHASIS ON LANGUAGE EDUCATION

It is no accident that language has always been a major part of any formal education, as is shown by the fact that language education constitutes two-thirds both of the medieval trivium and of the traditional three R's. In many traditions, the existence of classical texts in archaic language led to an inevitable emphasis on language education. Jewish, Hindu, and Moslem traditions all give examples of the development both of linguistic studies and of systems of elementary language teaching in order to make the classical religious text available to new generations. For more than 2000 years, Jewish elementary education has involved learning a classical language (Hebrew) and later a vernacular (Aramaic) in which the basic religious texts were written. Similarly, for Hindus the learning of Sanskrit and for Moslems the learning of classical Arabic have had equal emphasis. In the western tradition, primary education has always meant first the acquisition of literacy in a classical or standard variety of language. For the Greeks, the classical texts of Homer were already archaic; for the Romans, the ability to read Greek was a fundamental aim of education; and throughout the Middle Ages, the first goal of schooling was to acquire Latin. In Chapter 2, Lewis points out that the standard varieties of the world languages have taken over the place that Latin held in the medieval world. There is hardly a school in the modern world that does not have as its first aim that its pupils should be able to read and write a standard language.

Even in nontraditional societies, there is great respect for those who can master a status variety of the vernacular or use it effectively in accordance with traditional rhetorical rules. The man of words or orator in St. Vincent (Abrahams 1972), the talking chief in Samoa, and the Navajo story teller all share in the respect due not just to someone who can use language well but to someone who has acquired this skill through a long process of education.

THE CHOICE OF A LANGUAGE EDUCATION POLICY

The simplest situation for establishing a language education policy is in those comparatively rare cases where the language and variety spoken in the home are identical with the language and variety that schools will require. In these cases, language education is simply a matter of adding control of the written medium (and even this often takes place in the home in such cases) and sharing with the home in the gradual expansion of a child's control of the standard variety. Such middle-class monolingual education works well up to a certain point. Its major linguistic problems arise when control of some extra language is added. The great difficulties that regularly accompany attempts to teach foreign languages in schools, of course, result from such a situation. Serious as the problems may be, they do not approach the difficulties encountered when a school requires, as its first goal, that all its pupils acquire mastery of a language or variety different from the one they learned at home. For the Aramaic-speaking Jewish children of 2000 years ago, the learning of Hebrew was a first barrier to education, just as for the Yiddish-speaking children in East European 19th Century Jewish communities, both Hebrew and Aramaic were a first task. Throughout the Middle Ages, any western education had to start with the learning of Latin, just as throughout the world now most children are expected to acquire a standard variety before their education can even begin. Difficult as this task is, it is clearly exacerbated when there is more than one vernacular as when children in Belgium or Ireland or Canada come to school speaking one of two languages, or in Micronesia where they come speaking one of seven, or in the British Solomon Islands where a choice must be made among 70, or in newly independent Papua New Guinea, which faces the problem of choosing among 700.

When there are differences in the varieties that the children coming to school speak, or when the children's home variety differs from the one that society thinks they should speak, the essential dimensions of the choice of language education policy are whether to use one or more languages for instruction and which language or languages to use. For each language chosen a number of questions must be resolved: Which variety of the language should be used? For how long? For what purposes and for what subjects? By what persons and by what means?

The choice is complex enough: various attempts to set up descriptive models (e.g., Mackey 1970) show that there is no simple way to categorize educational programs as monolingual or bilingual, but rather a need to describe in detail how the various languages and varieties fit into the situation. Even more complex are the factors that influence or lead to a choice. In the following section, I will set out briefly a model for describing these factors and try to analyze how the various parts may be interrelated.

A MODEL FOR THE DESCRIPTION OF BILINGUAL EDUCATION

The model that we have developed (Spolsky, Green, and Read 1974) is an attempt to map all the relevant factors onto a single integrated structure and to suggest some of the lines of interconnection. The model is based on a hexagonal figure. Each side of the hexagon represents a set of factors that may have a bearing on, or be affected by, the operation of a bilingual program in a particular situation. The six sets of factors are labeled psychological, sociological, economic, political, religio-cultural, and linguistic. Not all of the factors will be equally (or even at all) relevant in an individual case, but since our aim has been to make the model as widely applicable as possible, the full range of factors is presented with no special concern for their relative significance. It is important to note that the various factors overlap and interact with one another in a manner that cannot be adequately represented without sacrificing the simplicity required. For this reason too, there is a certain arbitrariness about placement of the categories in relation to one another around the figure. In the center of the figure, we locate a seventh set of factors, the educational ones. This is not done to assert the primacy of these factors. In fact, one of our purposes is to show how relatively insignificant educational considerations may be, both in the decision whether or not to establish a bilingual program and in the evaluation of a program's "success" in reaching its goals. However, we are engaged in the study of an educational activity and it is appropriate to recognize this by placing education in the middle as the focus of the figure, while the other factors circumscribe and shape it on all sides.

The three dimensions of the model may be thought of as ordering each of the factors in three major levels. The first level represents the total situation of a community before a bilingual program is introduced. Community here should be understood to include any relevant socioeducational entity—a village or neighborhood, a school district, a geographically focused ethnic group, a province, a region, a whole nation. The model is intended to be broad enough to deal with the consideration of bilingual education in any of these. This level then sets out the whole range of factors that should, ideally, be taken into account in deciding on the establishment of a bilingual program. The second level includes those factors more or less under the control of the people administering a bilingual program, or those which may be directly influenced by the operation of the program. The prime factor here is a central element of the whole model, the use of two languages as media of instruction and, in particular, their distribution in the school curriculum. The first level, then, represents factors that predate and are independent of a bilingual program, whereas the second deals with factors involved in the interaction of the school with the outside world upon the introduction of bilingual education. Thus it includes the sources of the program's basic needs (funds, personnel, materials), the constraints within which the administrators have to work, the program's contribution to the community, and the potential reasons for the program's failure.

On the third level we place the perceptions that those responsible for the program might have of its outcome. The perceptions might be of effects on the individual participant or on the community at large. Included here then are the goals of those who have planned the program, whether explicit or implicit. Clearly, it is possible that different participants might have different views of the outcome: thus, the community might feel one way, the educators another. To illustrate the working of the model, and to give some view of the multiplicity of factors involved in bilingual education, in the sections that follow I will try to give examples of factors and of their relevance to specific programs.

LINGUISTIC FACTORS

In describing what is essentially language education policy, it is appropriate to consider first the linguistic factors. Various suggestions have been made for the description of a speech community, however small or large it is, and of its communicative networks (e.g., Fishman, 1971, 1972a). The data which form the base for a sociolinguistic description necessarily include a statement of the languages or significant varieties spoken, the numbers of speakers of each, the domains in which each is used, and the modes (spoken or written). The description might focus on the complete community or start with the individual child. In any case, it must distinguish between the school and the people who make it up (the administrators, the nonprofessional staff, the teachers, and the students) and the community outside the school. From this description will emerge a general configuration of languages within the community concerned.

Usually, there will need to be some distinction between standardized and local varieties or languages; often, the complete pattern will form one version or another of diglossia. The description of the sociolinguistic situation will need to focus specifically on literacy in each of the varieties of language. Going beyond this, it will describe the opportunities to hear or read each of the varieties in the public media: radio, television, newspapers, and books. The first focus in this area of linguistic description should be language use: in order to measure the situation, language testing of functional skills might be called for (cf., Cooper 1968, Spolsky et al. 1972). A second dimension of the linguistic situation will be the state of standardization and development of each of the languages (Fishman 1974).

Of the various types of languages, three are most relevant: world languages, standardized languages, and local vernaculars. A *world language*, that is, a language used over wide areas of the world, provides access to modern culture, science, technology, and economic life: in Lewis' words, it is a language associated with a civic culture. A *standard language* is accepted for full use within the political unit involved and permits expression of a wide (though not necessarily complete) range of cultural, scientific, technological, and economic notions. A *local vernacular*, or a social dialect, or a regional dialect, tends to be unstandardized and to lack vocabulary and possible styles to handle significant areas of technology in modern life. While the whole range of possibilities clearly is a continuum, there are two related but separate dimensions: the provision of access to advanced science and technology and the provision of access to literary and modern life. The description of the varieties in these terms will usually refer to the existence of dictionaries, grammars, established orthography, and provision for lexical elaboration and standardization.

In this last area, in particular, the language situation is modifiable and most often must be modified in order to meet the demands of a bilingual education program. The various processes of language planning, language standardization, and language modernization might be considered the focus of a purely sociolinguistic model of bilingual education (e.g., Paulston 1974). That is to say, where in this model we have chosen to make language choice (an aspect of curriculum) our central factor, language planning would probably be the key aspect of a sociolinguist's involvement.

A bilingual education program might be seen as having three possible outcomes that could be labeled linguistic: it might involve either language maintenance or language shift and in either case it may also call for language development (modernization and standardization). The goals of a bilingual program may be transitional bilingualism, partial bilingualism (one form of which is monoliterate bilingualism), or full bilingualism. These linguistic outcomes may be reflected in the public media, in terms of a demand for new opportunities to hear and read the language varieties being used in bilingual programs. A careful analysis of the linguistic situation will generally reveal that it is much more complex than is often assumed.

Belgium often is considered an example of simple bilingual education, and as a country where the key question is whether instruction should be in Dutch, French, or both. In fact, as is pointed out by Bustamante, Van Overbeke and Verdoodt (in press) the vast majority of children in Belgium receive education in a language of instruction other than the mother tongue. There are three distinct northern dialects generally grouped under the term Walloon, one group of German dialects in the east and, in Brussels, a hybrid language which is a mixture of French and Dutch. In the past, educational policies have ignored the existence of these dialects, concentrating only on the official standard languages. There are no reliable data on the extent of their use. But recent trends involve the recognition at least in Flanders of the dialect and some official use of it as a method of obtaining control of the target language, French.

In many parts of the world, the linguistic situation is considerably more complex. Each district in Micronesia has a different major language and one or more minority languages. The ultimate in complexity is found in the British Solomon Islands with 120,000 people who speak at least 70 different languages, or Papua New Guinea, with 2,000,000 people who speak 700. But there are many other parts of the world where children come to school speaking several different vernaculars. In other cases, like Indonesia, a language has been selected which is not the language of the majority or, like the Philippines, one of several major languages is given national status.

The kinds of linguistic goals that are possible depend, naturally, on the situation. All school systems aim at mastery of the standard language: the nature of the bilingual program depends on the attitude taken to the other language. Theoretically, the choice is limited to maintenance, shift, or revival. If a language is to be maintained, a decision must be made as to the functions for which it is to be maintained whether limited, or of equal value with the standard language. Similarly, if a language is to be revived, a decision must be made on the domains for which it will be intended. Given the choice of linguistic goals, the particular kind of language planning activity that will be needed (standardization, development of orthography, lexical elaboration, development of literacy) can be determined.

While it is obvious that linguistic factors are basic to the situation in which bilingual education takes place, and that linguistic areas require modification if a program is to be implemented, it is, I believe, much rarer for a linguistic outcome to be the basic motivation for a bilingual program. For the linguist, and for a few other language romantics, the maintenance or revival of a language is a sufficiently important value in itself. For most of those concerned, however, language serves a secondary role either as a symbol or as an instrument for one of the other factors that will be described later in this chapter.

The Navajo situation is typical of many in which the need for bilingual education arises. There have been several recent studies of Navajo language maintenance (Spolsky 1970, 1975). As a preliminary to our study of the feasibility and effect of teaching Navajo children to read in their own language first, we carried out a survey of the language use of six-year-old Navajo children entering school. In 1969 and again in 1970, we asked teachers in a hundred or more schools on or near the Navajo Reservation to rate on a simple five-point scale the language capability of their six-year-old pupils. The 1970 survey included over 3600 children, more than 80% of the six-year-old Navajo children in school that year. The survey showed that 30% of the children were judged on entering school to be monolingual in Navajo, compared to 5% monolingual in English. Another 40% were reported to be dominant in Navajo, knowing a little English but not enough to do first grade work in it; and another 20% were considered to be equally at home in either language. On this basis, one could guess that 70% of the children came from homes where Navajo was the only language used, 20% from homes where both languages were used, and 10% from homes where English is now used. The data also revealed a clear distinction between Bureau of Indian Affairs schools, where the normal situation is for a child to come from a Navajo-speaking home, and public schools where about 20% of the children seem to come from English-speaking homes and another 30% from bilingual ones. Analysis suggests that this reflects the relative accessibility of the school and the nearest town as factors in the spread of English. On the basis of these surveys, it is possible to make some general guesses about the speed of language loss. Assuming, conservatively, 1949 to be the last year when almost all Navajo children would have come to school monolingual in Navajo, we find by 1969 that 30% have some serious exposure to English before they come to school. With near universal education, the proportion knowing English will continue to increase rapidly. Given present trends, one would very soon expect to find three clear divisions among Navajos: English speakers living away from the Reservation whose children know Navajo; bilinguals in the more urbanized parts of the Reservation whose children speak English but hear Navajo from their grandparents; and a continually decreasing group of Navajo speakers in rural areas whose children will start learning English at school.

An orthography for Navajo was developed in the late 1930s and there have been various attempts at developing literacy in it. A dictionary and grammar were published in 1942, and a new edition of the dictionary is presently being compiled. There remains however comparatively slight use of written Navajo. While a vast majority of speech heard on the Reservation is Navajo, most writing is done in English. The tribal council conducts its business in Navajo, but the minutes of the meetings are written in English. The official tribal newspaper is in English, but there is a great deal of radio broadcasting in Navajo. Written Navajo then is largely restricted to some religious use (there is a complete Bible translation) and to the slowly growing number of bilingual education programs. Lexical elaboration required for modernization has probably been associated mainly with the work of interpreters and the tribal council and with the new bilingual education classrooms. With these modifications, the basic linguistic situation involves a largely unstandardized vernacular used for speech and a dominant standard language (Holm 1972 and Kruis 1975).

Even when a second language in a community is a world language, it often happens that the particular variety of it spoken is an unstandardized vernacular or dialect. It then becomes of critical importance to know whether there is a continuing availability of a standard variety. It is instructive in this regard to contrast the situation of French in Canada and of Spanish in the southwestern United States. The particular variety of French spoken by the inhabitants of Quebec easily is recognized (and often is attacked) as a local dialect. However, throughout the period of French in Canada, cultural, educational, and religious institutions have maintained the use of standard French and contact with its culture. There have been schools, colleges and universities doing all their teaching in French; there have been newspapers, theater, and a well developed intellectual life conducted in the language. It has been possible then in Quebec to consider bilingualism as teaching of two standard languages. Spanish in the southwestern United States, on the other hand, has long been kept as a home language with little access to the literary and cultural heritage of the world language. As a result, it has become what is sometimes referred to as a roofless dialect or, rather, as one where the standard variety is another language. While Spanish has continued to be widely used for internal family and communal life, English has become the language for literature and public activities even among nationalists. In this situation, a bilingual program is challenged by the need both to teach the dominant standard language and to develop access to the standard variety of the minority language.

Bilingual programs also arise in situations where the minority language is virtually extinct. Among many American Indian groups, it is now the case that no children are being brought up speaking the traditional language: there are many groups whose youngest speaker is twenty, forty, or even sixty years old. In such cases, a bilingual program will necessarily be involved not in language maintenance but in language revival. A number of the programs coordinated by the Alaska Native American Language Center under the direction of Michael Krauss are of this nature. There are very few, if any, young speakers of Haida, Tlingit, or of a number of Athabaskan languages. With support from the federal and state governments, and with great enthusiasm from a number of the people, linguists have been working at various aspects of language preservation and possible revival. In each case, this involves a linguist working with one or more elderly native speakers, organizing workshops, developing word lists and dictionaries, establishing an orthography and, training the native speaker to write his or her own language. The materials so prepared are then used in order to teach some of the younger members of the group their own language. Considering the smallness of the numbers involved, the chances of serious language revival are slight.

The call for education in Maori in New Zealand faces similar problems. While Maori, like Cherokee, was a language in which high literacy was developed in the mid-19th Century (by 1900, there had probably been more material published in New Zealand in Maori than in English) school policy in the late 19th and early 20th Centuries and a strong movement of urbanization both led to rapid language loss. There are very few if any communities left in New Zealand where children grow up speaking Maori as their primary language. However, for a number of reasons, including the recent emigration to New Zealand of a large number of Polynesians who still speak their own languages, there has been increasing interest in the revival of Maori culture and values in general and of the language in particular. It is this cultural and possibly political emphasis that provides encouragement for various attempts to teach the language to young Maoris and to other New Zealanders.

The two best known cases of language revival both arose out of strictly political nationalism. The efforts to establish Irish as a national language were associated with the movement for Irish independence. The general effect, better to be discussed when one considers political matters, appears to have been politically successful but linguistically less successful. While Irish continues to be a national symbol and while great numbers of people are expected to learn it, it is not used to the extent that its supporters originally hoped. The revival of Hebrew has been considerably more successful. It quickly became the language of cultural and political integration and has achieved significance not just in use within Israel but in Jewish communities throughout the world.

SOCIOLOGICAL FACTORS

As has been well demonstrated by recent studies in sociolinguistics, the language pattern of a community is a close reflection of its social structure. Whatever distinctions are made within a community, whether on the basis of sex, race, social class, or ethnic group, they almost always tend to be reproduced in linguistic variety. While often this marking is comparatively subtle as in the case of social or sexual dialects, it is also very common for it to be reflected by actual language differences. In considering the relevance of these factors for bilingual education, we need to look at the degree of ethnic or other social integration of a given community, the social status of the speakers of the various languages of the students and of other people associated with the school, and the basic functioning of the school within the community.

In terms of goals, the essential contrast is between a model that calls for basic and ultimate assimilation and a model that recognizes pluralism in one form or another. A number of examples will help make clear the general outline of possibilities.

In many areas, there is a degree of social elitism (often reflecting political or economic power) in the standard language. Studies of attitudes to language in Quebec made clear that not only the English-speaking minority but also the French-speaking majority attributed higher status to English than to French and higher status to continental French than to Canadian French (Lambert 1972). Given this fundamental attitudinal situation, even a bilingual program aiming at cultural integration has a long way to go. While there is by now considerable support for French immersion programs that will make English speakers bilingual, there are as yet few signs that the linguistic program is having much effect on the social situation. English-speaking children are learning French well, but they are not learning Canadian French nor do they seem to be developing the social relations with French Canadians that would be a prelude to an integrated society. In this case, bilingualism does not seem to threaten pluralism (Swain 1974).

This is not usually the case with immigrants. The bilingual programs for immigrants in the United States and Europe work essentially within an assimilatory framework, resulting usually in such a low status for the immigrant language as to discourage its use.

Of considerable importance is the degree to which a school system is an alien or integrated institution. For much of the world, schools of the present kind are something that have been introduced during a period of western colonization. In an extreme case, as on the Navajo Reservation, schools have, until recently, remained essentially alien institutions. Physically, they are differentiated from the rest of the Reservation not just by high wire fences but also by a basic difference in design and arrangement of building. Navajos traditionally prefer to live in a reasonably scattered way, each hogan a considerable distance from the next. The cluster of government houses built for teachers around the school compound stands out most clearly. The linguistic isolation has been equally marked: of all institutions on the Reservation, only the school has continued to insist on English in all its domains. Similarly, most of the staff of the schools have been Anglos coming from elsewhere to work in Reservation schools. A principal effect of developing bilingual programs in Navajo schools has been to place Navajos in various roles within the school, first as aides, but now as teachers and even administrators. Sociologically, the greatest effect of this has been the opening up of the school to the community. It now is possible for a Navajo parent to come into a school building and find someone to speak to. As a result, the school is much more open to community influence, and is seen less and less as an alien institution.

With their economic power, schools are also capable of influence on the social system. In developing societies, the school teacher is often one of a very small group of people who can expect cash wages. With this income can go the change in status. In Samoa, the traditional social system would seem to have been preserved largely by making sure that those people obtaining status in the school system as administrators are themselves chiefs with established social status in the older community. In Ponape in Micronesia, the educational administrators seem to form a new social class different from but respected by the traditional chiefs. In Ponape, a natural alliance in favor of bilingual education seems to have developed between some of these Ponapean administrators and chiefs: for the former, bilingual education is a method of asserting their superiority over the monolingual English-speaking American administrators they are replacing; for the latter, it is a way of providing access for the traditional community to what is clearly a powerful institution.

It would then be a serious mistake to underestimate the importance of sociological factors both as causes and effects of bilingual programs.

ECONOMIC FACTORS

One of the first economic factors to be considered is who is prepared to pay the costs associated with a bilingual program. Bilingual programs are expensive for a number of reasons. First, they involve training teachers to be able to work with more than one language. Second, they involve having available two sets of materials. Third, they are likely to involve extra costs in language planning and language modernization. For this reason, a bilingual program often must wait for some additional source of funds. In the United States, this source has been the Bilingual Education Act. For the last few years, the federal government has been willing to put some of its resources into the establishment of bilingual education programs. With the impact of federal initiative, there has been a slowly increasing willingness on the part of state governments to take some share in the operation. Most recently, there has been judicial action to force local authorities to use their regular resources to assume some costs of bilingual programs.

Bilingual education can be perceived as having two kinds of economic outcomes: the one long term, and the other short term. In the long term, schooling may be seen as a preparation for employment. To many parents, the learning of the standard language is seen as the principal method of obtaining access to good jobs. Navajo parents want their children to know English because they see that people who speak English have much better jobs than those who don't. Similarly, immigrants and other socially underprivileged minority groups put a great deal of emphasis on school as a method of upward social and economical mobility. Among these groups, there may well be suspicion of bilingual education all the time that it seems to suggest less emphasis on teaching the standard language and more on preserving the native language, for they fear that the kind of social pluralism involved will also be marked by economic discrimination.

There are, however, immediate economic effects that are of considerable importance in many cases. As I mentioned above, the school is often one of the principal employers in an underdeveloped community. Bilingual education provides jobs for members of their community for it insists on using native speakers rather than bringing teachers from elsewhere. The first programs established under the Bilingual Education Act placed emphasis on training classroom aides. When there was talk of the possibility of career training for these aides, all the time that it was clear they were not a threat to established certified teachers, there was little problem. However, in recent developments, emphasis has moved toward training certified bilingual teachers. The potential impact of this in such a case as the Navajo Reservation is very great (Read et al., 1976). There are over 50,000 Navajo children in school, served by about 3000 teachers. In 1969, no more than 100 of these teachers were Navajos. Any kind of bilingual education program, even a transitional program in the first three grades, would call for the training of a good number of Navajo teachers. The Navajo Division of Education took as its goal the training within five or ten years of 1000 Navajo teachers. The economic effect is clear. Generally, the standard of living of Navajos on the Reservation is below the poverty level. In order to obtain salaried employment, a Navajo usually had to be prepared either to leave the Reservation or to take a job in a develping semi-urban settlement, such as Window Rock or Shiprock. The call for bilingual programs and bilingual teachers in schools throughout the Reservation has opened up 1000 potential jobs for Navajos close to home. The economic effect of this change will be very great: beyond the economic effect, there will be the development of a significant new middle class spread throughout the Reservation.

Sensitivity to this kind of issue has been displayed in the approach taken by the New York City Teachers Union. The Union has accepted the need for bilingual education, but has called for teaching Spanish to present certified teachers rather than training and certifying Spanish-speaking members of the local community. Similar reactions are reported in Toronto.

POLITICAL FACTORS

In looking at the political factors involved in bilingual education, one may choose to focus on one of a number of levels. The focus may be international, national, regional, local, or ethnic, depending on the political or linguistic make-up of the community involved. As an example of international focus, one may point out the considerable interest in foreign language teaching and in various forms of elite bilingualism taken within the European economic community. The most common political focus is national: here, the integrational effect of a national language in contrast to the potential disintegration in support for regionalism and regional languages is a common consideration (Fishman 1972). The move for community schools has led to even more local political concerns in bilingual education. Finally, one of the effects of the new ethnicity has been the call for some degree of ethnic education even where an ethnic group is not regionally based.

Two of the four stages of bilingual education proposed by Lewis (1975) are particularly concerned with varying political roles. While the first stage is instrumental and the third individualistic, both the second and fourth are based on an attitude to national goals. The second, according to Lewis, is the phase of cultural assimilation: the stage at which the principal aim is the creation of one nation. The fourth stage reverses this in some ways for it is essentially the phase of pluralism. One of its principal goals is to establish not just individual equality but equality of all groups.

The tension between centralized and local control and between pluralism and diversity has been well illustrated by Lewis (1975) in his study of Soviet policy on multilingualism and bilingual education. There have been pressures in the two directions: a steady pressure for the establishment of Russian as the first language for all of the Soviet Union and, at the same time, pressure for recognition to various extents of various accepted national languages. Similar tension between a national and several regional languages has created many of the difficulties of education in India.

The importance of language as an instrument of national integration has been perceived by many 19th- and 20th-Century movements for national independence. Fishman (1972) has pointed out the way in which the vernacular languages came to serve both as the medium and as part of the message of nationalism. The vernacular was used to communicate with the illiterate masses and also became one of the central symbols of the nationalist movement serving as a link with the great tradition of the past and as a method of distinguishing the national group from others. The slogan that "language equals nationality and nationality equals language" became central to great numbers of movements for national independence and liberation. In many cases, the choice of a national language has been difficult and involved in new nations in considerable difficulty and expense. But the symbolic value for Israel of Hebrew, for Indonesia of its national tongue, for African states of Swahili, is of sufficient worth for political leaders to take on this additional cost. There is very real conflict between the political needs for a national language of integration with the economic need for using a well established and highly standardized language; the latter language, however, often is likely to be associated with the colonial power and so with values that the new nation is attempting to alter.

The difficulties of language planning in a new nation can be well illustrated with the case of Papua New Guinea. The two million people of Papua New Guinea, are said to speak 700 distinct languages. None of these languages has wide enough currency to make it a reasonable choice for a national language. Two creolised languages are widely spoken: Pidgin and Police Motu. The new nation is faced with a choice between English (which very few people speak and which is, of course, not a suitable symbol of national integration) and the two creoles. At the same time, it will be necessary to give schooling in as many as possible of the vernaculars (Bulu 1975).

Bilingual education can be used as a method of establishing political power. The example of Navajo illustrates this. The move for Navajo independence works in a number of domains but one of the most successful so far has been education. It is not coincidental that each of the independent community-controlled Navajo schools has placed a good deal of emphasis on bilingual education. Nor is it coincidental that the Navajo Education Association and now the Navajo Division of Education have argued for Navajo control of the educational system as being a goal closely associated with the establishment of bilingual education. As I mentioned earlier, bilingual programs can offer a community access to its own schools and, in appropriate circumstances, control of those schools.

The situation at Ramah, New Mexico, follows these lines exactly. The move toward a community-contracted school started in 1970 when the McKinley County system proposed to close the high school at Ramah. The Ramah Navajo School Board was responsible first for conducting the high school: this past year, it has taken over the elementary school and the control of the Bureau of Indian Affairs (BIA) dormitories. At the same time, it has taken control of a good number of other functions previously carried out by the BIA agency. It is now active in social services and economic development, conducts a radio station, and rapidly is becoming a corporation with political and economic control of most public community functions. In these activities, some degree of conflict is already developing with the Navajo Tribe and its Division of Education. A school like Ramah, where local parents already have political power, is, naturally, far from enthusiastic about the development of a strong centrally controlled educational system, even if that central control should be Navajo rather than non-Navajo. By now, it would be an exaggeration to claim that bilingual education is the focus of the move for community power at Ramah, but it is clearly seen as an integral part of the process.

PSYCHOLOGICAL FACTORS

The psychological factors relevant to or affected by establishment of a bilingual program fall into two principal groupings: those concerned with the students' learning process (the educational psychological factors) and those concerned with attitudinal factors (social psychological factors).

A good deal of the work in the psychology of bilingualism has been concerned with the effect of bilingualism on the individual. Lewis (1975) suggests that this focus follows because the studies were made in the United States in particular during what Lewis calls the third phase of bilingual education: the period during which emphasis was on individual effects and on the fullest development of the individual. Much research was carried out to determine whether there were psychological advantages or disadvantages to being bilingual or educated bilingually. Elsewhere in this volume, Norman Segalowitz reaches two important conclusions:

> Studies of the effect of bilingualism on measures of intelligence do not indicate any deficits when factors such as social class, educational background language proficiency, etc., are carefully controlled.

Failure to keep these other variables distinct has led to much of the controversy and the existence of studies that make contradictory claims about the intelligence of bilinguals. Similar failure to take into account sociological factors may be at the base of questions raised about the relationship of bilingualism to affective factors. Segalowitz concludes:

> Research on the effects of bilingualism on personality and social development suggests that maladjustments observed to accompany bilingualism usually originate in the social environment rather than from bilingualism as such. Language is often perceived by the community as an important symbol of identity and in this regard the bilingual may feel it difficult to identify with two groups at the same time (the groups in question may make it difficult for him to do so). There is also some evidence to suggest that intensive learning of another language may lead to feelings of normlessness or alienation with the bilingual feeling dissatisfied with his social environment. However, it is not known how long these feelings last and in any event they are more likely due to the bicultural aspects of his experience than to the fact of knowing two languages.

This brings us to the attitudinal questions. Essentially, there is a wide range of differences possible in a society with two or more languages. A bilingual program can arise from or affect attitudes of the dominant society, of the local community, of the parents, or of the students to themselves and other groups, to varieties of language and their speakers, to education as a whole, and to bilingual education itself. Studies by Lambert and others in Montreal showed why it was that for so long speakers of French were ready to acquire English while speakers of English were reluctant to acquire French. Each group, some of Lambert's earlier studies showed, accepted the higher status of speakers of English and the greater benefits from speaking it. Without necessarily changing these basic attitudes, the political reality in Quebec has managed to overcome these attitudinal factors to some extent so that now the vast majority of English-speaking children are being exposed to some version of a French immersion program. There is not yet clear evidence that these bilingual programs are leading to changes in the attitude of English speakers nor have there yet been reports of fundamental changes in the status of the French language.

When a minority language has been associated for a long time with the lowered status of a minority group it takes some major change for social attitudes toward it to change. Particularly if the minority language does not have a major public culture associated with a world literature or a major educational system, it takes quite some time for the school and the community to accord the same status in educational affairs to the minority language as to the majority one. The very arguments presented for the minority language (that it is related to folk culture, that it reflects the warmth of the home) are ones that prepare it for a second class status in an institution like school where the formal values (written literature, the modern technological world) have first place.

In essence, perhaps the major attitudinal claim put forward for bilingual education is that it encourages the pupils' self-respect to discover that their home language, in which they have invested so many years and with which they have such warm associations, is respected or at least not maligned by the school system. There are frequent claims—though I am not sure of evidence—that the improved attitudinal relationship can lead to better educational achievement; at least, it is clear that it will lead to a much more pleasant situation with fuller respect for each individual and group making up the school and the community.

CULTURAL FACTORS

Attention has been drawn to the importance of cultural factors by the use of such terms as *bilingual bicultural* and *bilingual multicultural* education. These terms make clear that (1) it is not enough to teach in two languages unless the school also recognizes the cultures associated with each language, and (2) it is possible to teach in only one language and still recognize the existence of two or more cultural groups in the community. Both of these arguments, I suspect, have more to do with political or educational reality than with the issue of culture itself. The former argument is put forth most strongly by people who are not satisfied with bilingual programs that have formal teaching of the minority language by non-locals. That they are fluent in a world variety of the local minority language is not enough: not being members of the community, they are unable to deal adequately with the local culture. This might be seen then as simply another argument for ethnic or community control of the school. The other argument—that of biculturalism without bilingualism—may arise in cases where few if any of the members of the ethnic or community group qualified to teach in the schools are still fluent speakers of the minority language. One approach to such a situation is, of course, the kind of language revival program I have referred to earlier: a second is a bicultural program taught by relatively assimilated members of the minority group but in the majority language. This is not the place to go into the complexities of cultural questions to be faced within the curriculum. However, it must be pointed out that teaching about the local minority culture whether in the majority or the minority language is not the same as finding a way to integrate minority and majority cultures.

RELIGIOUS FACTORS

I have already referred to the fact that formal education in a religious context often involves teaching a classical language in order to provide access to a sacred text. Religions, like other social institutions, very often are associated with specific language. The dissociation of a classical sacred language from religion is considered a major step. Only recently has the Roman Catholic Church taken the step of accepting vernaculars for the Mass: future historians will be able to judge the effect of this. One innovation of 19th-Century Reform Judaism in Germany was to switch from Hebrew to the vernacular. The principle was retained in Reform Judaism in the United States but in the last 20 years or so, since the creation of the State of Israel, there has been a marked increase in the use of Hebrew even within the Reform movement. Thus, Jewish religious education for all groups has come to mean a variety of bilingual education, that is to say, some degree of instruction in the Hebrew language, so that Hebrew School is a normal term for a Jewish religious school whether Reform, Conservative, or Orthodox.

While there are cases where religious pressure is exerted to favor some variety of bilingual education, the converse can also be true. A group may consider it quite inappropriate to bring a sacred language and sacred culture into the profane and alien environment of the school. The paradox is highlighted most clearly in the Indian pueblos. In some pueblos, very few children are still learning the native language at home. In some of these then the community—including the more conservative members—is not unwilling to have the school teach the native language so that the children might be better equipped to take part in major religious ceremonies. In other communities, where there has been stronger language maintenance, there remains opposition to the use of the native language in school lest this give the school and the strangers it employs and represents access to the religious secrets of the community.

EDUCATIONAL FACTORS AND CONSTRAINTS

Just as I have argued that it is a serious mistake to leave out of account factors concerning bilingual education that are not formally considered strictly educational, so it would be equally wrong to minimize the importance of factors that are directly concerned with the school. Here, I do not wish to go into the full details of the complexity of the implementation of a bilingual education program or of the evidence about its various effects on the school and on the pupils. Rather, I would like to sketch and illustrate three major factors: those concerning students, those concerning teachers, and those concerning curriculum. Within the model that I have outlined above, we could look at each of these as situation, operation, or aim. However, it quickly becomes apparent that we do not need to consider in equal detail the nine cells of a possible matrix but rather to concentrate our attention at this stage on situational constraints that need to be overcome in the case of teachers and curriculum and of educational aim in the case of students.

Let me take curriculum first. The development of suitable curriculum material for a bilingual program usually poses a serious problem. The only simplifying circumstance is likely to be when the two languages involved are both standard languages and it is then possible to build a curriculum around two sets of materials each developed in a different country. But even this turns out to be a much more complex issue. When it was decided to develop bilingual Spanish/ English programs in the United States, one obvious strategy in the curricular area was to obtain materials from Latin America for use in the bilingual classrooms. Numbers of problems emerged. First, the materials available did not always seem as sophisticated as the English materials that had been developed. Second, and perhaps more seriously, there remained basic linguistic and cultural differences between curriculum materials developed for Latin America and those suitable for the various Spanish-speaking groups in the United States. Anyone who has heard New Mexico state legislators denouncing the use of curricular materials developed in Miami will be sensitive to the stronger feeling of opposition to foreign materials. One key force behind support of bilingual education is a kind of regional or local or ethnic patriotism: materials from another area or another country can often be seen as in conflict with this principle. Even greater problems are faced in the development of curricular materials for a nonstandardized language for, as has been mentioned earlier, a great deal of work in terms of language planning, standardization, and modernization is called for when it is decided to develop a vernacular language to be used in school. Often, arguments of expense and impracticality rather than arguments of theory or desirability make it inevitable to choose a transitional bilingual model rather than to aim at biliterate bilingual education.

The need for teachers able to work bilingually, or in what Fishman (1976) refers to as the marked language, is a similar constraint of considerable importance in making bilingual programs feasible. In few situations can one have the luxury that Mackey (1972) has described for the bilingual program in Berlin where all teachers can be assumed to be fluent and literate in both German and English. The establishment of bilingual education almost always entails a major effort in training teachers in one language or the other. One common process is to look overseas for teachers: the bilingual French immersion program for English speakers in Quebec has made extensive use of French-speaking teachers from France, from French North Africa and from the French Caribbean. Here, the religious division of school systems slowed down the hiring of French-speaking Catholics for the English Protestant schools. In the United States, the development of Spanish/English bilingual programs has been hampered by the absence of Spanish speakers with good enough training and high enough literacy to be acceptable in the schools: for this reason, the emphasis of the bilingual education program has moved to teacher training.

The potential of teachers for bilingual education is influenced in some measure by the level at which teacher-training is carried out. In the United States, the decision to require a university degree of all elementary school teachers allows very few members of the disadvantaged linguistic minorities to qualify as teachers. Those few who have managed to make it through the system usually have done so only at the cost of giving up their linguistic and ethnic identification. Such teachers often turn out to be strongly opposed to bilingual education. Emphasis now is moving to teacher-training programs that do not break cultural ties and social attitudes.

In other parts of the world, while teacher training is at a lower academic level (post primary or even earlier), it is still often the case that the teachers have been prepared to teach only in the standard language and lack the willingness or skills to use their mother tongue in other than informal settings. An excellent example of this is Micronesia. In principle, all education has been in English for some time now; all textbooks and all curricular materials assume this. The teachers, however, are probably not themselves sufficiently fluent in English to use the materials with ease and their pupils certainly do not know enough English to understand the textbooks. Thus one of the several vernaculars is used informally. However, there is little official recognition or support for this actual realistic compromise.

The programs for training Navajo teachers reflect similar difficulties. In the past the handful of Navajos who qualified as teachers in general were firmly convinced of the need to teach only in English. The recent programs supported by Title VII funds or by the Navajo Division of Education all have assumed bilingual education as a goal: however, in practice, while the emphasis has been on training Navajo teachers, very few of the newly qualified teachers are yet committed to or experienced in bilingual teaching. The implementation of a bilingual program is a long and difficult process.

Of all arguments presented in favor of bilingual education, the most common one is that it benefits the student. As we have seen, it is probable that there are much stronger reasons in support of the program. One suspects that the debate over the effect on students is not quite as serious as one would hope. Certainly it is true that it is difficult to find good data bearing on the question of the effect of a bilingual program on pupils' educational achievement. It is easy to make a good case for the need of a bilingual program when students come to school speaking a language other than the school language. It must be obvious to all that incomprehensible education is immoral: there can be no justification for assuming that children will pick up the school language on their own, and no justification for not developing some program that will make it possible for children to learn the standard language and for them to continue to be educated all the time that this is going on. Similarly, very clear arguments can be made for the value of teaching children to read in the language that they speak rather than attempting to teach a new language and initial reading at the same time. As Patricia Engle (1975) has made clear, however, it is harder to produce empirical data in support of these claims than it is to make them. Two current studies deserve mention, however. The recent immersion programs in Canada have shown that in appropriate conditions it is possible to develop bilingual programs without evident cognitive disadvantages to the students who become bilingual rather than monolingual. Second, cautious studies at Rock Point Community School have shown clear and significant gains in English reading ability for Navajo students whose initial reading work was in Navajo. As more evidence accumulates, it is hoped that more clarification of this most vital factor will be obtained.

CONCLUSION

In this paper, I have been able to do little more than sketch the complexity of education of children in multilingual societies. It has become clear, I hope, that the language education policy adopted depends on and has ramifications for a multitude of factors beyond those normally considered in looking at the school. Any planning or evaluation that fails to take into account this full complexity will miss some important effects that bear on a program decision. Not all factors are of equal importance in any particular situation but the full matrix assures that factors of potential importance are not overlooked.

II

Bilingualism and Bilingual Education—

The Ancient World to the Renaissance

E. Glyn Lewis

Note. This study was completed with the help of a research grant by the Ford Foundation whose generosity is gratefully acknowledged.

INTRODUCTION

The Significance of Bilingualism

Polyglottism is a very early characteristic of human societies, and monolingualism a limitation induced by some forms of social change, cultural and ethnocentric developments. It is doubtful whether any community or any language has existed in isolation from other communities and languages. In Europe and elsewhere and at all times there have been bilingual groups and this is reflected in the regard with which the possession of more than one language has been held in even remote countries and undeveloped educational systems. For instance, a Norwegian Speculum Regale of the Middle Ages claimed that mastery of many languages, especially Latin and French, was necessary to an educated man (Sommerfelt 1954: 25). In New Guinea and in vast areas of South America and Africa languages, though they are restricted to individual villages or groups of villages, are held to be mutually intelligible over varying distances—one-day languages or one-week languages (Hockett 1958: 326). Many tribes like those of the North

American Indians were so small that voluntary or obligatory exogamy was encouraged or made obligatory to ensure survival. The complexity of the linguistic patterns which resulted must have been formidable. Nor was the condition of Europe in earlier times different from what we may observe today in many parts of the world. Indo-European was not a single homogeneous language but a congeries, a reticulation of several dialects and languages. Furthermore, the speakers of those languages conquered and settled lands in the Middle East for instance, where non-European languages in equal diversity were spoken (Atkinson 1952: 8).

Contact between languages and consequent changes in personal and group attachment to particular languages result in a proportion of the population becoming bilingual, invariably for so long as it takes to complete the shift of attachment, and usually longer. It is not only those parts of the population actually in contact which become bilingual: at all stages the need to become bilingual is brought home to those who are far from the point of contact but have need for social intercourse with those who have become bilingual (Meillet 1951: vol. II, 77): there is a form of linguistic "Brownian" process. The specifically linguistic consequences, especially the problems of *substratum*, "though vexed questions which it is now the fashion to minimize" (Tovar 1954: 221) have not been ignored to the extent that the social and historical contexts of language contact have been.[1] Yet, because of the frequency of such contacts in the past as well as the current fluid social and linguistic state of many communities which are products of the history of those contacts, a study of that history and of the attempts of those interested in education in its efforts to cope with the consequences of bilingualism needs to be encouraged.

One possible consequence is reflected in the claims that languages influence the speaker's habits of thought—

> The fact that we and the French share to a peculiar degree a common linguistic tradition has inevitably created similarities of mental processes, of methods of thought and presentation of ideas that link us together in close spiritual affinity. (Orr 1953: 42)

On the bold assumption that the major premise of this assertion is correct the argument has important implications for childhood education. Others, while agreeing that language tends to govern mental processes, allege an adverse effect, "an absence of mental precision." Because of bilingualism in Medieval Europe, it is argued, "people were forced into perpetual approximations in expressing their thoughts . . . forced as they were into an incessant movement to and fro between the two planes of languages." (Bloch 1961: 78). It is difficult to conceive how such an allegation can be validated or what criteria should be employed in any attempt to do so. Bilingualism has rarely been absent from important levels of the intellectual and cultural life of Europe and nearly all European languages have had long and, in some instances, several successive periods of language contact.

Bilingualism has been and still is nearer to the normal situation than most people are willing to believe. Imprecision of thought and expression, if it is a consequence of bilingualism in Bloch's argument, is therefore a normal not a pathological condition. These generalizations, and many like them are commonplace but the authority behind them makes it necessary for us to understand the historical roots of bilingualism if a realistic policy for bilingual education is to gain approval.

The study is made even more imperative by some of the characteristics of the present age. On the whole, the apotheosis of language loyalty during the last two centuries has not been uniformly advantageous. Language is peculiarly endowed to enable communities to assert the separateness as much as the identity of their interests. Of the various ties that bind mankind a common language can claim no privileged status: other bonds protect the language rather than language them. Those who press the national inviolability of a language usually are an elite or intelligentsia for whom "national languages constitute a huge system of vested interest which sullenly resists critical enquiry" (Sapir 1949: 118), and it is easy to underestimate the power of such mental insularity. Sapir could hazard the guess that "revivalist movements" and the investment of great emotional and intellectual capital in the effort to save languages from the consequences of contact "would come to be looked upon as little more than eddies in the more powerful stream ... which set in at the end of the medieval period" (Sapir 1949: 88). But these eddies are still strong and possibly hazardous: a transient phenomenon, it may still turn out to be but hardly an insignificant one.

Linguistic Pluralism or Exclusiveness?

Though it has profound social and educational importance, the identification of language with national or group self-interest is, if not peculiar to the modern era, far more characteristic of it than it was of an earlier age. Little is more alien to ancient and early medieval traditions than such views as were attributed by Daudet to the schoolmaster in his "La Dernière Classe," prompted by the substitution of German for French in Alsace Lorraine: "We must keep it alive amongst ourselves and never forget it: because when a people is imprisoned, as long as it looks after its language it is as if it holds the key to its cell."

Such views have their origin to some extent in the growth of nationalism at the time of the Renaissance, as Sapir implied. Ronsard was among the first to speak of the "treachery" of abandoning "le langage de son pays ... c'est un crime de leze majesté." Du Bellay argues that "la meme loy naturelle qui commande a chacun defendre de lien de sa naissance nous oblige aussi de garder la dignité de notre langue." This novel consciousness of the close ethnic and national associations of a language were reinforced in the Age of Enlightenment as well as by "Romantic particularism" conjoint with the idealization of the "folk" exemplified in the writings of Von Humboldt (1903-1936: vol. VII, 42), for whom the essence of ethnic identification is the associated language:

> The spiritual characteristics and the linguistic structure of a people stand in a relationship of such indissoluble fusion that given one we should be able to derive the other from it entirely.

It is but a short step to the identification of language with political nationalism such as we find in the Irish 19th-Century writer Thomas Davis; "a people without a language of its own is only half a nation" (Davis 1914: 173). The Romantic (Idealist) aspects of philosophy, linguistic nationalism and the development of modern philology are not only linked historically but draw their strength from the same epistemological sources.

Elitist nationalism and exclusive attitudes to languages, derived from the views of Romantic philosophers about the uniqueness of ethnic groups were necessary but not sufficient preconditions of the present identification of national self-interest and language, an identification which justifies bilingual education in the eyes of many. They needed to be reinforced by those factors which put a premium on the growth of interest in the vernacular, namely the rise of a powerful and self-conscious middle class, the invention of printing which made the vernacular a viable literary language, the rapid growth of industrialism which required a proletariat which was literate (necessarily in the vernacular to begin with) and an advanced process of social integration which fed on national self-consciousness as a means of ensuring acquiescence in the discomfort of social change. This combination of circumstances may have made linguistic nationalism inevitable, but inevitable or not it certainly resulted in a profound change in mental attitudes which have had vital implications for education. It is not unfair to say that the *refusal* to accept a pluralistic philosophy toward language in society is a reflection of a general philosophy of education in most of those countries where the consideration is relevant. What is more disturbing, such a unitary linguistic philosophy is taken as the most natural state of affairs and to be axiomatic by many educationists. Suppression of a language is assumed to be a necessary condition of the political integrity of the state. No doubt the first obligation of the state is to itself, and because of that it will seek to maintain untrammeled the paths of communication. However, its survival is simply the means to ensure the well-being of its constituents. Its "esse" is only the precondition of the "bene esse" of the groups of which it is composed: its integrity is justified solely by its capacity to accommodate diversity. Nor is it self-evident that an authoritarian, uniformist language policy does safeguard the integrity of a linguistically diverse state.

It would be patently absurd to argue that peoples and nations had never, until now, regarded their languages with pride and affection. But it was not until well after the Enlightenment that a sense of group identity was tied to the maintenance of its language, or that attitude to language became an ideology, thus ensuring that attitude to language not only reflected certain beliefs about that language but was transformed into a powerful tool of social action which often was only distantly associated with language. As late as the end of the Middle Ages, writers would abandon their native language temporarily in favor of another with higher claims to cultural or aesthetic preeminence. Many Italian poets used Provençal and a great Provençal poet in Dante's *Commedia* is revealed as singing in Italian. Dante's master, Brunetto Latini, wrote his great work in French. The Troubadour Raimbaut of Vacqueiras (*ca.* 1200) composed a five-stanza sonnet in Provençal, Italian, Northern French, Gascon and Portuguese in turn. In Spain, too, such alternation of language was practiced by Lope and Gongora in their sonnets (Curtius 1952: 32). Roman Vidal chose to write lyric poetry in French because it was the convention that the choice of language was determined by *genre* rather than the nationality of the author.

In the Classical world, group differences and especially those relating to cultural activities were not thought to require different languages for their expression. In the older Empires problems affecting choice of language were determined empirically and pragmatically rather than on grounds of fixed principle. The Greek language was claimed by barbarians, semi-barbarians and civilized alike. The Greek-speaking population on the Struma and Isker rivers were not brought into the Hellenistic political system until the advent of Claudius. Conversely, there were thoroughly hellenized peoples whose languages were Carian or Lycian, Lydian or Messapic. Claudian in the days of Honorius could write, "We who drink of the Rhone and the Orontes are all one nation," and language was never the criterion of membership. Convenience might indicate the desirability of using a particular language for the administration of large territories; but beyond convenience there were few, if any, other considerations that might induce the suppression of a local or the promotion of an intrusive language. While Latin became the acknowledged medium for the transmission of Greek culture in the West, the Romans refrained from dislodging the Greek language in any country where it was either the native tongue or a lingua franca. This was true of areas like Sicily and the Northwest coast of Africa, which were nearer to Rome than to Athens. Africa remained a Greek-speaking country through the 7th Century A.D. and in accordance with strict Roman practice the Edicts of Cyrene, even under Roman rule, were written in Greek.

Between the phase of Classical indifference (shared by even earlier civilizations) leading to tolerance of diversity, and our own hypersensitivity to diversity associated nevertheless with intolerance, there was an age, also tending to intolerance but in that instance arising from linguistic universalism rather than diversity. The extent to which Latin was a universal language is a matter of controversy, but it cannot be doubted that compared with the diversity and adherence to "pluralism" in the Classical world, the Middle Ages not only tended toward but pressed for uniformity in theory and practice. Compared with the encouragement which the Byzantines and the Eastern Church gave to the vernaculars, the Western Empire and its Church were singularly restrictive. It is true that within Greece itself the Byzantine policy was to hellenize the Slavs, but outside Greece they not only tolerated but did what they could to promote the vernaculars. Not till the 11th Century did the Roman policy of centralization succeed in uprooting that tradition of tolerance. The Slavophil policy pursued by the eastern imperial regime "contrasted with the uniform imposition of Latin upon Western Christendom in the Middle Ages" (Obolensky 1971: 147-151). Even as late as the Carolingian Empire educational and cultural enactments in the West were intended to ensure total subjection to an authoritarian policy (Heer 1953: 40). Latin, the sacred language, was the sole safeguard of man's store of culture, science and faith. In the whole period down to the 12th Century, though what it was associated with was a beleaguered culture which found its refuge in monasteries and elitist and aristocratic schools, Latin was virtually the only vehicle of communication on an intellectual level. The world of Western Europe, unlike that of pre-Classical and Classical times, or of the later Byzantine Empire, was "a closed world of grand forms," the frontiers of which were defined by the currency of Latin. Our own era prefers "closed national worlds of limited forms."

Once a policy favoring uniformity is articulated and a highly cogent rationale for it argued at the highest levels, any divergence from it, to be effective, also needs to be formalized and made explicit so that attitudes to language become polarized. Once the political will and the economic power to maintain a universal regime (linguistic, ecclesiastical or political) were enervated, as at the end of the Middle Ages, what was proposed as a substitute had also to be rationalized and presented as an alternative ideology. However, just as there were undercurrents of conflict in Classical and Medieval times so today the grounds for linguistic exclusiveness are being eroded. The accelerating diffusion of a language tends to "denationalize" it. English, Spanish, and Russian (at least in the vast complex of the U.S.S.R.) have tended to loosen their historical associations with their native and traditional cultures. They and others have come to be adopted by other nations, with their own important traditions and languages, not for the historical and national associations of those languages but as vehicular languages of wider communication. For instance, at the inauguration of a new medical school in 1838 the Ottoman ruler reminded the students:

> You will study scientific medicine in French. . . My purpose in having you taught French is not to educate you as French men; it is to teach you scientific medicine and little by little to take that into our language. (Lewis, B. 1961: 83).

Any system of education has to attend to this ambivalence if the tension which so frequently characterizes the discussion and formulation of policies for bilingual education is to be avoided or resolved. Thus, attitude to English in Wales is distorted by failure among many of the Welsh intelligentsia to acknowledge that English need not in all situations be regarded as a "national" language. They might then cease to associate it so ineradicably with English national dominance.

LANGUAGE CONTACT AND LINGUISTIC UNIFICATION

The Mediterranean as an Area of Contact

The historical study of contact cannot in theory, or very well in practice, be limited to any one area, however extensive, of the world. Nevertheless some areas and the languages native to them represent an identifiable and close-knit web of contacts which are very well recorded. In some cases, too, these contacts have placed an indelible imprint on the world far beyond the geographical location of speakers of those languages.

Prior to the Christian era there had been three periods of linguistic unification and of consequent widespread, though not necessarily "mass" or "popular" bilingualism. Moreover, each period necessitated bilingual education for some of those minorities who were required to operate the machinery of political and administrative unification. The three periods correspond to the ascendancy of Akkadian (the Babylonian language), Aramaic, and Greek. The successive moves toward unification and the pattern of language contact and consequent bilingualism occurred in areas of considerable linguistic diversity. In Asia Minor there existed a substratum of ancient languages such as Lydian and Lycian over which flowed a series of linguistic influences from the South represented by the Semitic languages, and from which emerged Babylonian, Hebrew, and Aramaic. From the North and Northeast came the Indo-European languages—Hittite, Phrygian, Thracian, and Armenian. During the Christian era we can recognize the continuing influence of some of the earlier languages of unification, especially Greek, as well as newcomers to the category, for instance Latin and Arabic. In all these phases of unification, early and late, bilingual schools were an important formative factor though they involved only a minority of those who were bilingual in varying degrees. Upon the East Mediterranean during successive historical periods a large number of different linguistic influences converged, which interacted to produce a variety of contact situations and types of bilingualism.

In fact, the history of the Mediterranean constitutes a key to study of bilingualism and bilingual education not only in Europe (Western, Central and Eastern), Asia Minor, Russia (and, by association with Russia and Iran, parts of Central Asia) but also in large areas of the New World—Latin America and the United States and Canada as well. The cohesion produced by these contacts had more wide ranging influences.

> These same waters remained through many centuries the axis of the Roman world. A senator from Aquitania could make his career on the shores of the Bosporous, he could own vast estates in Macedonia. The great fluctuations of forces that shook the Roman economy were felt from the Euphrates to Gaul. . . . On the other hand anyone crossing the Rhone found himself in a strange and hostile land, the vast territory of the Barbarians. (Bloch 1961: XIX)

Whether the direction of linguistic movement and influence is from the Northeast with Celtic, from the East with Greek, from the South with Latin, or the West with Latin influence on the Slavs, all forces appear to converge upon or radiate from the Mediterranean: it is "the sum of the individual voices of Europe."[2] And these multifarious voices are heard not only in the total context of Europe, but in many small localities. Because of the convergence of linguistic influences down the centuries there is hardly a bay that is not a unique, complex linguistic community. To that complexity contributed not only the languages of the Mediterranean peoples but those of the Portuguese, Normans, Bretons, Dutch, Flemings, and English who were drawn to it. This fact suggests an important conclusion about the bilingualism of the Mediterranean: it was of two kinds or, rather, it existed on two levels. First there is the bilingualism which results from "maritime contact"—a series of contacts with considerable influence but tending to lack continuity. Such contacts are brought about quickly but are impermanent: for instance, Western penetration by the Greeks, the establishment of Phoenician centers, the later extension of Venetian influences to the East, and in the Aegean Archipelago the confluence of the Byzantines, Venetians, and Genovese. The story of the Corsican and Sardinian complex is that of a succession of Etruscan, Greek, and Carthaginian contacts, and Sicily exemplifies the same interrelationship of Greek, Arabic, Norman, Angevin, and Spanish languages. Maritime contact produced a "conjuncture" of languages and this was due to the fact that while the sea promoted such contacts, the Mediterranean lands are isolated by high mountain ranges, obstacles to be overcome before language contact could be consolidated and perpetuated.

The second level of bilingualism in the Mediterranean is "territorial," reflecting the gradual appropriation of a firm and expanding base. It is slow to develop but permanent in its historical influence—it creates a "structure" rather than a conjuncture of linguistic contacts. Whereas the maritime contacts tended to be motivated by trade and commerce and for that reason produced a *reciprocal* bilingualism where both groups had to learn of each other, *territorial bilingualism* resulting from conquest, partial displacement of native populations or migration tended toward assimilation and the creation of *unilateral transitional* bilingualism which hardly affected the newcomers. Celtic and Germanic territorial penetration to the West, Latin domination of Italy, Gaul, and Spain, so far as permanence of linguistic influence is concerned, compared very favorably with the maritime influence of Greek in the Western Mediterranean.

The Mediterranean area constitutes a unity in the sense that the sea and the surrounding mountains provide a frame for or a set of limitations to the constant flux of peoples and languages. The sea promoted, or at least facilitated, movement and provided the means whereby trading colonies were constantly reinforced. The mountains placed constraints on such movements and ensured the concentration of the intrusive languages in limited areas. Reinforcement and concentration helped consolidation. Furthermore the mountains provided the "proletarian reserves," a countervailing linguistic influence in such areas as Southern Italy or in Massilia, or on the Eastern shores of the Mediterranean where Greek and the local languages, for geographical reasons, co-existed for several centuries. The Mediterranean because of this interaction of mountains and sea constrained the contact of languages so that the influences of Aramaic, Greek, Latin, and Arabic in turn were not dissipated. It is true that these constraints did not work so effectively inland so that we cannot speak of a similar coherent pattern of contacts for the whole of Europe, but what coherence there is has been derived in considerable part from the influence of the Mediterranean.

This chapter is based on the belief that while we cannot wholly break with the tradition which seeks for the origins and derivations of contact, it is more profitable to understand how people have achieved their unity: starting as heterogeneous elements and moving into a new and coherent pattern. Bilingual education is only partly and, to my way of thinking, only secondarily concerned with simple maintenance and conservation. If it is to be worth anything bilingual education needs to make certain that out of the discrete cultural elements a new unity is born. This is what we witness in the history of bilingualism in the Mediterranean.

Akkadian

The scene of the earliest instances of linguistic unification was Mesopotamia which, during the 3000 years of its early recorded history had close contacts with several other civilizations, some of them quite distant. The region of direct and indirect contact stretched from the Indus Valley across Iran, Armenia, and Anatolia to the Mediterranean and into Egypt. It was criss-crossed by pressures and influences exerted by kindred ethnic groups as well as foreigners. Akkadian, the most influential of the early Mesopotamian languages, appeared in rock inscriptions in the Zagros mountains, on statues on the Euphrates, on clay tablets in Anatolia on the trade route through Upper Mesopotamia, in Alalakh and other localities in the Middle East. However, prior to the establishment of Akkadian as a language of unification, the earliest Semitic Amorites had been infiltrating from the desert for a long time, and had succeeded in ensuring the use of their language in Babylonia; but it is doubtful whether their particular language replaced the existing vernaculars entirely. The Semitic languages belong to several closely related groups. The main division separates West and East Semitic. The West Semitic group includes Ugaritic, Canaanite languages (Phoenician, Carthaginian, Moabite and Hebrew), and the southern "Aramaic" languages (Syriac, Samaritan, and Nabatean, among them). The West Semitic includes Arabic and the ancient languages of southern Arabia. The members of the other main group, East Semitic, are the ancient languages of Mesopotamia—Assyrian and Babylonian, the general name for the two almost identical languages being Akkadian, derived from the old Sargonic Kingdom of Akkad.[3] Akkadian takes us back a considerable but not the entire distance of the history of this civilization. Sumerian allows us earlier glimpses. And both Sumerian and Akkadian provide linguistic evidence of even earlier culture levels. Additional earlier Semitic evidence suggests the presence of speakers of several early Semitic languages near to or along the course of the Euphrates.

Not only was there a long history of overlapping languages and civilizations but there is also evidence of divisions of function between, as well as within, these languages. There is also every likelihood of a considerable difference having existed between the written language of the scribes and that spoken in the daily business of living in towns and villages. Sumerian and Semitic languages were found in close association from the earliest historical times and the two languages were not used exclusively by each ethnic group. For instance in 2600 B.C. Sumerians in Southern Mesopotamia wrote inscriptions on Semitic votive tablets and there were Semitic names on Sumerian tablets (Moscati 1959: 48). The distinction of languages was made according to locality, and to some extent according to the subject of communication, Sumerian being the language of learning, religion and literature. The growing preference for the use of Akkadian rather than Sumerian reflects a conflict which had therefore little to do with the ethnic or political associations of the two languages, but reflected, rather, two different social systems and two spiritual orientations. Because of these differentiations of function it is difficult to obtain a clear picture of the Akkadian language. For instance, such texts as those which came from Susa are all rather specialized as if the use of Babylonian had been admitted only for specific purposes (Oppenheim 1972: 69). This is an interesting example of very early "diglossia."

During the first half of the third millenium before Christ this civilization reached a high level, enriched by a literature employing the newly invented cuneiform syllabic script. Akkadian, when it emerged as the heir of this political dominion, introduced a new element into an already richly varied pattern of contacts. The result of a fusion of Sumerian and Semitic cultures in Mesopotamia, Akkadian, hitherto the tongue of a minority of Mesopotamian Semites spread rapidly, partly because its literature became associated with the court and the ruling classes. Between 2350 and 2150 B.C. it is attested over the whole of Mesopotamia from South to North, co-existing with South Sumerian, the other language of unification, as well as languages of local provenance. Collections of tablets, like the great "library" assembled by Assurbanipal (668-627) at Nineveh as well as several other collections in Assur and Harran in the North, Ur and Babylon in the South give evidence of the existence of important bilingual scribal schools in which the native Akkadian and the traditional Sumerian were taught. In the Sumerian (as well as Egyptian) literature there are frequent references to the craft of the scribe whose importance in society is extolled. There is hardly anything of the like nature in Akkadian, although there is evidence that among them the occupation descended from father to son, and was clearly prestigious.

The bilingualism of the scribes is reflected in more than a hundred Sumerian incantations and prayers that are given interlinear Akkadian translations.

Educational handbooks, some of them bilingual, also were used to maintain the standards of the schools and the technical proficiency of the diviners (Oppenheim 1972: 17, 21). The shift from Sumerian to Akkadian prepared for by such bilingual texts occurred in stages: in the first stage, traditional material like the Royal hymns are most frequently written interlinearly; in the second stage, texts appearing in Akkadian only are nevertheless adaptations of Sumerian originals—mythological and epic texts; in the third stage, the texts are Akkadian originals—the Codes and royal inscriptions. During the last third of the old Babylonian period translations from Sumerian ceased, and the only texts then produced were Akkadian. This meant that the bilingual education of the scribes becamse even more important since they, almost alone, had access to the older Sumerian traditions.

> The traditional bilinguality of the scribes was maintained by the training in which a great deal of Sumerian material was used. Interest in Sumerian grammar and lexicography was effectively kept alive. (Oppenheim 1972: 249)

The scribes were educated to deal with every kind of composition, as is known from the bilingual texts that describe the wide variety of topics which made up the curriculum (Kramer 1949: 199-215). These topics have been categorized as follows: first, records of administrative arrangements, taxes and the entire work of the vitally important bureaucracy; second, codification of laws which need not then depend for their effectiveness on an oral tradition. Several Sumerian, Akkadian and Hittite codes, some of them bilingual, are extant. Third, sacred lore was preserved, and it is here that much of the Sumerian/Akkadian bilingual material is of interest. Fourth, the scribes produced the contemporary annals; they wrote the letters, edicts and public pronouncements, many of which had to be bilingual. In addition to all this the scribes produced a considerable body of writing concerned with ceremonial and ritual (mortuary texts and inscriptions) many of them bilingual, carved beside streams and on rocky slopes.

The texts which were used in teaching the scribes developed in an interesting fashion over the years. Lists of signs or words in narrow vertical columns began simply as a means of enabling the scribal student to learn to write while memorizing the pronunciation of the sign, but as time went on the lists became a complex apparatus for the higher linguistic education of the scribes. One type of advanced syllabary, comprising 40 tablets, had in addition to the three vertical columns ordinarily used (pronunciation, sign, sign name) a fourth giving the Akkadian translation of each logogram, often several Akkadian translations of the same sign. There are other more complicated multilingual systems evidenced by at least 16 tablets, and the trend toward such texts increased with the development of the Akkadian civilization. One group consists of Akkadian/Sumerian synonyms, the Akkadian column governing the arrangement. There are also topically arranged bilingual word lists and there are a number of grammatical texts designed to teach Sumerian morphology to Akkadian scribes (Oppenheim

1972: 246-248). The teacher used "school tablets," small discs on which he wrote a sign, a word or a short sentence on one side or above a line. On the other side, or below the line the pupils copied the example, or produced a translation. The text of larger tablets consisted of excerpts from literary material which were copied and sometimes translated. The study of Akkadian entailed the study of Sumerian also, specific writing and translation habits into and from both languages. The course was fairly uniform everywhere, as is known from evidence discovered in Hattusa, in Alalakh and Ugarit. As a result the scribes could write to allies of their master, to overlords and to the governors of dependencies either in the native language of the recipient or in the Akkadian lingua franca.

Hittite

In 1595 Babylon fell to the Hittites and Hammurabi's dynasty ceased. With the arrival of the Hittites "European peoples penetrated the civilized world for the first time," and "thus signalled the first historical conflict between East and West" (Ceram 1955: 3-5). Their coming was profoundly significant for within a relatively short period of about 400 years they became such a powerful nation that their writing was used from the Aegean through Anatolia and deep into Syria. Yet it was not unified by the possession of any single language: in Boghazkoy (Hattusa), the capital of the Hittite Empire, traces of eight languages have been found and at least four of these were used widely. Hittites did not possess a unified script: they developed their own hieroglyphic script, but cuneiform, which they employed for ordinary purposes, they borrowed from the Assyrians. According to some scholars it is probably because of this uncoordinated linguistic diversity as well as a lack of religious unity that the Hittite empire of the second millenium B.C. made no lasting contribution, so far as we can tell, and was buried in oblivion for many centuries. With the single exception of the "Prayers in Time of Plague" of Mursilis there is no Hittite literature.

After the arrival of the Hittites, Akkadian had to contend with a "host of proletarian vernaculars—Hyskos, Hittite, and Kassite" (Toynbee 1950: vol. 5, 485). Northward, the land between the Zagros Mountains and Lake Van was inhabited by the Hurrians who even before the Akkadian period had infiltrated quietly into areas bordering on Mesopotamia and as far as the Mediterranean, submerging Assyria and sweeping through Syria. On their southern flank they were in close contact with the Semitic Hyskos who conquered Egypt. To the north of them was the Hittite Kingdom of Anatolia. In spite of their numbers and their military power few of these groups formed lasting political units, though there is evidence of the influence of Hurrian, a language of the South Caucusus. Many of these diverse peoples, some literate in Akkadian, settled in Assyria, Phoenicia, other territories of Asia Minor, and Egypt. By means of the Akkadian script the contributions of these other language groups, Hittites, Hurrians, and Cretans for instance, were disseminated widely. The native lore of many peoples was transcribed and translated so that the Akkadian language came to serve a vast polyglot urban population in many lands. The Akkadian-Hittite contact was strong and the latter language assimilated many Sumero-Akkadian loanwords, and more significantly countless *Akkadograms*, words taking Akkadian form but meant to be pronounced as Hittite translations. It has been claimed that it was the Akkadian impetus that carried Anatolian culture and the Hittite language over into the Aegean (Gordon 1962: 59-63). The Hittites were unlike another of the mountain people who came down from the Northeast, bringing their own language, namely the Kassites who usurped the rule of Babylonia for 400 years but nonetheless assimilated the language and culture of the local people, and bestowed great care on the maintenance of the tradition of scribal education. The Kassites had also been infiltrated by the Hurrians in the Zagros Mountains, and this fact is attested by the occurrence of Hurrian elements in Kassite names.

The Hittites were an independently minded people who preserved their culture and maintained their linguistic identity. There are bilingual Hittite-Akkadian documents of the reign of King Hattuclis X; and Hittite scribes composed trilingual glossaries of Sumerian, Akkadian, and Hittite (Sturtevant and Hahn 1951: 2-4). Their situation was complicated by the fact that in addition to two methods of writing, Cuneiform and Hieroglyphic, the Hittites had two major native languages, Hittite and Khattish. Hittite was the dominant language of the empire and its sphere of influence extended from Halicarnassus to Zion. A Hittite enclave flourished around Hebron in the days of Abraham. They dominated an important section of the polyglot populations of Ugarit.[4] A long bilingual inscription in Phoenician and Hieroglyphic Hittite was discovered in eastern Cilicia also (Sturtevant and Hahn 1957: 6). Ugarit had accommodated a Mycenean settlement and the whole area, including Alalakh, was a cultural entity with an overlapping pattern of languages. Through Cypriot Myceneans the population of Ugarit was in linguistic contact with the mainland Greeks (Webster 1958: 66) as well as Mesopotamia. Ancient Syrian literature is completely identical with Ugaritic (Moscati 1959: 213). Though Akkadian was the language of international communication, diplomacy and law, and Hurrian was the language of religion, the normal language of local and everyday affairs was Ugaritic (Gordon: 1962: 131ff). Around 1190 B.C. the city of Hattusa was demolished and the Empire of the Hittites disintegrated under the pressure of a new migration into the area. The first of these invaders, "the peoples of the sea," may have spoken Mysian (Thracian) and Phrygian.

The writing of the cuneiform script, knowledge of Akkadian as a lingua franca (together with Sumerian and/or Hurrian), meant that educated people were bilingual and possibly trilingual. But though numbers of even ordinary people needed some oral command of more than one language, formal instruction was restricted to a privileged and specially selected group. Trilingual vocabularies, used in the education of the scribes, have been discovered at Ugarit, and at least two examples of vocabularies in four languages—Sumerian, Akkadian, Hurrian and Ugaritic—have been discovered (Gordon: 1962: 60). In the Royal Colleges of Babylonia and Assyria students received this very efficient linguistic education during a period of three years, after which they were expected to be proficient in several languages. Like other captive Hebrews in Babylon, the prophet Daniel, after being selected for a scribal education by Nebuchadnezzar, was able to communicate in the most important languages of the Empire as well as in his native tongue. The linguistic requirements of those graduating from the Royal Colleges varied considerably, but the course was intensive and well organized. Even those who confined themselves to writing the business documents and so-called "letters" received some instruction in the ancient Sumerian language as well as a thorough grounding in their mother tongue. No one could read or write cuneiform otherwise. In addition to this, their work demanded some knowledge of Semitic dialects other than their own.

Phoenician

Before moving to the next phase of linguistic unification, the Aramaic, some mention should be made of the influence of Phoenician (later Punic), if only because it is a good example of the impermanence of "maritime bilingualism." The actual commencement of Phoenician history coincides approximately with the event which more than all others created the linguistic complexity and flux of the ancient Near East, the invasion of the "peoples of the sea" around 1200 B.C. Restricted to the strip of land between the Mediterranean and the mountains of Lebanon, hemmed in by the arrival of powerful states (the Hebrews and the Aramaens), the Phoenicians were compressed into a unified people and simultaneously compelled toward the Mediterranean (Moscati 1968: xxii). Thus the civilization of the Phoenicians emerges partly as a consequence and partly as a component of the cultural and linguistic complex of the Near East, as well as the intermediary between the Eastern and Western Mediterranean. Their language is undoubtedly closely related to other Semitic languages of the Syro-Palestinian area, though its remarkable geographical distribution and history of contact with non-Semitic languages helped to create dialects which correspond to different phases of the development of the Phoenicians.

After the collapse of the Mycenean empire in the 12th Century, the Phoenicians made sure that eastern influence, linguistic, cultural, and economic, did not flag. Classical writers ascribe the Phoenician colonization of Cadiz to 1100 B.C. and of Utica to 1101. They preceded the Greeks in Sicily. From the 6th Century B.C. it was the Phoenicians in concept with the Etruscans who defended the trading depots of the West against Greek colonization. The history of Etruscan culture begins with an orientalizing phase which has usually been attributed to Phoenician influence. There are bilingual Etruscan/Phoenician inscriptions at Pyrgi. Inscriptions in Zincirli and Karatope show the spread of the Phoenician language into southern Anatolia. In the territory of Carthage, while the zone closest to the city was in the hands of Punic settlers, cultivating their vines, orchards, and olive groves, they had very close contacts with the native Libyans who remained in possession of the hinterland. Consequently we observe a marked divergence between the conservative official language and Vulgar Punic in which there are clear divergences from the Semitic norms, especially in syntax, due to the influence of the languages with which it was in contact. If the Punic background affects the Greek language in Sicily, it is even more true that the Greek element permeates and is sometimes indistinguishable from the Punic. This is a characteristic of the Phoenician culture on the island (Moscati 1968: 201). However, the almost exclusively maritime communication network of the Phoenicians limited the possibility of permanent linguistic and cultural influence so that the second great phase of linguistic unification belongs to the Aramaic language.

Aramaic

Pressed by Aramaic during the 8th Century, Akkadian was on the retreat as a spoken language (Moscati 1959: 70). Beginning with the 12th Century B.C. we meet Aramaic-speaking tribes from the Euphrates to the coastal regions of the Mediterranean; they penetrated downstream into Babylonia proper and across the River Tigris. Masses were transplanted by Assurnasirpal into Assyria. In the Northwest they did not accept the civilization of the Mesopotamian region or its language and its style of writing. In the Southeast they tended to be assimilated, accepting Akkadian names and, at the beginning at least, the Akkadian language and writing system, though eventually the Aramaic language and its writing system prevailed. This system, of Western origin probably, and first attested in Ugarit, gradually spread into the heartland of Mesopotamia and usurped the old cuneiform scribal tradition.

They established a series of Aramaen cultural zones with their own written language, using the Phoenician script. Aramaic-speaking merchants came to replace Phoenician traders, and eventually, supported by Assyrian military power, Aramaic became the vernacular of the whole Fertile Crescent, including Palestine and Phoenicia. In Nineveh, the capital of Sennacharib's empire, men from the Northwest jostled with Medes and Elamites and the royal scribes were hard put to transcribe the strange words from so many languages. In fact the keepers of the royal records added Aramaic glosses to facilitate interpretation later (Smith 1935: 95). By the end of the 8th Century Aramaic had supplanted Akkadian, after co-existing with it for three centuries, as the diplomatic language of southwest Asia and Egypt. Since the two languages were of the same Semitic family it was comparatively easy for speakers of Akkadian to learn Aramaic. The transfer was made easy because of the superiority of the Aramaic alphabet over cuneiform. This facilitated the development of Akkadian/Aramaic bilingualism exemplified by bilingual inscriptions dating from the reigns of the Assyrian Shalamanaser V, Sargon and Sennacherib (Dupont-Sommer 1940: 82, 84, 86, 88).

Although the role of Hellenism as the originator, transformer and carrier of ideas cannot be overestimated it is necessary to keep in mind that another 'international' movement preceded it. This is the still incompletely known network of Aramaic-speaking-and-writing groups which covered approximately the same territory and must have represented not only international trade but also a measure of intellectual contact. (Oppenheim 1972: 90)

This international value of Aramaic was promoted by the Achaemenian[5] Monarchy which established a universal Empire stretching toward India in the east and Lybia in the west, a single empire built up of diverse peoples among whom Aramaic, a well tried lingua franca, co-existed with a large number of local languages which it was the policy of the Empire to tolerate. Aramaic was the official language in all provinces, certainly west of Iran. It was used extensively in Egypt, and it appears at the same time in Anatolia. Eventually Aramaic came to be the dominant partner in a large number of contact situations. The kind of bilingual patterns so created is illuminated by a fresco of the 9th Century showing an Iranian imperial official dictating to two secretaries, who simultaneously with the dictation, translated onto clay and parchment (Dupont-Sommer 1940:86-89). The area within which Aramaic supplanted the local languages was not so extensive as that in which it was used simply as a lingua franca, but even so, people over the whole of the northern fringes of the Arabian steppe gradually transferred their affiliation to it. The Nabataean inhabitants of Petra were Arabic speaking, but the official language of their scriptions was Aramaic. The Jews first adopted Aramaic as an auxiliary language, but after a lengthy period of transitional bilingualism abandoned their own native tongue in its favor, retaining Hebrew for the sanctified texts originally composed in it, although finally Aramaic, too, was admitted to the pale of sanctity.

The Nile and the Aegean, the Indus and Jaxartes, the African desert and the frontiers of China were the limits of the expansion of the Achaemenian Empire and it might be expected that the Persian language would have been promoted as the language of unification in that area—an adstratum to Greek, Egyptian, Hebrew, Phoenician, Assyrian, Phrygian, Lydian, Median, Armenian and Aramaic. However the Persians had no lingua franca of their own to help consolidate their hold on so vast a territory with such varied vernaculars. They depended upon the liberal recognition of languages of limited currency together with the official recognition of Aramaic as the major international language together with localized official support for Persian at Persepolis, Assyrian at Babylon, and Neo-Susan in Elam. The co-existence of Aramaic, Greek and the local languages is evidenced not only among the denationalized inhabitants of Babylon and the towns of Syria but in remote and backward areas as well, where cities were rare and village life the rule. Scribes and administrators were brought up in specialized "government schools," which used bilingual lexicons and texts, to be literate in Aramaic as well as the local vernacular, though the emphasis was mainly on reading and writing Aramaic. Consequently, it has been claimed that Aramaic, the language of the Galilean, could carry those who knew it northward as far as the Amanus, eastward as far as the Zagros, and westward as far as the Nile, in the certain assurance that whatever the vernacular of any area, there would be sufficient speakers of Aramaic with whom to communicate.

Just as Phoenician exemplifies a category of impermanent maritime bilingualism, Aramaic is an excellent illustration of *territorial bilingualism*, slow to develop but enduring for centuries. It was not until the Babylonian exile (586 B.C.) that the Jews, for instance, began to replace Hebrew with Aramaic as the language of normal conversation. Even as late as 170 B.C. Hebrew was used as a literary language, and we can be certain therefore that it was understood by the people. After the return of the exiled Jews, until about 160 B.C., Aramaic continued to exert an important influence on Hebrew, so that Hebrew/Aramaic bilingualism lasted a long time. Meanwhile Aramaic came to be challenged by Arabic, and though it is difficult to determine the period of the shift to Arabic, it is probably true that Aramaic was still spoken up to the middle of the 8th Century. Some claim that a variant of Aramaic is still spoken in Syria, Azerbaijan, and Kurdistan. Others insist that after a prolonged period of Arabic/Aramaic bilingualism the latter was completely replaced by Arabic in the 5th Century A.D. In any case Aramaic had a long history of contact with other languages and contributed to a significant phase of unification and bilingualism.

Egypt

The Egyptians, though they exercised nothing like the imperial sway of the Persians, were similarly involved in a complex pattern of linguistic contacts from early times. They were an amalgam of African linguistic groups, wandering Semites and Asiatics. The Helu-nebu who made recurrent appearances in Egypt were, it has been claimed, Greek in origin (Montet 1964: 131). After gaining independence from Persia, Egypt opened its doors to the outer world; large numbers of Greeks entered, some of whom settled in Egypt as merchants, and some possibly as artisans. Beside those immigrants who were elevated to the upper strata of Egyptian society, large numbers earned their living in agriculture and as clerks. Consequently different immigrant bilingual groups came to be significant in Egyptian society (Rostovtzeff 1941: 82, 331). Further, the attitude of the Egyptians encouraged the injection of these new influences, because they valued their contacts with other nations—

> "The North wind is a life giving wind,
> He has been given to me and from him I derive life"
> (quoted in Montet 1964: 208)

From as early as 3000 B.C. Egyptians had regular contacts with Byblos where a temple served a permanent settlement (Gordon 1962: 104). Relations between Cretans and Egyptians were close for several centuries, and their contracts, treaties and diplomatic communications were bilingual (James 1920: 58).

Sometimes their contact with other peoples and other languages was not of their seeking. Invasions by the Hyskos are a case in point. [The Hyskos were a people or group of peoples actively involved in a complex succession of migrations, conquests and acculturations during the first half of the second millenium B.C. in Lower Egypt, Palestine and Syria. It deeply affected the political and cultural character of the region.] Egypt was invaded and occupied by these Asiatic hordes, and the period of their domination witnessed the movement of Semitic tribes into Egypt. The biblical account of Joseph probably refers to the end of the Hyskos era. During the 18th Dynasty, the language of these invaders was used widely, a fact which was responsible for changes in the Egyptian language which were not unlike, though they were less radical, perhaps, than those which saw the transformation of Latin into the several Romance languages after similar periods of bilingualism (Montet 1964: 201). Contact between Egypt and the Hebrew people became increasingly important during the period of the decline which followed the New Kingdom. Later, in the 7th Century a colony of Jewish mercenaries was established near Aswan, and this continued until the end of the 5th Century. From this site as well as from Suggura, Edfu, and Hermopolis have come a great mass of letters, business and legal documents written in Imperial Aramaic, revealing considerable Egyptian influence. After 301 B.C. Ptolemy brought back many Jews from his Palestine campaigns and he employed Jewish soldiers in Egypt, giving them land and so establishing a semi-permanent Jewish influence. Solomon's reign witnessed considerable economic expansion as well as many social and political innovations. Because of these he required an enlarged and better educated cadre of administrators whose training was influenced by Egyptian models on account of Solomon's ties with Egypt through marriage.

Egypt had a long tradition of didactic treatises designed for the sons of officials who were trained to enter government service. These treatises, entitled "Teachings" in Egyptian were the textbooks of the scribal schools and were used to teach reading and writing together with the habits of correct speech. The 10th Century, which witnessed the rapid development of the Israelite state under David and Solomon, owed much to the introduction of scribal schools patterned on those of Egypt and they adapted Egyptian "writings" into the Hebrew language.[6] Nevertheless, in spite of these known developments and the fact that the Egyptians were from time immemorial in contact with Semites who have left written records almost as old as Egyptian ones, it is noteworthy that the "Egyptian language made only a relatively slight impact on the languages of the ancient world" (Cerny 1955: 197). This may be due to the "impermanency" of Egyptian contacts. The Egyptians used rather than incorporated the Jews. The lack of Egyptian linguistic influence to the west and south is not remarkable for the languages of those areas left no written records, and were superseded by the languages of invaders or immigrants (Cerny 1955: 197).

Another reason for this slight impact of the Egyptian language is the Greek reluctance to admit Egyptians to the privileges of citizenship. Egypt was made use of rather than hellenized. While there were important areas of contact, Egyptian life on the whole remained centered on the temples and villages and existed side by side with Greeks without mixing (Preaux 1971: 322). This served to keep the Egyptian element in the population separate. Even in the time of Caracalla those who infiltrated into Alexandria could still be distinguished easily by their "rustic" language. Yet under Greek rule Egypt became the most important mixing place of East and West, for the Ptolemaic Empire at its high tide included not only Egypt but Cyrenaica as well as parts of Ethiopia, Arabia, Phoenicia and Cyprus. Although it drew elements of its population from all these countries, the bulk of the people were Egyptians while the top strata of society consisted of Greeks and Macedonians. It is no wonder, therefore that the large cities, Alexandria for instance, were polyglot. Greek dialects predominated there, though in the native quarters Egyptian was the language of the inhabitants. In the Jewish wards, Hebrew and Aramaic were the prevailing languages. Other Semitic languages and even some Indic dialects could be heard as well (Rostovtzeff 1941: 418). These facts were reflected in the linguistic aspects of the school curriculum of the middle and upper class children of all ethnic groups.

Greek

East Mediterranean

The Greeks represent another of the main waves of the linguistic influence with which we are concerned. The beginnings of the hellenization of Greece cannot be stated with any precision, though in the early years of the first millenium B.C. the influence of the Greeks prevailed in that area. They were themselves the products of prior linguistic contacts and mergers, which began as far back as the second half of the 12th Century B.C. with the arrival of the "new people" in what had been the Mycenean area. There is good evidence for a pre-Greek population in this same area. These were the Pelasqians, who according to Heroditus adopted the Greek language. The series of intrusions resulted in the merging of populations and in the close contact of their languages and dialects (Nesborough 1964: 259-260). Meanwhile, the Northwest corner of Asia Minor was the scene of similar incursions from Thrace. During the beginning of the first millenium that area became the home of the Phrygians and related populations like the Mysians who maintained close linguistic contacts with the native peoples. A second wave of Thracians followed and settled in the land to which they gave their name, Bythynia (Magie 1950: 303). There is ample evidence of the contact established between the various linguistic groups of Mesopotamia and the Aegean area, arising partly out of the existence of mediating groups of Greeks who established themselves on the Bosphorous and the shores of Euxene Sea, as well as of Ionians who colonized areas of the Propontes. The Near East became an area of special colonizing interest. At Mina, at the south of the Orontes, existed the most important Greek settlement, led possibly by the Eoubeans bringing with them slaves and setting up a regular trade.

 The Greek colonizers must have been a minority, and because of this they had to learn the local language. These mediating expatriates involved in normal trade and commerce helped to spread the results of linguistic contacts over the whole of Asia Minor. As the language grew in importance with the rise of Greek political influence, it was confirmed as the bond between the different linguistic groups of the Eastern Mediterranean and Asia Minor, and consequently as the one common factor in very many different bilingual situations. Nevertheless it would be unwise to exaggerate the currency of the Greek language. For instance, the discovery of a substantial funerary inscription in Greek and Georgian near Tbilisi dating to the 2d Century A.D. does not permit us to extend Greek linguistic influence so far. Nor does the use of Greek in official documents in Inner Asia (for instance, in Mylasa) argue that the language was firmly established in that area. There are cases enough of the use of the conquering Greek tongue in places where there can have been no Greeks or very few to speak it (Tarn 1948: 226).

Of all these languages and cultures, it is about the Phrygians, the heirs of the Hittites, that we know most. They seem to have exerted the main influence in Anatolia in the 8th Century. But really close contacts between them and the Greeks do not appear before the 7th Century, by which time the Phrygians were able to adapt to their own language the recently developed Greek alphabet. By the 6th Century the Phrygians, defeated by the onslaughts of the Cimmerians, handed on their political and cultural supremacy in that area to the Lydians, whose capital, Sardis, lying very much closer to native Greek cities, became an important focal point of linguistic contact (Cook 1961: 27). The Lydians during their period of ascendancy employed many Greek mercenaries, against Egypt for instance, and thus helped to spread language contacts. Like the Phrygians, the Lydians also adopted the Greek alphabet.

At about this time, too, the Aeolian Greeks arrived among the Thracian population of Samothrace, and the Carians were also brought into close contact with them. In Greek tradition the latter were regarded as natives of the Aegean, though they themselves claimed to have arrived from Asia Minor. It is now thought that their language belonged to the Luvian group. There are many references to their contact with and displacement by the Greeks, together with evidence of intermarriage between Greeks and Carians. This is not surprising in view of what Xenophon called the "mixo-barbarous" character of the small towns along the coast (Cook 1961: 22-23). The most important of these communities which welcomed Greek cultivators and industry was at Halicarnasus, reputed to be the scene of the first regular meeting place of Greeks and Carians, and where, from the beginning, Greek as well as Carian was spoken. The Carian population of the settlement, witnessed by the proportion of personal names recorded by Herodotus, was as numerous as the Greek. This was an example of a thoroughly bilingual community, one which had absorbed a considerable native element without diminution of its hellenism.

Furthermore, because of the traffic between Greek and Carian settlements and cities, it is not surprising that some Carians were residents of Greece itself, as the Carian-Greek bilingual inscriptions on an Athenian statue suggest (Boardman 1964: 101). Even before the 4th Century the West Carians had taken to the Greek way of life and its language. By the end of the 4th Century most Carians had followed their example. Consequently the Greek language dominated the pattern of contacts (Cook 1961: 22-23), partly because the Greeks themselves, like the English in the 19th Century as well as present-day Russians in Central Asia and elsewhere in the U.S.S.R., were reluctant to learn local languages. They might not insist on others learning Greek but they had a high regard for their native tongue. The monoglot Greek possessed the superior culture and the fact that he did not seek to understand the language of Phrygians or Syrians or Carians made for unilateral bilingualism on the part of the latter. Their urban proletariat had good opportunities to acquire a smattering of Greek, and though the class was small their hellenization was remarkably thorough. Greek rapidly became the universal language of polite society, and most hellenized orientals were bilingual insofar as they could talk to their humbler compatriots in the local languages (Jones 1937: 32).

West Mediterranean

Almost simultaneously, with the consolidation of their relations with the peoples of the East Mediterranean seaboard and its hinterland, the Greeks penetrated to the West Mediterranean. The Greek colonization of Southern Italy, Sicily, the coasts of Gaul and Spain constitutes the third and perhaps the most important of the unifying influences in the Mediterranean. It began in the Tyrrhenian, as it did in the Aegean and Black Seas during the 8th Century, and under the same economic and social causes which compelled the dispossessed populations to seek their fortune abroad (Glotz and Cohen 1955: vol. 2). They belonged to several dialect groups, Chalcidians of Euboea for instance, and they established their first colonies at Cumae and Naxos, their aim being not so much the acquisition of territory as the development of a market and the safeguarding of their trade routes. From there they dominated the hellenization of the Etrurian coasts. There is evidence, according to Pliny, of Greeks living in Etruria, marrying Etruscans and becoming prosperous merchants there. After the 6th Century (and the Ionian trouble), many Greeks emigrated and settled in Etruria, while Etruscans in their turn came to work among the Greeks at Cumae (Boardman 1964: 102).

The Etruscans, little though we know of their origins,[7] contributed a novel and undoubtedly extraneous element to the pattern of contact in Italy. On the one hand there was some emigration from the East, which produced a dynamic minority to work on the indigenous culture. On the other hand, whether it was trade or colonization, the Western Mediterranean from the Mycenean era onward was constantly furrowed by ships coming from many directions. By 700 B.C. they were established in Central Italy which had rich mineral resources and for that reason had attracted Greeks and Phoenicians. The centers of Etruscan civilization were the towns which were the focal points of a primitive Etruscan industrial revolution. Etruscanization of Northern Italy coincided with the progressive acquisition of Etruscan consciousness—"a sense of political, cultural and linguistic affiliation with the Etruscan world" (Heurgon 1973: 41-45). There is no clear evidence that all strata of the population within range of Etruscan influence spoke that language and it is far more probable that Etruscan was the possession of only an upper class minority who thus constituted the bilingual element in the society, the majority speaking only the local languages. Their sea power limited Greek colonization to Southern Italy until about 600 when the Phocaeans opened up their lines of communication, only to be parried by a combination of Phoenician with Etruscan forces. The Etruscan borrowed from Greek and from Italic dialects, but its own contribution may have been far more considerable. During the period of Etruscan domination Latin assimilated a number of loanwords from that language, relating to religion and divination, the drama and music. The Roman naming system originated with Etruscan. It was the Etruscans, themselves taught by the Greeks, who taught the Romans to read and write by introducing them to the alphabet. Etruscan influence beginning at the end of the 7th Century expanded throughout Provence, Languedoc and Catalonia. It was broken off about 580 with the foundation of the Greek city of Massilia in 600 B.C.

The Euobeans who settled on both shores of the Sicilian straits and in Eastern Sicily were followed by other Greeks—Dorian, Megarians, Corinthians, Achaeans, Lacedemonians, Rhodians, Cretans, and Ionians—so that Sicily was colonized by a variety of Greeks and to a very considerable extent. As in South Italy, some of the native population worked and lived in Greek cities, and Greeks may have lived in native villages—Tore Galli, for instance. The hellenic influence was not limited to the coastline. Morgantina in the center of the island was a hellenized city. The two populations intermarried, for they got on together well enough in spite of the basic master slave relationship. The Sicels took to writing their own language in the Greek alphabet: they used Greek names and ultimately shifted their linguistic attachment from Sicel to Greek after a considerable period of bilingualism. The inscriptions of Motye, a half-Greek town in the 5th Century, were probably cut for half-Greek inhabitants (Woodhead 1962: 22). Consequently bilingualism is claimed as being responsible for the replacement of Latin /d/ and /g/ by /t/ and /k/ in the Messina region of northeast Sicily and in South Apulia (Jungeman 1959: 475).

The linguistic complexity arising from Greek colonization was not limited to the interaction of Greek and the native languages. Sometimes a city together with some of the surrounding area might be colonized by more than one Greek dialect group—Chalcidians and Mycenians in Rhegium, Achaeans and Troezenians in Sybaris, Rhodeans and Cretans in more than one city. A late 8th-Century inscription from Pithecusae is written in the Ionian dialect of the Chalcidean colonists, strongly tinged with Homeric influences. Mingling with the local inhabitants and other Greek colonies served to undermine loyalty to their original Greek dialect. Himera spoke a mixed language halfway between Dorian and that of the Chalcidians. In Sicily this mingling gave rise to a Doric Koine in which Rhodean elements predominated. On mainland Italy the original dialects maintained themselves more distinctly (Heurgon 1973: 85).

Hellenization came about gradually by direct contact and by import trade. Instead of taking over an area inhabited by natives the Greeks let them live as neighbors, leading a life that was altered only by commerce with the colonists (Adamesteanu 1957: 20-46, 147-180). Nevertheless there are differences between Greek colonization and its linguistic consequences in Southern Italy and Southern France, at Massilia for instance. There the impact of the Greek language was less permanent than in either Southern Italy or Sicily, though it provided a center from which Greek influences radiated widely into Western Europe. Phocaeans colonized Massilia around 600 B.C. under pressure of their own small and poor land, together with the threat of the Persians under Cyrus. Their foundation of Marseilles was only one point in an ambitious program which many think may have begun in the south of Spain, moving to the coast of Provence because of the antagonism of the Phoenicians already established there, and controlled as well as reinforced from Carthage. The establishment of Marseilles not only exemplified the comparative impermanency of Greek influence in that part of the world but was the cause of continuing struggles between the Ligurians and later the Gauls. In spite of these struggles it was from contact with Massilian Greeks that the Gauls learned "a more civilized way of life and abandoned their barbarity . . . Their progress was so brilliant that it seemed that Gaul had become part of Greece rather than that the Greeks had colonized Gaul" (Dunbabin 1948: 187). It is well known that they were called "trilingues"—speaking Greek, Latin and Celtic. The example of Massilia encouraged the establishment of colonies like Nice, Monaco and Antibes, which still retain their Greek names. Consequent on the social intercourse of Greeks and Gauls, Provence came to inherit Greek linguistic influences and the same applies to Southern Italy. It has been argued that Greek enclaves in the West did not survive the 3d Century (Jones 1960b: II, 986). Yet observers in the 16th Century A.D. claimed there were 22 Greek-speaking localities there, and as late as the 19th Century there were still 12 such localities. There were, even more recently, Calabrian and Apulian villages which remained partly Greek in speech. These very late survivals were small and very scattered. Nevertheless, the existence of considerable Greek bilingualism, especially in Southern Italy, and of a Greek substratum is not to be doubted.

Hellenic Language Policy

Gradually as the various Greek dialects leveled themselves in the direction of a uniform "Koine," the influence of the language deepened and spread; and with the imperial advance of the Hellenes it penetrated far into the East and Egypt, where there was a considerable Greek social and linguistic element from early times, witness the story of the Samian merchant who around 638 B.C. made regular runs to Egypt. Herodotus records the use of Greek mercenaries by Egyptian kings. After such early beginnings, Herodotus claims, the Greeks settled down to close relations with the Egyptians. By about 575, Naucrates, at the mouth of the Nile, had accumulated a considerable polyglot population, including all sorts of Greeks—merchants, artists, poets and a variety of professional people and skilled workers. Such settlements, however large, were isolated and it was not until the arrival of the Macedonian kings in Egypt that the use of Greek became widespread. The dissemination of the Greek language is recorded in thousands of administrative documents drafted by village officials and thousands of private letters written, by persons of quite humble station. This is because the elaborate bureaucratic regime established by the Ptolemies required scores of minor officials with at least an adequate knowledge of Greek. It became worthwhile for the better class of peasant to learn enough Greek to justify a government post. Furthermore, apart from the inducements which fraternization with the Greeks held out to the fairly well-to-do Egyptians, almost everybody's affairs, at some time or another, were matters of concern to the government and involved some discussions in Greek. Consequently there must have been a fairly large number of Egyptians and Greeks who were bilingual, particularly for the purposes of administration. Many of the rural clergy, too, were bilingual (Rostovtzeff 1959: 882). The upper classes received a good education in Latin as well as in Greek and Egyptian. In the courts the judges and advocates, though local men, insisted on evidence being given in Greek. It was not unlikely that Greek was the normal language of town life for many people (Jones 1937: 995).

The nature of Greek influences in Egypt, as elsewhere, was determined partly by the attitude of the Greeks to their native language. They were liberal in their acceptance of other languages, especially in religious affairs. It was certainly this attitude which enabled the Jewish temples to transact their own business in Aramaic. But however they might react to the speaking of local languages by others, their purpose was to maintain the Greek language, and to secure a Greek upbringing for the younger generation. In the larger villages and the capitals of the provinces, surrounded by Egyptians, the Greeks established their own enclaves. In their long history they scarcely tried to hellenize anyone; the notion was generally foreign to them partly because it was unnecessary. If Greek colonization produced a certain amount of hellenization that was the result of natural symbiosis; natives became hellenized and Greeks orientalized. On the other hand, Greeks were intent on preserving their own language and avoiding complete assimilation. Consequently the new members of the Egyptian ruling class saw the advantage of acquiring the Greek language and conforming in some degree with a way of life which gave significance to the acquisition of the Greek language (Rostovtzeff 1941: 502).

An important item in the budget of any community was the cost of the gymnasium and of public education (Jones 1960a: 220). Many inscriptions show that the cities of the Greek east were extremely eager to secure for the youth of the cities an education on Greek lines, which though good was expensive. Huge sums of money were required to pay the teachers and to provide and keep in good repair the schools and athletic grounds. Nevertheless, wherever any significant number of Greeks congregated they made the gymnasium the focal point of their civic existence, and there are recorded petitions that they should be allowed to establish schools. Even the Greeks who lived in rural Egypt and who apparently had no state-recognized self-government had their own educational institution. Other communities under Greek rule aspired to obtain the same facilities. The progressive party in Jerusalem petitioned Antiochus IV to be allowed to establish a gymnasium at the same time as they requested that they should be incorporated as a city (Rostovtzeff 1941: 147). The Attalid kings provided Pergamum with three gymnasia, and cities like Salamis in Cyprus and Miletus had the same distinction (Jones 1960a: 220). To have pursued a course of instruction in a "palaestra" or to frequent a gymnasium was the distinguishing mark of an educated man. In Egypt those who had profited from the experience inevitably became bilingual and in consequence entered a special class of the population, which enjoyed privileges and rights of a high order. The youths of Alexandria who had been educated in this way were considered by the Emperor Claudius to be qualified for Alexandrian citizenship.

Such educated men lost interest in their local cultures, and though their native language remained for them a necessary means of communication with the majority of their own people, they gradually shifted their attachment in favor of Greek, at least so far as the more sophisticated aspects of life were concerned. Within their own class they normally spoke Greek, and were able to read and write that language only. Some texts have survived which refer to schoolmasters and their pupils, and they bear witness to the popularity of the Greek schools among the hellenized natives, as well as to the efforts that were made to teach children the Greek language in order to qualify them for the gymnasium. On the other hand, many Greeks became acclimatized to Egypt, and, taking an active interest in Egyptian affairs, learned the language also. The bilingualism of Egypt ran both ways, though there was, naturally, a much stronger flow in the direction of Greek (Jones 1960a: 220).

Large numbers of Greek settlements were established throughout the Oriental parts of Alexander's empire. Some of these, like the seaports of Gaza and Tyre, became the centers of trading and industrial interests. Such settlements were found throughout Iran, Bactria and the Punjab; and it has been emphasized that the size of the Greek-speaking elements of these populations, which kept in touch with the rest of the Greek-speaking world and were constantly reinforced by Greek-speaking groups, ought not to be underestimated. Initially the native and Greek-speaking populations might be segregated. The fact that at Thyateria the "Macedonians" are described as "around" the city, while those at Cobydele are noted as being "from" the communities suggest that though the language groups were at first segregated they were later in much closer contact (Magie 1950: 972).

Although an exception was made in the case of Judea the underlying principle of the policy of Antiochus (Ephiphanus) IV, was not to hellenize the oriental towns by force but to legalize a process of amalgamation between

Orientals and Greeks. But by spreading over their dominions a network of Greek settlements whose inhabitants belonged to the same nationality and spoke the same language as themselves the Seleucids[8] inevitably made Greek the *de facto* official language of the empire. Greek became the lingua franca. Trade with the West and North was conducted on the acceptance and official recognition of Greek documents: transactions in which one party was Greek and the other native were regulated by Greek law and recorded in Greek legal documents. Perhaps more important than commercial and administrative uniformity was uniformity in the mode of life. Boys were educated in Greek schools. There were Greek private elementary schools in all Greek settlements and the gymnasia were as fundamental an institution in the Eastern monarchies as they were in Greece and Asia Minor (Rostovtzeff 1941: 521, 1047).

Consequently the Greek settlements never lost their original character and even in the farthest outposts of hellenism, in the Parthian Kingdom, they preserved their Greek tongue. Alexander arranged that 30,000 youths in Bactria should go to school to learn Greek. It is a fair assumption that many of the native population as well as Greeks in India were bilingual in Greek and Prakrit; and Greek was alive there in the reign of Kajula Kadphises in the first quarter of the 1st Century A.D. An Indian who was a citizen in a Greek polis was bound to be hellenized to some extent; he would have to learn enough Greek for the purposes of daily life and understand something of Greek civic forms, and the educated had been taught to read some Greek literature. Conversely the Greeks knew some Indic languages. But the effects were not long-lasting, and they did not penetrate the system of Greek education in India (Tarn 1938: 375, 387). The sphere of Greek linguistic influence embraced Babylonia too: Herodicas' epigram to the effect that Hellas and Babylon were equally his homelands is well known. A Babylonian would add a Greek name to his own. He learned Greek and wrote the Babylonian language in the Greek alphabet. Some wrote their books in Greek because of the prospect of a better distribution throughout the whole of the eastern territories (Tarn 1938: 56). The Greek city of Sileucia had a large Babylonian population outside its walls with which it was in close communication. In Syria, Greek and Aramaic were closely intertwined, both languages being familiar to the more or less educated and denationalized inhabitants of that region.

Preservation of Local Languages

So far we have described the spread of Greek and other languages of unification, but bilingualism, if it is to be more than a temporary and superficial phenomenon involves the continued long-term existence of the local languages. Partly because of the permissive linguistic policy which the Greeks pursued, partly because of the class structure of the society which made linguistic stratification possible, and partly because of the simple facts of geography and the comparative inaccessibility of the majority of the people to an intrusive language, this was the case in the Mediterranean area. The displacement of the indigenous languages was an exceedingly slow process, and affected a whole host of languages which eventually made way for Greek—Bithynian, Cappadocian, Cilician, Galatian, Isaurian, Lycaonian, Mysian, Pamphylian, Pisidian, Phrygian, Pontic and Thracian, for none of which are there any literary records. Nevertheless Isaurian and Mysian are described as living languages late in the 6th Century, and others in the 4th Century A.D.

Western Asia Minor was a land of great natural contrasts with fertile river basins and highways terminating in busy ports where the Greek was at home with his commerce and industry, his complicated political machinery involving the hellenized and urbanized natives. On the other hand there were almost inaccessible mountain groups, peasants in the rural districts into which neither trade nor the Greek language penetrated deeply. For a long time the Greek population of pioneer settlements, Smyrna even, was quite small. Not more than 1000 free Greeks lived in the city, matched by an equal number outside. Miletus may have had a somewhat larger Greek element. This fact ensured the demographic, if not the functional supremacy of the local language. Greek influenced the masses because of its prestige, but the numbers of those who spoke Greek were small to begin with. Then again, the physical contour of the land, while it allowed for the Greek settlement of the fertile river basins in Western Asia Minor, preserved the comparative inviolability of the local languages in the mountainous interior. Though the Greeks built cities in which the indigenous were offered a Greek education, these were along the coast and Greeks did not proceed into the interior for a long time. Lycia's population of highland folk remained isolated in spite of their contacts with the ring of hellenized countries along the coast (Magie 1950: 144 et sec.). If, as was certainly the case, native languages survived well into the Byzantine age in some localities and among certain social strata, it is plain that Greek never completely dominated them.

Greek-based bilingualism was a matter of the cities and towns, therefore, and these were truly and remarkably bilingual. For instance, according to Strabo, in Cibyratis four languages were in use; besides Greek there were the language of the original Cabalians, Lydian[9] introduced by the first colonizers of Cibyra, and Pisidean spoken by invading tribes from the east. Pontus had such a heterogeneous population that it is not surprising to read that 22 languages were spoken within its walls. In Rhodes freedom and foreigners, including natives of Asia Minor, Syria, Phoenicia and Egypt, as well as a slave population drawn from a large number of language groups (Lydian, Phrygian, Cappadocian, Galatian and Armenian) formed the bulk of the population. But of all the polyglot communities, perhaps Dioscurus, in Colchis at the eastern end of the Black Sea, was the most remarkable. According to Pliny "it was once so famous that as many as 300 different languages were spoken in the settlement." Subsequently business was carried on there by the Romans with the help of a staff of 130 interpreters.

As has been suggested already, the attitude of the Greeks to their own and to the languages of the various localities was an important factor in producing long-term bilingualism. They were intent on remaining Greek, but they were not interested in displacing the languages of the areas into which they penetrated. Some of the languages, Lydian for instance, were superseded, but not as a result of any deliberate policy. Carian seems to have become obsolete before the beginning of the Christian era, but here too, there was no noticeable attempt at extermination or suppression. Other languages, such as those of Pamphylia, became unrecognizable because of Greek influence which was fortuitous and unplanned. The Lycians preserved their distinctive national culture, language and script down to the 4th Century B.C. In the 3d Century Lycian inscriptions disappear though the people did not lose their national pride when they succumbed to superior hellenistic forces (Jones 1937: 97, 289). The Thracians, on the evidence of John Chrysostom, retained their language until the first century of our era. (Chrysostom n.d.: 501). Although by the 2d Century the hellenization of the Galatian upper classes appears to have been widespread and Celtic names are not found thereafter, the peasantry continued to speak their ancient language and Jerome recalls that the Celtic Galatians still spoke their language in his day, and it probably survived until the end of the 5th Century A.D. Cappadocia remained, on the whole, a very backward country by Greek standards, and the Greek language made very slow headway there. It was still spoken in Strabo's day. Philostratus in the 3d Century notes the influence of the mother tongue of the Cappadocians on their second language, Greek. They spoke it with a thick utterance, confusing the consonants, shortening the long and lengthening the short vowels.

Phrygian, like Galatian, was spoken in the time of St. Paul and persisted to the end of the 5th Century A.D. Its preservation, until that time, shows that a native tongue may continue to be spoken for some purposes after the major responsibilities for communication have devolved on an intruding language. The city of Iconium was considered Phrygian even when Greek had taken over the transaction of public business, and many of the Iconians were bilingual since they retained a command of Phrygian (James 1920: 69). As Greek education spread among the towns and villages of Eastern Phrygia, radiating from the centers of Seleucid and Roman government, and reinforced by the extension of Christianity, Greek killed off the use of Phrygian eventually, but the two languages co-existed for a long time. There is evidence of this in the Neo-Phrygian texts which have survived. Many Greek words were borrowed into it—many more than has generally been supposed—and Greek influenced its syntax as well (Calder 1911: 164).

The same Greek influences were exerted on Egypt and Syria. There the survival and use of the vernaculars together with Greek are attested by the fact that in those countries the national churches adopted Coptic and Syriac as the literary and liturgical languages, the government-supported orthodox church language being Greek (Jones 1960a: 293). East of the Euphrates, in Osrhoene and Mesopotamia, Syrian survived not only as a spoken but as a written language as well, with a corpus of original literature. It was taught in the schools of Grammar and Rhetoric of Mesopotamia with Latin and Greek, and it was possible for even an educated man not to be inconvenienced if he knew no Greek provided he spoke Syriac and Latin. Mesopotamia was socially orientalized, and Syriac early established its supremacy there, though in political sentiment the population remained Greek. Harmonius laid the foundations of a vernacular literature in the 3d Century with his Syriac hymns, and Greek education declined with the emergence of Syriac as a literary language (Jones 1937: 223). Syriac was, therefore, more successful than Egyptian, which did not maintain a continuous literary tradition and could not contribute to the education of the young. The demotic script was less and less used in Egypt and died out before the end of the 3d Century with the result that Egyptian became the illiterate peasants' patois. Even when Coptic appeared after a long period of contact with Greek and adopted a modified Greek alphabet, Egyptian remained the language of the less educated lower classes. No educated Egyptian chose to write in Coptic if he could help it, and Coptic literature was limited to translations and lives of the Saints (Jones 1960b: Vol. II, 992).

Greek became a unifying language from Travancore to the hinterland of Marseilles, but it did so in partnership with a large number of languages which had a remarkable gift for self-preservation. Though, where bilingualism did exist the degree of oral competence was adequate for all practical purposes, the amount or the spread of Greek literacy among the various classes of society should not be exaggerated (Tarn 1950: 226). In some areas, indeed, the Greek language made very little headway: in Iran and Babylonia the Seleucids elicited only a limited response from the natives and little Greek influence has been found in Babylonian documents of the period (Tarn 1938: 55). It has also to be recognized that few of the vernaculars provided for literacy, though Syriac, as we have noted, survived as a written language. It was used for translating Greek theological works, as well as for original writing, mainly religious. In the Latin zone of the Empire, the only rival to Latin in ensuring any degree of literacy was Gothic, together with Hebrew among the Jews. But though the local languages could not compare with the languages of unification, the bilingualism of these centuries and in these areas, especially among the upper classes, cannot be underestimated. It is because of the inclusion of Greek in a number of bilingual partnerships that the Septuagint appeared in Greek, that Greek as well as Hebrew and Latin appeared at the Crucifixion, and St. Paul could communicate freely in the different lands through which he traveled. He could address a Roman Governor in Paphos because the one had learned Greek with Aramaic and the other Greek with Latin. He could stand before the Areopagus at Athens and address that distinguished body in its own language because it was, as it was for many of his countrymen, a well cultivated second language. In fact, though large numbers of various populations became bilingual to some degree or other, the contribution which language contact has made to a unified civilization, a shared sensibility and a set of common assumptions and practices in education derives from the existence of literate bilinguals, however few the elite who learned the dominant language in addition to their native tongue, whether for theocratic or administrative purposes, or simply because they belonged to a certain class.

BILINGUALISM IN WESTERN EUROPE

Celtic Contact with Other Languages

Italy

Whitney suspected that

> the prevalence of a peculiar and strongly marked linguistic disease known as Celtomania which is apt to attack students of the subject, especially those of Celtic extraction . . . leading them to exaggerate . . . the importance of the Celtic civilization, language and literature.

This is a point of view, which at the time when Whitney wrote, may have been received sympathetically. However, later linguistic and archeological research justifies a less critical note. Indeed it has been claimed recently that Celtic contacts with Germanic and North Italian dialects introduced "barbarian Europe into the advanced Mediterranean cultures and civilizations of the maturing ancient world" and that the "significance of the Celts in European civilization has no parallel in the early history of Europe" (Filip 1960: 191).

How the pre-Roman, Greek and other languages and dialects of Italy with which Celtic was in contact came to be there, whether as the result of three separate waves of migration moving from east to west as some have suggested, or of slow, uninterrupted and almost unperceived infiltration, it may be impossible to decide. However we are permitted to surmise that changes in the linguistic structure of Italy were not unconnected with the appearance of Indo-European in the Near East and Aegean about 2000 B.C., because of the pressure from the "peoples of the Steppes." There were two foci for the Indo-European invasion: the Danubian—Central European area, and the Pontic—Caucasian. Latin with Faliscan moved from the former center, Venetic appeared in Italy at about the same time, and in a second wave came Umbrian and Oscan. These migrations occurred between 1500 and 1200 B.C. Consequently up to the time that Latin became the official language of the peninsula and long afterwards, there existed in Italy a complex of different ethnic and linguistic groups. First there were the speakers of Italic dialects in central Italy during the first millenium B.C. These included Umbrian, spoken in the upper Tiber valley; Sabbelic dialects around Rome, Sabine in the middle Tiber and Volscian to the southeast of Rome; and in the wider area of southern Italy, Oscan.

Second, there were the pre-Italic dialects (those which prevailed before the spread of Latin). These included Messapic, spoken in Apulia and possibly related to Illyrian; Venetic at the northern end of the Adriatic; Rhaetic north of Lombardy and Piedmont, and, until it was displaced by the Etruscans and Gauls, in the middle valley of the Po. And finally Ligurian along what has become the Italian and French Riviera. The Romanization of Italy occurred during the period 4th Century B.C. to the 1st Century A.D. and naturally enough there was a great diversity of bilingual patterns since Latin hardly ever completely ousted the local language. Rome itself was a double city, a combination of three Latin villages on the Palatine hill and four Sabine villages on the Quirinal. Both Sabine and Latin were spoken by the population of Rome, though this would not entail great problems since the two languages at that late stage of their history were fairly close. Oscan was used extensively at the end of the 2d Century B.C. and was in fact the official language of the federation of allies opposed to Rome between 91 and 88 B.C.

For at least 40 centuries the Peninsula had witnessed the constant arrival and intermingling of currents of immigration, a successive and gradual displacement of groups infiltrating where the land was sparsely populated, establishing themselves near the local inhabitants and being assimilated wholly or partly: sometimes taking to the local culture, and sometimes exerting a great influence of their own so that not only in culture and religion but in language we witness a long and complex evolution. Right up to the 5th Century there was a continous arrival of elements that were new demographically and culturally (Francisci 1959: 129). What is equally certain is that the speakers of the languages maintained long periods of contact and co-existence with each other, with the result that we have layers of languages across Italy and various indications of bilingualism (Pulgram 1959: 345). The Celts had established very intimate contact with several Italic languages and this cannot have occurred much later than the 5th Century B.C. Successive waves swept down upon the valleys and as far south as the Tiber, with the capture and near destruction of Rome in 390 B.C. Those who came down into Italy came from the banks of the Rhine or at all events from Central Europe. Because of the same pressures other Celtic hordes surged toward the Danube (Grenier 1943: 212), plundered Greece and penetrated Asia Minor, where they established themselves in Galatia. Various Celtic groups mingled with the Ibero-Tartessian non-Indo-European indigenous groups in Spain, and so helped to form the Celtiberi (Bosch-Gimpera 1940: 245). It is not a question, therefore, of Celts occupying Iberia so much as a mixed race of Celts and Iberians, or Iberianized Celts who, in the 5th and 4th Centuries B.C. possessed a living unity of culture. Most of the territory of Ancient Gaul was occupied by Celtic speakers who helped to bring about a decisive change in the linguistic and ethnic character of the area.

They were also in long contact with Scythians, Thracio-Dacians and Illyrians. That the Celts migrated in large bands is unquestionable since a few stragglers could not have had even the short-term immediate influence they undoubtedly did exert. "Had they behaved not like the Etruscans before them but rather like the Romans, their successors, they might . . . have become masters of

Italy and altered the history of the entire world," including its linguistic heritage (Pulgram 1959: 204). Even so they did have an enduring influence. Long before the end of the 4th Century the Ligurians had been overrun, and Ligurian came to be spoken by a people whom it is difficult to distinguish from Celtic-speaking tribes. In other words an area was recognized in ancient times in which the two linguistic groups, an early Ligurian and an invading Celtic one were indissolubly intertwined (Whatmough 1933: 65).

The Augustan period was the principal time of Celto-Ligurian and Latin contact. Towns like Augusta Praetoria were founded by garrisoned soldiers in which the speakers of the native languages had their quarters and settled. Many of the inscriptions which witness to the Ligurian language came from town centers so that it would be safe to assume that its speakers took an active part in city life. The evidence of Latin in these inscriptions increases as the people became bilingual. At first they were written in Celtic script and from right to left. As the contact of the two languages became more intimate, there was an approximation to Latin forms and styles (Chilver 1941: 70). There are a number of Celtic borrowings in Latin and the Celtic names in the inscriptions of Cisalpine Gaul are frequent (Palmer 1954: 13-15). However, the importance of this Celtic contact is restricted to its influence on Ligurian and other northern dialects, showing itself perhaps as a substratum influence on some modern "Gallo-Italian dialects" (Pulgram 1959: 204).

Along the valley of the Adige in northeast Italy, another Celtic language, Raetic, was spoken, its speakers having intermingled with those of Venetic and Illyrian, a language which survived both Celtic and Latin contact to form the base of Albanian. Raetic shows the results of considerable contact with Etruscan, consequent on the exercise of an Etruscan overlordship. The bilingual inscription of Voltino on the western shore of Lake Garda is an indication of Raetic contact with Latin also. The contact of Latin with another Alpine language is revealed by the bilingual inscription found at Todi (Tuder), which reveals the existence of Lepontic in Apulia (Whatmough 1933: 175). This was where, as Horace illustrates (Satires, 1.10.30), the contact of Latin, Greek and another Italian language, Oscan, was made. The latter derived from the conjunction of Umbrian and Sabittic, a dialect spoken by the Samnites after their conquest of Campania (Pallatino 1955: 25-26).

By the end of the Second Punic War, the Romans had overrun the Celtic-speaking areas of Northern Italy and founded Placentia and Cremona. What remained of the Celtic dialects of the Alpine area was overlaid by the Latin speech of the conqueror. By the end of the 2d Century the Romans had taken control of the whole of Italy and had established their linguistic hegemony. Though practical measures were never adopted with the view to Latinizing others, Roman soldiers, Roman officials and teachers carried the language of public administration throughout Italy so that their language found access into homes and marketplaces where, nevertheless, the local languages continued to be spoken. Large sections of the population who were conquered by the Romans passed through longer or shorter periods of bilingualism according to the local language they spoke. They adopted Latin as a second or third language at different times.

The ultimate shift to Latin lasted about 500 years and it is interesting to note that for centuries after the ethnic and political assimilation of the conquered people bilingualism between speakers of Celto-Italic dialects, and between Latin and other Italic dialects, was still strong, and at a later point expanded to include Latin with Greek as in the case of Tarent after the Roman conquest in 272 (Honnyer 1957: 415-420). This widespread Latin-related bilingualism led to several linguistic consequences: the adoption of a foreign alphabet for instance, considerable place name changes and much lexical borrowing, accompanied by radical phonetic changes to accommodate these new lexical items. Furthermore, as Plautus and Lucilius witness, grammatical interference of several languages with each other occurred quite frequently. A bundle of isoglosses running east and west from Lucia to Ancona separates the Gallic-Italic dialects of Emilia, Lombardy, Liguria and Piedmont, from Tuscan in the South. North of a line from Rimini to La Spezia is an area which shows the influence of Latin and Venetic phonology (Pulgram 1959: 162). In a wide region of central Italy substratum influences are considered reasonable where the phonological development of /-nd/ /-nn-/ and /-mb/ /-mm-/ are concerned, affecting Oscan and Umbrian; such substratum influences are only slightly less probable where the survival of Etruscan pronunciation habits are concerned (Hall 1974: 63).

Spain

In our ignorance of the demography of pre-Roman Spain we are unable to map the distribution of the indigenous languages or even to distinguish many of them with any confidence. It was not a question of the indigenous ethnic groups living as separate entities. The Celts intermixed with many such groups to produce a mixed race of Celts and Iberians who in the 5th and 4th Centuries possessed a living unity of culture and language, fertilized by Greeks and Phoenicians. The influence of Celtic on the language of Spain was reinforced later from association with Gaul. Contemporary Greek and Roman writers in Spain distinguished the languages of the Tartessians in the South and Southeast, Iberian in the East, Celtic in the extreme Northwest, and in the center Celtic and Iberian in mixed and bilingual communities. We are confronted with a multilingual pre-Roman Spain in which the Celtic language as an element in Ibero-Celtic played a significant role and did so until contact was established with Latin. Celtic had probably ceased to play an independent role by the time the Romans arrived, having been absorbed socially and linguistically by the earlier inhabitants (Malmberg 1961: 72). By the end of Augustus' reign (A.D. 14), Latin was fairly well established, and it was spoken throughout the peninsula except by the Basques. When the Empire came to an end (476 A.D.), Spain was as Latin as Italy, and surviving linguistic evidence of the existence of Celtic is more tenuous than it is in Italy. It has been claimed that only one word of proven Celtic origin is peculiar to the peninsula (Entwistle 1936: 39-40).

Britain

Romano-British. It is to Britain and mainly to the fate of Welsh that we must look if we are to find contemporary evidence of strong Celtic influences and a long-surviving Celtic linguistic tradition in spite of contact with other dominant languages. Bosch-Gimpera speaks of a Celtic invasion of the whole of the Western province of the Hallstatt civilization amounting to a military occupation. Though the establishing of the Gallic peoples in Gaul spread over more than a thousand years, it was the 5th Century which marked the decisive turn in the peopling and the linguistic development of France. Then occurred a new influx of settlers who, like those who crossed to Britain about the same time, were undoubtedly Celts.

While the great proportion of the speakers of Celtic dialects remained on the continent, two waves descended on Britain, the first in the 6th Century B.C. speaking a variant of Brythonic from which Welsh, Cornish and Breton[10] derive; followed, a considerable time later, by Goedelic-speaking Celts, from which are derived Irish, Scots Gaelic and Manx.

Of the languages spoken in Britain before the arrival of Celts we know as little as we know of the pre-Roman languages of Spain but Celticists would have no objection to admitting

> that the more securely the Celtic invasions are anchored within the half millenium between 600 and 100 B.C. the more incumbent it becomes upon them to admit the existence of some prior language, let it be non Indo-European or an earlier form of Indo-European than that which we recognize as Celtic. (Adams 1940: 21)

When the Romans arrived in Britain, therefore, Celtic and possibly some vestiges of a non-Celtic language in the far north were spoken throughout the islands. To the end of the Roman occupation Celtic continued to be spoken by the vast majority of the population either as their sole language or in conjunction with Latin. It has been argued that there is "ample evidence that Latin was spoken by all classes of the population, not only in the towns but also in the rural country houses and the farms" (Zachrisson 1927: 25). Celtic was presumably the mother tongue of the Romano-Britons and there is no clear evidence as to what proportion of the population were bilingual or mainly Latin speaking. However there can be no doubt that speakers of Celtic were in close contact with the Latin language and considerable bilingualism resulted.

The Latin language must have been used in government and the administration of the law. The native upper classes, who came to play an increasingly important part in local government and official life, were encouraged to learn Latin. Latin was the language of the army and its Celtic recruits. Those who administered to its needs would need to know some Latin. The language of all large-scale trade and commerce would be Latin, though the local markets would probably be dominated by Celtic. In the Lowland zone all education and writing would be in Latin. The cities and towns in the same zone were always very strong buttresses of Latin since they were the centers of administration and government. As time went on their influence spread in ever-widening circles into the surrounding countryside. It has been shown that the great expansion of town life in the Flavian and later Antonine periods had considerable influence on the contact of the languages (Collingwood and Myres 1931: 194-195). The language of the Church was Latin and with the advent of Christianity it became to a large extent the quasi-official language of the country. Elsewhere in the agricultural Lowland Zone (apart from the Villas) and the whole of the Highland Zone, where Latin was confined to the military encampments and garrison areas, there was very little Latin (Jackson 1953: 97-105).

In Britain the system of education was very similar to that of Gaul and Spain. The sons of the nobility were gathered together and educated as Roman citizens and eventually local initiative may have carried on what was started officially. The process is well known from Spain where it started early in the 1st Century B.C., until by the end of the 1st Century A.D. even small mining centers had elementary schools and *grammatici* and *rhetors* were at work in most towns (Liversidge 1961: 150). The children who passed through such schools were taught very conservatively by schoolmasters who insisted on strict speech habits, unlike the Vulgar Latin spoken by traders and lower class townsfolk. The families of these children provided many of the *decurions* who would have to speak in the *ordo* on public occasions, and many of the children completed their studies with professors of rhetoric, many of whom were Gauls. Juvenal (*Satires* XV. 112) ridiculed the fact that "the whole world has its Greek and Roman . . . Eloquent Gaul has trained the pleaders of Britain and distant Thule talks of having a rhetoricum."

Anglo-British. With the collapse of the Roman occupation in the 5th Century A.D. the Celts whom we may now conveniently identify as British were opposed and overrun by Germanic invaders speaking dialects with phonological and morphological systems which differed considerably from the Celtic languages. The Angles, Saxons and Jutes began to settle in Britain in the middle of the 5th Century and moving from the Southeast and Northeast they progressed west, ultimately taking under their control the whole of what is now England. By the last quarter of the 7th Century the linguistic divide between England and Wales had been established on a line which is to all intents and purposes identical with the present administrative boundary. The whole of Wales and the extreme western areas of England remained Celtic speaking for the next 500 years but the areas occupied by the British in England, whatever contact there may have been, did not offer much opportunity for the continuance of the Romano-British forms of education. Enclaves of British survivors have been identified but these were in inhospitable areas—forest, swamp and bare hills. In any case there was probably little place for urban life in the England of the later 5th and 6th Centuries. Nowhere did the Roman cities (with their schools) carry on any tradition of civilized life, and in many instances their sites were desolated and abandoned.

Nevertheless there is linguistic evidence of considerable Anglo-Celtic bilingualism, at least among the British survivors. The nature of the sound change affecting place names adopted by the English "could only mean that the natives learned Anglo-Saxon thoroughly and accurately, so accurately that they had to mangle their own names to suit the language of the conquerors rather than the reverse" (Jackson 1953: 242). Jackson concludes that the following features characterized the linguistic contact situation at that time.

> The British learned the language of their conquerors and they acquired the sound system and vocabulary very completely, their own phonetics having no discernible effect on the new language and their own vocabulary very little. There must have been at least some degree of close relationship and intermarriage, through which British personal names were taken into Anglo-Saxon. All this suggests a bilingual stage, when the British knew both Anglo-Saxon and their native language though it is not likely to have been a long one, especially in the east of England; and it is not probable that the conquerors learned very much of the language of the conquered. (Jackson 1953: 245)

Norman-Celtic. Later the British were brought into contact with the Norsemen, represented by the Normans. The Norsemen, without having any lasting influence on the civilization or languages of mainland Europe, had raided and later settled in parts of France. Their principal area of operation apart from Britain had been Northern France and the Lowlands though they had penetrated as far south as the Lower Rhone, Pisa and Fiesole as well as western Spain and the Balearics. They drove to the Loire and the Seine in 885, and in 924 were able to appropriate parts of what is now Normandy when the King handed over to them the Bessin, and in 933 the dioceses of Avranches and Coutances, thus establishing the shape of the province. However, within about 60 years of their settlement in France, by 940, their language was no longer spoken among the Northmen of the Seine and although in the Bessin, where they may have been reinforced, the language lasted longer, it was abandoned there too. By the year 1000 the process of assimilation was complete. Neither the Romance dialect of Normandy nor any other dialect of French was affected by the language of the Norsemen.

Nor was the situation radically different in Britain. Though the island was conquered by descendants of the Norsemen (the Normans) and though the language the Normans spoke had a profound effect on the development of English and produced a considerable degree of bilingualism both informally and officially, in England this was not the result of the use of even a diluted form of the Nordic language but of Romance. So far as the remaining element of the Celtic population of Britain is concerned, namely the Welsh, the principal consequence of the arrival of the Norman-French language was to stratify, linguistically, the whole of the population of Wales. In the areas of Wales occupied by the Normans the native Welsh language was sustained almost exclusively by the common people. These areas were the Marches (along the English border), the Vale of Glamorgan, and nearly the whole of Monmouthshire, as well as the lowlands of southwest Wales. The aristocracy, "bonedd," turned to English or left for London. In the western and northern highlands Welsh remained the only language and was sustained by the princely families as much as by the common people (Roberts, G. 1567: 163). After consolidating their position the Normans were not prepared to attack these almost impenetrable mountains, especially since their conquest offered them few advantages. Thus, at the beginning of the last century nearly 600 years after the Norman Conquest, the "language divide" in South Wales still separated the Norman settlement areas (the Englishry) from the hilly north (the Welshry).

The Tudor conflict. The major threat to the Welsh language from the Anglo-Normans happened after the Tudors, a dynasty of Welsh descent, came to the throne of England in the 15th Century. For most of the time the Normans had ruled through powerful but local families. The Tudors, faced with possible attack from abroad, pursued a very different, highly centralizing policy. They thought that a strong, united Britain was possible only by subordinating powerful, local families, creating a uniform legal, administrative and ecclesiastical system, and by permitting the use of only one language, namely English. The Act of Union for the first time provided that

> no person or persons that use the Welsh speech or language shall have or enjoy any manner office or fees within this realm ... unless he or they use and exercise the English speech or language.

This meant the ambitious gentry's gradual alienation from the language, as well as the attenuation of the related culture. The use of Welsh was virtually proscribed in all prestigious contexts. Yet as one Welsh scholar complained, "if there be no learning, wisdom or piety in a language what better is it than the churn of wild fowls or the bleating of beasts" (Salesbury 1547). Although the Welsh aristocracy transfered their preference to the English language, Welsh was still the native tongue of nearly all the common people of the Principality. Even an English diocese, Hereford, was enjoined by Parliament to see that copies of the Welsh Bible and prayer book were available in the Churches; and as late as 1660 there were complaints in the same diocese that the Welsh were not offered services in their own language (Williams 1967: 177).

With the Act of Union and the departure of the Welsh aristocracy for the Tudor court, the literary cultivation of Welsh and the tradition of education which had been prescribed by the Celtic bards went into a decline. With the Renaissance a different kind of influence was exerted. Many Welsh scholars were recusant Catholics who spent considerable periods in exile in France or Italy. They were well aware of the controversies which had exercised the minds of writers on the continent for many years concerning the use, the development and "embellishment" of national languages and the "vulgar tongues." They argued the case for Welsh in much the same way as the case for Italian had been promoted by Dante and Petrarch a little earlier. The scholars saw the peril of Welsh losing its former status in the world of learning and scholarship, and feared that English would be the sole medium for those purposes. "Do you suppose," asked one of them "that ye need no better words and no greater variety of expression to set out learning and to treat of philosophy and the arts than you have in common use in daily converse when you buy and sell and eat and drink . . . ?" (Salesbury 1547).

But although Renaissance humanism and scholarship promoted the cause of a literary "embellished" Welsh, there was considerable native opposition to it. Of all nations, one writer claimed,

> none is so indifferent or opposed to the preservation of its language as the Welsh. . . Among the educated aristocracy and the learned leaders of the Church there is scarcely one in fifteen who is able to speak and write the language. (Edwards 1651)

This is not surprising, because education at all levels was available only in the English language. With the accession of the Tudors aristocratic parents sent their children to schools across the border. The less privileged used the new foundations in Wales itself, which were almost invariably either near the border or in towns that were historical centers of Norman influence, and were modeled on those in England. Not until the religious revival of the 18th Century and the creation of Circulating Schools by religious organizations did the common people who were predominantly Welsh speaking have an opportunity to learn to read and write their native tongue, and so begin a new era of bilingual education.

Greek and Latin Bilingualism

The Survival of Greek in Italy—Societal Bilingualism

After their original colonization of areas of southern Italy the Greeks of Magna Graecia made contact with the Latin language toward the end of the first half of the 4th Century and from that time onward they remained in close contact both in Italy itself and in the Eastern Mediterranean, homeland of the Hellenes. There are three stages in the development of Latin/Greek contact, the first of which concerns us at this point. This was of a direct oral kind compared with the learned contact of the second stage. In the third stage, of the later Empire, the contact became direct again, mainly affecting the Romans in the East and the Christian missionaries in Rome. From the end of the 4th Century B.C. to 148-146 B.C. when Macedonia and homeland Greece were subjugated and certainly up to 272 B.C. when Magna Graecia surrendered at Tarentum, the Greeks appeared as very serious contenders for the domination of Italy. This is reflected in the frequently quoted lines of Horace:

"Graecia capta feram victorem cepit et artes
Intulit agristi Latio."

(Greece though conquered conquered her barbarous conqueror and brought arts
to Rustic Latium.)

After 150 B.C. the Greeks were moribund as a political power. It was this political power which had supported the spread of Greek and, in association with trade, maintained it overseas. Meanwhile the Romans began to exert their influence in the Mediterranean and Latin penetrated the lands which they occupied.

The Greek language continued to be spoken in certain parts of Italy, particularly in the South, for the Greeks made every effort to retain their tongue and never ceased to regard Latin as a barbarous language. Other nations learned Greek, and for that reason, among others, the Greeks never made any concessions to Latin. They despised it and learned it only when economic circumstances made it necessary for them to do so. The Romans for their part, in spite of Augustine's remark that "the victorious Romans imposed their own language upon the vanquished for the sake of peace," were completely under the spell of the Greek language. They made no effort to set up Latin in rivalry to it or to Latinize their political and military gains. This reluctance to undertake any degree of linguistic proselytization was due in part to a simple sense of their own superiority, which induced them not to impose Latin, but rather to consider its acquisition by foreigners a privilege to be sought, like citizenship. The inhabitants of Cumae, for instance, had to request permission to use Latin in public affairs and in the pursuit of trade. After the Punic wars the earlier Roman rural ethos and pride in simplicity was overtaken by hellenistic innovations and technology. The aristocracy maintained a strong opposition and this is reflected in such references as "bibite, pergraecamini" (*carouse* or, literally, act as the Greeks do). But eventually even the most conservative like Cato began to learn Greek, even at 80 years of age, and it was the aristocracy, later, who promoted Greek most effectively. For several reasons, therefore, Greek came to exert an increasing influence even in Rome itself. As early as the 2d Century B.C. the city was permeated by Greeks, a large proportion of them slaves. The Greek-speaking Christians who formed a significant element in Rome carried the Greek language everywhere, and the highest ranking officers of the Empire adopted hellenistic models of culture and speech. For instance, Sempronius, father of the Grachi, was able to deliver a Greek oration before a highly critical audience at Rhodes, and in 281 the Roman envoy addressed the people of Tarentum in their native Greek (Cicero: Tusc. IV. 4).

While this attitude was characteristic mainly of the aristocracy, it was not restricted to them, for the whole of Rome was drawn under the Greek spell. The language of serious life may have been Latin, but Greek was the language of pleasure, of frivolity and of the lightest kinds of entertainment. The talk of the Scipionic circle, we are told, was full of Greek words. Words with a Latin root and a Greek termination like *ferritribaces* (galled with iron) are found. Lucilius writes in Greek characters Greek words governed by Latin verbs, just as Ausonius does in the 4th Century A.D. It is significant in the history of bilingualism that Plautus expected his audience, which must have included a considerable popular element, to understand Greek phrases, as is the case in the "Bacchides." Juvenal declaims against women who irritate their husbands by talking Greek:

> What can be more disgusting than to find that not a single woman considers herself attractive until she has been transferred from a Tuscan into a Greekling? . . . They talk nothing but Greek. . . Greek is the language of their fears, their quarrels, their joys and anxieties. In Greek they pour out their souls.

It is not surprising, therefore, that in the Mediterranean areas Greek persisted as a parallel lingua franca with Latin for a considerable time though, as was to be expected, longer in the East than in the West. Latin was certainly regarded as the official language of administration; in actual practice Greek was frequently used even in the courts of law. The Roman Emperors, after Diocletian, endeavored to promote Latin as the language of imperial unity, and there is evidence that they attempted a strict enforcement of its use in official business and to promote its acquisition (Seutonius). But time went on, and as the numbers of Latin-speaking settlers in the East declined, the enclaves of Latin influence were submerged (Rostovtzeff 1959: 187). Though the Byzantines, for instance, were anxious to call themselves Romanoi, their education was bilingual but predominantly Greek. This was particularly true in the higher professions, such as law. In the 5th Century the teaching of law was in Greek but the students had in their hands copies of the Latin texts as well. The languages of the conquerors and vanquished continued to be yoked together in an uneasy partnership, and the Empire in the East functioned to the very end as a bilingual or diglossic state.

The Teaching and Use of Greek—Bilingualism in Education

In the light of what we have described, it is no wonder that in the West, from the 2d Century onward, Greek-Latin bilingualism was reflected clearly in the education of the young. This was true of the provinces, of Africa and of Rome itself, as Ausonius illustrates (Epistles XXII). Greek remained prominent for a long time after the true potential of Latin had been revealed by orators and writers like Cicero. Ennius, born in Messapia, had been brought up to be trilingual, which is hardly surprising, for his native city, Rudiae, according to Strabo, was still Greek 200 years after Ennius' death. Italian by birth, Greek by education, he used to refer to his "three hearts"—"Quintus Ennius tria corda habere sese dicebat quod loqui Graece et Osca et Latine sciret" (Aulus Gellius). Some Roman children and young people were sent to Athens for their education, or to Massilia because of that city's Greek character. For the parents who could not afford to send their children away to school, there were the immigrant Greek teachers to whom Polybius (XXXI, 23) refers as "this tribe of teachers flocking over just now from Greece to Rome." Among these were Greek slaves like Livius Andronicus who, on receiving his manumission, set up a bilingual school (Jerome 1929: 187a).

There were also Gallic bilingual teachers whom it was the custom of the

Romans to employ because of the excellency of the Gallic schools. Juvenal writes "Gallia considicos docuit facunda Brittannos, de conducendo loquitur iam rhetore Thule" (Eloquent Gaul has trained Britons as lawyers and in Thule there is talk already of engaging a professor of rhetoric). There were popular wandering *rhetors*, and Aulus Gellius describes pupils accompanying the teacher from place to place. They were engaged by literary clubs where they perpetuated the methods of the bilingual rhetors—"rhetorious sophista, utrius que linguae callens."

Such a provision of education for bilingual children prevailed for a very long time. As late as the 5th Century the sons of aristocratic parents were still taught Greek, and some of them were taught entirely in Greek. So important was Greek that the nobleman Symmachus decided that "while my son is being taught Greek, I will join him and like a young scholar share his labours" (Jones 1960b: 937). Aemilius Paulus, father of the younger Scipio, was noted for the care he took to give his son a thoroughly Greek education. Cornelia, the daughter of the elder Scipio, provided her sons with the best Greek tutors of her day (Gwynn 1926: 38). It is not surprising that Paulinus, the grandson of Ausonius, brought up by Greek slaves, is reputed to have been able to read Homer and Plato when he was only five years of age. And there must have been many children like Fulgentius, in Africa, who acquired a perfect Greek accent (Jones 1960b: 987). In the 4th Century, Greek was still part of the curriculum not only of the aristocratic boys but of the middle class student like Augustine, though it was not continued at a higher level under a *rhetor*. Even in the 5th Century boys from aristocratic homes still learned Greek. Sidonius Apollinarius read Menander to his son in the 60s of the 5th Century.

At the beginning Greek was not simply a subject in the curriculum but was regarded rather as the foundation and core of the child's education. It was taught before he was introduced to any formal instruction in his mother tongue, and this is illustrated by the case of the child Delmatius. He died at the age of 7, but though he had only begun to learn the Latin alphabet, he already knew Greek (Carcopino 1950: 115). Such children were put in the care of Greek slaves or servant-tutors, and as Quintilian (Institutio 1935: 1.i.4) remarked, the child's first step in education would be in the slave's speech. Cicero preferred Greek to Latin as the language of his son's instruction, and Quintilian (Institutio 1935: 1.i.10, 12) advised that Greek lessons should begin as soon as the child could speak, and certainly before he gained any marked control of Latin.

This early instruction in Greek was assumed to be at least as good a foundation of the child's intellectual development as his mother tongue could be. It had the advantage of ensuring the easy and firm acquisition of a necessary second language and it was regarded as a satisfactory means of improving the child's control of his mother tongue. Naturally every Roman child picked up Latin in the ordinary course of events, so that when he reached the age for attending school he was thoroughly bilingual (Quintilian, Institutio 1935: 7 1.i.10, 12) and could profit from formal instruction in both languages, though it was with Greek that such formal instruction began. The grammar classes were conducted in Greek and Latin, but the rhetoric classes were almost entirely in

Greek. Later, parallel but separate Latin and Greek schools, rather than parallel instruction in both languages in the same school, became attractive. Cicero (1901-1903: *De Rhet.* 2) remarked to Titonius that he remembered the first teacher of Latin, L Plotius Gallus, and he regrets that older and more traditionally minded people interfered to prevent him from attending Plotius' very popular classes. Until a late period, then, Roman children were brought up as if they were Greeks, but were instructed in Latin as well, though even so, that Latin curriculum was modeled on the Greek course. It was for such schools that bilingual textbooks were prepared, the "Hermeneuamata Pseudo-dositteana." These contained a Greek-Latin lexicon arranged alphabetically as well as according to subjects and topics. Short, easily understood passages of prose were also arranged bilingually. Having acquired a firm grounding in the parallel short texts, the students were given the classics to read (Marrou 1956: 263).

There was, of course, considerable antipathy to bilingualism, and especially to a bilingual education. The linguistic gaffs, mistakes in declension and gender, etc. in the conversations recorded by Petronius in "Cena Trimalchionis" are due, it has been suggested, to the author's wish to satirize the inept bilingualism of the Greek-speaking residents of Rome. Plutarch wrote that Marius the demagogue never learned Greek well nor used it for any cultural or civilized purpose, thinking it foolish, as Plutarch continues, "to learn a language that was taught by men who were themselves slaves." Of the same man's relatives, Cicero (*Letters*: VII.i.3) wrote, "You care so little for all things Greek that you would not even use the Via Graeca to get home to your villa." The Romans themselves recognized some of the more pressing difficulties of their form of bilingual education. Quintilian noted that if formal instruction in the mother tongue were too long delayed in order to help the child consolidate his Greek, he might come to speak his native tongue with a foreign accent. And we know from other sources that this fear was not exaggerated. Cicero, for instance, took care to caution his son, who was being educated in Athens, not to neglect his Latin exercises. There is evidence that, as a result of very early Greek instruction and the use of that language, educated Romans tended to introduce some features of the Greek tonic system into their Latin speech. The poor quality of the Latin spoken by bilingual Greeks who, apart from actually teaching Latin would as servants or child-minders often provide the earliest models the Roman child would hear, is referred to by Quintilian (Institutio 1935: x.5, 2-3). Then again, there is evidence that many felt that the acquisition of two languages simultaneously was an intellectual burden. A child's time and capacity are limited, it was argued; and even from the teacher's standpoint, it was thought quite impossible satisfactorily to keep instruction in the two languages going simultaneously. For many pupils, it was even more difficult and frustrating: Paulinus of Pella, the grandson of Ausonius, was in this predicament. He wrote,

Quae doctrine duplex sicut est potioribus apta
Ingeniis, gemenoque ornat splendore peritos,

Sic sterilis nimium nostri, ut modo sentio, cordis
Exilem facile exhausit venam

(To be asked to learn two languages ia all very well for the clever ones, for they
get a double glory. For the average school boy like me the need to keep up both
languages is trying and exhausting.) (Quoted by Haaroff 1920: 226)

It was argued also that as a contribution to general education, apart from its
value to men of letters, "Greek studies were barren and fruitless." Augustine
(*Confessions* 1954: 1.13) criticized the futility of a system of bilingual education
which imposed the exclusive use of the second language as the medium of
instruction for the young, for this led to boredom and drudgery. It was unnatural:
while Latin came to him in the course of nature—"inter blandimenta nutricum et
ioca arridentium et lactitias alludentium" (with his mother's milk), Greek was a
mechanical imposition. And this has been the burden of the remarks of many
scholars to this day. Haaroff refers to thoughtless and unscientific pedagogy, and
of the teachers in this tradition "regarding the child as a receptacle for external
and ready-made ideas (a kind of) spiritual militarism. . ." (Haaroff 1920: 227). A
contemporary classicist writes of the

well organized educational system of the Empire having for its main aim to
teach the two literary languages and to inculcate in the minds of all its pupils
the established methods and the desirability of imitation. . . Among the reasons
why the Empire failed we ought probably to number the intellectual failure of
its educated classes. Hampered by their traditionalism and by the strict linguistic
discipline which they imposed upon their minds, the members of that class
could not solve their immediate problems.

He concludes that "a smaller nation would not have been so prodigal of human
effort" (Bolgar 1954: 24, 59).

The social and educational dissatisfaction with, and the Augustinian-type
criticism of the practice, apart from other circumstances, made the continuance of
Greek-Latin bilingual education impossible. As early as the 4th Century
competent teachers of Greek were hard to come by, certainly in the provinces. As
Latin continued to realize its literary potential, the impetus toward learning Greek
for cultural purposes slackened. By the end of the 5th Century its acquisition was
a symbol of an outmoded tradition rather than a response to a realistic appraisal
of educational need, or to the existence of social forces which at one time may
have justified its position in the curriculum. Even so, though the instances we have
adduced must be only a very slight indication of the spread of certain types of
bilingualism, it would be wrong to exaggerate the support for such bilingualism
among the masses even when it was most prevalent. The education which
prevailed was based on an aristocratic way of life and this meant a limited
opportunity for any form of literate bilingualism for the vast majority. Greek was
taught, as time went on, less as a "second language" for which there was a
supporting background in the community, and more and more as a foreign
language.

The Triumph of Latin

Factors Involved

The diffusion and ultimate triumph of Latin in the West was the result of several factors, among which was the element of military conquest. The auxiliary regiments of the Roman armies were composed of provincials who had learned Latin. The *castella* which they usually built and inhabited were surrounded by villages and small towns, *canabae*, from which new recruits were drafted and which gradually assimilated Latin-speaking foreigners, mostly soldiers. They settled down there, organized a community of like-minded people and introduced Roman habits and the Latin language (Rostovtzeff 1959: 245). These settlements provided for administration, legal offices, schools, markets and, by no means least in importance, places of amusement. The local people would acquire a sufficient facility in the new language to enable them to benefit from the amenities and services which were offered. Latin spread, gradually and thinly it is true, to more outposts and outlying hamlets, thus ensuring a degree of bilingualism.

But though military occupation was important in itself in spreading bilingualism, it was even more important in facilitating trade and commerce. During the civil wars several waves of Roman immigrants settled as organized groups in the conquered territories of Gaul, Spain and Africa. Some groups were led by the instigators of the revolution, but others settled voluntarily as traders, and agents of the tax-gathering concessionaries. They were the necessary bridgeheads for the penetration of Latin into the vernacular areas. Many of these *negotiatores* followed the legions, but instead of returning to Italy they remained, occupying themselves in local affairs and becoming models of Latin behavior and speech, to be emulated by the natives.

The presence of the military, the promotion of trade and commerce, and, especially after the civil wars, stability and safety of communication along increasing numbers of good highways produced a high level of urbanization. Gaul was fairly densely settled in the rural as well as the urban areas and the march of Latin was irresistible, though it took centuries for Latin to replace Gaulish. The cities were more amenable to Latin than was the countryside, and so were the upper classes compared with the others. The former were anxious to take advantage of the Roman schools which taught Latin and Greek, and large numbers of them graduated into the service of Rome, military and civil. The successors of Augustus encouraged provincials to migrate to the towns and cities, where they had to learn Latin in order to participate in the normal activities of urban life. Latin was, if not imposed, at least a superimposition, introduced more and more in a vulgarized form and in permanent conflict with the native language. Economic disintegration led to a more active bureaucracy, and to an extension of education. A passage in the Digest of Ulpian mentions village schoolmasters (Auerbach 1965: 251). The process of linguistic assimilation is not difficult to envisage: the highly developed public life, access to administrative and legal offices, markets and daily meetings—in the streets, the places of amusement, theaters, public baths, gymnasia and palaestra (which were open to most inhabitants who wished to gather there)—all were sufficient incentives and provided opportunities to acquire Latin. Conversely, the need to trade with the provincials was an equally powerful motive for the Romans to acquire some proficiency in the local languages. There was a gradual intermingling of the two languages and an increasingly rapid diffusion of Latin into the countryside. Their languages had for a long time influenced and been influenced by the Celtic languages. Germanic terms like *rik-a, frei, leder, erbe* have a Celtic origin. The Celtic La Tene culture was responsible for the contribution to Germanic of the names of such materials as lead and iron. Similar and even closer contacts were established between the Germans and the Romans.

However, the rural population was in no way completely absorbed by the cities and there was always a very extensive pool of proletariat monolinguals to ensure that the local language made up in strength what it lacked in prestige. The survival of the Gallic language into the 3d Century is attested in a passage in the Digest of Ulpian (222-228): "Fideicomunissa quo qunque sermone relenqui possunt, non solum Latina vel Graeca, sed etiam Punica vel Gallicana vel alterius cujuscum que gentis." St. Jerome's comparison of the language of the Treveri to that of the Galatians, and the inscriptions in the Temples at Treves, appear to indicate that Celtic was still in use in that area at the end of the 4th Century. In the same period Postumanius, in reply to a young priest who had apologized for the rusticity of his Latin in talking about St. Martin of Tours, said "Talk in Celtic or in Gallic so long as you talk about Martin." The diffusion of Latin geographically and socially and the retention of Gallic by the majority of the population ensured in every region a period of bilingualism during which the emphasis shifted from the vernacular to Latin.

Impact of the Germanic Tribes

The Romans were not allowed to continue undisturbed in their assimilation of the Celts and their language, and the interruption ensured that there were in fact two periods of prolonged bilingualism, the second of which was due to the presence of a new linguistic element brought by the Germanic tribes (Meillet 1951: II, 77).

After the 3d Century small Germanic groups and later whole tribes were invited to enter Roman territories and settle within the boundaries of the Empire. Some were recruited into the Roman army, others were made slaves. The system of "laeti" allowed for the settlement of Germans who sought refuge and in this way considerable numbers of Germans, bred on Roman soil, came to be able to speak their own languages and Latin. There were as many as 14 settlements in the cities of Northern Italy, Apulia and Calabria and nearly half as many again in Gaul (Jones 1960b: 620). In addition there were many penetrations of Gallo-Roman settlements by Germanic groups, while the promotion of commerce brought opportunities for linguistic contact between the two groups.

Between the mid-3d and the mid-5th Centuries the decline of the Empire helped to accelerate the movement of these and other tribes into the Empire.

There were massive immigrations of large non-Roman peoples in search for new homes, the so-called *Vokerwanderungen*. Rome itself was captured successively by the Goths (410 A.D.) and the Vandals (455 A.D.). However these peoples did not succeed in establishing permanent or even long-lasting independent states or governments. The Visigoths remained in Italy only from 401 to 410, when they moved to South Gaul (410-507) and Iberia (456-711). In Italy they were supplanted by the Ostrogoths (493-555). The Burgundians were defeated by the Romans in 437 and resettled in areas around Lyon and Geneva, and later near Vienne and Besancon. Because they had undergone a process of Romanization from such an early date, they were fairly easily assimilated in the transalpine areas and did not experience any lengthy period of bilingualism. This fact is reflected in the slight influence which their language had upon Gallo-Roman (Elcock 1960: 224). There is every likelihood too that the Visigoths also profited from their early contact with Rome so that the greater part of their nobility, although they spoke Gothic in ordinary discourse, understood, spoke and some even wrote a little Latin. The lower classes understood it less well in the early years of their settlement, but even they soon adapted to the new linguistic circumstances.

The Lombards were the most successful within Italy itself, remaining in the areas of Pavia, Spoleto (on the Po and the Tiber respectively) as well as east of Naples. But their influence is almost entirely confined to Italy. In Western Europe as a whole the most influential were the Franks who by the 8th Century occupied the land from, and including, Bavaria to the Low Countries and northern Gaul. They were the last to appear on the Gaulish scene and influenced the dialects of their areas considerably, the evidence relating mainly to lexical items in Old North French, though some syntactic survivals have been claimed (Hall 1974: 90). Unlike the Lombards they were continually reinforced from their homelands, and unlike the Burgundians and Visigoths they had not been under any considerable Latin influence before their permanent settlement. For these reasons theirs and the Gallo-Roman language contrived a lengthy period of co-existence, based on the numerical superiority of the one and the political, administrative and cultural prestige of the other (Meillet 1951: 92). The Suebi, from what little evidence we have, influenced Galician in the main, and was caught up in the complex of Ibero-Celtic dialects.

Thus, linguistically, the impact of the Germanic invasions varied in intensity and permanence. In Italy they played a relatively insignificant role partly because of the relative fewness of speakers of Germanic dialects in the area, the disunity and fratricidal proclivities of the invading tribes, the low prestige of the culture related to their languages compared with the culture of the Romans, which the invaders were reluctant to destroy because the educational provision favored the Latin language as it did in Gaul. But the speakers of the Germanic dialects even in Italy were bilingual at some stages, and many of them must have remained so for long periods. The immigrants probably spoke their native tongue among themselves, but with the failure of the reinforcements necessary to the survival of Germanic in the invaded territories, the social and cultural pressure of Latin prevailed and the shift to that language could not have been delayed beyond the second or third generation, around the 10th Century. The Germanic dialects, for the reasons already given, were not strong enough to affect any radical changes in Latin. There is only very doubtful evidence of any influence on the phonetics of Italian, and the most identifiable effects were on the vocabulary (Pulgram 1959: 230).

Elsewhere, during the whole of the Merovingian and the greater part of the Carolingian periods, the Germanic dialects were sustained. But with the coming of Christianity and its reception by the rulers, as well as the increasing attractiveness of the Gallo-Roman civilization, Latin became the common language. The conquerors found themselves obliged to use the language of the vanquished: there was a Latin secretary in the Burgundian court, and Theodoric the Visigoth was greatly drawn to Latin literature. Romans were used in administration and Romans of high rank became popular. The native nobility naturally followed the example of the courts. In spite of edicts to the contrary, intermarriage is known to have occurred. By the 5th Century many of even the common people must have known Latin or they could not have been able to worship or follow addresses from the pulpit. In the 6th Century the majority of the Franks would be compelled by the necessities of day-to-day business to adopt the language of a population which immensely outnumbered them (Dill 1926: 277-278). Latin continued to perform a unique function in spite of it being the language of a minority. The life of a period, as late as the 12th Century for instance, found expression in Latin hymns: polemical literature, chronicles and mystical speculations were written in that language. One has to conclude with Pirenne (1937: 112) and Curtius (1953: 25) that the Germanic peoples did little if anything to change the essential characteristics of the languages or of the intellectual character of the Mediterranean area: they disturbed the surface but did not affect the enduring patterns of linguistic and therefore of intellectual contact. They not only brought no new ideas with them, they "also with the exception of the Anglo-Saxons allowed the Latin language to remain the only means of communication wherever they settled. Here as in all other spheres they assimilated" (Pirenne op. cit.: 112).

By the end of the 7th Century many factors had helped to sway the advantage permanently in favor of the Gallo-Roman dialects and facilitated the shift to what was now emerging clearly as Romance. One of the factors was the accentuation of the very long-standing differences between spoken (vulgar) Latin and the written language. The argument, until comparatively recently accepted by very many scholars, that the Romance languages developed as they did because of the shaping influence of the local languages on Latin, is now largely discounted. Though it would be unrealistic to believe that the local languages did not have a material effect on the development of Romance, they are now seen to be in the main the result of the growing disparity between the spoken and written variants of Latin.

From the time of Cicero onward grammarians recognized different varieties of Latin, especially the differences between elegant *sermo urbanus* and the everyday *sermo usualis, sermo vulgaris* or *sermo rusticus.* The Latin variants refer back to a source which, although it was not identical with Classical Latin, was very close to it. The two variants, classical literary usage and everyday informal speech, diverged about the middle of the 2d Century B.C. (Hall 1974: 16). There was never any sharp separation, but from the 1st Century B.C. onward classical usage became even more conservative and was distinguished by its homogeneity and selectivity (Auerbach 1965: 249), while the popular idiom developed according to the demands and pressures of everyday affairs, as well as because of the influences of the local languages. It was natural, therefore, that just as the original classical Latin had produced its own variants, the popular variant should . generate dialects which reflected the differences between the languages and the environments of the several ethnic groups who spoke it. Thus it came about that one form of Latin, *sermo urbanus* was a superimposition standing over and against the everyday *sermo vulgaris.* Toward the end of the 5th Century the last remaining groups of the Roman-educated aristocracy had assimilated in terms of the popular Latin, and though the other variant lived on as a written language it meant that the separate development of the vernaculars, now becoming increasingly "Romance," was facilitated.

So, "in the early middle ages there was no literary public and no generally literary language" (Auerbach 1965: 23), and the undoubted bilingualism which prevailed at that time was with very few exceptions an entirely oral bilingualism. The degree of this bilingualism is best measured by a consideration of the geographical extent of the *sermo vulgaris.* In the 4th Century, for instance, it was used throughout Italy, Iberia, Sardinia, Corsica, Gaul (with the exception of the Celtic Brittany), present-day Switzerland, Germany south of the Rhine, the Main and the Danube, Southern Austria, Croatia, Serbia and Dacia (Hall 1974: 109).

A second factor influencing the shift to the vulgar tongue was the consciousness of illiteracy and the need to eradicate it. This consciousness characterized the elements of society to whom the rise of feudalism had given a new status. This was comparable to the desire for literacy among the rising Middle Classes in England during the 16th Century, a desire which promoted English in preference to Latin in the new Grammar Schools. Though none of the local languages apart from Gothic produced a literature, the German dialects invited attention from many among the clergy and some of the courts, who would in any case be well versed in the use of Latin.

The earliest connected sentences in a clearly Romance language are the Oaths of Strasburg (842) pronounced by Louis the German and the Soldiers of Charles the Bald. Documents, difficult to date, include sermons and short religious poems. For several hundreds of years after the break-up of the Empire the normal written language continued to be the *sermo urbanus*: it was not until 813 that the Church, alerted to the failure of communication with the common people, issued an edict at the Council of Tours that priests should translate their sermons "in rusticam romanam linguam aut theotiscan" (into the rustic Roman, or German tongue). As late as Charlemagne the same need was felt, this time in the secular sphere. Wishing the common people to understand the laws by which they were governed, he decreed that they should be translated (Auerbach 1965: 266). We possess writings in Romance languages from the 9th, 10th and 11th Centuries but even in the 12th Century they are still fragmentary. Further, none of what was written in the vernaculars before the end of the 12th Century was addressed to the readers, who even at the end of that century were exceedingly rare. Those who could read at all read the "high variant" or *sermo urbanus*: what was written in the vernaculars was intended to be read aloud to the illiterate (Auerbach 1965: 280, 284) and this group includes a large number of the nobility.

The bilingualism of these centuries, we must again stress, was very largely if not almost exclusively an oral bilingualism; those who could read read only one language. Nevertheless this phase of Western European bilingualism left its mark upon the linguistic map, especially on what has become contemporary France. Bilingualism or bidialectalism was a pronounced phenomenon for several centuries. As late as the 16th Century, it has been remarked, bilingualism existed among a large number of Frenchmen, and the ancient vernaculars subsisted in familiar intercourse, especially among the less well educated. The same condition is reflected in the way in which *le français commun* is even now spoken in the various provinces, for instance in Provence (Meillet 1951: 101-102). During the early Middle Ages, therefore, the conflict between the languages Romance and Latin did not mean that classical language ceased to be spoken and was used only for reading and writing. The position was that Romance was the "native" language and Latin a second, the former not being employed generally for reading and writing. The latter was taught and spoken in the schools, where the pupils were punished if they even inadvertently slipped into the Romance vernacular. It was also the official language of the Church, the law, and the customary language of commerce.

The interest of the Empire in schools during the period of its decline was largely due to the need for an increased bureaucracy, especially in the 3d Century when the administration was centralized and enlarged. Elementary education was then greatly extended and we hear, for instance in the Digest of Ulpian, of the village schoolmaster as an influential figure. The schools served first of all to accentuate the difference between the two variants of Latin, and at the same time helped to ensure the survival of the "elegant language" and therefore of bilingualism. Thus, these schools catering of, necessity almost, for students who were bilingual or were anxious to become bilingual, were maintained by the municipalities but supervised by the central imperial administration. Such schools as were established at Narbonne, Toulouse, Arles, Lyons, Autun, Treves, Bordeaux, Vienne and the other large towns were attended, generally speaking, by young noblemen, though inscriptions show that the trading classes were attracted to them as time went on (Pope 1952: i). The schools were mainly interested in refining the language of the students. The sons of the Celtic nobility could learn the "correct" Latin of Rome itself, with standards which diverged more and more from the vulgar Latin of traders and soldiers who were the ubiquitous tutors of the mass of the population. Their educational program was characterized by the distinctive methods of the bilingual Greek-Latin-speaking rhetors, thus the schoolmaster of the West was the ally of the Empire to the extent that he ensured the Romanization of the Gauls: and as more schools were built this Romanization of the Celtic and Germanic tribes was intensified.

THE BYZANTINE CIVILIZATION AND SLAVIC CONTACTS

Safeguarding the Greek Inheritance

The concept of the Mediterranean as a culture unit and as a framework for a coherent pattern of language contacts may be exemplified in a consideration of the contribution of the Byzantine civilization to the history of bilingualism and bilingual education. Byzantium came to be the only center where Greek and Roman civilization was still alive and the respective languages were cultivated assiduously by large numbers of bilinguals. After the passage of the Goths through Dacia and the Balkans in the 4th and 5th Centuries, new large scale migrations of Slavic groups took place in the 6th and 7th Centuries. Their incursions extended as far as Greece and the Peloponnesies and they settled permanently in the Balkans, the Central and lower Danube valley and Dacia. The Latin-speaking population of Dacia probably remained in Transylvania in close contact with the Slavic-speaking invaders (c.f., Hall 1974: 82). A little later, the Arab conquests of the 7th Century on the shores of the Mediterranean, because of the changes they precipitated in France and Italy, ensured that the remnants of the Roman Empire in the West and of Romanized Gaul had little influence on their German conquerors: they were prevented from transmitting to them the Graeco/Roman literary and linguistic heritage. Charlemagne in the North did what he could to try to salvage something of what was left, but access to the source of Graeco-Roman civilization was barred by the Arabs, the Avars and the Slavs, who were holding Central Europe and the Balkans (Dvornik 1949: 183). The Byzantines not only helped to safeguard what remained of the classical world but constituted themselves consciously as the mediators between that civilization and the "barbarians." They also ensured the renewal of classical culture in the Renaissance. "The world Renaissance was invented in Italy by a Byzantine clique" (Neuman 1969: 36).

Economically and culturally the Greek cities on the north coast of the Black Sea in classical and Hellenistic times linked the Greek world to the steppes of Western Eurasia. From as far back as the 7th Century B.C. there were commercially oriented Greek settlements there. Those cities were then, as they were later to the Byzantines, outposts of Hellenism—"the hem of Greece sewn on the folds of the Barbarians" (Cicero, *De Republica*: 11.4). The Byzantine Empire was situated at the junction of communication between Asia and Europe, and Europe and Africa; all routes, by land, sea or river connecting Eastern Europe with the Mediterranean passed through Byzantine territory. In some senses, political and military, they were vulnerable on this account. But from the standpoint of commerce its centrality was an inestimable advantage, and by the same token it constituted the focal point for the convergence of many languages.

The Byzantines safeguarded an inheritance, linguistic in particular, and enabled those with whom they were in contact to profit from it. They enabled the South Slavs to survive for centuries of Ottoman occupation. Further, Russia, it has been claimed, was Byzantine's greatest spiritual conquest (Portal 1969: 4). They thus expanded considerably the limited range of the Graeco-Roman influence of later centuries.

> The world of Justinian's time was larger than that which the West knew in the Middle Ages. In Justinian's time men were acquainted with Scandinavia and could distinguish between Swedes and Norwegians. They used the trade routes through Russia to the Baltic. The peoples of Russia from Finns and Letts in the North to the Mordvins, Iranians and Altaic nomads were no strangers to the Byzantines, nor for the same reasons were Russians unacquainted with other nations. Early Russian urban centers had German, Jewish and Armenian together with Varangian quarters. In Central Asia the Byzantines knew the great Turkic realm stretching from Persia to China. Byzantines visited West Turkestan and Sogdiana regularly. (Haussig 1971: 101)

The work of the Chronicler John Malatas (7th Century) was preserved in the papyrus documents and records of Barbarian princes beyond the Empire. What the Aramaic language, Greek in Hellenistic, and Latin in Imperial times had done to create a unity in the Mediterranean, and to extend its influence in the West, the Byzantines (using Greek but also the Slavic languages) did in bridging the West and East Mediterranean, and extending the Mediterranean influence northward and eastward of the Black Sea and throughout Central and Eastern Europe. The pattern of linguistic contacts so created was as complex as that of Western Europe, and since it involved at least the fringes of what is now the Soviet Union, it was vastly more extensive.

The history of East-West relations up to the present even was written by those early Byzantines who, while maintaining and promoting the Greek language and its associated culture, acknowledged also the necessity of using the local Slavic dialects. The Kievean tradition so greatly indebted to Byzantium helped, after the Mongol interruption, to fix Russian in the cultural system of Byzantium and the Hellenes. This was not an easy matter, or was its Western orientation ever a foregone conclusion. Dostoevski saw the dilemma of East and West. In his view the conquest of Asia by the Russians

> is necessary because Russia is not only in Europe, but also in Asia: because Russia is not only a European, but also an Asiatic. Not only that: in our destiny it is perhaps precisely Asia that represents our main way out. (Dostoevski 1896)

Trubetskoy thought Russia was fundamentally related to the East and Peter the Great's reforms were sterile (Trubetskoy 1927: 34-53). Roman Jakobson has followed his master in stressing the eastern linguistic affiliations of Russia (Jakobson 1969: I, 144-201). None of these comments is false: what they do in fact is to represent what, without the Byzantine influence, would have been an ineluctable and irresistible attraction away from Europe. Nor is it the history of Russian alone which reflects the contemporary power of the Byzantine heritage. The misunderstanding which, after the Yugoslav unification, still divided Croats and Serbs was in the last analysis explicable only in terms of the conflict between the Byzantines and Rome. The quarrel still separates the Roman Slavs (Croats, Slovenes, Slovaks, Czechs and Poles) from the Byzantines (Serbs, Bulgarians).

> The dissemination of Byzantine civilization among Slav peoples is of general historical significance—more so than the transmission of Byzantine culture to the West and to the Armenian and Caucasian peoples, for it has continued to determine their development to the present day. (Haussig 1971: 302)

The Byzantine expansion depended on trading contacts rather than conquest, so that there had to be mutual respect for the languages of the participants. For instance, behind the conflict between Persia and the Byzantine Empire lay the struggle for access to the central Asian routes to China and the silk trade. The Byzantines depended entirely on trade: traders stayed in special quarters in cities—Turkic traders from Central Asia as well as Persians. They also traded with the Altaic tribes in Russia and Siberia. Their communication network embraced the peoples of the Caucusus and West Turkestan. The Iberians in the Caucusus were strongly attached to Byzantium. On the eastern shore of the Black Sea the Lazgins, Abaz and Zichians were converted to Christianity by the Byzantines in the 6th Century and this proved a powerful cultural influence. Trade was not the only factor which promoted Byzantine Greek. The development of Byzantine civilization was possible only with the elevation of Christianity as a state religion and so in Armenia and the Balkans the language was the instrument of political influence: in the former countering Arabic influences and in the latter forestalling Frankish and Latin Papal overtures. However the Byzantine Church's influence was greater than its political power. Its missionaries transmitted its culture: religion meant the introduction of the Graeco-Roman tradition, and Orthodox Christianity meant the cultural assimilation of the Slavs, reinforced by the use of the Greek language. In Italy, Byzantine Greek was reinforced by three waves of immigration, the first consequent on the Slav penetration of Greece, the second from Syria and Palestine because of Arabic pressure and the third from Greece, Asia Minor and Constantinople because of religious or iconographic controversies. Whatever the reasons, Byzantine Greek influence spread.

The Encouragement of Slavic Languages

The decline in the influence of Rome meant the shift of the linguistic, cultural, economic, and military center of gravity from Italy to Asia Minor and the provinces of the lower Danube. The language of trade, including the slave trade, was Greek. For the slaves from Syria, Asia Minor, Egypt and Roman provinces of Africa, Greek was a common language, as it was among the traders. In the first half of the 7th Century Latin was replaced by Greek as the official language of the Byzantine Empire, though Roman traditions remained strong and enclaves of Latin persisted for several decades in the East. However, even more important than the predominance of Greek over Latin was the eventual breakdown of the monopoly of both languages, brought about partly by the system of military command on the borders, which gave a good measure of local autonomy, partly because of the establishment of new and important industries in the eastern provinces, but mainly because of the evolution of local Christian churches. These had begun as early as the 3d Century when it became possible to speak of Anatolian, Syrian, Egyptian and Roman churches, all distinguished by linguistic differences. There was a corpus of Syriac Christian literature at the beginning of the 3d Century, as well as Coptic (Egyptian) translations of the Bible.

Although it is "the fashion in Western Europe to underestimate its influence" (Miller 1952: 326), it is the Byzantine relationship with the Slavs which introduces the principal new element into the history of bilingualism. Their precursors, the Antae, appeared about the 3d Century when the Scythian and Sarmatian civilization was destroyed by the Goths. Even that antecedent Slavic culture was impregnated with Hellenistic influences, and those very early Slavs, the Antae, formed a link between the Hellenic-Scythian-Sarmatian civilization on the one hand, and that of 9th-Century Kiev on the other. Contemporaneously with the Norman invasion of Western Europe and the collapse of Charlemagne's work, the Slavs advanced to the South, West and North far into the eastern Alps and the Dalmatian coast. They possessed in time almost the whole of Greece. In Macedon up to Thessalonica and even to Thrace and Graeco-Roman provincial population held out only in scattered enclaves in towns on the lower Danube. In the face of the advancing Slavs the rest of the Romanized Illyrians retreated into the mountains until the end of the 12th Century when they settled as farmers and began the foundation of the Rumanian nation. Most of the Greeks retreated too, and others fled to Southern Italy. By the 9th Century the pattern in the area of present-day Yugoslavia and Bulgaria is a mosaic of peoples in which the Slavic element predominates. Baudel has called it an "ethnic conglomerate." The Byzantines were ringed by Slavs from the Alps to the Black Sea and from the Adriatic to the Aegean, in Eastern Thrace, Thessally and Epirus.

Furthermore these Slavs maintained their ethnic identity and their Slavic dialects, in some places within Greece up to the 15th Century. Thessalonica, the native town of Constantine/Cyril and Methodus, the Balkan missionaries, was a bilingual city in the 9th Century. It received neighboring Slavs within its walls and had close contact with the Slavs of the surrounding countryside. It is not surprising that the two missionaries were multilingual—both spoke Latin, Arabic and possibly an Altaic language as well as the Slav dialect of the Thessalonian area. Constantinople was even more polyglot. The city attracted people from every country—ambassadors and kings, traders and merchants, adventurers and merce-naries. It was the home of the foreigner, and the cauldron of languages.

Although trade as well as political and military considerations entered into the Byzantine-Slav relationship, it was religion and especially the work of the missionaries which dominated the interlingual situation. On the eastern shore of the Black Sea the Lezgins and the Abazins were converted to Christianity in the 6th Century by Byzantine missionaries and it was their mediation which enabled the Greek language to penetrate Georgia and to influence the Iverians. The Byzantine renaissance of the 9th Century provided the impetus for the Orthodox Church missionaries to carry the Greek language to the peoples of Central and Eastern Europe. Orthodox Christianity was a means of assimilating the Slavs culturally and this was reinforced by the use of Greek as a liturgical language, the consequence being the indelible imprint of the Greek language upon Old Church Slavonic. Nevertheless, though in Greece itself Byzantine policy was hellenization, elsewhere they exercised a remarkable degree of tolerance of Slav dialects. What linguistic conflict there was existed between Slavic and Greek, but principally between Slavic and Latin and was expressed in arguments and practices concerning the liturgy.

One consequence of the Byzantine presence and of its tolerance of the local languages outside Greece itself was the difference in the education provided compared with Western Europe, where in the centuries we have reviewed book learning was drawn from Monastic sources. In the Eastern Empire, J. B. Bury claimed "every boy and girl whose parents could afford to pay was educated," reflecting St. Gregory of Nazianzeu's belief that "all those who have sense will acknowledge that education is the first of the goods we possess." This education was provided for those whose native tongue was not Greek (the language of instruction) and was therefore a type of education for bilingual children. But there was an element of bilingualism in the education of the Greek-speaking child also, since the aim of the education was the complete hellenization of the speech and mind of students and the defense of classical Greek against the popular language—an early form of diglossia. Such an education began between the ages of six and eight and the child studied locally with teachers of the elementary school. Beyond this primary stage many never progressed, but for those who did there was "grammar" and all that it implied in the middle school, and "rhetoric" and philosophy at the University.

The old Bulgar language was transcribed in Greek characters. They had no script of their own and the majority of transcriptions, even in the 9th Century, were in the Greek vernacular so that even there Greek must have survived the barbarian invasions from the East. It was used as the official language of the Bulgar state in the first half of the 9th Century. Young Bulgars were sent to Constantinople to school for a solid grounding in Greek secular education. The conflict of Latin and Greek and antagonism to both tended to handicap education and the development of a literature. At first, Latin and Greek sources were transposed into Slavic idioms. When Bulgar areas fell under Byzantine domination

Greek became the language of education, though a survival of a Slav national tradition is evident. It was from Bulgaria that the new written language, in Cyrillic, went out to become the Greek-rite ecclesiastical and educational language in Kiev. The development of a national literature with the help of Byzantine works transmitted through Bulgarian translations led to the formation of the old Russian koiné based on the Kievan dialect, which by the 11th Century was influenced by the idioms of the local dialect. The Bulgarian literary language together with Greek had been in evidence at the Kievan Court since the 10th Century. In the 11th Century it gradually became the Russian literary language with a strong Kievan (Byzantine) influence. Following the decline of Kievan supremacy the Moscow parizans of Latin or Greek respectively were in conflict but the Byzantine influence remained too strong, so that the Russian language, in developing its excellent philosophical vocabulary, relied on Old Slavic translations of the Greek Holy Fathers. By the introduction of the Slavonic liturgy into the Russian state, indirectly from the work of Cyril and Methodus, the Russian Slavs inherited the Old Slavonic literature bequeathed by the two missionaries to Moravia. As a result in the 10th, 11th and 12th Centuries Kievan Russia grew into the center of culture in the Latin West at that time, partly because of the great inheritance the Byzantines transmitted, and partly because they were not simply willing but anxious to employ the Slavic languages as a means of transmission.

Bohemia was biliturgical and its religious rites bilingual in the 10th Century. Although Poland was under intense German (Latin oriented) pressure, and although Latin was the language of learning and the official language, we may assume that besides Latin priests there came to Poland priests educated in the use of the Slavonic language. Even Wenceslas, committed to a westward, Latin orientation, had no quarrel with Slavonic liturgy, literature and language. The Slavonic language was centered on Prague whereas it was at Budech, out in the country, that the Latin language was established in educational institutions. The same conflict of language affiliation is exemplified in the South. In the 6th and 7th Centuries B.C. the Southern Slavs, Slovenes, Croats and Serbs spread over the eastern Alps, the Danube basin and the Balkan toward the Peloponnesies clashing with Romanized Graeco-Illyrian peoples. Elements of the latter adopted Slav. Other areas along the Dalmatian coast resisted Slavicization. While in the East the South Slavs took in Turco-Tatar elements to form the Bulgarian people, in the western areas they were assimilated into the Greek-speaking population.

Dalmatia was populated by a variety of peoples including, from the 4th Century B.C., a colony of Greeks. It was conquered by Rome and enjoyed a brilliant civilization until the 5th Century A.D. It became Christian in the 3d Century and, hardly touched by German influence, it came under Byzantine influence in the time of Justinian, and was submerged by Slavs in the 6th Century and with some exceptions it was completely Slavicized. Slavonic was introduced into the rites of Dalmatian Croatia by the 9th Century and many priests were educated in Bohemia. At the same time the Latin Bishop of Dalmatian Croatia was under the jurisdiction of Rome. Yet the strength of the favorable attitude to Slavonic was so strong that he showed no animosity to the use of Slavonic. The

Croat Church, following its abandonment by the Byzantines, turned to Rome and this had a powerful influence on the education of the young. Education became the province of priests and monks who substituted Latin as the teaching language. The Benedictines provided many schools and libraries along the coast. Dominican schoolmasters appeared later. Nevertheless there was a significant language conflict in their schools. Though Latin predominated, Croatian literature during the early Medieval period evolved entirely in the Glagolitic writing. Slavic dialects, Čakavština and Ikauština persisted and enabled communication to be maintained with the Serbs. The subjects taught to Slavic-speaking children were very much the same as those taught in the Latin schools of the West. Latin constituted the foundations but Glagolitic as well as Latin script were used.

Although the Eastern and Western Churches differed fundamentally in their policies for language in school and society, the former being liberal and the latter conservative, and although they also differed in the degree of ecclesiastical control they exercised over education, the former being favorable to a secular system while the latter insisted on a completely ecclesiastical control, they shared one thing in common, namely: the promotion of whatever language was favored, Latin in the West, Greek or the local languages in the East, was undertaken in the main by missionaries. Augustine was typical, perhaps the prototype. In addition to Latin and Greek he spoke Phoenician and knew something of its affinity with Hebrew. He insisted on his Bishops speaking or knowing Phoenician. Cyril and Methodus were in that tradition to which Jerome also contributed. The missionary's awareness of language led to the preparation of religious texts in local languages and this helped to standardize and stabilize many of those which were in very close contact with other languages and under intense pressure to change rapidly. They also helped to maintain those languages. Apart from the major languages, Latin, Greek and Aramaic, they produced texts in Coptic, Gothic, Old Church Slavonic, Armenian, Georgian, Albanian and Finno Ugrian. But perhaps as great as any other contribution they made to the stabilizing of language contact situations in the Old World is their work in similar linguistic situations in the New World. Although this aspect of bilingualism and bilingual education is beyond the scope of the present essay, it may be that it is no more than the extension of the influence of the languages of the Mediterranean and a reflection of the same issues which were experienced in the Old.

JEWISH BILINGUALISM

The Middle East

The history of bilingualism and bilingual education in a limited area which we have attempted to trace has been governed by the interaction of one or another of three "imperial" languages. Aramaic, Greek and Latin on the one hand, and on the other many languages spoken in limited areas, like Phrygian or Lycian in the Middle East, the Italic languages, Celtic on the continent or in Britain, and the Slavic languages. The Jews have spoken or written Hebrew for well over 3000 years, and have been in close contact with the three "imperial" languages as well as very many of the "localized" languages in the Middle East, West, Central and Eastern Europe. Hebrew is not an "imperial" or is it simply a local language: it has had an international provenance from very early times, but it has not had the political, military or massive economic reinforcement which has enabled the imperial languages not only to survive for many centuries as Hebrew has done, but to dominate the local languages as well. Successive waves of linguistic influence swept over the Jews—Hebrew, Aramaic, Greek and Arabic. While these linguistic tides ebbed and flowed the speakers of Hebrew and Aramaic were in close contact with the Hittites, Phrygians, Thracians, Armenians and many others. Educational influences originating in several different countries were experienced by them. For instance, Egyptian pedagogic treatises, "Teachings," exercised a marked effect on Jewish education under Solomon, whose need for increased numbers of trained scribes on account of the expansion of his bureaucracy caused him to turn to Egyptian practice and theory.

The extensive and varied bilingualisms which have characterized the social and religious life of Jews from the beginning of their history to the present time is not to be doubted or underestimated, but because of the unique status of Hebrew among Jews, together with their additional and intimate linguistic affiliations at various times and in different areas, the pattern of bilingualism among the Jews is both different from and far more varied than that of any other people. Furthermore, Hebrew-related bilingualism runs like a single, clearly identifiable strand through the texture of bilingualism in Europe, which is the limit of our present concern. Hebrew never died in any of the areas where Jewish communities were established, and for over 1300 years it was the everyday language of the Israelites. (Fellman 1973: 250) Even when its status as the vernacular was undermined and it was replaced as a spoken language by Aramaic and Greek, after 200 A.D., Hebrew still remained a living language. From 500 A.D. onward written Hebrew was a vital means of secular communication within and between the Jewish communities of different countries, while remaining the sanctified language of study and religious observances. Long before the 9th Century the language was scientifically studied and its proper usage established. In some places it was also a spoken language, used by Jews either to emphasize their separateness from the gentiles, or as a means of international communication among Jews from different areas of Europe. Consequently, Hebrew was the one stable or consistent element serving to ensure the continuity of the Jewish people. Nevertheless, while religious and historical literature, like Ecclesiasticus, Maccabees I, Esther and David, continued to be written in Hebrew, it ceased to be their only or even their most frequently used language.

Aramaic became their dominant spoken language and gradually became a literary and even a co-sanctified language. As Hebrew lost some of its familiarity for the Jews, their scriptures had to be translated into Greek to be comprehensible to large segments of the population. Their late classical literature, for instance the last three books of Maccabees, was written in Greek and even modeled on Greek genres. The protracted Greek rule in Judea, the patterns of the Ptolemaic and

Seleucid regimes, the material achievements of the Hellenistic civilization in finance, agriculture and city building combined to produce far-reaching changes in language affiliation among the Jews. Yet hellenization, normally supported by the Jewish aristocracy, the Greek princes, the Maccabees (Hasmoneans) and Herodian rulers of Judea under Roman patronage, was resisted by the masses, so that Aramaic was able to co-exist as a vernacular with Greek, together with Hebrew as a language of different status. The co-existence of Greek- and Aramaic-speaking settlements in Egypt was an important aspect of Jewish bilingualism at that time. The highest class was undoubtedly Macedonian and Greek, but there were many Jews whose influence was only slightly less (Sarton 1950: 17). In the Herodian city of Caesarea there were Jews who read the Shema in Greek.

The Rabbis knew Greek well and as to the masses, though they were not favorable to Greek, their knowledge of that language was unlikely to be less than that which other nationalities in the Middle East possessed. The attraction of the cultured Jew toward Greek is suggested by the prohibition, expressed in Rabbinic regulations, on the teaching of Greek, while the importance of the Maccabean revolt was as much linguistic as religious (James 1920: 64, 65). The study of Greek was considered a prerequisite for leadership among the Jews of Palestine, since that task involved the needs and problems of the Hellenistic-Roman Jewish Diaspora, and contact with gentile rulers and authorities. However, although elementary education in the Talmudic period points to contact between educational institutions of the Greek cities and the educational institutions of the Jews, the general Jewish school system for all Jews dealt with neither Greek culture nor their language. Greek was studied in Palestine only by the narrow aristocratic circles, and it was, therefore, very much an elitist bilingual education that was provided (Safrai 1971: 148, 153). The great majority of the Jewish people lived in scattered towns and distant urban areas within and beyond the boundaries of the Roman Empire, in Persia, and the Arab kingdoms along the Red Sea coast.

Meanwhile the Jewish affiliation to Aramaic became less firm with the rise of Arabic. Though many scholars have maintained that Aramaic remained as a spoken language among the Jews down to the 8th Century, and others claim that dialects of Aramaic are still evident in Syria and Iraq, it is generally believed that the Jews ceased to use Aramaic after the 5th Century and turned to Arabic (Shaffer 1972: 320). In the large cities of the Middle East, Jews and Arabs were not segregated, the two communities often shared property and Jews occupied land bordering on Muslim or Christian properties. There was enough face-to-face contact to prevent a closed linguistic group, but at the same time enough concentration around the Synagogue to ensure absolute commitment to their own language (Gottein 1971: 175). Great numbers of Jews worked in Arab academies and other educational institutions, and they took an active part in the cultural rebirth of the Orient (Keller 1971: 145).

During 300 years after the rise of Islam the Hebrew bible had been translated into Arabic more than once, the tenets of the Jewish faith had been set forth in the language of Islamic theology, and the rabbinical law had been formulated with the aid of Muslim legal terms. Jews were intimately involved in the development of an Arabic culture. Simultaneously Judaism, too, developed in every respect, and the Hebrew language was cultivated (Gottein 1971: 170, 172).

Spain

With the development of national languages in Spain, Italy, Northern and Eastern Europe the Jews were involved in even more and novel patterns of bilingualism. Before the coming of the Barbarians there were sizable Jewish communities in Rome, Naples and in Sicily, while in Milan, Verona, Genoa and other northern Italian cities they preserved their communities under the Ostrogoths. In Gaul the Jews were mixing with the native populations of Marseilles, called the Hebrew city, Narbonne in the Auvergne, Arles, Orleans and Bordeaux. They had been in Spain for centuries before the arrival of the Visigoths. In Northern Spain the headstone at the grave of a young Jewish woman named Miriam is inscribed in Hebrew, Greek and Latin. With their long history of close relations with Arabs it is not surprising that the Muslim invaders of Spain were supported by the Jews. Neither is it surprising that the Jewish system of education took Arabic into account while maintaining Hebrew. In Spain, no less than in France and Germany, the basis of Jewish education was a knowledge of Hebrew prayers, the Bible and the Talmud. A knowledge of Arabic was presupposed in all the syllabi as was a knowledge of Latin, later. The pedagogical program was discussed in Hebrew and Arabic writings. The intimate relations of Christians, Jews and Muslims in Spain is witnessed at the intellectual level by the production of the Mozambic haragat, bilingual refrains in the Ibero-Romance dialect to Hebrew and Arabic verses (Hall 1974: 117). Two centuries after the Muhammadan conquest was a golden age for the Jews in Spain (Keller 1971: 174), especially in Seville, Granada and Toledo. Cordoba was the seat of an important Jewish academy with students from all over Spain and North Africa engaged in the study of Hebrew and Arabic, and acting as involuntary intermediaries between the literatures of the two languages, for instance the introduction of Arabic metrical forms (Keller 1971: 181). The importance of Spanish centers of learning helped to preserve Hebrew because the confluence of so many students from the various European countries meant that Hebrew became the lingua franca but it cannot be doubted that, but for the use of Hebrew in worship, that language might have been lost in Spain. It was complained at the end of the 13th Century that the younger generation spoke only the language of the country, and that the majority of male adults even could not speak Hebrew. The Hebrew poets, grammarians, and Bible exegetes were indignant over the neglect of formal instruction in Hebrew, and deplored the superficial knowledge of the language among the masses. In Sicily they spoke the local language, Greek and Arabic.

This was very different from the situation of the Jews of Provence, the geographical situation of which made it an ideal meeting palce for their development under Spanish Arabic influence.

> Provencal Jews were initially immersed head and shoulders in traditional
> learning . . . unlike their co-religionists in Moslem Spain where in addition to
> rabbinic learning Jewish scholars welcomed and absorbed the culture of the
> Muslims and emulated them in poetry, comparative linguistics . . . the Jews of
> Provence were scarcely exposed to secular (influences). (Ben-Sassoon
> 1971: 195)

Nevertheless it was Provence which provided the center for the transmission of Judeo-Arabic achievements in philosophy and philology. It was the clearing house and center for translations from Arabic, and its schools were involved in the dissemination of secular linguistic learning.

This was the result of the shifting of the Jewish center of gravity northward in Spain as a consequence of the transfer of political mastery in the Iberian peninsula from the Saracens to the Christians. Spanish was the tongue of the now dominant population and Spanish was also the vernacular of the Jews in the reconquered areas,[11] though as late as the 14th Century the Jews spoke and wrote Arabic in Toledo, just as in Sicily Arabic was still spoken by Jews long after the departure of the Saracens. Sicily continued in the 13th and 14th Centuries to be a great center of Jewry.

It is no wonder that of the Jews of Spain and Provence it was claimed "they knew Persian, Arabic, the languages of the Franks, Spaniards, and Slavs." But it was Romance which the Jews cultivated as their secular native languages and it is they which were referred to as "our language." Both Catalan and Castilian in their different ways left their traces on the response literature.

> As if prompted by a premonition of their destiny the Jews of the Iberian
> province adhered to their beloved language all the more tenaciously as the
> century of doom and exile advanced upon them. It became increasingly the
> language in which they formulated the statutes and regulations of their social
> and communal life. They also made it the literary medium of their lighter vein.
> (Neuman, 102)

Meanwhile they preserved the use of Hebrew and many continued to read Arabic.

Italy

Jewish communities were to be found solidly established in many Italian cities when the Empire came into being. The revolt against the Romans in Palestine and the fall of Jerusalem resulted in the enslavement of many thousands of Jews who were brought to Italy, 97,000 to Rome alone. The increase in the Jewish population of South Italian cities like Taranto was enormous, and the cities north of the capital were also recipients of large numbers of Jews. Therefore the Jewish community in Italy, centered on Rome, were descended from Jewish families established in the country from Imperial times and constituted one of the oldest recognizable elements in the ethnic constitution of the peninsula. About 96-100 A.D. Rabbi Mathea ben Hevesh was sent to organize the Italian communities and he introduced an apparently new system of education which while it preserved the Jewish languages also took account of local vernaculars. It is not surprising, therefore, that with increasing cultural and linguistic acclimatization an Italian vernacular literature makes its appearance among them. The language employed is evidence of the interaction of the Jewish and local languages, and the linguistic characteristics of this contact have been perpetuated in the Judeo-Italian dialect. This was attested in. medieval documents and in scattered Italian dialects, especially in Leghorn (Hall 1974: 30).

In the 8th and 9th Centuries it is obvious that there was a remarkable revival of interest in Hebrew language and literature in Southern Italy. The Jewish scholars and educated lay members of the population were at all times in close contact with Palestine, partly because of commerce and pilgrimage interest. It is not surprising therefore that inscriptions in the southern towns and in Rome itself are in choice Hebrew displaying a wide knowledge of the literature and a scholarly acquaintance with the language (Roth 1946: 59). In Southern Italy there appears to have been a prolonged cultural ferment. The Latin, Italian, Byzantine and Muslim elements combined with the Jewish to keep in being a high level of intellectual excitement. The contribution of the Jews was important mainly because of their wide linguistic knowledge which enabled them to translate from Arabic, sometimes via Hebrew to Latin. This "renaissance" could not have been achieved so well but for the openness of the Mediterranean area. "Multiple lines of communication of whose abundance we had till recently no idea ran between Italy (especially Rome) Byzantium and Sicily" (Heer 1953: 105). With the expulsion of the Jews from Spain, Sicily, and later from Portugal, this Jewish element in Italian intellectual life was greatly enriched. Italy was the only land in Christian Europe open to them. In Rome in addition to the several old established Italian congregations and those maintained by immigrants from northern Europe, synagogues following the Castilian, Catalan, Aragonese and Sicilian rites were established. A similar process occurred in the North, where in addition to a few Spanish refugees—Sephardim—there was a constant immigration from Germany and Central Europe, and in the 15th Century from Rhodes. Holland experienced an influx of Ashkenazim from Germany so that the situation in Holland as in Italy reflected two types of Jewish linguistic characteristics—Spanish-speaking Sephardim who had been there for a long time, and German/Slavic-speaking Ashkenazim.

By the time of the full flowering of the Renaissance the Jewish population of Italy had been profoundly Italianized in both language and culture. Jewish immigrants from Spain, Portugal and Northern Europe retained their former "national" languages for some considerable time, but they too were assimilated like the Italian Jews. The Jews in Italy nevertheless tended to preserve, as they did in other countries, an early stage of the development of Italian based on the Roman dialect and affected very little by the fashionable Tuscan. Together they constituted a rich and varied pattern of bilingualism, for though they would speak Spanish and Portuguese, and would learn Italian as well, they also retained Hebrew not only for use in their prayers and other aspects of worship, but for limited domestic purposes, in an archaic form. Frequently they wrote Italian in Hebrew characters and an interesting corpus of Judeo-Italian literature has been preserved. This dialect was comparable in many ways to Yiddish (Judeo-German), and Ladino (Judeo-Spanish). At the same time the linguistic interests of Renaissance scholars affected the Jewish attitude to Hebrew. The linguistic works of Elias Levitas, Solomon d'Urbino, and David de Pomi, most of them bilingual and thus available to the non-Jews, assisted in laying the foundation of Hebrew linguistic purity, and so made the language available for non-Jews to study in the Renaissance, as they studied Latin and Greek.

The contribution of exiled Spanish and Portuguese Jews enriched the linguistic pattern of areas other than Italy. From 1450 onward they made a deep and lasting impression on the Levant. Spaneol (Spanish with Hebrew loanwords) displaced the Greek formerly spoken by the Jews of that area. It became the lingua franca throughout the Near East. Thus, around 1550, a Spanish businessman, Gonzalo de Ilesiar, reported:

> The Jews have transplanted our language to Turkey. They have faithfully preserved it down to the present time, and speak it perfectly. In Salonika, Constantinople, Alexandra, Cairo and other cities, they employ Spanish alone in trade and otherwise. In Venice I met Jews from Salonika, very young people, whose Castilian was as fluent as mine. (Quoted in Keller 1971: 272)

In the 15th Century the historic Jewish communities of South Italy were scattered far and wide. Apulean and Calabrian congregations were distinguished by peculiarities of Hebrew pronunciation—they did not distinguish Hebrew sounds ch/ and h/. They long preserved enclaves along the Dalmatian coast, in Constantinople and in other centers of the Turkish empire. To Corfu the Italians brought their own dialect of Italian which continued to be spoken among the Jews of the island almost to the present day.

The influence of the Byzantines and of Germany, and later the Ottomans in the Slavic world carried with it a Jewish component also. The immigrant Ashkenazim brought their language with them from Germany and established it in Poland. Yiddish became the lingua franca, so that in time, even among Jews long settled in Poland, it gradually displaced the national language, though not entirely. Indeed, with Hebrew, Yiddish was considered virtually a sacred language. In the south-Slavic areas and in European and Asiatic Turkey the Spanish of the Sephardim from the Iberian peninsula became the prevailing language of the Jews.

A perusal of this very brief outline of the linguistic vicissitudes of the Jews will be enough to support the proposition that the linguistic sophistication of their education had a considerable effect on the development of the Jews. On the one hand it led inevitably to what has been called a "levantization" of Jewish speech habits. On the other, Jews were induced very early to pioneer in comparative linguistics. Their familiarity with several languages may, indeed, have awakened their grammatical consciousness precociously, for they were among the first to know the *techne grammatice* of Dionysos of Thrax. The Moseitic obligation to preserve the accuracy of the Biblical text was a fundamental factor in all this, but there can be no doubt that their voluntary and involuntary acquaintance with so many languages also helped. They could not help noticing the differences between the various languages, and they were educated, because of their knowledge of Arabic grammarians, to elucidate texts in one language by comparisons with similar texts written in other Semitic languages and dialects. From here it was but a short step to comparisons with non-Semitic languages, with Arabic and the unrelated Berber, Persian and other Indo-European dialects. In the earlier Muslim era more intense contact with the Arabs promoted interest in linguistic analysis. Points of grammar became the subject of passionate debate among all educated persons. "Spanish Jews following a widespread fashion among their Arab neighbors heatedly debated philological minutiae in their social gatherings" (Baron 1967: 3-4).

THE EFFECT OF BILINGUALISM ON THE DEVELOPMENT OF WRITING

Inter-relationship of Scripts and Linguistic Unification

Reference has been made to the written systems of languages in contact and to the process of unification facilitated by several overlapping patterns of bilingualism—Sumerian with Babylonian, Babylonian with Aramaic, Aramaic with Greek, Greek with Latin, Latin with Celtic and other Western languages. Such contacts are important irrespective of the written systems involved. At the same time the development of writing has exercised its own independent influence on the contact of languages and the associated cultures. Contact of languages does not necessarily imply, especially in the modern world, contact between different writing systems, and so one of the advantages of the historical study of bilingualism in education is that we are made aware of the contribution of the development of writing to the unification of mankind and more particularly to the homogeneity of Western civilization. The systems of writing represented by languages in contact influenced each other. For instance Sumerian cuneiform dissolved into the Akkadian but only over a very long period during which the Sumerian non-Semitic co-existed with the Semitic Akkadian and therefore had every chance of influencing how the latter was written. The Hittite script is inspired probably by the older system of the Egyptians and in turn influenced the Cretan and hence the Greek writing system (Evans 1895: 33).

Probably the most important influence on the Greek system, however, was the Semitic Old Phoenician and because of the spread of that Greek script via the Etruscan to Italy the Semitic script has helped to bring close together the whole of the Western World, and the Western to the world of the Middle East. The Etruscan was borrowed and adapted by the Latins who developed the Faliscan and Latin alphabets which have dominated Western Europe. At one time it looked as if the Latin alphabet might even replace the Cyrillic, Iranic and Arabic alphabets in the Soviet Union. Even so the Greek original of the Latin script is still represented in many of those employed in the Soviet Union. The Armenian was developed by the Missionary Mesrop "after the system of the Greek syllables." The Uigurs, a Turkic people developed their system under the influence of the ancient Sogdian, a Middle Iranian dialect, and that in turn from the Aramaic. Thus the writing systems of the Western world, the Middle East and many parts of Central Asia constitute a net woven of links represented by many scripts in different types of contact situations.

The Influence of Bilingualism on the Development of Scripts

When a script was borrowed from one language by another, or when an attempt was made to adapt one script to another, anomalies were bound to arise—the two might not have the same sound system, for instance, and for that reason some signs might not be needed and so might be used to symbolize sounds not represented in the intrusive script. This is the kind of phenomenon one experiences when learning to hear and speak a new language. Thus, the Ugaritic cuneiform alphabet had been created originally for a non-Semitic language. When the Semites took over the alphabet they had to make changes in the vowel signs (a, i, u) as well as in other respects. The Cypriot syllabic script, Jensen (1970: 76) maintains, was "highly unsuited to reproduce the Greek language: for example long and short vowels are not differentiated . . . and nasals before consonants are not indicated." In addition normal Greek consonant clusters are disrupted in the new script. These anomalies may be due to the fact that the syllabic system was probably developed for an earlier Cypriot language, alien to Greek, and only gradually was it adapted to the needs of the latter. A similar situation arose with the influence of Greek on the Avesta script of Iran during the Sassanic period (3d Century A.D.) when signs for vowels were introduced.

But perhaps the largest number and the most complicated set of script anomalies occurred because of Sumerian/Akkadian non-Semite/Semite bilingualism. The Semites took over all the Sumerian idographic word signs but substituted for the Sumerian word the Semitic equivalent. Thus the sign for *name* was read no longer as *mu* but as *sumu*. At the same time the Akkadian retained the Sumerian pronunciation of the sign but contrary to the practice of the Sumerians they used it as a syllable and disregarded its meaning, so that a sign of a meaning (a word) became the sign of a syllable (no fixed meaning). Consequently they could treat the sign *mu* (name) as an ideograph (to give meaning) and therefore read *mu* as *sumu*, or they could regard it as a syllable sign (phonetically only) and continue to read it as *mu*, without attaching the original, or for that matter any particular, meaning to it. No wonder it has been claimed that "in many respects the Sumerian script sits on the Semitic Babylonian like an ill fitting garment" (Jensen 1970: 83).

Such changes were cumulative in the sense that, because of the complex interrelationships between scripts to which reference has been made, whatever changes occurred in one script, for instance those which occurred in adapting Sumerian to Akkadian cuneiform, tended to prepare the way for another set of changes, for instance, the change from Semitic cuneiform to Semitic alphabetic (Aramaic) script. This diffusion of change is noted when a script is "exported" to a colonial or conquered territory. For instance, the wide-ranging and much-traveled Phoenician script developed a number of variants just as the language it recorded developed different dialects in the Mediterranean area. "Wherever the Punic script was deprived of its . . . proper native soil . . . completely new forms arose" within the script. The same is true of the Aramaic which up to the 2d Century B.C. appears to have been a homogeneous script. Thereafter, because of political disintegration and the formation of politically and culturally independent communities it gave rise to a variety of derivatives, the Hebrew square script, Palmyrene, Syriac and Arabic and these to a considerable extent reflected other linguistic and script influences.

However the best example of the modification of a script to accommodate the different linguistic needs of distant localities is the Greek, which never appeared as a uniform script for any length of time, but as a congeries of very intimately related but also considerably different local variants. These have been classified (Buck 1955) as the archaic of the Dorian Islands and the southern archipelago, closest to the Phoenician script; eastern alphabets which included Ionian or Milesian and Corinthian; and third, and most interesting of all, the western alphabets which comprise the scripts of the non-Ionian colonies and South Italy as well as the scripts of Laconia and Thessaly. All these possess markedly different signs made necessary by the need to accommodate other languages and their different sound systems. This is even more marked in the Greek-influenced scripts of Asia Minor—Phrygian, Lycian, Lydian and Carian, all of which were probably non Indo-European, and all of which if they were to cater for Greek, needed signs which did not belong to the original scripts.

SOME IMPLICATIONS

Language and Culture-alliance

An important characteristic of the successive phases of linguistic contact in Europe, as we have seen, is the overlap of several major languages. For many centuries there was an interpenetration of cultures and languages which extended from India to Rome and farther west. Contacts between India and the Mesopotamian region had existed from the Sargonide period of Sumerian history (2500 B.C.). A historical, religious and linguistic complex extended from the Nile Valley to beyond the Syro-Palestinian coastal strip, the table lands of Anatolia and Iran. Its influence, linguistic and cultural, irradiated from the East toward Greece and Anatolia. The overlap of languages ensured there was no cleavage between East and West, but rather a pronounced continuity. "When Greek civilization comes into flower the Near East has thousands of years of history behind it," from which Greeks profited (Moscati 1959: 314). At the time in the 2d Century B.C. when Greeks moved across to Bengal, the Romans established the

Graeco-Roman civilization on the coasts of the Atlantic. Linguae francae allowed ideas and moods to sweep the area, so that the Mediterranean destiny was to provide coherence to our civilization—to establish a center and to connect epicenters with one another and epicenters with the center itself. Social habits became more and more alike; cities and the houses of upper classes had a similar appearance. Celtic forces, though they were submerged, except in Britain, made enduring contributions in Bohemia, Western Europe and especially in Wales and Ireland. Celtic artist-craftsmen were sought after in the mature Graeco-Roman cultures of the South. The Celtic contribution to the Christian Church, whether in art (e.g., the 8th- and 9th-Century illuminated manuscripts of Ireland) or in missionary work, has its own unique character. "The significance of the Celts in European civilization has no parallel in the early history of Europe" (Filip 1956: 199). In the Eastern Mediterranean where the language remained Greek and education was based on Greek classics, centuries of Roman influence and the presence of Latin produced a network of institutions and established common ideals and assumptions regarding man and his work which were embraced by the Byzantines. The barbarians brought into the cities on the northwest of the Black Sea appeared as the outrangers of Hellenism. The consequent Graeco-Slav influence, linguistic and cultural, was to provide a channel for the transmission of Byzantine civilization to Medieval Eastern Europe (Obolensky 1971: 141).

All this was made possible by the intricate web of languages in contact and it was mediated by educational systems which, though highly selective, took account of those differences in language. In a very vital sense our concept of education, the paedeua which with all its faults has promoted the advancement not of the Western world alone, derives very largely from this complex pattern of languages in contact. One language might be in contact with several others simultaneously, so that it is difficult to identify a period of history when important cultural consequences did not derive from such a matrix of intertwined languages over vast territories. It is partly because of this that there has emerged a *European semantics* as an expression of such contacts:

> the common denominator of historical styles of semantic expressions of civilization which in the course of time have been superimposed the one on the other to make up the fabric of that semantic koiné which allows a person speaking one European language to master semantically any other. (Spitzer 1948: 7)

These are Aramaic, Greek, Latin, Celtic and German. They constitute what Gilbert Murray (1946: 66) referred to as "the inherited conglomerate." The phrase implies that the principle of linguistic and cultural interrelationships such as we have described is agglomeration, not substitution. A new pattern of contact seldom effaces the old completely. These languages, because of their cumulative interacting influences, have helped to ensure a fairly homogeneous system of semantic reference, underlying whatever cultural differences there may be.

In the semantic overlap other linguistic traits have been diffused, helping to create what Trubetzkoy called a language alliance, a *sprachbund*. The disintegration of the various Empires and the long period during which the smaller countries matured under varying conditions produced many European cultures, but because of the linguistic overlap and the complex contact situations we may venture nevertheless to speak of a European society and even of a European Hochsprache (Auerbach 1965: 338). There is a linguistic alliance which in part provides the possibility of a consistent system of ideas and values which we call our Western civilization. And though there is currently a widespread call for a transvaluation of Western values, those values and the Western system of education are influential throughout the world.

Education

Increasingly, different linguistic groups are determined to participate in bilingual education. In 1962 a survey of six nations revealed that a majority of Dutch and Belgian adults claimed a speaking competence in one or more languages other than their native tongues. Of the German and French who were questioned, 25% and 33% respectively made the same claim (*Sondages* 1963: 41). Russian is the second language of 16 million non-Russians. The same urge to establish communication outside one's own group is characteristic of less sophisticated peoples also. In Central Africa, it has been claimed, the natives set out consciously to extend their identities beyond their native villages by deliberately choosing to incorporate in their own conversations a vocabulary other than that of their native dialect (Samarin 1966: 199).

These facts illustrate the tendency of civilizations to increase progressively the radius of communication and point to important consequences for education. Lord Bryce saw this tendency in exclusively European terms. The new sort of unity being created among mankind, he contended, was the result of the dissemination of Western European languages and the culture and science related to them (Bryce 1914: 2). But there is now no reason to believe that the world pattern of language contact of the kind that Bryce had in mind will be dominated by Western Europe. Russian in Central Asia as well as Arabic and Chinese are increasing their range and, doubtlessly, others will emerge into prominence. In the pattern of present and probably future bilingualism, it is likely that a few languages of this kind will enter intensively into complex contact situations and partnerships far beyond the areas where national territories have common boundaries. This development will affect not only the relatively small proportion of highly educated men and women but those whose professional or occupational interests bring them into immediate contact with speakers of other languages, professional soldiers for instance in integrated military organizations, as well as even comparatively low grade industrial operatives employed by international industrial concerns. The introduction of a second language at lower levels of primary education in increasing numbers of school systems, and mass media of many kinds available to increasing numbers of young people have reduced the obstacles of mountain ranges, oceans, and rivers. Further, these emerging contacts are not simply fortuitous as they have been in the past, but planned and engineered as part of national and international social systems, mediated through educational institutions.

If there is one thing we learn from a historical study of languages in contact it is that the languages which appear to contribute most and survive longest, those which constitute the *adstratum* rather than the *substratum* are usually supported and reinforced by powerful institutions, of which the schools, monastic institutions, royal households serving an educational function, and specialized higher institutions like those to which the legal professions were attached are among the most influential. But the fact that bilingual education has contributed so much in the past is due to its having been directly or indirectly a factor in the lives not only of the privileged classes but of the middle and lower classes also. They participated in the process of Romanization in the West and Hellenization in the East. Some of them wrote Latin or Greek. Though it is improbable that the urbanized workers or the isolated inhabitants of rural areas shared the education with which the others were provided, they could not fail to profit from their example. And we cannot ignore the experience of the most depressed class of all, the slaves. A considerable proportion of them, 10 thousand in 4th-Century Athens for instance, were absorbed into domestic service and in many cases, apart from becoming the tutors of the children of the family, they became formally recognized teachers. Others were employed in a professional capacity as secretaries and bank managers (Jones 1956: 185-199). Formal bilingual education might have been limited but its influence was diffused among the total population.

The schools could not fail to provide a conservative influence in the fluid situations created by the social conditions which promoted bilingualism: "cette instabilité des habitudes . . . qui est une caractéristique des régions et des milieux bilingues" (Malmberg 1961: 74). It is through the schools that the vernacular can achieve the desired status once the demographic situation which makes its use necessary in the attempt to integrate hitherto depressed elements in a nation is recognized. The schools are also the means whereby the traditional values associated with a prestige language are made available to nourish the emerging vernacular. Nevertheless, a bilingual education should involve not only the survival of the customary but the exploration of new modes of thought and feeling.

If a system of education is a necessary emollient in social-conflict situations and a bulwark against the coarsening of the languages which are traditionally associated with education in any particular country when they come into contact with other languages, it needs also to be an insurance against the possibility that the survival of the traditional language does not create a chasm between a "refined" and a "vigorous consciousness." The Carolingian reforms in education were motivated by the awareness of the Latin compromises with the vernacular which pre-Carolingian texts reflected. But in attempting to preserve the traditional, the new system suffered from the same defects which had been revealed in the Roman system of bilingual education: the insistence on correct Latin (like the insistence on Greek) cut the feeble ties of communication between Latin and the vernaculars and between a sophisticated and a realistic education. Even "the leading classes of society possessed neither education nor books nor even a language in which they could express a culture rooted in their actual living conditions" (Auerbach 1965: 254-255).

This is one of the prevailing problems of all bilingual education programs— how to ensure that the teaching of the language which encapsulates a traditional culture is not divorced from contemporary life. And at the same time how to avoid such a commitment to the emerging vernacular that education does less than justice to the continuity of the great traditions or the "world of commanding forms." Bilingualism can be a handicap and it inevitably leads to the possibility of conflict. We are unwilling to accept the fact that languages may be as exposed to natural laws of decline as human beings. Others refuse to believe in the value of a pluralism which acquiesces in the co-existence of several languages among one people. They are apt to level the indictment which was leveled at the Jews who "having held sincere after Babel yet with temporizing with Egypt, politicizing with Chaldea, merchandizing with Syria and idolatrizing with Canaan . . . grew out of knowledge among people" (L'Isle *n.d.*: ii). It is for this reason, partly, that a historical study of bilingualism is needed to supplement what we have been accustomed to: it ensures greater objectivity and a perspective which allows us to detach ourselves from an ethnocentric vision. In most instances the history of one nation is very much the record of its contacts with neighbors, and the history of its language cannot be understood in isolation from an understanding of its contacts with other languages:

> l'histoire de l'allemand en France nous semble etre un complement necessaire d'histoire du Français en France . . . l'histoire linguistique de la France ne se limite pas a une simple histoire du Français en France. (Levy 1950: vi)

Past and Present—The Universal Significance of Bilingualism and Bilingual Education

The whole set of issues associated with the promotion of unification or of linguistic diversity, partly through the agency of bilingual education is only one aspect of a more general, indeed a universal, conflict of principles reflected not only in contemporary life but at all stages of history and in different ways. The conflict is sometimes seen as expressing the clash of the *jus rebellandi* (disenchantment) with tradition conceived as "the treasury of arcane revelations within the closed circle of a ritual community." It expresses itself in the form of heresies (Heer 1953: 8). Sometimes the conflict expresses itself as the revolt of subjectivism against rationalism. Sometimes it expresses itself, however disguised, as a political conflict. When the much discussed Carolingian educational and cultural legislation was promulgated it was an attempt to reestablish the traditional Latin language over the proliferating vernaculars. But it was equally an attempt to subject the new nations to the authoritarian rule of one man, Charlemagne. He however saw it as a religious issue, seeking to revivify the Christian Church and to re-establish its authority against heretical churches and against disavowal of the cult of the mass, and the Roman liturgy. These were all aspects of the conflict between the values of uniformity and diversity, and simultaneously it expressed itself in different attitudes to language policies, and in the philosophical treatment of language.

As against the authoritarian attitude to language, to the universalism of the Carolingian educational reforms, the medieval philosopher Ockham conceived language as a democratic convention between free individuals who reach understanding by means of open discourse. "Thinking no longer meant repeating the sacred words, reproducing the sacred meaning of each individual thing by reference to its link with the universal" (Heer 1953: 16). This nominalism was built into the way in which they regarded the languages to be related to communities, and was at the root of the rise of national states. It was more than a new logic or even a new way of looking at language; it was the expression of a fundamentally different way of looking at man from that which motivated the educational and linguistic policy of the Carolingians.

Looked at from this standpoint, two opposed orientations have influenced thinking about society since people began to engage in that activity. On the one hand there is commitment to the search for unity: the first good of man, it is maintained, consists in some mode of assimilation to one ideal and authoritative way of life and mode of thinking. Although there were important divergencies and conflicts among the philosophers and theologians of the Middle Ages, it is this belief in the overriding value of unity which best characterizes it, and it is this belief which is reflected in the attitude of the Middle Ages toward language in Church, school and society. It was the idea of a controlling *Law* of Nature rather than the liberating *Rights* of Nature which officially dominated the period. This is not unconnected with the austere, uniformist Stoic school, emphasizing order, unity and restraint as well as the patrician norms of behavior and the acceptance of the authority of one language. It is a rationalist philosophy which stresses universals in thought and language. It has always drawn powerful minds in all ages, our own included. Its danger is a tendency to remoteness from the crowded marketplace of life.

The other point of view is concerned to cultivate richness, variety and exuberance rather than strict conformity with formal pronouncements and rational prescriptions. It is a reflection of the belief in *diversity* rather than *unity* as the most important value. It accords with the insistence on *plenitude*, a decentralized, infinite and infinitely varied universe. This attitude became increasingly characteristic of the two centuries following the Renaissance but its apotheosis occurs with Romanticism, when it was argued not only that diversity is an important aspect of society but that it is the essence of the excellence, which it should be the object of social action to encourage. The world is the better the greater its variety. Between the Renaissance and the 18th Century the key concept *nature* ceases to be mainly a *regulating* and becomes mainly a *liberating* principle. Both as an aesthetic and moral aim the effort to enter as fully as possible into the immensely various range of thought and feeling in other men is emphasized in the use of languages. Romanticism, nationalism and the rise of modern philology are contemporaneous and associated features in the 19th Century Revolutionary period. And it is in their ambience that contemporary "ethnicity" emerged as an ideology and a sociological theory. It is the ambience also of the rise of plural and relativist theories of language for it tends to influence scholars toward an acceptance of the uniqueness and comparable value of every language and dialect. It also tends to direct the scholar's mind away from the unity underlying languages, *universals*, toward differences: "unity of language is the most fugitive of all unities whether it is historical, geographical, national or personal" (Firth 1935: 78).

Attempts have always been made to find a middle way between the belief in the social universe as abundance (plenitude) and the social universe as unity. Such an attempt is made by Clyde Kluckhohn who argues that in

> the realm of human psychology, social life and culture there are similarities as well as differences ... We must indeed recognise similarities within differences... The inescapable fact of cultural relativity does not justify the conclusion that all cultures are in all respects utterly disparate and hence strictly incomparable entities. There is a generalized framework that underlies the more apparent and striking facts of cultural relativity. (Kluckhohn 1962: 284, 293)

But the fact that many scholars in several disciplines look for the middle way does not negate the fact that there are profound differences between the two points of view we have described, as the belief in the world as unity and the belief in the world as variety, as explanations of the social universe. And these two opposed points of view have governed the formulation of rationales for bilingual education since the need for such rationales was first felt.

NOTES

1. For a useful summary of the issues involved and the current consensus see Cassano (1973) whose treatment is broader than is suggested by the title.

2. No one acquainted with Baudel's seminal studies will fail to recognize the indebtedness of this section to his researches. It is not only a duty to record that debt, but a pleasure to express gratitude for many exciting hours following the paths he has pioneered.

3. Many scholars prefer to speak of Assyrian and Babylonian as two dialects of Akkadian (cf. Oppenheim 1972: 9, 389).

4. The language of Ugarit is a Semitic dialect whose relationship to other languages of that group has not been determined. Tablets unearthed in Ugarit contain Akkadian texts and word lists which contain Sumerian/Akkadian items, and Hurrian translations of words in the language of Ugarit. Hittite texts were also found.

5. The Achaemenid dynasty ruled Iran from the middle of the 6th Century B.C. (having conquered the Medes) to 331 B.C. Under Cyrus II (The Great) they acquired an empire extending into Anatolia and Syria and including Babylon (in 539 B.C.). Cambyses, his son, conquered Egypt and Cyprus, while Darcus I moved east into India and West into Lybia.

6. One of the most successful mimes written by Herondas named "The Schoolmaster" gives a good commentary on the school texts which are found among the surviving papyri. A roughly contemporary textbook was unearthed at Faiyum, and is an example of the kind of dictation the teacher used in class (Roberts 1971: 363).

7. It is generally considered that the account given by Herodotus is correct: that the earliest Etruscan immigrants to Italy came by way of North Africa from Asia Minor. If this account is accepted the argument that the Etruscan language is of remote Indo-European origin and related to Hittite is more tenable, though many scholars remain skeptical (Poultney 1968: 340-341).

8. This civilization seems to have grown from a fusion of native Mesopotamian, imported Syrean or Aramaean and superimposed Greek elements during the dynasty of Seleucis I Nicator (died 281 B.C.), ruling large areas of the Middle East from a new Mesopotamian capital, Seleucia.

9. The language is known from more than 50 inscriptions excavated from its former capital Sardes, all dating from the 4th Century B.C. or earlier. A bilingual inscription (Lydean/ Aramaic) suggests affinities with or the influence of Hittite.

10. Although most Celtic scholars support the assertion that Breton is a variant of Brythonic, some Bretons, particularly Falc'hun (1968), maintain that it is a vestige of ancient Gaulish since the two languages have almost identical features.

11. Valuable discussions of the relation of the Jewish Spanish dialect to medieval and pre-Renaissance Spanish have been provided by Wagner (1930).

III

The Sociology of Bilingual Education

Joshua A. Fishman

Note. The preparation of this report and the empirical work discussed therein were supported by a grant from the Research Section, Division of Foreign Studies, Institute of International Studies, USOE-DHEW (Contract DEC-0-73-0588).

The bulk of the current bibliography on bilingual education is either psychological (Lambert and Tucker 1972; Lambert, Tucker and d'Anglejan 1973, Mackey 1972, Macnamara 1966), educational (Andersson and Boyer 1970, Andersson 1971, Anon 1971b, Gaarder 1970, John and Horner 1971, Lange 1971, Noss 1967, Special Subcommittee 1967 and Swain 1972) or linguistic (sections of Kelly 1969, Saville and Troike 1971) in nature. Although undoubtedly there has been *some* sociolinguistic impact on the field (particularly in Anon 1971a, Cohen, 1970, Fishman and Lovas 1970, Kjolseth 1972, Mackey 1970, Macnamara 1973, Ramos, Aguilar and Sibayan 1967, Spolsky 1972) nothing has appeared until recently that is an avowed sociology of bilingual education. (See my *Bilingual Education: An International Sociological Perspective*, Newbury House, 1976 which has appeared since this chapter was written.) This paper represents an attempt in that direction, both theoretically and empirically. Among the byproducts to be hoped for from the development of a sociological component in this field are improved understanding, practice and evaluation with respect to the *thousands* of bilingual education programs now underway in the U.S.A. and elsewhere.

HISTORICAL AND COMPARATIVE PERSPECTIVE

The stress on *thousands* of programs immediately indicates that a worldwide perspective is in order if we are not to confuse *sociology* with *American society* and the particular constraints that it has imposed on bilingual education.[1] Of course we want to understand, implement and evaluate American bilingual education better, but in order to do so we must first know how it differs from and is similar to bilingual education elsewhere in the world. There are countries (e.g., Singapore) in which bilingual education is omnipresent and there is no other kind. There are countries (e.g., Ireland) in which it is very widespread but in which there are other alternatives as well. There are countries (Wales, parts of non-Russian U.S.S.R.) in which it is not very common but a recognized alternative. There are countries (e.g., Belgium, Switzerland) in which it is rare and viewed as enriching for elites and others (e.g., Andean Latin America) in which it is rare and viewed as compensatory for the poor. Certainly such basic differences in the societies in which it exists must be built into a universally relevant sociology of bilingual education. Doing this will provide useful heuristic perspective on the *American situation.*

Diachronic perspective is also likely to be needed, in addition to the comparative synchronic perspective just mentioned, in any sociology of bilingual education. From the earliest records of education in all classical societies we find ample evidence of the predominance of bilingual education (Lewis, Chapter 2). Most often all formal education was elitist, and, therefore, so was bilingual education. Most often the target or textual language differed from the process or mediating language. But, in any case, the variation to be noted across time is as important to us as that to be noted across cultures, both in devising a sociology of bilingual education, on the one hand, and in benefiting from it for the purposes of American education on the other.

AN INITIAL SOCIOLOGICAL TYPOLOGY

Reflecting this concern both for historical and comparative (i.e., diachronic and cross-cultural) perspective a beginning typology was derived based upon the interrelationships among four dichotomies first to one another and then to rated success in the languages of primary and secondary emphasis.

Dichotomy 1: *Language Given Primary Emphasis* vs. *Language Given Secondary Emphasis* (LPE-LSE). Because languages are not functionally equal or identical almost all bilingual education programs devote more time to one than to another. It would seem, on intuitive sociological grounds, to be important to distinguish between the bilingual education *inputs* and *outputs* for LPEs and those for LSEs.

Dichotomy 2: *Mother Tongue* vs. *Other Tongue.* Just as most bilingual education programs are "unbalanced" in the emphasis each language receives, so most classrooms within such programs differ in the mother tongue—other tongue status of these languages for the students receiving bilingual education. It certainly appears sociologically advisable to examine the impact of this distinction on bilingual education inputs and outputs.

Dichotomy 3: *Minor* vs. *Major Language.* The five official languages of the United Nations (English, French, Spanish, Russian and Chinese) were considered "major" languages on the world scene. The distinction between smaller and larger (broader and narrower) seems well worth considering in any sociological typology.

Dichotomy 4: *Out-of-School Formal Institutions.* A language of organized or official importance out of school (regardless of whether it is the mother or other tongue of students) obviously can have a far different claim on students, teachers and school authorities than a language that has no such out-of-school reinforcement. The sociology of bilingual education must be concerned with the power differentials of language in the real world.

FIRST PRELIMINARY FINDINGS

Interaction among these dichotomies results in 2^4 or 16 potential societal contexts for bilingual education. These 16 contexts were applied to the literature. I and several colleagues and advanced students (20 judges in all) rated jointly the 60 instances of bilingual education that we collectively knew best (whether on the basis of the published literature or case studies derived from our collectively shared and corroborated experiences). These ratings (averaged and rounded) were then used to predict criterion ratings that we jointly applied to each instance or case, these criteran being "success relative to LSE and LPE goals" as rated on a four-point scale. The resulting multiple predictions may be viewed as a first approximation of the value of macro-societal contextual factors such as those that we have indicated thus far.[2]

SIX-PREDICTOR RATINGS "APPLIED TO THE LITERATURE"

Notwithstanding the limitations which such data admittedly have, it would seem, nevertheless, that, as preliminary and provocative indicators, some importance can be ascribed to them and to the findings derived from them.

It is quite evident from Table 3-1 that our sample of cases is such that, insofar as attainments are concerned, a clear distinction must be made between the language of primary and the language of secondary emphasis. For the language of primary emphasis it leads to greater rated success when the language is the mother tongue $(r = .41)$ and when it (the mother tongue) is the language of important formal institutions outside of the school ($r = .28$). For the language of secondary emphasis, it leads to greater rated success when the language is the mother tongue ($r = .35$) and when it is a major language on the world scene ($r = .40$). Note, however, that the degree of rated success with respect to one language is significantly related to that with respect to the second.

Several interesting implications derive from the foregoing. Unless both languages—or neither—can be societally viewed as mother tongues (not as much of a logical impossibility as is implied by our typology),[3] there would seem to be a built-in conflict within bilingual education in that both languages require mother tongue students for success to be optimized. This state of affairs may actually be viewed as an equalization of educational success (or access) rather than as a conflict. Insofar as bilingual education is a reflection of the need to cater to two different mother tongue groups then it may be viewed as an opportunity to provide some appropriate degree of success to each. However, in addition, the language of primary emphasis must be officially in evidence in society (i.e., it cannot merely be home- and school-based) and the language of secondary emphasis must also be of worldwide significance (it too cannot be merely of home and school relevance) for maximum success to be achieved.

In conclusion, we should note that this crude, "first approximation," sociological model yields multiple correlation coefficients in the high forties and fifties. Thus, having accounted for approximately one-fourth to one-third of the variance in "rated success" we are encouraged to search for a more complex model.

A SOMEWHAT MORE ADVANCED SOCIOLOGICAL MODEL

Seven more variables (variables 6 to 8 and 10 to 13 in Table 3-1), each of them continuous, were also rated by the same judges and at the very same time that the first six, described above, were rated for the 60 cases under review. Two of these focused upon the language of *primary* emphasis and the language of *secondary emphasis* insofar as goal intensivity was concerned (Fishman and Lovas 1970), that is, upon the extent to which *full* bilingualism was a goal. Another variable among the additional six pertained to the entire educational context, rather than to one or another of the languages of instruction alone. It asked whether admission selectivity was high, medium or low. Finally, two quite provocative sociological variables were rated, separately for LPE and for LSE, namely (a) the extent to which either the language of primary or secondary emphasis was dependent on school instruction (rather than on more general societal participation) in order to be *learned* and (b) the extent to which there was nationalist or other heightened socio-political sentiment on behalf of either language of instruction.

The general purpose of these last two variables, as well as of the one dealing with "selective admission" (the other side of the "drop-out" coin), is to increase our sensitivity to the social nexus of education as a whole and to societal pressures

Table 3-1   Six predictors and two criteria: Intercorrelations ($n = 60$) (Circled values are significant at the .05 level.)

x	Variables	1	2	3	4	5	6	7
1.53	1. Language of Primary Emphasis: other $t = 1$, mother $t = 2$	—						
1.62	2. Language of Primary Emphasis: minor = 1, major = 2	-.12	—					
1.48	3. Language of Secondary Emphasis: other $t = 1$, mother $t = 2$	(-.97)	.15	—				
1.47	4. Language of Secondary Emphasis: minor = 1, major = 2	.00	-.09	-.04	—			
1.48	5. Language of Formal Instit. Emphasis: other $t = 1$, mother $t = 2$	.24	.01	-.20	.03	—		
2.61	6. Evaluation of success re goal for LSE (hi = 4, lo = 1)	(-.31)	-.03	(.35)	(.40)	-.03	—	
3/42	7. Evaluation of success re goal for LPE (hi = 4, lo = 1)	(.41)	-.07	(-.38)	.16	(.28)	(.38)	—

Cumulative Multiple Prediction:

LSE: Criterion 1

1. V4 = LSE: minor = 1; major = 2 $r = .40$
2. V3 = LSE: other $t = 1$, mother $t = 2$ $= .54$
3. V1 = LPE: other $t = 1$, mother $t = 2$ $= .57$

1. V1 = LPE: other $t = 1$, mother $t = 2$ $r = .41$
2. V5 = LFI: other $t = 1$, mother $t = 2$ $= .45$
3. V4 = LSE: other $t = 1$, mother $t = 2$ $= -.47$

Table 3-2   Cumulative Multiple Predictions
(based upon 12 societal predictors)

1. V7	Extent to which LSE is school-dependent	R	= 44
2. 4	LSE: minor—major		.57
3. 11	Goal re LPE		.63
4. 10	Selectivity		.69
5. 16	Evaluation of success re LPE		.71
6. 12	Extent to which LPE is school-dependent		.74
7. 13	Extent of nationalistic movement for LPE		.75

1. V12	Extent to which LPE is school-dependent	R	= 53
2. 15	Evaluation of success of LSE		.60
3. LFI	other—own		.65
4. 11	Goal re LPE		.67
5. 8	Extent of nationalistic movement for LSE		.68
6. 1 LPE:	other—own		.71
7. 4 LSE:	minor—major		.72

upon the languages of instruction in particular. Certainly bilingual schools in which there is careful selection of students face a different type of task than those in which bilingual education is considered to be desirable for one and all. Similarly, where only the school is available to teach a particular language of instruction a far different task is faced than when society at large, and most particularly when organized forces within society, reinforce or stress that language.

TWELVE PREDICTOR RATINGS "APPLIED TO THE LITERATURE"

As the body of Table 3-2 reveals, the addition of seven more predictor ratings yields several interesting results. Clearly both LSEs and LPEs are very widely school-dependent when they are *not* the students' own mother tongues ($r = -.66$ and $r = -.59$ respectively). Similarly, they are more likely to be supported by organized socio-political movements when they are themselves minor languages on the world scene ($r = -.37$ and $r = -.39$). Presumably, they are only recognized by educational authorities because of the support of such movements. Finally, the two languages are likely to be school-dependent in inverse degrees ($r = -.72$), that is, if one is, the other is not. Thus, on the whole, bilingual education is frequently concerned with one societally stressed language and one school-stressed language. The former is more likely to be the children's own language, regardless of whether it is major or minor. However, for a minor language to be present in the curriculum it is necessary for it to have organized socio-political support, whether it is the students' mother tongue or not. Presumably, without such support either one major language or two would be taught, even if neither were the students' mother tongue.

Table 3-3   Twelve Sociological and Two Psychological Predictors in Conjunction with Two Criteria ($r = 60$)

1. *Variables*

1.	Language of Primary Emphasis: other = 1, mother = 2	1.53
2.	Language of Primary Emphasis: minor = 1, major = 2	1.62
3.	Language of Secondary Emphasis: other = 1, mother = 2	1.48
4.	Language of Secondary Emphasis: minor = 1, major = 2	1.47
5.	Language of Other formal Institutions: other = 1, mother = 2	1.48
6.	Goal re LSE: 1 = transitions or monoliterate; 2 = partial; 3 = full	2.15
7.	Extent to which learning LSE is school-dependent (1-3)	1.98
8.	Extent to which there is a nationalist movement for LSE (1-3)	1.52
9.	Adequacy of teaching methods/materials for LSE (1-3)	1.07
10.	Selectivity (academic standards) for admission to bilingual program (1-3)	2.33
11.	Goal re LPE: 1 = transitional or monoliterate; 2 = partial; 3 = full	2.87
12.	Extent to which learning LPE is school-dependent (1-2)	2.00
13.	Extent to which there is a nationalist movement for LPE (1-3)	1.52
14.	Adequacy of teaching methods/materials for LPE (1-3)	2.22
15.	Evaluation of success re goals for LSE (1-4)	2.62
16.	Evaluation of success re goals for LPE (1-4)	3.42

2. *Intercorrelations* (Boldface intercorrelations are significant at .05 level. Intercorrelations *above* diagonal are *not* significant as zero orders but *are* significant in final cumulative multiple correlations.)

Variables	1	2	3	4	5	6	7	8
1.	—							
2.	−.12	—						
3.	**−.97**	.15	—					
4.	.00	−.09	−.04	—				
5.	.24	.01	−.20	.03	—			
6.	**.32**	−.03	**−.33**	**.36**	.22	—		
7.	**.67**	−.01	**−.66**	−.09	−.05	.10	—	
8.	−.20	**.26**	**.26**	**−.37**	.22	−.23	−.20	—
9.	−.08	.05	.08	**.64**	.12	**.34**	−.09	−.03
10.	**−.26**	.13	**.25**	.17	.02	.00	−.04	.02
11.	−.17	**.40**	.18	−.03	**.28**	.11	−.01	.14
12.	**−.59**	.25	**.62**	.07	−.07	−.06	**−.72**	.16
13.	**.25**	**−.39**	**−.28**	.12	−.09	.06	−.01	**−.36**
14.	.14	**.42**	−.10	.18	**.35**	**.30**	−.04	**.34**
15.	**−.31**	−.03	**.35**	**.40**	−.03	.13	**−.44**	−.00
16.	**.41**	.07	**−.38**	.16	**.28**	.23	**.38**	.09

Table 3-3 (continued)

3. *Cumulative multiple prediction of criteria* (significant variables)

LSE = Criterion 1 (V15)

V9	Adequacy of teaching methods materials re LSE	R = .53
V2	Extent to which learning LSE is school-dependent	= .66
V11	Goals of LPE	= .74
V13	Extent to which there is nationalist movement for LPE	= .76
V10	Selectivity re entering BEP	= .77

LPE = Criterion 2 (V16)

V14	Adequacy of teaching methods/materials re LPE	R = 59
V12	Extent to which learning LPE is school-dependent	= 75
V2	LPE: minor/major	= .78
V7	Extent to which learning LSE is school-dependent	= .81
V15	Evaluation of success re goals of LSE	= .82
V10	Selectivity re entering BEP	= .83

9	10	11	12	13	14	15	16	Variables
								1.
							−.07	2.
								3.
								4.
								5.
								6.
								7.
								8.
—								9.
.38	—						.09	10.
.10	.05	—						11.
.17	.17	.05	—					12.
.00	−.14	−.26	.02	—		−.07		13.
.37	.05	.32	−.12	−.34	—			14.
.53	.34	−.28	.42	−.07	.11	—	.03	15.
.30	.09	.09	−.53	−.13	.59	.38	—	16.

A glance at our criterion variables reveals that both LSEs and LPEs are rated less successful when *they* are school-dependent ($r = -.44$ and $r = -.53$) and more successful when the *other* is school-dependent ($r = .42$ and $r = .38$). In addition, LSE is rated more successful when it is more selective vis-à-vis admission ($r = .34$) and less successful when LSE goals are minimal ($r = -.28$). Thus, at this stage, we may add to our earlier general findings, which implied that LSE success is likely to be high if the language of secondary emphasis is the student's own and is a major one, the additional finding that it is rated high when it is not fully school-dependent and when minimal goals are set for the language of primary emphasis. Although nationalist movements may be important determinants of whether LSEs are used in education at all (particularly if they are minor languages) they do not determine whether LSE goals are successfully attained.

Turning to LPE success we may add to our previous findings that it is rated high when it is the mother tongue of the learners and when out-of-school institutions also employ it, a further underscoring of the conclusion discussed in the last paragraph. If instruction in the LPE is highly dependent on school, it is as likely, or perhaps even more likely to be unsuccessful in the case of the LSE. School use of a language is just *not* enough.

Finally, looking at cumulative multiple predictions based upon our somewhat expanded model, it is quite obvious (from Table 3-2) that such prediction is much better than it was with the first and smaller set of variables. From multiples in the high-forties and mid-fifties we have now gone to multiples in the low and mid-70s. However, our earlier more primitive variables do not seem to do as well in predicting LSE as they do with respect to LPE, once the extra predictors are added in. When we try to predict LSE success only the major status of the language continues to play a role, but not as important a one as whether LSE is school-dependent. Finally, with the exception of the factor of selectivity all other significant multiple predictors deal with LPE (*its* goals, *its* school-dependency and *its* nationalist roots). Obviously, LSE success is largely dependent on LPE circumstances (whereas the reverse is slightly less so). Further, it is striking to note the extent to which similar, parallel or identical variables are called for in the multiple prediction of success with respect to LPE and LSE alike. Indeed, although the relative rankings of significant predictors are often different even this is not always so. Thus school-dependency is once again the major independent variable, and LPE goals and LSE major-minor status are still important in raising the cumulative prediction. Once again, also, the *other* language's goals and its involvement in a nationalist movement are cumulatively important. Indeed, only two significant predictors really differentiate between the cumulative predictions of LSE and LPE. In the former case it is selectivity; in the latter, that the learners' own language be that of formal institutions outside of the school.

ON THE ADEQUACY OF SOCIOLOGY ALONE

So far, we have examined sociological predictors alone. This has been quite legitimate because we have been seeking to develop a sociology of bilingual education. In so doing, we have come up with a number of interesting and potentially important sociological findings (or in view of the fact that we are only interpreting other people's data, perhaps "hypotheses" rather than "findings"). The negative importance of school-dependency is clear: the more a language of instruction is entirely dependent on the school and lacking counterparts outside it, the less it is rated successful in achieving its goals regardless of whether it is LSE or LPE. Related to this is the fact that the learner's own language must be that of *formal* institutions outside of the school if LPE goals are to be maximally attained, and that LSE benefits most from being a major world language.

By adding a few additional societal variables we have explained over half the variance in rated LSE and LPE success. Although this is most encouraging, it is appropriate to ask whether the addition of psycho-educational variables would result in a substantially different picture, quantitatively (i.e., in terms of magnitude of multiples) or qualitatively (i.e., in terms of variables contributing significantly to the cumulative multiple prediction).

As Table 3-3 reveals, the answer to both questions is negative insofar as LSE is concerned and positive insofar as LPE is concerned when adequacy of teaching methods/materials is introduced to reflect psycho-educational dimensions. In the former case the resulting cumulative multiple prediction is raised only from .75 to .77 and no predictors are brought into the final set that were not originally there—although two are displaced from it: V4 (LSE: minor - major) and V12 (extent to which LPE is school-dependent). On the other hand, in connection with LPE the introduction of a psycho-educational predictor boosts the overall cumulative multiple from .72 to .83 and brings several other variables into the final set, namely V2 (LPE: minor - major), V7 (extent to which LSE is school-dependent) and V10 (selectivity). This is an interesting finding, implying as it does that LSE success is more societally determined and LPE more respondent to psycho-educational factors.

Note, however, that the final set of cumulative predictors is still quite similar for both LSE and LPE, adequacy of school materials, extent of school-dependency, and selectivity being important in both cases. Beyond this similarity only LSE success is uniquely influenced (negatively) by intensity of LPE goals and (negatively) by the presence of a nationalist movement supporting LPE. On the other hand, only LPE success is influenced (negatively) if it is a minor language, by the extent to which LSE is school-dependent, and the extent to which LSE goals are successful. From the foregoing it should be clear that both psycho-educational and socio-educational manipulation may be required for successful bilingual education.

FURTHER EMPIRICAL STUDY, SELF-DESCRIPTION AND OBSERVATION

Obviously we have gone as far as we should, if not beyond that, in deriving leads from the literature for quantitative or semi-quantitative methods. The leads must now be refined and extended using empirical data. A beginning in this direction has been made via the International Study of Bilingual Secondary Education. It has, to begin with, established a register of some 1200 bilingual secondary schools or school programs throughout the world. From this register it has selected 100 schools, in various settings, for intensive follow-up by questionnaire that will cover the same factors we studied from the literature, and will investigate many other hunches that we derived from sociological and sociolinguistic theory more generally. A dozen or so schools will be studied in more depth using personal visits and direct observation to further test the validity of the findings derived from the questionnaire responses. All in all, therefore, three types of data, at differing levels of abstraction and detail, will be compared. This, in itself, is an important undertaking since it will shed light on the constant suspicion that findings about bilingual education are limited by the sampling and methodological differences from one study to the next (Macnamara 1973). A sociology of bilingual education must be even more concerned with such suspicions than must psychologically or pedagogically oriented investigations. Since it seeks to systematize much of the situational and contextual variation that is otherwise regarded as error variance, it must be more certain that its situational and contextual data are wide-ranging and reliable. Whether or not the International Study of Bilingual Secondary Education can accomplish all that is needed to do this, it is clear that a "sociology of bilingual education" is beginning to appear even from its early stages.

NOTES

1. Bilingual education is here defined as use of two or more languages of instruction with particular students (whether these be all or only part of a given cohort group), in subject matter other than language instruction itself. Whether this subject matter is closely allied to language (e.g., the literature or "culture" uniquely encoded via a particular language) or basically unrelated to it (e.g., mathematics or physics) is itself a variable to be investigated, just as are other questions prompted by this definition, for example, the precise number of languages of instruction involved ("two or more") the proportion of all students involved, the number of years involved, the number of subjects involved, etc.

2. Two admissions are called for at this point. To begin with, the predictor ratings and the criterion ratings were made by the same raters (the last mentioned being made *before* the first mentioned by half of the judges and last by the others), thereby introducing an unknown degree of spurious consistency in the data which would tend to inflate the final multiple correlations obtained. Second, an approximately equal number of cases of each type were

sought, thus effectively counterbalancing or ruling-out type itself as one of the possibly important factors in the success of bilingual education. Both these limitations are overcome in more advanced research reported below.

3. Societies marked by widespread and stable diglossia may qualify on this score. In this connection, see Fishman 1967.

IV

Linguistic Perspectives on Bilingual Education

J. Donald Bowen

Bilingual education, the significant use of two languages in the basic educative process, typically has been viewed as often necessary but always unfortunate. This opinion is forcefully expressed in the oft-quoted report on the UNESCO-sponsored meeting of specialists on the use of vernacular languages in education, convened in Paris in 1951, where experts agreed that a child's home language is the best possible medium of instruction in formal education:

> It is axiomatic that the best medium for teaching a child is his mother tongue. Psychologically, it is the system of meaningful signs that in his mind works automatically for expression and understanding. Sociologically, it is a means of identification among the members of the community to which he belongs. Educationally, he learns more quickly through it than through an unfamiliar linguistic medium. (*The Use of Vernacular Languages in Education*, 1953: 11)

Though the report states unequivocally that "all children should at least begin their schooling in their mother tongue" and that "they will benefit from being taught in the mother tongue as long as possible," (p. 50) the experts recognize practical difficulties that will interfere with the ideal solution of a completely mother-tongue education. But the difficulties are seen as problems to be overcome, such as the preparation of adequate texts and materials, the development of teacher-training programs, planned expansion of vocabulary, etc., and when all the problems are solved, we can confidently implement the preferred pattern of vernacular education.

It is an appealing view, supported by logic and the combined experience of the monolingual societies of the western world, which, in general, have operated their schools through the medium of the mother tongue. Most educators would no doubt agree with the thesis of the appropriateness of the mother tongue as the language of education, as do Saville and Troike in another context of vernacular education: "An axiom of bilingual education is that the best medium for teaching is the mother tongue of the student" (Saville and Troike 1971: 1). Andersson and Boyer (1970: 45) cite several precedent studies and conclude that

> educators are agreed that a child's mother-tongue is the best normal instrument for learning, especially in the early stages of school, and that reading and writing in the first language should precede literacy in a second.

The same thought, and assumption of general acceptance, is echoed by Gaarder of the U. S. Office of Education in his statement made in Congressional hearings that "... there is an educational axiom, accepted virtually everywhere else in the world that 'the best medium for teaching a child is his mother tongue'." (Gaarder 1961; cited in Andersson and Boyer 1970: 51). It is interesting to note how frequently the word "axiom" is used to underscore the general acceptance of vernacular superiority for educational purposes.

When vernacular education has been questioned, it has been on grounds of feasibility rather than preference. In his review of the UNESCO Monograph, Bull points to the staggering problems of implementation (very many minor languages, extensive number of languages not written, severe lack of adequate teaching materials, limited availability of trained teachers, etc.) and concludes that there is no possibility of a significant increase in vernacular education in the present century. Further,

> What is best for the child psychologically and pedagogically may not be what is best for the adult socially, economically, or politically, and, what is even more significant, what is best for both the child and the adult may not be best or even possible for the society which, through its collective efforts, provides the individual with the advantages he cannot personally attain. It would seem appropriate, as a consequence, to contemplate the fact that while getting educated is a personal matter, in contrast, providing a modern education is a social enterprise. (Bull 1955: 290)

Bull rightly points out that linguistic self-determination as a general policy in the face of the reality of thousands of languages is hopelessly unattainable in terms of the economics of modern education, that stress on benefits to the individual endangers meeting the needs of modern society. But he doesn't deny the basic premise of the desirability for the individual of an education in his mother tongue.

It is interesting to see a paternalistic note in the UNESCO report, as the experts recommend that "Educational authorities should aim at persuading an unwilling public to accept education through the mother tongue." (*The Use of Vernacular Languages in Education* 1953: 69). One often notes in developing countries that the children of men on the policy-making level do not always attend the public schools which are required to follow official curricula, but rather go to private schools which offer a wider range of linguistic and curriculum choice. But that's another problem.

Where social, political, and economic considerations have overridden psychological arguments and a second language has been used for education, it is generally assumed that students have paid a price for their instruction, either in linguistic competence in their first language or in their overall cognitive development, or, more likely, in both. This opinion, widely shared by many scholars, is expressed persuasively by Macnamara (1966: 136) as a "balance effect"—that skill in one language is paid for by a deficit in the other, and that the use of a second language as the medium of instruction involves retardation in subject matter without affecting attainment in either language. Whatmough (1967: 55-56) offers a confirmation, saying that "Rarely is either of two languages . . . learned as well, even in childhood, as either one would have been if the child had confined himself to only one of them."

The experience of Macnamara, Whatmough, and others compels them to conclude that there is only so much linguistic capacity available, and that exposure to a second language that involves any responsibility has the effect of diluting this capacity to the detriment of both languages, and of course to the speaker, whose concentration is attenuated and who therefore suffers a disadvantage as a student in mastering subject matter content. It is a matter of observation that educational programs in a second language have not produced great quantities of scholars whose studies have significantly moved back the frontiers of knowledge, that the outstanding writer producing in a language other than his mother tongue (Joseph Conrad or Henrik Willem Van Loon, for examples) is very much an exception.

The upsurge of interest in bilingual education in the 1960s and 1970s in the United States seems to be largely prompted by the conviction that the home language of the child must be given a significant role in the educative process, that children from linguistic minority groups have been disadvantaged by the necessity of attending schools that ignored (or worse yet, denigrated) the mother tongue, forcing students to rely on a second language as the only available means of securing an education. The facts of disadvantage are incontrovertible, and they have been adequately documented by statistics that reveal social maladjustment: dropout rates, delinquency, prison populations, welfare rolls, etc.—all of which testify to limited achievement and indirectly to lower expectations for upward mobility by members of linguistic minorities. It has been natural to assume a relation between lack of opportunity for vernacular education and limited socio-economic achievement, and efforts to correct such injustices by any promising means should be applauded and supported.

Bilingual education, then, has been considered as a means of increasing opportunity for those who demonstrably need help. The attention and concern shown by the growing number of bilingual programs probably will generate the desired effect, at least in the initial stages of optimism, that at last we are addressing the problems that should concern us most. It is at least possible that this success will be less in evidence after a period of educational experimentation, when the exciting novel programs have settled into channels of routine. Other signs of reverse Hawthorne effect may come when bilingual education is so thoroughly accepted that politicians can no longer attract headlines by publicly offering their support, having done their bit and redirected their attention to some new issue of public concern. That will be the real test of bilingual education: whether it can survive the effects of acceptance and neglect.

Legislatively mandated programs make me uneasy. Politicians seeking public approval want immediate and spectacular results, and have the means of financing anyone who convincingly promises to "deliver." (cf. note 3) But all is quickly forgotten when delivery fails to meet expectations and the politicians look elsewhere for notice. A most appropriate example is the Casey Bill in California, which required foreign-language instruction for sixth, seventh, and eighth graders in all public-supported schools in California. It was a beautiful promise— intercultural understanding through international communication, taking advantage of the prepuberty child's natural ability to learn a foreign language. But it evaporated like dry ice, and today there is no trace of its effects.

Will the same fate overtake bilingual education? We can hope not, but the record of politically motivated support is not promising. Perhaps this time educators will find both the patterns and the means to effect permanent improvements. Time will tell.

With all the evidence being amassed and presented for the advantages of education in the vernacular of the students and with so many examples of limited educational achievement in a second language, we might consider the question of the most appropriate language for the medium of education as essentially decided. But there is other evidence. For one thing the correlations of language and educational pattern are not always clear. Often there are other factors that could have an effect, typically considerations of status: the position in the social hierarchy of the concerned group, lack of tradition of formal education, a philosophy that does not include delayed rewards for the investment of time, resources, and effort, an unenviable economic position that imposes the necessity of early participation in wage-earning activities, lack of incentive based on a history of nonachievement, etc. Perhaps some of these factors are at least in part responsible for the failures of the students who have been taught through the means of a second language.

As a kind of empirical support for the thesis that education in a second language may be responsible for the limited achievement of disadvantaged students, a number of vernacular-language experiments have demonstrated their advantages: case histories cited in the UNESCO Monograph, *The Use of Vernacular Languages in Education,* include the Tarascan project in Mexico (pp. 77-86), Pidgin English in New Guinea (pp. 103-115), the first Iloilo experiment in the Philippines (pp. 123-131). Subsequent experimental programs of vernacular education have lent additional support, such as the study of three Indian groups in Chiapas, conducted by Nancy Modiano (Modiano 1968), the impressive literacy projects of the Summer Institute of Linguistics (Andersson and Boyer 1970: Vol. 1, 44), and a "transitional bilingual" program for Quechua speakers in rural Peru (Burns 1968).

Where vernacular education has been tried experimentally against a tradition of second-language education, it has indeed often proved advantageous. The first Iloilo experiment is a good example, reporting "faster educational maturation in the mother tongue, together with age increase caused, in the third grade, speedier learning in English in about six months than in the same language in two years and six months." (*The Use of Vernacular Languages in Education,* 1953: 129). Other advantages are cited, such as more interest in school, greater ability to organize and express thought, better school attendance and health habits, and very significantly, better relations and cooperation between school and home. There was an aura of enthusiasm in the entire experiment:

> Instead of confining themselves to teaching the three Rs, teachers visited homes and taught parents to build water closets, to plant vegetables and raise poultry and pigs, construct drainage systems, prepare balanced diets, tend children and the aged, and improve the privacy of the homes. In class, teachers made these activities the basis of studies—reading, language, arithmetic, and civics. Pupils visited home gardens, the town post office, the doctor's clinic, the agricultural experiment station, and other public places. Later, discussing what they had learned through observation, they were led to show their parents how their knowledge could be applied to the problems of the home and community. Then, children and adults, using the same language, began to work together to improve living standards. The teachers acted as guides, also using the native language, and exemplified in their own homes the practices they had preached. (op. cit., p. 131)

This was undoubtedly a significant educational endeavor; one can sense the excitement, and I know from several years of close professional collaboration what an impressive educator Dr. Jose V. Aguilar is. His design and conduct of the first Iloilo experiment was a milestone in Philippine education. At the same time I feel it is only fair to point out that the enthusiasm that sent teachers into the community no doubt had a considerable effect on the outcome of the experiment and the conclusions it reached.

I have suggested that there are factors other than linguistic (the choice of language used as medium of instruction) that may have affected experimental studies—mainly social and psychological factors, and that enthusiasm for a new idea may influence the testing of that idea even under experimental conditions. But what really confirms for me the thesis that the choice of language to be used as medium of instruction is not the determining factor of pedagogical success is the availability of counterevidence, experiments where students studying in a second language matched or excelled over those studying in their mother tongue. This would not be expected to happen if Macnamara's "balance effect" operates.

The first counterexample I wish to cite is from the Philippines, another experiment in which Aguilar was involved in planning and design, referred to as the Rizal experiment, after the province where it was carried out. Fifteen hundred Filipino children were followed through six years of elementary school instruction. The experiment is reported fully in a Philippine Center for Language Study monograph (Davis 1967). Briefly described, the children were divided into three groups: one beginning their schoolwork in grade I in a second language, English; one beginning in the mother tongue, Tagalog, and switching to English at the beginning of grade 3; and finally one beginning in Tagalog and switching to English at the beginning of grade 5. All students had both English and Tagalog as school subjects each year. The experimental design was planned carefully to control for differences in home environment, school facilities, teacher preparation, class attendance, language-learning aptitude, etc., and a broad pattern of language and bilingual subject-matter tests were administered through the six-year period. Teams of curriculum writers prepared what was hoped would be comparable material for each language stream. One could certainly expect a native-language advantage to be reflected in the test results.

But the test results (Davis 1967: 74) show that the unexpected happened:

First, whether the tests were given in English, in Tagalog, or bilingually, the group that used English as the medium of instruction in Grades 1-6 displayed at the end of Grade 6 subject-matter achievement that is significantly greater than the achievement of the groups that used Tagalog as the medium of instruction in Grades 1-2 or in Grades 1-4. The differences in achievement are large enough to be of both statistical and practical consequence. So different are the levels of achievement of pupils in Group 1 from those of pupils in Group 3 (regardless of the language used for measuring achievement) that a pupil who stood at the middle of a Group-1 class in achievement would exceed 75-80 per cent of the pupils in a Group-2 or Group-3 class. Or, putting it another way, if a pupil who ranked at the middle of a Group-2 class in achievement were transferred to a Group-1 class, he would find that 75-80 per cent of the pupils were superior to him in achievement. Differences in achievement levels of this magnitude cannot be ignored if one is interested in the social, cultural, and economic welfare of school children and, perforce, of their nation.

It is possibly of some significance that the results interpreted by Davis in the paragraph above came as a complete surprise, and consequently were not supported by the aura of expectation. The established language-media pattern for the elementary school at the time of the experiment was two years of Tagalog followed by four years of English. The experimental design took this standard (2-4) as the central point and established comparison patterns with both more English (0-6) and less English (4-2). It never crossed anybody's mind that the all-in-English 0-6 group might excel. (Had this been considered a possibility it is not unlikely that the inclusion of this group would have been opposed, since it was not politically expedient to favor any extension of the use of English in the schools. Indeed no such extension came, in spite of the significantly superior performance of the all-English group.)

One test was given a selection of the Rizal experimental classes that was not in the original plan, a literacy survey conducted in grade 4. Randomly chosen experimental and nonexperimental classes were given a literacy test in English and Tagalog. Results from the schools where an experimental class was matched with a nonexperimental class showed the following percentages of students judged literate:

	English	Tagalog
Experimental	79.42	93.76
Nonexperimental	39.26	69.04

As Aguilar points out, these differences are highly significant (Ramos, Aguilar, and Sibayan 1967: 88). The results are undoubtedly influenced by a Hawthorne effect, but it is still interesting that Tagalog literacy measures which averaged in the performance of students who had never used Tagalog as the medium of instruction were still almost 25% higher for the experimental classes.

It is interesting and instructive to note, as the literacy data cited above suggest, that the Rizal experiment indicates no advantage in fuller mastery of the vernacular from its use as a medium of instruction. Aguilar (op. cit.: 97) states:

> The second of the major conclusions drawn from the data in the Rizal Experiment is: "The average level of literacy in Tagalog is not closely related to the number of years in which it has been used as a medium of classroom instruction" [as is the case for English when English is the medium of instruction]. It is probably safe to generalize this finding to any vernacular. For example, at the end of Grade 4 or of Grade 6, the pupils in Groups 1, 2, and 3 of the Rizal Experiment were about equally literate in Tagalog even though the pupils in these three groups had used it 0 years, 2 years, and 4 years, respectively, as the medium of classroom instruction.

But Rizal is not the only example where education in a second language has been conspicuously successful. In a longitundinal study that has become a classic of design and execution, Wallace Lambert and Richard Tucker and their colleagues at McGill University have conducted a home-school language switch program at the St. Lambert School on Montreal's south shore (Lambert and Tucker 1972). The program was begun on the initiative of English-speaking Canadian parents who, realizing the importance to the next generation of Canadians of bilingual skills, were concerned about the relative ineffectiveness of the French language teaching available to their children. The program has been reported in technical detail, and there is no need to repeat those details here. Suffice it to say that for the English-speaking Canadian children there has been no linguistic retardation in their home language (they are doing as well as the

English-speaking control children); progress in second-language skills has been very satisfactory—experimental children are confidently able to communicate with their French-speaking age mates (in striking contrast to English-speaking Canadians who have studied in the traditional French-as-a-Second-Language classes); there has been no subject-matter deficit in other (non-language) school courses. The experimental children rate their training high and express satisfaction with the program, which they want to continue; they are fairer and more charitable toward French culture, less ethnocentrically biased than English-speaking controls and seem to think of themselves as both French and English Canadians.

The success of this program is especially striking for the reason that both the experimental and the control children were volunteered for participation in the experimental group, offering assurance that the experimental group was not directed by special motivation. One very significant feature was the participation of the parents in planning a voluntary program. Those working at policy-making levels might be especially aware of the enhanced probability of success if they take into account the wishes and desires of their followership, rather than just "persuading an unwilling public to accept" whatever they in their wisdom wish to decree.

But Lambert and Tucker realize that the Montreal pattern of home-school language switch won't necessarily work everywhere, that there are special circumstances in Canada that may not exist in other situations.[1] The English-speaking Canadian students are obviously emotionally secure and culturally stable; they are not concerned about their identity, and they are supported by homes where parents recognize the values of biculturalism. Other patterns would be needed for other circumstances; Lambert and Tucker offer as a generalization the guiding principle of giving priority in early schooling, in situations of incipient or developed biculturalism, to the language least likely to be developed otherwise—to the language most likely to be neglected (Lambert and Tucker 1972: 216). Again this illustrates what I believe is the major point: that the choice of language as the medium (or media) for educational purposes should be determined by social conditions—not by a preconceived notion that the mother tongue should per se be used.

One additional example of a second language used as medium of instruction was inspired by the Montreal experience—a home-school language switch program in Culver City, in greater Los Angeles.[2] In its third year, this program's results for the most part were comparable to those in Montreal. One remarkable difference was the lack of any special outside funding. In spite of its obvious research value, this program was unable to attract any financial support (it deals with children who are not the object of particular social concern), and its success is a tribute to the interest and devotion of teachers and research assistants who paid their own extra expenses for the privilege and satisfaction of working in a challenging and significant program. It is particularly interesting to see an outstanding research success, which in many ways has outperformed others which have had the advantage of almost unlimited amounts of federal and foundation research support.[3]

Not only was there no special funding, there was no specialized training for the teachers, no special curriculum or hardware, no teacher aides (other than graduate students gathering data for their research studies). Materials were usually makeshift, and the Anglo kids just "tagged along" as their teachers taught them the regular curriculum, presented in Spanish. There haven't been a lot of studies reporting this program, but more are appearing, the most informative by Russell N. Campbell and Andrew D. Cohen, the UCLA staff members who have worked most closely with the project.[4]

Again this is not the place to report details that are available elsewhere (Cohen 1974). But as in Montreal there is no evidence of any native language or subject matter retardation; in fact, the immersion group was significantly better than comparison children at story-telling and reading. In Spanish the Anglo children were reasonably able to communicate after two years. Surprisingly, though they are not quite as good, they are not statistically inferior to a comparable (age, socioeconomic class, time in school) group of Spanish-speaking children in Guayaquil, Ecuador. Within the pilot group there is a correlation of English and Spanish reading scores (good evidence for transference of reading skills). The English reading catch-up was accomplished by the end of grade 1, earlier than at St. Lambert.

Parents of the immersion students are enthusiastic, as are the children. One very significant result was accidental. When attrition lowered the number of an already rather smaller than usual class at the end of the kindergarten year, school authorities looked around for additional students who could be assigned to the immersion group. The answer was a group of children from Spanish-speaking homes, who were transferred from a discontinued special program at another school. This fortuitous circumstance has provided a very satisfying development, since these children have been received as friends and accepted as models. Although they make up approximately one-fourth of the class, they are not resented for their linguistic advantage. It is no surprise that the Anglo immersion students tested significantly more positive toward Mexican cultural items on a cross-cultural inventory than Anglo control students, with the positive and extensive interaction between the Anglos and Mexican Americans in the immersion class. (For more details, see Cohen 1974.)

The results of the Rizal, Montreal, and Culver City experiences suggest strongly that bilingual education is a good thing in itself, not just as a creation to allow instruction in the mother tongue, or as a device to develop cultural pride and identification (though granted it may be useful for these purposes), or as a bridge to competence in a dominant official or national language. Rather we can conclude that bilingual education is good even for those students who, strictly speaking, don't need it.

But a nagging question persists: how can Rizal, Montreal, Culver City, etc. produce such encouraging results when essentially the same curriculum pattern has proved completely unproductive, even unworkable, for extensive groups of students in the United States, particularly the American Indian and Mexican-American students? Part of the answer has to be that the difference is not a matter of language—either of mother tongue or medium of instruction. In other words, it is not strictly a linguistic problem. This is not an easy point to make, given the considerable amount of research reporting on the advantage of the mother tongue and the general belief that "bilingual" really means learning English by speakers of other languages. John and Horner describe bilingual programs as needing teachers "able to teach English as a Second Language, to teach primary subjects in the mother tongue, and to teach the history and culture associated with the mother tongue" (John and Horner 1971: 108). There is not even a glimmer of English *being* the mother tongue in a bilingual program.

So the vernacular advantage theory continues to be applied, and such farcical assumptions as the "forced early learning of English" are offered as explanations for unsatisfactory performance, documented by numerous corroborating experimental studies (ibid.: 169-172). Occasionally a hint of other possible explanations occurs—one suspects inadvertently, since they are never acknowledged as relevant. Thus the statement "school may be a frightening and frustrating place for the young non-English-speaking child" (ibid.: 164), while undoubtedly true, can also be applied to English-speaking children, as many uneasy mothers who were advised to walk out and leave their crying child in kindergarten can recall. Must we assume it is frightening and frustrating only to children who are non-English-speaking and therefore *because* they are non-English-speaking? The authors (ibid.: 165) continue by discussing the social and emotional consequences of "speaking a language that may be downgraded by the school and by society as a whole." Aye there's the rub! It's the downgrading, not the "non-English," that reveals the cause—and it's the whole society, not just the school, that bears the burden!

If it is true that "bilingual" is loosely synonymous with "Spanish-surname or individual assumed to be of Mexican ancestry" (ibid.: 166), then we can understand the status implications for speaking two languages. I hold that one very effective way to give status—which is the real social question involved—is to use the minority language in a significant role in the dominant culture. It has certainly proved out in Culver City, where Spanish-speaking parents are proud (and surprised) that Anglo parents are willing for Spanish to be used as the language of instruction in their children's education. If Spanish (or Navajo or Tagalog or French or . . .) can be shown to have real status, much of the apprehension may disappear (as it does for virtually all English-speaking children), and with it the stigma that inspires feelings of inadequacy.

Status—really acknowledged status in the society—is one explanation for the limited performance of minority-language students, but there are others. We have good research evidence that indicates teacher expectations have a potent influence on student achievement (Rosenthal and Jacobson 1968; Rist 1970; "Pattern Transmission in a Bicultural Community" 1967). Apparently, if we expect low performance from a group of students, they will oblige us. This proposition gets unexpected support from a surprising source: native American English-speaking students of other languages compared to minority students' achievement in English. While true that there is little cause to rejoice over the achievements of minority-language students of English, they are as a group light-years ahead of students in our foreign-language classes. The explanation, to me at least, is perfectly clear: we expect our Indians, Mexican Americans, immigrants, foreign students, etc. to learn English; we don't expect our indigenous English speakers to really learn Spanish, French, Russian, Chinese, etc., and in fact we are surprised if they do. I once had a job that included interviewing persons to be offered language training. A standard set of questions enquired about foreign-language competence, language study, experience abroad, etc. Typical student answers were "Yes, I took French for four years, but it was just school French." They did not expect to learn, nor were they expected to by their teachers. How ironical that the minority-language students excel (compared to the favored majority) in precisely the field of our concern for their educational welfare!

But whereas the minority students do better in language, they do not do as well in general education, and general education is what really counts in terms of career planning, professional preparation, job markets, etc. How can we, then, go about expecting more? I submit that this problem is related to the overall problem of status, that something significant will have to happen in the society in general. I don't think we can just say to our teachers "Expect more" and have the result we wish. Some of the things being done are certainly appropriate and promising, such as more fully recognizing the contributions to American (and universal) culture of our Indian and Mexican-American subcultures. There is material to build pride and understanding, and we should encourage both.

But I return to the idea of two-way bilingual education. If bilingualism can be shown to be advantageous *per se* as a human condition, as I think it can, and if the choice of language of instruction in our schools is linguistically irrelevant, as I think it is, then we can move in the direction of clarifying and removing some of the massive misunderstanding and bias that surrounds language as a school subject and as a medium of instruction. But meaningful bilingual programs, either of the home-school language-switch type or of the employment of a minority mother tongue as an instructional medium type should be organized only on the initiative of an informed parent group. And I specifically exclude the method of informing parents by officially "persuading an unwilling public to accept education through the mother tongue." In my view the best way of persuading anyone is to show the advantages through an action program: an opportunity for a two-way bilingual program that recognizes the intrinsic value of bilingualism as a social, political, and economic resource that is appropriately rewarded nationally and locally. Then our students can meaningfully hope to become citizens of the world, leaders in intercultural communication, which we need so desperately. (Today we depend on an immigrant for our Secretary of State; tomorrow we may develop bilingual Kissingers in our own schools.)

There is some evidence to support the conclusion that bilingual competence is an advantageous human condition, that speaking two (or more) languages is a liberating experience that increases a person's ability to perceive, analyze, and compare. Far from constituting restrictions imposed by an overloaded intellectual capacity, competence in a second language seems to make available an additional conceptual network that encourages the development of flexible and imaginative responses, more diversified reactions, with faculties for greater initiative and versatility.

The McGill team cautiously conclude "the data suggest that the home-school language switch program in the early school years may well have had a salutary effect on [the Experimental children's] intellectual development, particularly their performance on measures of cognitive flexibility" (Lambert, Tucker, and d'Anglejan 1973: 149). Also, "there are signs that [the Experimental children] may be developing more flexible or creative strategies for problem solving than the controls" (ibid.: 156). We can speculate with Lambert and Tucker, following the arguments of the Russian scholar Vygotsky, that an intellectual advantage may be expected as the children approach bilingual balance, presaged by the reliably faster performance of Experimental children over Controls at certain grade levels in producing associations in English (Lambert and Tucker 1972: 210,204).

In my opinion the benefits of study in and through another language should be available to any student, provided he is motivated to want bilingual skills, and the most promising way to develop bilingual competence, to make a person proficient in another language, is to use that language in a significant function. The most successful attempt to provide an adequate opportunity for bilingual skills that I am aware of, is an immersion program where early education is given fully or substantially in a second language.[5]

In summary, the linguistic perspectives in bilingual education are that we have more choices than we may have thought. I don't mean to say that the choice of the language or languages of instruction in our schools doesn't make any difference—it does. But that choice is determined not by linguistic factors, but by social and practical considerations, such as public attitudes, opportunities made possible by bilingual populations, the availability of teachers and materials, and encouragement in the form of support by government bodies (but without hoopla, legislative mandating, public posturing by politicians looking for votes, etc. that will probably disappear when some new fad catches the public eye). We need professional leadership, solid research and evaluation, strict avoidance of amateurism and hobby horses, the ability to see the forest *and* the trees, and the wisdom to follow our successes.

NOTES

1. The St. Lambert project has been criticized as perhaps applicable only to middle-class students and not generalizable to other students, particularly to those who come from working-class homes. A recent extension of the home-school language-switch idea to a less advantaged area of Montreal tentatively indicates that even children with language learning difficulties can benefit from bilingual training in an immersion program: ". . . to date our preliminary results indicate that the children with language learning disabilities in French

immersion classes fare well. They have learned to read in both English and French. Their school achievement is adequate. They can understand as well as communicate in their second language with some facility. Furthermore their first language ability does not appear to have been retarded by this educational experience" (Bruck and Rabinovitch 1974: 124).

2. Other examples could be cited, such as the New Primary Approach in Kenya, a highly successful shift from vernacular to English instruction in the late 1950s, which "was an immediate and resounding success," for many reasons, such as a new philosophy of child-centered instruction, better texts and teaching materials, provision for adequate teacher training and supervision, etc. (See Prator, 1967.) This success has been repeated in other African countries, recently in Zambia, where instruction in English has been widely adopted for practical and political reasons. In general these programs have been considered improvements on the vernacular-medium instruction they replaced.

3. Wright 1973: 153 notes that $400 million was originally authorized in the Bilingual Education Act of 1968 for a period of six years and that $117 million of that amount has been spent. The authorization for fiscal 1973 was $135 million, of which $35 million was spent to support 213 projects in 32 states and territories, involving 100,222 students (an average of $349.22 in special funds per student). It is apparent that there is no lack of money—that indeed if more could be spent, it would be made available. This may not be good since easy money may encourage careless administration and poor accounting, sometimes even dishonest handling of funds if the wrong kind of personnel are attracted to the program. An additional disadvantage that I have observed is the inculcation in the minds of students of the belief that there are no restrictions on supplies, materials, etc. so that they actually are taught profligacy instead of the careful use of material resources.

4. The article by Cohen (1974) is the source of most of the information included in the present description.

5. At a general session of a TESOL Convention (March 5-10, 1974 at Denver, Colorado) Richard Tucker presented a paper titled "TESOL Research in the Middle East," in which he reported that a secondary-level course in mathematics is being offered in Jordan with English as the medium of instruction as a means of providing a significant context to reinforce and give meaningful substance to English language teaching.

V

Psychological Perspectives on Bilingual Education

Norman Segalowitz

This paper reviews the psychological literature related to two aspects of bilingualism. The first concerns the consequences, if any, that bilingualism may have for the cognitive and social functioning of the individual. The second concerns the psychological factors that may facilitate or hinder second language mastery.

Feelings have always run high about the psychological implications of being bilingual. For example, Weinreich (1953: 116-122) presents numerous examples of fears that people have entertained regarding the dangers of bilingual education: bilingualism leads to stuttering, left-handedness, bilinguals are likely to suffer "conceptual poverty" and develop personalities characterized by "mercenary relativism." On the other hand, some writers have argued that there are valuable psychological advantages to be derived from being bilingual. Early bilingualism might increase the facility for acquiring new languages later in life and may have beneficial "spin-off" effects for mental development, such as enhancing creativity and general intelligence.

These opinions appear to rest on two assumptions. The first is that human mental processes are highly dependent on linguistic processes. That is, in some important way language is believed to lie at the core of all or many of our intellectual abilities. The second assumption is that language functions differently in bilinguals than in monolinguals. Those who believe the difference is unfavorable for the bilingual make the further assumption that conflicts arise between the linguistic processes subserving each language, conflicts which, in turn, have detrimental effects on the general mental functioning of the individual.

As Weinreich (1953) is careful to point out, many of the hopes and fears expressed about the consequences of bilingualism for the individual are not based on strong evidence. Often they are prompted by viewpoints owing more to nationalistic feelings than to dispassionate scientific inquiry. Both in cases of positive and negative sentiments it is usually simply assumed that many psychological processes other than those directly related to speech will be affected by bilingualism. The purpose of this chapter is to review the theoretical and empirical material related to this assumption. As we shall see there are a number of theoretical perspectives in the literature supporting the contention that bilingualism could have important effects on the psychological functioning of the individual. However, it will also rapidly become clear to the reader that psychological theory concerning the relationship between language and thought is still in its infancy.

The plan of this review is the following. The chapter begins with a consideration of five major theoretical positions in psychology that are relevant to an understanding of the psychological consequences of bilingualism: Vygotsky's theory of language and thought, Whorf's linguistic-relativity hypothesis, a Piagetian approach to language and thought, associationist approaches to language and, finally, cognitive network theory. Following this two issues regarding the bilingual individual are considered. The first concerns whether the bilingual brain functions differently from the monolingual brain. Here the individual is viewed in isolation from the social context and attention is focused on the effects bilingualism may have upon neurological and cognitive aspects of mental processes. The second concerns whether the bilingual person functions differently from the monolingual person. Here the individual is viewed as a social being and attention is directed to the effects bilingualism may have on interpersonal relations. The fourth section considers whether there are constitutional or experiential factors that predispose some people to success in language learning. The final section is a summary and discussion of the material covered.

A word about the definition of the term *bilingual* is in order here. Here, people are considered to be bilingual if they possess sufficient skills in a second language to permit a significant part of their social and/or intellectual activities to be conducted through the medium of that language. Of course, this includes many bilinguals who are considerably less skilled in certain respects in their second language than native speakers of that language. In most cases our concern will be with so-called *balanced* bilinguals—those having equal skills in their native and second languages as measured by tests of reading speed, pronunciation skills, speed of word recognition, vocabulary size, and so on.[2] Such bilinguals differ from second language learners who are still in the process of attaining bilingual skills and "weak" bilinguals who have completed second language acquisition but are definitely more skilled in their native language.

PSYCHOLOGICAL THEORY

Vygotsky's Theory of Language and Thought

Vygotsky's (1962) theory has not been directly concerned with bilingualism but it does provide a basis for thinking that bilingualism could affect cognitive development differently from monolingualism (e.g., Lambert and Tucker 1972: 207, acknowledge the influence of Vygotsky's notions in their ideas on bilingual education; see also Belyaev 1965).

Vygotsky proposed that the acquisition of language brings about a radical restructuring of mental processes, with the result that human intellectual functioning falls into a qualitatively different category from the intellectual functioning of lower animals. Psychological development is a joint function of biological and social development, and language plays a critical role in shaping the way biological and social factors interact. Language first develops in a social context in which child and parent learn to verbally control each other's behavior. This social use of language to control other people's behavior continues to develop as the individual becomes involved in increasingly more complex social relationships. However, in parallel with this socially rooted development of language there is a second type of language development in which language also becomes a tool of thought, an instrument in the operation of cognitive processes. Thus instead of remaining only a means for affecting the behavior of others, language is also used by children to control their own behavior. At a certain stage in development children begin to guide themselves with self-generated verbal instructions (many of the so-called egocentric utterances of young children are examples of such self-guiding speech, according to Vygotsky). In adults this self-guiding speech is completely internalized and usually is inaudible (called *inner speech* by Vygotsky).

One major implication of Vygotsky's theory is that the internalization of language for such self-regulatory purposes brings about a restructuring of many mental processes. Memory is enhanced by the availability of verbal mnemonics, perception is affected by the existence of linguistically defined categories, and problem-solving strategies become more rational and sophisticated when they can be verbalized. It is as though the organism with language has available to it a special mental calculus—a set of symbols and a set of rules for manipulating the symbols—that not only extends the power of mental operations but radically alters their character.

For our purposes Vygotsky's theory is interesting because it claims that important facets of intellectual functioning are intimately linked to language development. What effects, then, can we expect multilingualism to have on intellectual development? With more than one language available to mediate intellectual processes one could argue that psychological processes would be enriched. The mental algebra would contain more symbols, perhaps even a more sophisticated differentiation between symbols. The increase in quantity and quality of the linguistic apparatus available for mediating thought could lead to an enhancement of memory, perception, intelligence, creativity, and so on (Bain 1973). On the other hand, the profusion of linguistic symbols available to mediate thought might give rise to a great deal of confusion producing a lack of clarity of thought and a slowing down of those processes which utilize linguistic mediators. In this case multilingualism could have a deleterious effect on intelligence, creativity and other aspects of mental functioning.

Vygotsky did not address these issues directly except to suggest that in foreign language learning there will be a transfer of conceptual abilities from native to second language meaning systems. Knowledge of foreign languages should enhance knowledge of the native tongue by "facilitating the mastery of higher forms of the language" (1962: 110). Unfortunately he does not provide specific examples of what he has in mind here. One claim that Vygotsky has made about language development has, however, been mentioned frequently in the literature on bilingual development (Ben Zeev 1972; Ianco-Worrall 1972; Imedadze 1967; Leopold 1953-54). This is that there is a stage in language development when a child is not yet aware that words are arbitrary labels for concepts and not inherent properties of the referents named. For them the name is not dissociable from its referent (they cannot pretend that a cow can be called "dog"). Some theorists have argued that bilingualism may accelerate the onset of this awareness.

Vygotsky's theory suggests that language, as a mediator of thought, is intricately bound up with the mechanisms of thought. His theory also is an historical one, emphasizing that man is able to create higher order processes from the interaction of language and thought to replace processes acquired earlier in development. It is these aspects of the theory—the suggestion about possible mechanisms for thought and the emphasis on man's ability to transcend certain modes of intellectual functioning by creating new processes—that have particularly excited psychologists (Bruner 1962) and that possibly provide an interesting perspective on how multilingualism could affect an individual. However it should be pointed out that recently the theory has run into both empirical and theoretical difficulties. Predictions from the theory have been supported in studies by Luria (1959, 1961), Kohlberg, Yaeger and Hjertholm (1968), and Schubert (1969). However, Miller, Shelton and Flavell (1970) report failures to replicate some of Luria's work. As well, Fodor (1972) points to some conceptual difficulties in the theory by suggesting that Vygotsky has made incorrect assumptions about what exactly constitutes mature adult forms of conceptual ability. Fodor argues that the differences between the adult's and child's conceptual skills reflect quantitative differences in the range of situations to which cognitive processes may be applied rather than qualitative differences in kind. Leontiev and Luria (1972) and Sinclair (1972) provide some replies to Fodor's objections. Despite this controversy however, the idea that certain intellectual functions may be heavily mediated by linguistic processes has remained an intriguing one to the student of bilingualism.

Whorf's Linguistic Relativity Hypothesis

According to what some have called the strong form of the Whorfian hypothesis (Whorf 1956, Fishman 1960; Hoijer 1954) the language we speak sets certain limits or constraints on the way we perceive. If the speakers of one language have available to them a linguistic categorization of certain objects in the world which speakers of some other language do not have, these objects will be perceived differently. Our perceptual habits are thus held to be conditioned in some way by the linguistic categories available to us.

The Whorfian hypothesis has often been in the minds of those who theorize about the effects of multilingualism (see, for example, the discussion in Alatis 1970: 40-45, Carroll 1963a, and Christophersen 1973). As Haugen (1956; also in Alatis 1970: 41) indicates, bilinguals often feel that there is an element of truth in the notion that one's perception of the world changes depending on which language one is speaking. But no one has yet been able to specify precisely what this difference is (beyond giving subjective characterizations) or what mechanisms cause this difference to exist.

While experimental efforts to demonstrate that visual perception is affected by language categories have only achieved very modest success (Brown and Lenneberg 1954, Carroll and Casagrande 1958, Lantz and Stefflre 1964), it might be argued that we are more likely to find linguistic relativity effects in social perceptions. For example, speakers of a language containing honorifics will be forced to recognize important status characteristics of the interlocutor in order to ready themselves with the appropriate way of speaking. Speakers of a language lacking such honorifics might fail to note such characteristics and their behavior with the individual might take a different turn.

Similarly, cultural patterns sometimes accord a word certain emotional connotations that are lacking in its usual translation in some other language. For example, the word *church* in language A spoken by a very religious community may have a different meaning from the word *church* in language B spoken by a group that is not basically church-going. Bilinguals speaking languages A and B might come to appreciate the different nuances these words have for monolingual speakers of A and B. This awareness might have the effect of encouraging them to discover other subtle linguistic differences with the result that perhaps they will develop perceptual habits not usually found in monolinguals. These new perceptual habits will not depend so much on the particular languages involved but rather on the fact that they have been exposed to two languages and therefore made aware of possibilities not otherwise so evident to monolinguals. The important factor is the bicultural experience; the language differences serve to make the cultural differences more salient. The same effect could be produced by exposure to people of another culture who speak a different regional variety (dialect) of the same language.

In general, the main contribution of the Whorfian hypothesis in this area has been to focus attention on the possibility that bilinguals may have linguistic and cultural experiences that alter their perception (and hence appreciation) of their environment. The major difficulty remains, however, in distinguishing the effects of cultural experience from linguistic experience as the principal factor responsible for this altered awareness.

Piaget's Approach

Piaget has not written specifically about bilingualism, but his approach is included here because his theories of cognitive development have been and continue to be of major importance in psychology.

Piaget's views of language differ from both the preceding approaches in a way which is fundamental to the issue of multilingualism (Piaget 1959, 1970, 1971; Sinclair 1967, 1969, 1971). Language is neither a tool of thought in Vygotsky's sense nor a shaper of perception as proposed by Whorf. Rather, language is just one of many symbolic systems available to the child with play, mental imagery, dreaming, and various forms of imitation being other channels for symbolic functions. All these develop structurally and in the range of areas to which they can be applied as the child develops intellectually. Language thus provides one channel among several for interacting with the environment (primarily the social environment) and, at certain stages of development, for operating on the environment symbolically rather than physically. In this view language development *follows* cognitive development and not vice versa.

If linguistic development merely reflects cognitive development, rather than being a factor guiding or shaping it, then one wonders whether the acquisition of more than one language would have any special consequences for psychological development. Ben Zeev (1972) argues in favor of the idea that there could be special effects. First, she points out the importance in Piaget's theory of internal conceptual conflict for cognitive development. The young child is constantly involved in accommodating activity, that is, adjusting (accommodating) internal representations of the world to fit new information received from interactions with the environment. All language learning also involves such accommodating activity since the linguistic environment will often be discrepant with the child's current internal organization. In the case of bilingualism there is the additional element of conflict within the linguistic environment itself since the child must adapt to two languages (Ben Zeev 1972: 67). Thus for the bilingual child, the element of conceptual conflict that triggers accommodating processes in cognitive development should be heightened compared to monolinguals.

Second, language is a highly structured symbolic system and in some respects (e.g., the acquisition of a transformational rule system) its development may proceed faster than the corresponding development of other cognitive structures. Thus in learning to manipulate the structure in language, the child may learn a general cognitive manipulative skill useful in other domains. In bilingual children linguistic structure is all the more salient because of the contrast between their two languages, so the development of cognitive skills should be accelerated. According to Ben Zeev (1972: 83), then, the cognitive conflict that triggers accommodation processes and the cognitive structures that are necessary for the assimilation of new information are enhanced in the bilingual child and cognitive development is correspondingly enhanced (see also Genessee 1974).

Associationism

The associationist approach to language has had an important influence on how psychologists have viewed the way language is represented in the brain. Of particular relevance is the formulation by Ervin and Osgood (1954) of the different ways multiple languages may be represented in the brain depending on the type of bilingual upbringing the individual has been exposed to. Since their theory has generated a great deal of research and controversy over some of the possible consequences of bilingualism it will now be reviewed in detail.

Ervin and Osgood (1954) made a basic distinction between two different ways words and meanings can be associated in the brain of the bilingual. In *compound bilingualism,* a word in language A and its translation in language B are associated with the same internal mediating neural event that is supposed to represent the meaning of the two words. Such a relationship between words and meanings arises, according to Ervin and Osgood (1954), from language learning situations typical of the classroom (e.g., learning Russian words via English meanings) and home language acquisition where the two languages are spoken interchangeably by the same people in all situations.

In *coordinate bilingualism* there exist separate meanings for each of the words in the two languages. Thus a pure coordinate bilingual would function like two monolingual speakers to the extent that the meaning systems are relatively distinct. This situation is thought to arise when learners acquire two languages in very different settings, or deliberately avoid the use of translation methods.

Although there have been numerous attempts to demonstrate that compound and coordinate language acquisition histories really do have different behavioral consequences for the bilingual, the evidence gathered to date is ambiguous at best. Some studies claim to show that compound bilinguals, who supposedly possess merged meaning systems, have less difficulty than coordinates in switching from one language to another and show greater transfer effects between languages on a variety of tasks (Jakobovits and Lambert 1961; Lambert, Havelka and Crosby 1958; Lambert and Rawlings 1969; Segalowitz and Lambert 1969). Support for the distinction also comes from Ervin's (1964) study which showed that bilinguals who acquired their two languages in different cultural settings told qualitatively different Thematic Apperception Test stories depending on the language they were asked to speak in. Lambert and Fillenbaum (1959) report data on bilingual aphasics providing qualified support for the compound-coordinate distinction.

On the other hand, Kolers (1963) reports a bilingual word association study failing to support the view that word-meaning links across languages depend on the language acquisition history of the speaker. Dillon, McCormack, Petrusic, Cook and Lafleur (1973), using a bilingual adaptation of the release from proactive inhibition technique (Goggin and Wickens 1971) failed to find a predicted difference between compound and coordinate subjects. As well, Arkwright and Viau (1974) did not find compound-coordinate differences in an adaptation of the Lambert and Rawlings (1969) study.

Serious theoretical criticisms have been leveled at the compound-coordinate distinction concerning (a) the extent to which the distinction is applicable to different facets of language; (b) the psycholinguistic theory underlying the distinction; and (c) problems in the classification of subjects.

Macnamara (1967a, 1970) has pointed out, for example, that behavioral differences between compound and coordinate bilinguals appear most reliably in semantic differential rating scale experiments (Lambert et al. 1958; Jakobovits and Lambert 1961). It is generally accepted that the aspect of meaning that the semantic differential deals with is restricted to the affective or emotive side of meaning (Weinreich 1958) and that the denotative aspect of meaning is not amenable to semantic differential analysis. It is thus misleading to conclude that the difference between these two types of bilinguals lies in the way words and meanings are linked. "Meaning" is a very broad and complex component of language, and a theory claiming to account for the relationships of words in one or more languages to meanings would necessarily have to deal with more than just emotive meaning. Moreover, these studies have only examined the relationships between meanings and single words. Words derive meaning from both the linguistic and nonlinguistic contexts in which they occur and so there is a need for an account of the contextual determination of meaning in bilinguals.

The second type of criticism leveled against the Ervin and Osgood (1954) approach concerns the use of psycholinguistic notions derived from stimulus-response theories. A number of linguists have pointed out that these approaches fail to capture the creativity of language, the grammatical structure of language and the basic fact that semantic and syntactic environments are extremely important in the determination of word meaning (Chomsky 1959, Fodor 1965). The general shortcomings of stimulus-response theories of language are necessarily the shortcomings of the compound-coordinate theory formulated in these terms.

Macnamara (1970) has further pointed out that the Ervin and Osgood formulation is very Whorfian in nature. Unfortunately this means that it too shares the shortcomings which prevent the Whorfian hypothesis from providing a viable approach to the language and thought question in psychology. Purely coordinate bilinguals would have different mediating processes underlying their verbal expressions in each of their languages. This suggests that when such bilinguals speak one language they might find it impossible to switch to the other and continue their discourse coherently unless there were some third set of processes linking the distinct mediating processes underlying the representations of each of the languages. We know that bilinguals do not have such difficulty but it is not clear just what such linking processes would look like in this type of associationist theory.

Finally, it has been pointed out that there are inconsistencies in the application of criteria for deciding whether a bilingual should be classified as compound or coordinate (Diller 1967). Lambert et al. (1958) used type of language acquisition context as the criterion while Arkwright and Viau (1974), Lambert and Rawlings (1969) and Segalowitz and Lambert (1969) used age of acquisition. Moreover it is not clear that either criterion is clearly enough defined to be useful. For example, Lambert et al. (1958) found behavioral differences between unicultural and bicultural coordinate bilinguals. The age criterion is also ambiguous. One can learn both languages at the same time in either compounded or separated contexts (e.g., both languages spoken at home versus one language at home and another on the street). It is a weakness of the compound-coordinate distinction that there is no way of telling how important or unimportant these differences in language acquisition contexts can be.

Cognitive Network Theory

The final theoretical framework that deserves mention is the cognitive network theory of Rumelhart, Lindsay and Norman (1972) as applied to issues in bilingualism by Taylor (1974).

In the cognitive network, ideas (information, meanings of sentences, etc.) are represented as a network of concepts linked together in special relationships. An important concept that is acquired early in language development is the concept "label," the concept that speech noises (words) can name objects and events. Taylor suggests that the relationship between words and objects or events is more stable in a monolingual environment than in a bilingual one since everything has more than one name in the latter. This makes the abstract concept "label" more difficult to acquire for the bilingual since the recurring patterns of association between uttered names and perceived referents are less uniform. Taylor thus predicts that children brought up bilingually from infancy will exhibit a delay in the onset of greater ability to acquire new words because of the delay in acquiring the mediating concept "label." On the other hand, once bilingual children have acquired this concept they also acquire the concept of multiple labels and that these can be involved in different conceptual networks. This means the cognitive network will be more easily differentiated into separable languages, presumably an aid to efficient acquisition of even more languages.

Related to this is the prediction that it would be easier to learn a second language together with the first than to learn it at a later date. The reason is that it would be difficult to differentiate an already developed cognitive network into two relatively distinct ones since new labels and syntactic processes would have to be built into the network where perfectly satisfactory ones already exist.

The cognitive network theory offers an interesting perspective on bilingual development but as it is a relatively new approach there is available little experimental research that speaks directly to the issues raised by the theory. The main advantage the theory has over other associationist approaches is that it attempts to deal with structures in language. The disadvantage is that the theory is too broad as it now stands. We need to know whether some concepts in the network can be learned more easily than others and what specific learning conditions facilitate the emergence of new concepts. Hopefully research in the near future will be directed to these questions.

COGNITIVE AND INTELLECTUAL FUNCTIONING

This section considers the evidence relevant to the hypothesis that the bilingual brain somehow functions differently from the monolingual brain. A basic issue here is whether the representation of multiple languages places a burden on the space and processing requirements of the brain as suggested by Jespersen (1922). Two types of approaches to this question will be considered: one emphasizing underlying neurological mechanisms and the other emphasizing processes at the cognitive level. The final part of this section reviews literature dealing with the overall intellectual performance of the bilingual, quite apart from the issue about how more than one language is represented in his brain.

The Bilingual Brain

At present there are no neuroanatomical theories about the representation of multiple languages in the brain. The best we can do is to consider some of the possibilities which seem appropriate in the light of what is known about the representation of a single language in the brain. Most current theories about the latter reflect the view that language results from the intricate coordination of a number of so-called brain centers each of which is specialized for particular functions involved in linguistic reception, production and comprehension (see, for example, Geschwind 1965; Luria 1966, 1970; Penfield and Roberts 1959; Whitaker 1971). Some theorists appear to favor a relatively narrow localization of function in which some particular aspect of language processing is carried out in a carefully circumscribed region of the brain (e.g., Whitaker 1971). Others place emphasis on the coordinated integration of these centers while remaining somewhat less explicit about the exact functions ascribed to any particular speech area (Penfield and Roberts 1959).

There appears to be general agreement on three main points. First, it is believed that there is no such thing as one neural center in the brain responsible for all language. Second, certain regions of the brain are more specialized for language functions than others. For example, the left hemisphere in most people is more specialized for language production activities (Gazzaniga 1970; Milner, Branch and Rasmussen 1964) and a region in the left temporal lobe is more particularly specialized for speech comprehension. The third point is that these specialized areas must operate in some coordinated fashion for successful language processing implying that a good deal of the brain is involved in language functioning. (An exception to this viewpoint is provided by Schuell and Jenkins

(1959) who argue that the brain has a general language capability not localizable to any specific region or interaction of regions of the brain.)

No one has yet been able to pinpoint areas of the brain responsible for this or that particular syntactic rule, articulatory pattern, semantic relationship, and so on. Thus it is impossible to point to neurological facts in answering the question about whether the neural representations for the phonological components of a person's two languages are spatially separate in the brain or whether they share the same underlying neural mechanisms.

One possibility is that, indeed, they are neurally independent of each other. In the multilingual brain neural mechanisms normally subserving one language might be divided between the languages spoken by the individual with the result that less neural material is available for each. Or, neural material not normally subserving language functions might be recruited for this purpose with the consequence that "less brain" is available for other functions. In this case injuries to the brain could selectively impair the functioning of just one language. Belyaev (1965: 176) cites Chlenov (1948) as support for this notion. A second possibility is that the mechanisms subserving multiple languages employ the same neural processes wherever possible. Thus from the neuroanatomical point of view, all the languages of the multilingual person are represented as one big language in the brain (cf. Penfield and Roberts 1959). This raises the problem of how the languages are so easily kept separate on the behavioral level. The third possibility is that languages have distinct but intermingled neural representations so that no particular areas of the brain can be uniquely identified with one specific language. This implies that while the representations of the languages are neurally distinct, an injury to the brain will never selectively impair only one language.

Obviously one cannot perform neurological experiments with multilinguals to explore these different possibilities, but occasionally multilinguals with brain damage from vascular accidents or penetrating wounds become available for study. In cases where the brain damage impairs language processes, it becomes interesting to trace the fate of the patient's several languages (see the review by Paradis, in press). In general, researchers have been guided by three notions in the consideration of bilingual aphasics. The first of these, known as the *rule of Ribot* (see Weinreich 1953: 76), holds that the first learned language will be the one more resistant to aphasic impairment. Lambert and Fillenbaum (1959), for example, found some support for this primacy effect among their Montreal patients. The second, known as *Pitres's rule* (Pitres 1895), is a habit strength rule that holds that the more practiced language will be more resistant to impairment. Pitres (1895), Lambert and Fillenbaum (1959) and, to some extent, Weisenburg and McBride (1964) report examples of this type of case. Of course it should be realized that in many cases the first learned language is also the more used language and so it is often difficult to find data that discriminate between the primacy and habit strength theories. The third approach is Minkowski's (1928) which predicts that the language to recover first will be the one with which the patient had the strongest emotional bond. Lambert and Fillenbaum (1959) cite as support for this view a study by Leischner (1948) in which a less used but emotionally important second language rather than the native language survived the aphasic injury. Hécaen and Angelergues (1968) also cite reports supporting this approach.

In general it is not easy to decide which of the bilingual's languages will be more resistant to impairment since a number of different factors may be operating in each individual's case. The data indicate, however, that different languages are not represented in widely separated and distinct areas of the brain since in the majority of patients there is severe impairment of all languages (see also Charlton 1964). This conclusion agrees with Penfield's (Penfield and Roberts 1959) contention that basically the same mechanisms subserving a single language also subserve several languages. In those cases where one language appears to recover faster than another there may have been psychological rather than neuroanatomical reasons for this selectivity (e.g., patients may be more strongly motivated to concentrate their efforts at expressing themselves in a particular language).

One interesting possibility for differences in the way multilingual and monolingual brains may represent language is in the degree to which the right hemisphere (normally not specialized for language production) becomes involved in subserving language. In young children damage to the left hemisphere results less often in permanent language impairment than in adults because the right hemisphere is able to take over the functions formerly carried out by the left (Lenneberg 1967). In many aphasic adults, recovery of language comes about from recruitment of neural mechanisms in the right hemisphere (Luria 1970). Left-handed and ambidextrous people are less likely to suffer language deficits from injury to the left hemisphere because their brain mechanisms subserving language are less strongly lateralized. Instead, both hemispheres are involved to a greater degree in left-handed people than in right-handed people. These considerations might support the speculation that early second language learning will create the need for recruitment of supplementary neural processes from the right hemisphere. For example, Lenneberg (1967) and Scovel (1969) suggest that young children are relatively more successful in second language learning than adults because language lateralization is not yet complete thus permitting greater involvement of the right hemisphere in language development. However, Krashen (1973) presents a dissenting view regarding the age of lateralization and Hill (1970) suggests that cultural factors may be more important than biological factors in this matter.

There have been few studies of the effect of bilingualism on cerebral lateralization. Arsenian (1945) reports a study by Saer, Smith and Hughes (1924) suggesting that bilingual children under the age of twelve make more confusions in tests requiring left-right identifications than do monolingual children. A more recent study by Hamers and Lambert (1974) investigated the ability of right-handed balanced bilinguals to identify the language of French and English words flashed in the right visual field (projecting to the left cerebral hemisphere) and the left visual field (projecting to the right hemisphere). Twelve of fifteen subjects demonstrated general left hemisphere superiority for language identification, one demonstrated more rapid language identification in the right hemisphere and two yielded results suggesting greater facility in identifying one language on one side but greater facility in identifying the other language on the other side. These results tend to support Penfield's notion that language representation in the multilingual normally involves one hemisphere as it does in the monolingual.

Thus, there does not seem to be strong neurological evidence indicating a basic difference in the way language is represented in the monolingual and bilingual brain. It appears that the same regions are involved in multi-language functioning as in single-language functioning. Lateralization does not appear to be affected by bilingualism. While it is clear that more studies are needed in this area, the evidence presently available does not indicate that a bilingual brain suffers some neurological burden that a monolingual brain escapes. From the strictly neurological point of view, a brain can handle two languages just as easily as one.

Cognitive Studies

Ervin and Osgood's (1954) theory of compound and coordinate bilingual systems is one of the earliest cognitive theories concerned with whether the bilingual's languages are stored together or separately in the brain. Although their claim that there are two types of bilingualism is now controversial the issue about whether multiple languages are functionally independent, as in the model of coordinate bilingualism, or are functionally dependent on shared processes, as in the compound model, is still important. Moreover, it is possible to identify several levels at which shared or separate processes may be found (Caramazza, Yeni-Komshian and Zurif 1974). For example, segregation by language of underlying processes may occur only at the speech production level when the person has to choose which of two languages to respond in. Or, it may occur at the input level making it possible to listen to one language and ignore information in another. Another possibility is that segregation of language processes occurs between input and output levels at the stage of comprehension where processing for meaning occurs in one of two functionally distinct systems in the bilingual.

As will be seen in the review below, the evidence supports the following conclusions. First, there is one semantic system in the brain subserving all the languages of the multilingual, rather than separate processes for each language. Second, the languages of the bilingual become functionally separate at the *speech production* end of the language process. This means that bilinguals cannot listen or comprehend selectively in only one language, whereas when speaking they can temporarily block certain mechanisms subserving the other language. This implies that linguistic conflict will manifest itself primarily at the level of speech production where there is the greatest separation of mechanisms underlying each language and not at the comprehension level. The studies relevant to these conclusions are presented below.

The first set of studies concerns whether the bilingual has separate meaning systems for each language. Penfield (Penfield and Roberts 1959) suggested that there is just one language switch triggered reflexively by the environment that puts the bilingual into one language mode or another. This implies that the two languages are somehow separable at the conceptual level in the brain. Early work in this area was interpreted as support for the idea that bilinguals do develop separate systems for each of their languages. For example, Kolers (1963) examined the pattern of same-language and cross-language word associations to see if a single mediating system could account for similarities in the associations given in each language. He reasoned that if subjects had only one instead of two ways of representing the meaning of the stimulus words then many of the associations made in one language should be semantically related to the associations made in the other language. Kolers found very little similarity across languages in the associations given and hence concluded that separate semantic representational systems underlie each of the bilingual's two languages. Lambert and Moore (1966) also found that bilinguals give different associations depending on the language of response.

While it is true that these studies present evidence that translation equivalents have different underlying representations this does not necessarily imply that the meaning systems underlying one language are functionally separate from the meaning system of the other. It is quite possible that there is only one general meaning system for all words, regardless of language, while so-called translation equivalents have relatively distinct representation (just as same-language synonyms have distinct representations). The behavioral implication of this view is that bilinguals will not be able to activate the meaning system of only one language since that meaning system is part of a greater representation subserving all meanings available to the brain.

Macnamara (1967c; Macnamara, Krauthamer and Bolgar 1968) reports two sets of studies which appear at first to support the idea of independent underlying representational systems subserving each language. Macnamara (1967c) hypothesized that if a bilingual's linguistic systems are independent then bilinguals should find it easier to confine speech to one language rather than to switch back and forth between languages (whether or not they are translating). To test this, Macnamara asked subjects to say as many words as they could in one minute in the same language or to alternate between two languages without translating. Macnamara found, as predicted by the linguistic independence hypothesis, that word naming was slowest when subjects had to alternate languages. It is possible, however, to interpret these results as being due to the effect of switching languages at the speech production level rather than at the conceptual level (the level at which the concepts to be named were chosen). A suitable control for the experiment described above might be to have subjects name words in a monolingual condition alternating speech output between high- and low-pitched responses or loud and whispered responses to see if switches in the response output mechanism by itself would yield similar decreases in the number of words named. Macnamara and Kushnir (1971) attempted to avoid this output problem somewhat by testing the comprehension of silently read passages which were themselves linguistically mixed (e.g., Les oiseaux have deux wings). They found, for example, that true/false judgments took longer to make with such linguistically mixed sentences than with monolingual sentences. However, Neufeld (1973), attempted to replicate this finding but failed to turn up differences in speed of judgments between bilingual and monolingual test conditions. Kolers (1966b) reports a study comparing bilinguals' comprehension of linguistically mixed passages (sentences composed of words in two different languages) with comprehension for linguistically uniform passages (all words in one language or the other). He found no differences in measures of reading comprehension but reading rates (reading aloud) were slower for mixed texts than for single language texts.

While these results do not provide clear-cut evidence on the issue of linguistic independence in the bilingual, there are a number of other studies suggesting more directly that meanings are not segregated by language in the bilingual brain. For example Kolers (1965, 1966a), Lambert, Ignatow and Krauthamer (1968) and Nott and Lambert (1968) report findings where bilingual lists of unrelated words were remembered just as well as equally long monolingual lists. These results suggest that bilinguals do not have separate memory systems for each language; with two independent memory systems, they would be able to recall twice as many items from bilingual lists as from monolingual lists. As well, keeping track of a word's language in this condition does not place a serious burden on memory. (Tulving and Colotla (1970) present evidence showing that trilinguals recall *less* from multilingual lists of unrelated words than from monolingual lists of unrelated words. They suggested that when subjects attempted to assist memory by forming higher order units among words—that is, organizing the words into subjectively meaningful groupings—they found it more difficult to associate words of different languages than words of the same language.)

Dalrymple-Alford and Aamiry (1969) and Lambert et al. (1968) also report that when stimulus words were potentially organizable by language and/or taxonomic category (e.g., names of animals, parts of the body) clustering by common membership in taxonomic categories facilitated recall more powerfully than clustering by language. However, clustering by language also facilitated recall demonstrating that subjects could keep track of the language of each word. It also appears that keeping track of the language of a word does not block the facilitation effects of category clustering.

Kintsch and Kintsch (1969), Kintsch (1970), Saegert, Obermeyer and Kazarian (1973), Young and Navar (1968) and Young and Saegert (1966) report further memory studies which support the idea that bilinguals do not segregate their languages into separate semantic systems even though, as Kintsch (1970) has demonstrated, they can and do use language cues rather than semantic cues if the task requires it. Of particular interest are the findings of Kintsch and Kintsch

(1969) that when the task involved short-term memory subjects could easily keep track of words by language since here the important features of stored items are primarily acoustic. When the task involved longer term memory there were many interlingual confusions since here words are coded semantically rather than by the acoustic characteristics that can serve as language tags for the words.

There have been other approaches as well to the study of language organization in multilinguals. Kolers (1964) and Dalrymple-Alford (1967) report studies that attempt to find out whether learning a cognitive skill for tasks in one language (in this case, repeating the alphabet backwards) transfers to performance of a similar task in another language. Kolers found no such transfer and presented this as evidence for segregated language systems. Dalrymple—Alford showed, however, that by changing certain parameters of the experimental design such transfer could be demonstrated.

Treisman (1964) reports a study in which subjects had to shadow (repeat back immediately what they hear) a tape-recorded message delivered to one ear while ignoring a message delivered to the other ear. In this experiment the message to be ignored was in a different language from the message being shadowed. Treisman found that bilingual subjects who knew the language of the message in the unattended ear experienced a great deal of interference in trying to shadow the target message, whereas there was relatively less disruption when they did not know the language. This result suggests that bilinguals cannot selectively "tune out" one language.

One series of experiments has used a technique known as the *Stroop procedure* (after Stroop 1935; see also Jensen and Rohwer 1966). In the original Stroop experiments words which named colors were written in colored ink that did not match the semantic referent of the word itself. For example, the word "red" might be written in green ink. The subjects' task was to name the colors of the ink as quickly as possible from a display card containing many color names printed in noncongruent colored inks. It is reliably found with this technique that the color named by the word itself interferes with naming the color of the ink the word is written in, and naming ink colors this way is slower than naming the colors of a series of non-word color patches.

In one bilingual version of this technique, words are written in one language (e.g., "rouge" in French but in green ink) and the subject has to name the color in English (green). Other bilingual variants of this technique are possible as we shall see. The procedure in this bilingual form is used to measure the amount of cross-language interference as an indication of the degree of functional separation of the languages. Dalrymple-Alford (1968), Dalrymple-Alford and Budayr (1966), Dyer (1971) and Preston and Lambert (1969) all report that such cross-language interference is found when bilingual subjects perform this bilingual version of the Stroop task.

Hamers (1973) and Hamers and Lambert (1972) report some auditory adaptations of the Stroop procedure that further support the idea that semantic systems of the bilingual are not functionally distinct. Hamers and Lambert (1972) had bilingual subjects say whether a recorded word was spoken in a high- or low-pitched voice. The voice would say the words "high" or "low" in English or French and the subjects had to respond in a specified language. The finding of interest is that subjects were unable to attend solely to the physical characteristics of the stimulus. The semantic properties (meaning of the word) produced a significant amount of interference even in this seemingly simple task. Hamers (1973) reports other tasks where language names ("anglais," "French," and so on) were presented to subjects who had to name the language the words were written in and ignore the language named by the word. In other studies a boy's voice or girl's voice would say "garçon," "girl," etc. and the subject had to say whether it was the boy or girl who spoke. Errors could be made by the subject both in the response given (naming the wrong language, for instance) and in the language of the response (answering in French when the answer was supposed to be given in English). In general, however, Hamers found errors were made in the meaning of the response rather than the language of the response. This provides further evidence that bilinguals have difficulty keeping their languages functionally separate at the input and processing levels but not at the level of speech output.

   These cognitive studies suggest that except at the level of speech output, there is little functional separation of the two languages within one brain. Concepts are not tagged according to language and consequently it does not make sense to say that a bilingual can think in one or the other language as Belyayev (1965) suggests. Perhaps the subjective experience of being able to think in a particular language arises from the fact that when one subvocalizes or thinks about how to articulate a certain thought one chooses words from one language or the other. This may be due to greater familiarity with that language or due to a greater appropriateness of the labels in one language for the concepts evoked on that particular occasion. But this does not mean that the concepts themselves are segregated by language. Subvocalizing is a language production activity and it is at the level of production that languages are relatively segregated.

   More importantly, according to this view one does not expect there to be confusion due to linguistic interference at the conceptual level. The smooth functioning of the conceptual system should not depend on whether all of the concepts involved in a particular cognitive activity had their origins in a common linguistic context. Both monolinguals and bilinguals acquire many concepts in many different contexts and there is no evidence to date to suggest that linguistic differences between concept acquisition contexts have any greater effect on the flow of thought than nonlinguistic differences between these acquisition contexts.

   The evidence points to the production level as the place where a mechanism exists for keeping the languages separate. It is possible, however, that for some, even at this level, the languages may not be functionally separate (suppose there has been little practice in switching between languages). In this case the attention one would have to pay to speech to reduce overt linguistic interference may be so distracting that it interferes with the smooth flow of thought, as suggested by Macnamara (1967c). This could be disruptive to thought processes involving elements heavily tied to verbalization, such as mental arithmetic. This may also apply to bilinguals who are not balanced (probably the majority of the world's bilinguals) in their two languages and who therefore resort to a great deal of subvocalization in the weaker language (Sokolov, 1969, reports studies on subvocalization).

Intellectual Performance

We now try to obtain a more global look at the functioning of the bilingual brain by asking whether mental abilities in general (apart from an ability to use one or more languages) are affected by bilingualism. Inquiry into this area has focused on several specific issues. One concerns the relationship between bilingualism and intelligence as measured by I.Q. tests. As we shall see, work in this area has perhaps been the least fruitful although studies on this topic outnumber studies on most other psychological aspects of bilingualism. A second concern stems from Leopold's (1953-54) observation that for the bilingual the linguistic form of a word (its sound) is more completely dissociable from the meaning of the word than it is for monolinguals. Studies in this area have also drawn on Vygotsky's (1962) ideas about the way children conceive the relationship of sounds to meaning. The third issue concerns the effect of bilingualism on the course of cognitive development in general. Drawing on Piaget's theories, some researchers have suggested that the bilingual's verbal and cultural background is inherently richer because of its binguality and thus produces an earlier occurrence of certain experiences critical to intellectual development.

The relationship between bilingualism and intelligence has been a long-standing preoccupation of educators and psychologists, with studies dating back to the early part of this century. (See Arsenian 1945; Balkan 1970; Darcy 1953, 1963; Haugen 1956; Jones 1959, 1966; Macnamara 1966; Peal and Lambert 1962; and Weinreich 1953 for comprehensive reviews of this literature.) The early findings tended to show that bilingual children attained lower scores than monolinguals on tests of verbal intelligence while they did not differ on tests of nonverbal intelligence (see, for example, Darcy 1953). It is important to realize, however, that most of these early studies were marred by fundamental methodological flaws. Often no attempts were made to control for differences between bilinguals and monolinguals in social class background or to measure the language proficiency of the bilingual, especially in the language of the intelligence test itself. Since many of the bilinguals tested were children whose parents had relatively little formal education and often were from lower social class environments it is easy to see how factors other than bilingualism could affect test performance. In general the validity problems one faces in this area have been similar to those encountered in the present-day attempt to relate race and intelligence. When social class and ethnic differences are involved, factors such as identity of the tester, expectations of the pupils taking the test, familiarity with test-taking procedures and community expectations become potentially critical determiners of the test outcomes. (See, for example, Anastasi 1968; Jones 1966; Kamin 1974; Peal and Lambert 1962; Richardson and Spears 1972 for discussion of these factors.)

A more serious problem is the concept of intelligence itself. Two main issues are relevant here. One concerns whether intelligence is a unitary characteristic of an individual or whether it consists of many relatively independent abilities. The second is about whether the intelligence of any individual is biologically fixed, whether intelligence is a function of the child's early experiences or whether both the biological and experiential factors interact in some particular way (see also Anastasi 1968, Bayley 1970, and Kamin 1974 for reviews of these controversies). The early students of the relationship of bilingualism to intelligence appear to have taken the pragmatic but question-begging approach that intelligence is what intelligence tests measure. Dissatisfaction with this has led researchers to ask how bilingualism is related to specific abilities such as well defined verbal skills, cognitive flexibility, reasoning processes, and other abilities presumed to be relevant to understanding intelligence.

Peal and Lambert (1962) conducted a major study that has served as a point of departure for most of the more recent work in the field. They suggested several possible reasons why bilingualism could affect intellectual functioning. First, as other writers on bilingualism have proposed, knowing two languages may free one from the tyranny of words. The bilingual child is better able to dissociate the essential idea behind a thought from the particular form it assumes when verbalized. Such an effect should confer on the bilingual a degree of intellectual emancipation. Second, and in contrast to this, the linguistic interference that may occur between the two languages (Weinreich 1953) and the attention needed to keep the languages functionally separate might disturb conceptual processes. A third reason suggested by Lambert is that since the bilingual has richer linguistic and cultural experience than the monolingual, experiential factors responsible for the crystalization of certain components of intelligence may occur earlier for the bilingual than for the monolingual with the result that the former's intellectual processes develop at a faster rate. Peal and Lambert also suggested that perhaps the bilingual develops a learning set to switch from one linguistic channel to another, and in the process acquires greater cognitive flexibility. From these considerations they hypothesized that bilinguals and monolinguals should perform differently on a variety of subtests of intelligence, reflecting the idea that the structure of intellect will be different for the two groups. In addition, they hypothesized that insofar as bilinguals may suffer from linguistic interference, they might perform slightly worse on verbal I.Q. tests but should not differ from monolinguals on tests of nonverbal intelligence.

Peal and Lambert were considerably more careful in choosing their subjects than most of the researchers who preceded in the field. Subjects were ten-year-olds whose degree of bilingualism was determined by four separate tests. Intelligence was assessed by the use of three sets of tests together comprising a wide variety of different verbal and nonverbal subtests. School grades, information relating to the subjects' socioeconomic status and attitudes toward the two language groups were also collected. Their results indicated that the bilinguals had significantly higher nonverbal I.Q. scores and verbal I.Q. scores than monolinguals in contradiction to two of their hypotheses. However, in line with their predictions they found that monolinguals and bilinguals yielded different results on the subtests of specific abilities. The bilinguals performed better than monolinguals on nonverbal tests which appear to depend on concept-formation or what the authors call symbolic "flexibility." Peal and Lambert suggested that either the "freedom from the tyranny of words" hypothesis or the notion that bilinguals have a more enriched experiential background than monolinguals could possibly account for this superior mental flexibility. The authors concluded that contrary to the findings of most other studies, the bilinguals tested here appear to have a language asset instead of a deficit. They pointed out, however, that the results must be interpreted with a certain degree of caution. It is impossible to determine whether the bilinguals' more diversified intellectual structures, as revealed in the differences in the subtest scores and higher verbal and nonverbal I.Q. scores, were due to bilinguality or higher intelligence to start with. A selection factor operating here may have been that fluent bilinguals were those with superior abilities in general and the monolinguals were "failed" bilinguals (Ben Zeev 1972).

Balkan (1970) in a major study in Switzerland tested bilinguals and monolinguals aged 11-16 who were matched for performance on a general intelligence test and matched for socioeconomic status. His bilinguals scored significantly higher than the monolinguals on tests of numerical aptitude, verbal flexibility, perceptual flexibility (hidden figures test) and general reasoning. The bilinguals performed poorer than monolinguals on a word definitions test (*test de nuances*) but their performances were not significantly different from the monolinguals on a synonyms test. The conclusion Balkan drew from these results was that bilinguality is probably responsible for the bilingual children demonstrating superior abilities in certain abstract skills even though they were matched with the monolinguals on measures of general intelligence.

Together the studies of Peal and Lambert (1962) and Balkan (1970) have stimulated a series of investigations on the more abstract and creative intellectual abilities of bilinguals. Ben Zeev (1972), for example, derived a number of interesting hypotheses from Piaget's theory of intellectual development. She proposed that bilingual children undergo certain intellectual conflicts sooner than monolinguals and in the process of resolving these conflicts attain higher levels of intellectual development earlier. Two of the main hypotheses were that compared to monolinguals, bilinguals would show earlier development of concrete operational thinking and superior cognitive flexibility. (She also hypothesized that bilinguals would show increased ability to analyze syntax but her results did not support this prediction.) One test she used was originally developed by Warren and Warren (1966) in which a word recorded on a tape loop is listened to over and over. Adults typically report that the word they hear undergoes a transformation and that they hear different words from one moment to next. Warren and Warren

(1966) also report that the illusion usually appears with subjects above six years of age. Ben Zeev used English and Hebrew versions of this test with bilinguals and monolinguals aged 5-8. She found that compared to the monolinguals bilinguals perceived more transformations in the time allotted and that the onset latency for the appearance of the first perceived transformation was shorter. Ben Zeev interpreted these results as indicating that the bilinguals were more advanced than monolinguals in terms of perceptual organization and reorganization of verbal auditory material. Moreover, the ability to quickly abandon one interpretation of the material for another interpretation was taken by Ben Zeev as support for the prediction of superior cognitive flexibility in bilinguals.

In another test, Ben Zeev's subjects were asked to pretend that certain words in the language had been replaced by other words. For example, she had the children use the word *clean* instead of the word *into* in certain contexts (e.g., the child has to describe a situation by saying "the doll is going clean the house"). In other examples, the word *spaghetti* replaces *they, turtle* replaces *plane* and so on. Ben Zeev found that bilingual children could perform these symbol substitutions more successfully than monolinguals. She took this as further support for the hypothesis that bilinguals would demonstrate greater verbal flexibility.

In a third study, Ben Zeev reports the results of a transposition task (following Bruner and Kenney 1966) in which children had to remember the arrangement of a matrix array of different cylinders, reproduce the array transposed into a different orientation by filling in missing cylinders in the array, and finally explain why they placed the cylinders as they did. This last part of the task was especially interesting since correct explanations specifically involved isolating the two dimensions on which the cylinders differed. While she found no differences between bilinguals and monolinguals in success in reproducing the cylinder matrix, she found that bilinguals were better able to provide explanations of what constituted a correct solution.

Ianco-Worrall (1972) reports on a study involving English-Afrikaan bilingual children aged 4-6 that supports the idea that bilinguals develop an ability to dissociate sound from meaning earlier than monolinguals. In one experiment she presented her subjects with word triples (e.g., *cap, can* and *hat*) in which the first word had a close phonetic similarity to one of the other two words (e.g., *cap* and *can*) while the first and the remaining word resembled each other semantically (e.g., *cap* and *hat*). The children had to indicate which of the second or third words in the triple most resembled the first. She found a significant difference between monolinguals and bilinguals in the pattern of choices in this task, with the bilinguals showing greater preference for the semantic word match. Ianco-Worrall also conducted a version of the Vygotsky experiment in which children had to pretend that objects have new names. Unlike Ben Zeev, Ianco-Worrall found that there were no differences between bilinguals and monolinguals in ability to carry out this task in a play situation but when the children were asked about the relationship between the words and their referents the bilinguals revealed a significantly greater awareness of the arbitrariness of that relationship.

She concluded from this study that bilinguals do develop an earlier awareness that sounds can be dissociated from meanings and that the acquisition of this awareness precedes the ability to perform this dissociation.

Cummins and Gulutsan (1974) tested grade 6 bilingual and monolingual pupils and found in one test that bilinguals were more advanced in verbal ability and general reasoning, a result consistent with that of Peal and Lambert (1962). In a second test in which the subject within a given time limit has to give as many uses as possible for an object named by the experimenter, bilinguals demonstrated greater diversity (originality) in their responses (greater divergent thinking ability) (see also Jacobs and Pierce (1966), and Landry (1974) for evidence of superior verbal flexibility in bilinguals). Cummins and Gulutsan also explored John's (1970) speculation that bilingual children rely more on visual imagistic forms of symbolism than on verbal forms because of their need to escape from the linguistic conflict inherent in bilingual verbal systems. (See Paivio 1971 for a comprehensive review of literature related to this distinction between imagistic and verbal representations of word meanings.) However, their evidence did not support this notion. Their bilinguals did not differ from monolinguals on tests of nonverbal spatial abilities but did have higher scores on tests of verbal ability and verbal divergence.

This review of data concerning the effects of bilingualism on cognitive functioning suggests the following. Multiple languages appear to be represented in the brain much in the same way as single languages. Intellectual processes are not impaired and some may possibly be enhanced. However, more research is needed to broaden our picture of the intellectual functioning of the bilingual: evidence concerning creative abilities, reasoning skills, and cognitive style in general (convergent vs. divergent styles of thinking, problem-solving strategies, and so on). Studies are needed that will tell us if any intellectual gains associated with bilingualism have important consequences for future cognitive development or if they are relatively unimportant temporary accelerations in development. As well, research is needed on the effects of study in a weaker language. It is possible that cognitive skills relying on either overt or subvocal speech will suffer when performed with the use of the weaker language because, as noted earlier, the effort required to keep the two languages functionally separate in speech production may be disruptive to thought. Here, too, it is necessary not only to determine whether there are such problems with instruction in a weaker language but also whether the effects are lasting. (The studies in bilingual education of Barik, Swain and McTavish (1974), Edwards and Casserly (1972), and Lambert and Tucker (1972) suggest that deficits from instruction in a weaker language are *not* necessarily lasting.)

We turn now to consideration of the bilingual as part of a social environment.

SOCIAL PSYCHOLOGICAL FACTORS

Social and Personality Factors Responsible for Bilingualism

Two approaches dominate the area of research into social psychological factors responsible for bilingualism. The first concerns the bilingual's attitudes and motivations toward second language learning and toward the group of people who speak the language natively. The second concerns the particular social sensitivities individuals may have that might be helpful in second language learning.

Early studies in the 1940s and 1950s suggested that learners' attitudes may be as important as their aptitudes in determining success in language learning (e.g., Jordan 1941; Pritchard 1935). Jones (1949, 1950) examined the attitudes of English-speaking Welsh pupils toward the learning of Welsh as a second language and found that these attitudes were not a function of intelligence but they did correlate with language attainment. Jones also found that with increasing age, attitudes became more negative and that pupils exposed to Welsh outside the classroom were more positive in their attitudes than were those with only classroom experiences. Other reports about the social circumstances of particular individuals attempting to learn a second language (Lambert 1955; Nida 1956; Whyte and Holmberg 1956) also indicated that the learner's attitude toward the group of people who speak the language natively can be a powerful determinant of the level of language mastery achieved. These studies provided the background against which a series of extensive investigations were made of the relation between attitudes and bilingual attainment.

Gardner and Lambert (1959) reported a factor analytical study in which English-speaking high school students learning French were administered tests measuring, among other things, language achievement, language aptitude, verbal intelligence, motivations for studying French, attitudes toward French Canadians and motivational intensity (how hard they worked at studying French). The results indicated that there were two main independent factors which could be extracted from the scores they obtained. The first consisted of scores related to linguistic aptitude (achievement, aptitude, intelligence). The second consisted of items related to motivational factors, in particular to the desire to be liked by members of the language community who speak the target language. This latter factor also included achievement items indicating that motivation was highly correlated with language attainment. All in all, their results suggested that students with a motivation to be liked by the target language community—an integrative motivation—were more successful in language achievement than were students who wanted to learn French only for its usefulness—an instrumental motivation. Moreover, while this motivation factor correlated with achievement, it was statistically independent of the linguistic aptitude factor.

A number of other studies in widely differing social and cultural contexts involving different languages (e.g., English-speaking Jews learning Hebrew, Franco-Americans learning French, Filipinos learning English) have confirmed the general findings that ability and motivation in second language learning are relatively independent and that two types of motivation—integrative and instrumental—are important to language learning success (Anisfeld and Lambert 1961; Gardner and Lambert 1965, 1972; Gardner and Smythe 1974; Lambert, Gardner, Barik and Turnstall 1962; Randhawa and Korpan 1973).

The identification of these motivational and situational factors as significant sources of variation in language learning success is important for several reasons. It shows that success and failure in the acquisition of a second language is not simply a matter of inborn talent or the lack of it but of a number of other factors. This may have some interesting implications for bilingual education. For example, one way to reduce the occurrence of failures in second language study might be to structure the language program or bilingual curriculum in some way that takes account of the students' motivations. For example, Gardner and Lambert (1972) report that instrumentally motivated learners have more success with acquiring formal language skills (grammar, vocabulary) than native-like communicative abilities. Integratively motivated learners, on the other hand, have greater success in acquiring native-like phonological skills than do instrumentally motivated students (Gardner and Lambert 1972). Gardner and Lambert (1972: 130) point out, however, that whether teachers should capitalize on one type of motivation or another will often be a function of the setting. In North America, for example, fostering an integrative outlook toward the group that speaks the language being learned is generally more appropriate, while in developing countries an instrumental outlook probably more closely approximates the true motivations of language learners. The role of the teacher is especially important because he or she often provides the first emotional contact the learner has with the language. The teacher's attitudes and skill with the language will be an important determinant of how strongly the student identifies with the language learning activity (Gardner and Smythe 1974).

The matching of pupils' and teachers' goals sometimes can involve delicate matters of ethnic identity. For example, integratively motivated learners more often acquire native-like pronunciation than instrumentally motivated learners (since the former desire to communicate with valued members of the other group and perhaps even to "pass" as one of them). It may be, then, that in some circumstances learners who acquire native-like pronunciation will be perceived by their peers as potential "defectors" to the other group. Such a situation presupposes, of course, that the two linguistic groups are competing in some way so that the term "defector" is relevant (such competition very often occurs in regions where bilingual education programs exist). If people do make such judgments about their peers, then it is likely that social pressures, sometimes subtle, sometimes not so subtle, will be brought to bear against learners who appear to be learning a language "too well," that is, with a facility that is too native-like. Such factors could be very important in determining the level and quality of success of any given second language program, since such pressures may discourage high level of language mastery (Gatbonton, 1975, reports some studies relevant to this.) Alternatively, social pressures may encourage the learning of the second language, especially if the target language group is seen to be prestigious. Whether such pressures exist in any given context will naturally depend on a number of social, political and historical factors that cannot be discussed here (see, for example, Fishman, 1973).

The fact that such motivational and attitudinal factors are significant determinants of language learning success raises the question about what personality types are predisposed to having integrative or instrumental motivations. For example, Gardner and Lambert (1959) and Lambert, Hodgson, Gardner, and Fillenbaum (1960) found that bilingual subjects scored lower on measures of authoritarianism than subjects with weaker second language skills. This is entirely consistent with their findings that successful acquisition of bilingual skills usually accompanies highly positive feelings toward another linguistic group, an attitude not usually shared by people with a highly authoritarian personality. Presumably, authoritarian attitudes and ethnocentric values are learned early, perhaps even in the preschool years. Lambert (1967) suggests that a contributing factor to the formation of such attitudes may be children's preoccupation with contrasts between their own and other groups when developing a sense of their own identity (see also Lambert and Klineberg 1967).

Other personality factors mentioned in the literature (Gardner and Lambert 1972) but deserving more systematic investigation relate to need achievement and Machiavellianism. Relatively little is known yet about how these factors contribute to language learning success but there are good reasons to suspect that they might be important. For example, Lambert (1967) put forward the notion of the "linguistic spy," that is, the person who learns another group's language for the purposes of advancement in that group's circles without being noticed as a conspicuous outsider. Such motives are clearly integrative, but the really important considerations are the underlying determinants of that motivation—what types of success do such people strive for, do they succeed by manipulating people, and so on.

Another line of research has focused on empathy as a personality variable that may influence language learning success (Guiora 1972; Guiora, Brannon and Dull 1972; Guiora, Lane and Bosworth 1968; Taylor, Catford, Guiora and Lane 1971). Guiora and his co-workers view language as a symbolic system intimately involved in ego formation, that is, in how a person develops representation of the self. In Guiora's view (1972) language represents the highest level of self-representation because through the symbolism of language it is possible to achieve an integration of other representations of the ego (body image, ego representation derived from social interactions, and so on). In describing the structural facets of this language ego, Guiora assigns a special place to pronunciation (Guiora et al. 1972). According to his view, pronunciation is the most salient feature of the language ego (syntax and grammar providing a sort of "skeletal" structure, vocabulary being the "flesh" that hangs on the structure). Pronunciation defines the boundaries of the language ego and the flexibility of these ego boundaries are developmentally determined. The early stages of ego development are marked by great flexibility and so the child easily masters native-like pronunciation. In later stages ego development is more or less concluded and so its flexibility is diminished. Thus older learners have greater difficulty in acquiring native-like pronunciation in another language since that would require them to take on a new identity, that is, to alter the boundaries of their language ego.

Guiora's discussion of ego development is not very detailed and the other literature available on the role of ego development in language learning is small and often not directly related to points Guiora raises (see Wolff 1967; references in Diebold 1968 and in Haugen 1956). It is interesting to note, however, the similarities in the link he makes between identity and pronunciation skills in second language learning and the findings mentioned earlier that individuals with highly positive feelings toward the target language group tend to develop more native-like facility with a second language.

Guiora and his colleagues have attempted to test their theory. They reasoned that people who have a high degree of empathy (ability to gain an emotional understanding of another) should be most successful in acquiring authentic pronunciation in a foreign language. Empathy, in their view, requires "a temporary fusion of self-object boundaries" (Guiora 1967) and so a high degree of ego boundary flexibility as evidenced by a high degree of empathy should be accompanied by a similar flexibility in the boundaries of the language ego (Guiora 1967). The studies reported in Guiora et al. (1972) and to some extent in Taylor et al. (1971) found a positive relationship between measures of empathy and pronunciation mastery in a second language from which they concluded that people who are particularly empathetic are predisposed to acquisition of accurate foreign language pronunciation.

Bilingualism as a Factor in Personality Development

Early views of how bilingualism might affect character development tended to be negative (see Weinreich 1953 for an exhaustive review of this early literature). It was believed that the bilingual's personality is characterized by a conflict of values, identities and cultural outlooks because there are two languages in which to encode experiences: "the consequence (of bilingualism in children) is that the inner attitudes which are conditioned by language will not stand unconnected beside one another, but will enter into conflicting tensions in the child's soul. . ." (Sander 1934, quoted in Weinreich 1953: 120).

Others have pointed out that depending on circumstances, bilinguals may find themselves in a socially different position from monolinguals and that this fact, not the bilingualism *per se*, may be a source of important influences affecting personality development and adjustment. Spoerl (1943) found that the bilingual children of immigrants in the United States may suffer problems of emotional adjustment but she concluded that this was due to environmentally determined factors and not the result of mental conflict arising from bilinguality. Bossard

(1945) also argued that bilingual children who must maintain dual identities are likely to suffer the strain of keeping these identities intact. From a series of interviews he conducted with bilinguals, Bossard discovered some of the tactics bilinguals use to escape socially awkward situations stemming from the fact that they are bilingual. Soffietti (1955) also agrees that many of the difficulties bilinguals face are due to problems of biculturalism rather than bilingualism *per se.*

There has not been a great deal of research of a serious experimental nature on the question of how bilingualism affects personality adjustment but what there is suggests that the results are not necessarily always negative. For example, Aellen and Lambert (1969) compared the ethnic identification and personality adjustment of bilingual children of mixed English-French parentage in Montreal with monolingual children of either English only or French only parentage. They distributed semantic differential questionnaires to these pupils to measure a wide variety of variables related to social adjustment. The results indicated that in terms of parental identification (with mother or with father) ethnic identification (French- or English-Canadian), self-esteem and stability (including measures of alienation) there were no differences between children of mixed background compared with children of an ethnically homogeneous background. The mixed-background bilingual children perceived their parents as taking more interest in them and interacting more frequently with them compared to the other children of monolingual backgrounds. In this sense the bilingual children appeared to enjoy healthier relationships with their parents than the monolinguals. No differences between mixed- and homogeneous-background children appeared on measures of the quality of peer relationships, authoritarianism and ethnocentrism, or occupational aspirations. The general pattern that emerged for all the groups tested indicated healthy social adjustment, with mixed-background children showing no systematic disadvantage in any of the factors measured. All the significant differences that did emerge either reflected obvious differences in background (for example, the French-Canadian and English-Canadian children had different ethnic identity scores, as one would expect) or value patterns that were characteristic of all groups of subjects. The Aellen and Lambert (1969) study indicates that bilingualism derived from bicultural backgrounds does not necessarily lead to problems of social adjustment.

The theory of compound-coordinate bilingualism has also given rise to speculation that the bilingual might possess a kind of dual identity, each corresponding to a different language (Diebold 1968). In support of this, Ervin's studies (1964, 1967) can be cited in which primarily coordinate bilingual subjects responded differently to unstructured material (Thematic Apperception Test) depending on the language of response. For example, when speaking Japanese there was a tendency for speakers to talk about social relationships in a way that was more appropriate to a Japanese setting rather than an Anglo-American setting while the reverse was true when speaking English.

Ervin's bilinguals acquired their two languages in different settings whereas in Lambert and Aellen's study the subjects acquired their languages in the same (home) setting. Their school children did not show any signs of group alienation but perhaps learners who acquire their languages in distinctly separate settings would be more likely to experience a feeling of being pulled between two identities since a new set of norms and values must be acquired after one set has been fully internalized. Lambert et al. (1962) report a study that is relevant to this point. They examined the possibility that intensive study of a second language might engender a feeling of cultural conflict or a breaking away from cultural norms the learners previously felt close to. Their subjects were English-speaking students attending a French language summer school at which only French was spoken. The experimenters measured the subjects' feelings of anomie or normlessness (group alienation) both before and after the language course. The finding of principal interest was that with students in the advanced sections of the course, levels of anomie showed an increase after the course relative to levels of anomie before the course began and that these increases in anomie were positively related to increases in favorable attitudes to France. Lambert and his colleagues suggested that perhaps as the students gain more knowledge of the other culture they become more socially dissatisfied (more anomic) or that as they become more anomic they acquire a greater interest in the other culture. It thus appears that under some circumstances acquiring bilingual skills can lead to a certain feeling of normlessness or dissatisfaction with one's current social environment. However, it is not known how long such feelings last.

It is possible then that a person who becomes bilingual may also become bicultural with the consequence that feelings of solidarity with the first language group are weakened (become less exclusive to that group). Depending on one's political and social orientation this may or may not be a good thing. However, perhaps it would be useful to make a distinction between two aspects of this alteration of one's sense of identification that are logically independent of each other.

First, bilingualism might lead to a weakening of bonds between language and values. Constellations of cultural attitudes and values might become less intimately linked to a particular form of linguistic expression in the following way. The differences and similarities between cultures become psychologically more salient for the bilingual and bicultural person than for the monolingual because the former actually experiences these differences and similarities when switching between languages whereas the monolingual can only learn about a foreign culture indirectly. Because of this increased experiential salience the bilingual may be able to escape from the linguistic aspects of cultural values and develop representations of values and attitudes that are not closely tied to the particular ways they are verbally expressed. The most immediate way monolinguals can know about another culture is through a translation of other people's experiences into their own language. In this sense the monolingual is more dependent on words for understanding another culture than is the bilingual.

The second aspect concerns the consequence of this loosening of bonds between cultural forms and their linguistic expression. The major consequence for bilinguals will not depend on the fact that these bonds have been loosened but rather on how the people around them react to their binguality. In some circumstances they may feel a sharp conflict which they may attempt to counteract by emphasizing even more strongly the importance of retaining the link between language and culture for solidarity with the group. On the other hand, by being freed from the specificity of particular linguistic modes of expressing and representing cultural values, bilinguals may become more fully bicultural, not by having two distinct sets of cultural values but by evolving for themselves a cultural position that represents a synthesis of elements from both cultures. Thus, in the same way that the bilingual child is believed to become aware of arbitrariness of the relationship between verbal names and their referents, so the bilingual and bicultural person may develop deeper cultural insights by appreciating the commonalities between cultures once particular linguistic forms have been stripped away. As Lambert (1974) pointed out, the important similarities between different groups of people are often overlooked because these features are disguised in different forms. If the bilingual is able to appreciate this fact better than unicultural monolinguals, then bilingualism should be viewed as a potentially positive factor. Instead of becoming a marginal man (Stonequist 1937; Pieris 1951) without a culture or group to which to belong, the bilingual may rise above the limitations of particular forms of cultural expression, if circumstances permit.

THE SECOND LANGUAGE LEARNER

We now turn our attention from the accomplished bilingual to the individual still in the process of learning a second language. One critical problem in bilingual education is how to ensure that students master enough of the second language part of the program to successfully learn the content matter taught in that language. In this regard, there exists a great deal of variation between individuals in second language learning success. An understanding of the factors that govern this variability would be helpful in guiding the formulation of a bilingual curriculum. In the following pages we review the literature concerning possible sources of variability in second language learning success. In particular there are three types of factors that merit serious consideration: experiential and constitutional factors, motivational and attitudinal factors, and factors relating to communicative competence.

Experiential and Constitutional Factors

There is a commonsense view that one must have a good ear for languages to learn a foreign language well, or that one can have a knack for language. Such beliefs suggest that people differ in significant ways with regard to their physiological endowments in the language learning domain. Just as people can differ in intelligence, musical ability, athletic skill or what-have-you, so perhaps people can differ in language learning aptitude. One implication of this view is that bilingual education programs may have to be specially geared to take into account the individual's ability or inability to learn another language.

This commonsense view has been challenged lately by various psychologists concerned with second language learning and bilingual education (e.g., Gardner and Lambert 1972; Politzer 1970; Spolsky 1969). They point out first that virtually all human beings are successful in mastering their native language to a very high degree of proficiency. This fact alone suggests that all have a basic potential for language mastery; the problem is why this ability does not extend universally to second language mastery. In addition, theorists point out that our first language usually is mastered without formal instruction and that in many parts of the world second language mastery is the rule rather than the exception. Also, Carroll (1956, cited in Gardner and Lambert 1972: 2) reports a study of the relation between language aptitude measurements and grades received in language courses, in which he found that the relationship between these two sets of measurements was highly variable indicating that there is a great deal more to language learning than aptitude. Together these considerations present a strong *prima facie* case against the notion that individual differences in language learning success are primarily a function of individual differences in innate propensity to learn languages.

As yet no specific biological data support or refute the notion that constitutional factors are responsible for differences in people's language learning success. One could perhaps explore to what extent variation in such abilities is biologically determined by studying the second language learning success of separated monozygotic and dizygotic twins much as the matter of genetic contributions to variation in intelligence has been studied (Mittler 1971; but see Kamin 1974). However there are at least two reasons why such studies would be enormously difficult to carry out. First, the separated twins would each have to learn the same second language under roughly comparable conditions. Second, even if one could find a suitable population of second language learning twins there would still be the problem of interpreting the results. Suppose there were a greater correlation between monozygotic twin pair members in language learning success than between dizygotic twins. This could be interpreted as evidence for a genetic component in the determination of variation in language learning success. But another interpretation is possible too. If (as will be argued below) second language learning usually takes place in conditions that hinder the use of processes normally involved in first language learning, then the results may only indicate that there is a genetic component in the variation of language learning ability *under conditions* that are adverse for learning a language. Such results would indicate nothing about second language learning abilities under more appropriate and favorable conditions. Of course it is difficult to specify just what these favorable conditions are and at the moment there is considerable discussion about this very issue.

Does our ability to learn languages change with age? It could, for example, be argued that while each of us has sufficient aptitude to learn a language when we are extremely young this aptitude diminishes with age. Generally it has been observed that younger children do master languages more successfully. There is potential biological support for such a position in the notion of critical periods of development. According to this view the young developing brain is more flexible and hence more capable of second language learning, particularly in the period before cerebral lateralization is complete (believed by most to be about age 12) (Lenneberg 1967; Penfield and Roberts 1959). However, there is no direct evidence of biological limitations in post-puberty second language acquisition. All that has been observed is that post-puberty language acquisition seems to be considerably more difficult than pre-puberty language acquisition, but obviously factors other than biological ones may be responsible for this. Another difficulty with the view that younger children are more able to learn languages than older children is that no one has been able to identify which particular skills are supposed to diminish with age. There have been only a few studies comparing language learning skills of adults and children directly (Asher and Garcia 1969; Asher and Price 1967; Henmon 1934, and Grinder, Otomo and Toyota 1961, cited in Carroll 1963b; Yeni-Komshian, Zubin and Afendras 1968, cited in Jakobovits 1970) and these have not found children to be superior to adults. Carroll (1963b) believes that while children appear to learn accurate second language pronunciation more easily than do adults this may be because as a rule children spend more time on second language learning. In general, no one has yet discovered any particular skill (in memory, perception, imitation ability) at which children are better than adults.

Taylor (1974) made the interesting suggestion, noted earlier, that it should be easier to learn a first and second language concurrently than to learn them consecutively. The reason is that in learning languages consecutively the cognitive networks established for the first language have to be partially reorganized to accommodate the second. New semantic and syntactic relationships have to be established where perfectly good ones existed before. Thus very young children still acquiring their first language will have a greater facility with a second language than those who have already mastered a great deal of their first language. But here Taylor is talking about preschoolers. It is still an open question whether cognitive networks underlying the first language of the six-year-old entering a bilingual school are more adaptable to second language acquisition than are the cognitive networks of an older child.

Yeni-Komshian and Lambert (1969) report a study with teenage subjects comparing the learning of two artificial languages concurrently and consecutively. Their results indicated that in the conditions under which the two languages are learned at the same time, interference between the languages was considerably reduced depending on the opportunities available to the subjects to become aware of the critical contrasts between the competing "languages." When such contrasts could not be made, the learning of the two languages was faster in the condition where first one language was learned and then the other. Of course, as the authors themselves point out, one has to be cautious in generalizing these results since only vocabulary acquisition was studied. Moreover, the artificial languages were distinguished by color cues on the cards containing the nonsense syllables and not by phonetic patterns as in natural languages.

One last factor that may assist language learning that deserves mention is early experience with other languages. Most of the theories reviewed earlier predict that there could be a transfer of skills from early learning of two languages to later learning of other languages. For example, it was suggested that early bilingualism might lead to a greater separation of sound from meaning (Leopold 1953-54) facilitating the later attachment of new sounds to old meanings. Thus bilinguals may be better equipped to learn other languages than monolinguals.

Although there has been considerable theorizing about the transfer of abilities from one language learning situation to another (Jakobovits 1969; Politzer 1965) there is very little empirical evidence available on this topic. One study by Cohen, Tucker and Lambert (1967) provides support for the idea that bilinguals are more accurate than are monolinguals at perceiving phoneme sequences in a language not known to them. However, Lambert, Just and Segalowitz (1970) found that English-speaking children who followed their school curriculum in a second language (French) were not significantly better (although differences were in the right direction) than children in a regular native language program at a similar task in discriminating sounds in an unknown language (Russian). A further study by Davine, Tucker and Lambert (1971) also failed to demonstrate greater discriminative skills among bilingual children, but the authors suggested that at least five years of second language learning experience may be necessary for effects to be observed. This topic merits closer experimental investigation because transfer of skills is a central theme in the psychological learning literature and ought to be related to language learning.

Motivational and Attitudinal Factors

Because it has seemed unlikely that much of the variation in second language success could be accounted for in terms of aptitude factors alone, researchers have turned to motivational and attitudinal variables that might be relevant. As we saw earlier, there has been considerable success in isolating such factors that are statistically independent of intelligences and aptitude factors and that at the same time show a strong relationship with language attainment (see the discussion on instrumental and integrative motivations above).

These studies have all attempted to relate the students' longer term goals to language learning achievements. Thus, those who desire to be liked by members of the other language group or who wish to become members of that group are more likely to succeed in gaining a high level of language mastery than those who want only to communicate with them for specific utilitarian purposes.

However, as important as these long-term goals and broad attitudinal factors are, some theorists have begun to open a somewhat different but related line of inquiry into the factors determining success or failure in language learning. One reason for this shift in focus is that although the motivational variables are highly significant determinants of second language learning mastery, they often account for less than half the variance in the observed levels of language achievement (e.g., Randhawa and Korpan 1973). This means that there are still other important factors operating here. Second, there is an interest in the contribution of the specific learning situation to language learning success that is not captured by the study of the learner's longer term ambitions regarding the target language community. For example, there is the problem that classroom instruction often seems to be inferior to street learning. Also, while language mastery may be higher among integratively motivated learners, even they often do not achieve native-like control of the language.

Communicative Competence

Researchers have begun to examine the differences between the situational contexts of first and second language learning in the hope of better understanding why first language learning usually is much easier than second language learning and why young children acquire second languages more easily than older children. The hypothesis behind this approach is that young children and adults do not differ substantially in basic learning capabilities, but rather that young children, because they are young, find themselves in situations more conducive to language learning than older children and adults. The focus is the way learners develop a competence to satisfy the communicative needs arising in a given situation.

One approach to the study of communicative competence has concentrated on the cognitive side of communication. Both first language learners and second language learners in informal learning contexts have specific information to transmit and understand and, what is important, they have a genuine need to convey or comprehend this information (e.g., Macnamara 1972, 1973; Tucker and d'Anglejan 1970). From the point of view of these learners what is being learned is not phonology, syntax and vocabulary, but rather the uses of language and the meanings associated with these uses. Children learn a language by "learning to mean" (Halliday 1973: 24; see also the discussion in Kelly 1969: 55) because for them the most important thing is to succeed in getting the message across or in understanding the message correctly. The situation in the classroom contrasts sharply with this since there the emphasis is on linguistic performance. The information conveyed is very often not really important to the learner in the sense that failure to communicate has no serious psychological consequences. Even in bilingual education programs, such as immersion classes where the curriculum is taught in a second language, the learner's situation is still different from that of first language learners in the sense just described, unless the pupil is genuinely absorbed by the subject material itself. In summary, the assumption of this approach is that the conditions that most facilitate language learning are those that provide conditions in which the learner develops skills to handle real communicative needs.

This "communicative needs" approach differs from the instrumental/integrative motives approach discussed earlier in that it focuses on the motivational characteristics that are relevant to the learner's *immediate* situation. The other approach focuses more on learners' long-term goals (e.g., how closely they want to identify with the target language group). However the two approaches do not conflict. One can, for example, think of the instrumental and integrative motivations of the learners as setting boundaries or limits on what will or will not be relevant communicative needs in any given situation. It is possible to imagine some situation in which both an integratively motivated learner and an instrumentally motivated learner will have the need to communicate certain specific information but where only the former has the additional immediate need to convey the impression of wanting to be considered part of the group.

Savignon (1972) has reported an interesting study which incorporated the communicative needs approach into language teaching. Students learning French by more traditional methods (drill, language laboratory, vocabulary list learning, cultural lessons about France) were compared with students learning the language through situational experiences. The results indicated that students acquiring French by the situational communication technique developed a superior overall communicative competence in the language.

A second approach to communicative competence emphasizes the sociolinguistic aspects of communication. Hymes (1971), in an analysis of the concept of linguistic competence, points out that to understand actual linguistic performance one must consider more than just what utterances are *possible* according to the rules of any given linguistic system or what utterances are *feasible* given the performance constraints of the human brain. He points out that it is important to consider the factors governing the *appropriateness* of an utterance and how the conditions that define what is appropriate are linked to the factors governing the possible and the feasible in determining the actual speech performance. Hymes shows that this is particularly relevant in contexts where more than one code (register, variety, style, dialect) is used, especially in the bilingual situation. Not only do such situations allow for the possibility of linguistic interference as described by Weinreich (1953) but there is also the possibility of communicative or sociolinguistic interference in which there is failure to make the correct choice of code, speech, style, or language according to the social norms governing code selection. All this clearly has important sociolinguistic implications for bilingual education (e.g., Frender and Lambert 1972; Hymes 1970; Philips 1970). However our concern here is with some of the *psychological* implications of the sociolinguistic aspect of communicative competence. Little has been written directly on this topic but one can speculate how these social approaches to communicative competence may provide some insights into psychological processes involved in bilingual development (in and out of school).

In normal conversation it is important to appear friendly, respectful and interested in what the interlocutor is saying in order to create or maintain a certain degree of harmony (Goffman 1957). There are many ways speakers do this, including the use of a rich repertoire of nonverbal gestures (hand movements, posture, smiles, controlling direction of gaze, etc.), careful selection of words (use of terms of respect or familiarity as appropriate) and so on. The process of code selection discussed by sociolinguists is relevant here. For example, if speakers choose a formal speech code then they convey a particular social message that is different from that signaled by the choice of an informal speech code. The situation helps to define the most appropriate code, but the speakers still must choose how they will speak. The interlocutors reveal by their manner of speaking to their communication partners how they perceive the current situation. A variety of examples of the way situational characteristics determine code selection can be found in Blom and Gumperz (1972), Cazden (1970), Ervin-Tripp (1972), Herman (1968), Hymes (1968), Rubin (1968) and Sankoff (1972) as well as other papers in the collections edited by Fishman (1968, 1971), Giglioli (1972), Gumperz and Hymes (1972) and Pride and Holmes (1972).

Hymes (1971) expresses a similar view when he writes:

> In speaking of competence, it is especially important not to separate cognitive from affective and volitive factors, so far as the impact of theory on educational practice is concerned . . . (W)ithin a comprehensive view of competence, considerations of the sort identified by Goffman (1967: 218-226) must be reckoned with—capacities in interaction such as courage, gameness, gallantry, composure, presence of mind, dignity, stage confidence . . .
> (Reprinted in Pride and Holmes 1972: 283.)

It is unfortunate that there is so little research to date on the place of this sort of competence in the development of second language skills; these affective and volitive factors identified by Hymes and Goffman may be very important factors governing second language learning success.

Linguists have found code differences (e.g., formal vs. casual speech) to be fairly systematic and their uses to be related to specific situations (Cedergren and Sankoff 1974; Labov 1970, 1971; Sankoff 1974). Moreover, they have shown that codes are generally distinguished in an individual's speech by a predominance of some forms over others rather than by the exclusive use of one form alone (Labov 1969; Weinreich, Labov and Herzog 1968). For example, in casual speech, a given speaker may sometimes pronounce voiced "th" as [ð] and other times as [d] with the latter form predominating. The relative frequencies of these two forms will shift when the same speaker uses formal speech. We might think of this variability feature of speech as providing a medium for adjustments, an area for linguistic movement. A speaker can switch codes in the course of speaking by adjusting the relative frequencies of the use of one form or another (increase or decrease the use of contractions, for example). Moreover, one can even adjust the relative occurrence of these forms without necessarily switching codes by avoiding changes that are too extreme. The speech can thus be viewed as continually fluctuating as the speaker shifts forms according to the rules governing linguistic variability.

The results of some recent studies concerned with "linguistic accommodation" (Giles and Powesland 1975) suggest this variability in speech may have important psychological functions. Giles (1970, 1971) discusses how two interlocutors who speak different regional varieties of a language tend to converge in the way they speak in order to reduce the differences between them. In one experiment, Bourhis, Giles and Lambert (1975) presented tape-recorded conversations to subjects who had to judge the personality characteristics of the speakers. The speakers began their conversations with relatively different types of speech (in one case it was English Received Pronunciation vs. Welsh Regional English; in another case it was familiar vs. standard Quebec French) and during the course of the conversation they either converged their speech forms (reducing some of the differences) or diverged (creating greater differences). British and francophone Quebec subjects attributed different characteristics to the converging and the diverging speakers.

Extrapolating from this we might expect people to make judgments about their interlocutors depending upon whether the latter signal by their code selection that they perceive the demands of the present situation (to be respectful, casual, tactful, indignant, etc.) the same way as the listener does. Speakers will be affected by the speech style the other person uses and will consequently adjust their own manner of speaking until an appropriate level is found, taking into account the relative status of the participants, the nature of the topic, the location, the speech style of the interlocutor, and so on. What this means is that while the speakers are exchanging cognitive information—the principal ideas expressed in the vocabulary and syntax of their sentences—they are also exchanging important social information. This social information may cause one of the speakers to change the form or even content of the cognitive message as, for example, when it becomes clear the listener does not understand or is receiving the wrong impression. The exchange of the noncognitive messages provides feedback to the interlocutors about the progress of the conversation.

In summary, we see that the cognitive message is embedded in an environment of social and affective messages which themselves play a great part in guiding the way the cognitive message is communicated. The development of a communicative competence thus involves the acquisition of skills both to send and receive cognitive information while at the same time being able to create and participate in an elaborate exchange of noncognitive background messages. One way these noncognitive messages are communicated is through the manipulation of the variability feature of language that sociolinguists have drawn our attention to.

One implication this view may have for the development of bilingual skills is the following. Second language instruction obtained in formal settings (such as the classroom) often provides little opportunity for the learner to experience or observe the way native speakers of the target language manipulate the variability component to transmit noncognitive messages. Thus learners often may lack essential receptive and productive communicative skills for use in situations outside the formal learning context. This means that the second language learner is effectively cut off from participating in the circulation of noncognitive messages when speaking to native speakers of the language outside the classroom. To be sure, there are ways to compensate for this—for example, by transmitting these messages through nonverbal channels (gestures, eye contact, etc.; see Argyle and Kendon 1967). It is possible, however, that a great deal of the awkwardness language learners experience when using their second language outside the class stems from the fact that they are blocked from the interchange of background messages that normally characterizes verbal interactions in their native tongue.

There is some tentative support available for this idea. Segalowitz (1976) placed English-speaking subjects with non-native-like but nonetheless functional skills in French in situations where it was appropriate to use either formal or casual French in conversation with an interlocutor. The results showed that when the sociolinguistic requirements of the situation favored the use of casual speech, a speech style that differed from the more practiced formal French subjects learned at school, the speakers felt uncomfortable and reported a less favorable impression of the French-Canadian interlocutor. This behavior contrasted with their reactions when speaking with an English interlocutor and with the response of subjects who listened to the interlocutor but did not have to speak back in return. These results suggested that failure to fulfill the sociolinguistic demands of the communicative situation can have negative effects on the interlocutor and consequently might discourage further cross-linguistic contact. It is important that further studies of the psychological consequence of *not* being able to manipulate linguistic variability be undertaken in an effort to determine some of the causes of students' reluctance to actively pursue the use of their second language.

SUMMARY AND CONCLUSIONS

One concern of this paper was the effect bilingualism might have on the cognitive, intellectual and social functioning of the individual. The following conclusions can be drawn from the studies reviewed.

First, two languages can be handled by one brain in much the same way it handles one language. The evidence suggests that multiple languages are not represented in separate regions of the brain and that the learning of two languages does not alter the development of the brain in any substantial way (such as altering lateralization). Evidence from a wide variety of experimental studies suggests that concepts are not segregated in the brain according to the language of the words to which they are associated but rather they are organized into one semantic system that underlies all the languages available to the individual. No evidence indicates that memory, reasoning ability or other verbally based cognitive functions are impaired by bilingualism; thus, fears that bilinguals may suffer conceptual confusions and mental conflicts do not seem justified.

Second, while studies indicate that bilinguals cannot selectively listen or think in just one language, it is well known, nonetheless, that they can keep their languages functionally separate when they speak. It appears that the language "switch" responsible for this separation exists at the speech production level and is used by bilinguals to reduce the amount of cross-linguistic interference. The operation of this switch does require some degree of effort, especially when the bilingual has to change back and forth between languages. Bilinguals who are not skilled in keeping their languages separate in overt speech or who are much more skilled in one language than in another may experience difficulties in operating this language switch when speaking in the weaker language. Efforts to reduce linguistic interference in speech output may then disrupt the smooth flow of thought that underlies their utterances.

Third, studies of the effects of bilingualism on measures of intelligence do not indicate any deficits when factors such as social class, educational background, language proficiency and so on are carefully controlled. In fact there is some recent evidence suggesting that bilingualism may even result in greater verbal flexibility and in an earlier development of an awareness of the arbitrariness of the relationship between words and their referents. These results have been interpreted by some as an enhancement of creative abilities and increased sophistication regarding further language development. The critical question that deserves attention now is whether these gains are slight in comparison to the variation in creative abilities that already exists in any population of pupils and whether these gains have a significant long-term effect on the development of the individual.

Fourth, research on the effects of bilingualism on personality and social development suggests that maladjustments observed to accompany bilingualism usually are caused by social factors rather than bilingualism as such. Language is often perceived by the community as an important symbol of identity and in this regard bilinguals may feel it difficult to identify with two groups at the same time (the groups in question may make it difficult for them to do so). Some evidence also suggests that intensive learning of another language may lead to feelings of normlessness and dissatisfaction with the social environment. However, it is not known how long these feelings last and in any event they are more likely due to the bicultural aspects of second language experiences than to the fact of knowing two languages. It also was suggested earlier that bilingual-bicultural individuals may derive certain advantages from their linguistic experiences by being more able than monolinguals to dissociate cultural value patterns from their mode of linguistic expression. Such an ability affords bilinguals greater understanding of their own and other cultures.

This review touched on factors governing the acquisition of bilingual skills. Little evidence suggests that biological factors are important in determining language learning success or that there are biologically determined critical periods of development during which languages are most easily learned. While it is true that children seem to learn languages more easily than adults the reasons for this probably involve social and environmental aspects of the learning situation rather than biological factors. Personality variables such as emphatic sensitivities to others, attitude factors such as ethnocentrism and authoritarianism, and motivational considerations such as whether the learner wants to be liked by members of the other language group or just wants to learn the language for utilitarian reasons appear to be important here.

The final topic discussed focused on the learning situation as an important determinant of language acquisition success. While some researchers have emphasized the cognitive communicative needs (the need to exchange certain information) others have discussed noncognitive needs to communicate in a way that fulfills certain sociolinguistic obligations (to speak in a certain way). It was suggested in the communicative competence approach to language learning that the optimal learning environment is defined by two characteristics. First, it is one in which learners pick up specific language skills while acquiring an ability to exchange both cognitive and noncognitive messages with an interlocutor. Second, the messages they exchange are genuinely important to them. The situation must not be one in which learners merely "play" at communicating; they must be communicating something that is truly important to them at the time they are speaking.

The material reviewed in this paper has the following implications for bilingual education programs. First, instruction in and mastery of a second language does not necessarily harm the cognitive or social development of the individual. On the contrary, high levels of bilingualism may even carry certain advantages beyond facility with more than one language; future research will tell us how certain we can be of this. It is important, however, to discover what sorts of mental skills may suffer, if at all, by training through the medium of a weaker language and whether any such disadvantages persist after complete bilingualism has been achieved. Second, in terms of whether the second language will be learned successfully in a given bilingual education program, the most important consideration seems to be what meaning the total situation has for the student. If learning a particular language means for students that one group is trying to assimilate them or if they believe they are learning the language of an inferior group then language learning will be relatively less successful than if they perceive language mastery as a means of access to a highly valued group of people. Many factors determine what the language chosen as medium of instruction will mean to the student—personality, home attitudes, community sentiments, political environment—but in principle it is perhaps easier for educators to deal with these types of factors than with biological dispositions to success or failure in language learning.

NOTES

1. The author thanks Elizabeth Gatbonton, Fred Genessee, Helen Gougeon, Wallace E. Lambert, Susan Lederman, John Macnamara and G. Richard Tucker for helpful comments in discussion and useful suggestions on earlier drafts of this paper.

2. The truly balanced bilingual may not in fact even exist. D'Anglejan and Tucker (1973) report a study in which fluent bilinguals who were professional simultaneous translators showed native-like ability in performing a "CLOZE" task (filling in the missing words in a paragraph form which every fifth word was deleted) in their mother tongue but deviated from native-like performance on material in their other language. Thus, even though these bilinguals

were perfectly fluent in both languages their performance in at least one language was distinguishable from that of native speakers of the language. This suggests that there may be more to knowing a language than complete mastery of the phonology, syntax and vocabulary; perhaps cultural experiential factors help to determine familiarity with aspects of language tapped by the CLOZE procedure. A comprehensive discussion of the problems of defining and measuring bilingualism can be found in Kelly (1969).

VI

Bilingual Education—An International Perspective

Charles A. Ferguson,

Catherine Houghton, and Marie H. Wells

Note. The preparation of this paper was supported in part by funds from the OEO Grant 30061 to the Education Study Center, Washington, D.C., and an earlier version of the paper appeared as part of the final report for that grant.

No one knows how many languages exist in the world. Some estimate there may be four to seven thousand. The majority have no written form, and only a small proportion of those that do are used in formal education. Yet most of the nations of the world are multilingual, and millions of children have their schooling in two or more languages.

From the earliest days of civilization, bilingual education has been important in the development of society and culture. There has hardly been a time in recorded history when a nation could flourish as a monolingual entity with a completely monolingual educational system. Soldiers and statesmen, poets and kings have always needed more than one language in which to communicate.

In ancient Mesopotamia, military and political expansion and the subsequent administration of new territories necessitated that rulers and their subordinates learn languages other than their mother tongues. Men of commerce needed more than one language for trade and business. Changes in population required mutual intelligibility and more language diversity for teaching and study. And bilingualism was essential to artistic and intellectual creativity.

The first evidence of children studying with two languages in their schoolwork comes from cuneiform tablets from Mesopotamia between 3000 and 2000 B.C. Inscriptions on these tablets not only describe a full-fledged Sumerian-speaking civilization but also show that Akkadian, a Semitic language, was in prevalent use by the end of the third millennium. As oral traditions were inscribed in written form, both Sumerian and Akkadian became languages of record and affected one another's written development.

By the second millennium B.C., there were Sumerian texts (many thousands of lines have been preserved) and the beginnings of an Akkadian literature. Textbooks for the teaching of Sumerian to speakers of Akkadian came to contain dictionaries and Sumerian texts with line-by-line Akkadian translations. Thus a pattern of bilingual education was well established.

The Mesopotamians' technique of writing with a stylus on soft clay was widely accepted by neighboring civilizations. Their method of training scribes and their bilingual tradition were prevalent throughout the Near East during the second millennium B.C. From Elam and the Bahrain Islands in the Persian Gulf, to the Hittite Kingdom in Central Asia Minor, to the western area between the Euphrates and the Mediterranean Coast, and to Cyprus and Egypt, scribes communicated in Akkadian. In many parts of this territory, patterns of bilingual education existed, with Akkadian in addition to local languages (Oppenheim 1967).

In the third century B.C. the grandeur that was Rome was adapted from knowledge of the glory that was Greece. Again it was not just the intellectual elite who had a working knowledge of two languages. Both upper and lower classes of Roman society enjoyed the comic poet, Plautus, who often created his humor with a play on Greek words. The earliest Roman historians, Fabius Pictor and Cincius Alimentus, wrote in Greek, indicating not only their own fluency in the language, but also that at least some of their countrymen could read it.

The Romans based their education on the study of literature in a foreign language. Their training in Greek set the precedent which higher education has followed to the present time. What Greek was to the Romans, Latin became to the nations of Western Europe, and "there has never been a time when much of the best training of the mind did not consist in the study of the thoughts of the past recorded in a language not the student's own" (Wilkins 1905).

Today the nations of the world continue the tradition of bilingual education, and many nations have even more complex patterns of multilingual education. In India, over 150 different languages are spoken. Fourteen are officially recognized as regional languages and are used as the medium of instruction in public schools. In Calcutta, for example, a child can choose Bengali-, Urdu-, or English-medium instruction within the walls of a single primary school. In the Punjab area, even three writing systems are used in the schools, depending on the religion of the pupils.

There are approximately 500 languages in South America. Spanish or Portuguese is the school language for many who speak Indian languages natively. In the Caribbean, French and English are used in school, although creoles are the spoken languages. In China, there are a number of separate spoken Chinese languages with a single written language.

Africa has at least 1000 languages—some 100 different Bantu languages in the Congo alone. Languages of wider communication, such as the trade language Swahili spoken by at least seven million people in East Africa, or the colonial language French in West Africa, are used from the earliest years of school.

Nor are multilingualism and bilingual education limited to the so-called Third World. Europe, excluding Russia, has some 50 major languages. Norway has two closely related literary standard languages, and local school boards have the option of choosing which to use in the schools, although there is now a single textbook norm. Switzerland's four official languages, French, German, Italian, and Romansch, are used in the schools, and German-speaking Switzerland has two distinct varieties, a formal "high" standard German, and the very different local *Schwyzertütsch*, or Swiss German.

In Great Britain, where English has been used for centuries, there are still pockets of Welsh bilingualism and functioning Welsh bilingual schools in Wales.

The Soviet Union lists 120 languages within its boundaries. A number of written languages with large bodies of literature are used in addition to Russian in the educational system.

Even in countries that are essentially monolingual, such as Sub-Saharan Madagascar, Lesotho, and Somalia, there is multilingualism and bilingual education. In Somalia, for example, everyone speaks Somali, which has its own oral poetic tradition but is not normally written, while Arabic is used for writing and formal purposes, with Italian and English as important languages of wider communication with the rest of the world. Bilingual education is available in all of these.

LANGUAGE FOR SCHOOL

In some sense, all formal education is bilingual, since the forms and ways of expression of written language never reflect the spoken language exactly. Words, ways of speaking, and forms of discourse are used in the school setting which are not used in ordinary conversation and in other non-school settings. The first aim of formal education since its beginnings in the third millennium B.C. has always been to teach the pupils a written form of language. Other goals may be added and even the simple goal of literacy may become very complex and have sub-goals which at some stage in the educational process may take precedence. The fact remains that the familiar culture complex of "school," with its features of teacher, pupils, instruments of writing, and patterns of recitation, questions and answers, and reward for attainment, was developed in response to the need for transmission of skills in the use of written language. The school has persisted for some 4000 years with its essential traits unchanged. In spite of superficial differences such as stylus and clay tablet vs. ballpoint pen and spiral notebook, or outdoor setting and a sunny climate vs. central heating, one feels that the modern American teacher or the ancient Akkadian teacher would essentially feel at home in the other's school in terms of expected behavior, goals, and social values. Presumably the school has survived the changes in culture, political organization, and technology largely because it has succeeded to a sufficient degree in meeting its fundamental aims. Although it may be true that the social conditions today and in the near future are bringing fundamental changes in the aims of education, it is certainly profitable to examine carefully some of the features of the traditional school before attempting major changes in either aims or methods.

When the child first comes to school, he brings with him an incredibly extensive and sophisticated competence in the use of language. He not only has mastered intricate details of pronunciation and grammar in his conversational language but he knows how and when to shout and whisper, to wheedle and instruct, and to put his language to use in a fairly wide range of situations and occasions. In school he must learn a whole new set of language uses appropriate for the situations and occasions of school life which he has not known before. There will be some features of pronunciation and grammar which he must add to his repertoire; he must learn when to speak and when to be silent in a new range of contexts. In short, he must learn a whole new "register" of his language.

The child may have become familiar with some elements of the school register before actually coming to school. Some parents act out school behaviors with their young children, some features of the school register may occur in other settings (the village storyteller or the TV screen), and children in many societies play "school" even before they regularly attend. It is instructive to note how the details of language structure and language use are altered from normal conversational practice in these play situations in which to some degree the school register is being attempted.

The difference between the language registers the child already has command of and the written language and classroom register which he must acquire may be relatively slight or staggeringly large. Sometimes the pronunciation and grammar of the school register are very close to that of the child's conversational language and the differences of register consist of features like full forms for contractions, new vocabulary, subordinating constructions, operational forms of discourse, and the like. Often the conversational language which the child has is in a local dialect while the classroom requires use of a national or international "standard" form of language. A German child in Munich, for example, must learn to use new vowels and new verb forms which differentiate his own dialect from the more standard language of school. Often the standard language of the classroom register is closer to the language of books and writing than the local dialect and the child must gradually learn that ordinary conversation can be held in something very like the book language in appropriate situations, such as talking with people from another town or talking with educated people on more formal occasions. In other cases where the language of books is very different from the child's conversational language and the classroom register is in between, the child must learn that no one uses the book language for conversation but that various intermediate forms must be used in talking with other people on various occasions. Thus the child who goes to school in Cairo, for example, must acquire the language of books and formal speech, and learn to use intermediate varieties in the classroom or in talking with Arabs from other countries.

Surprisingly often the language of writing and the school register are a totally different language from the one the child knows at home. For centuries in Europe the language of the school was Latin, regardless of the language spoken by the children. Today a child whose primary language is Breton finds the school conducted completely in French, and the monolingual Navajo child may find the school conducted in English and be forbidden to use his own language even in the playground. In many communities this difference of language is accepted: it may be regarded as inevitable or it may even be highly valued by the community. In other communities the language difference may be resented: it may be seen as an unnecessary and psychological obstacle or even as an act of oppression (Ellis and Ure 1969; Ferguson 1973).

GOALS OF BILINGUAL EDUCATION

In 1951 a UNESCO study asserted that every child has the right to begin his formal education in his mother tongue and to continue in it as long as the language itself and the supply of books in the language permitted. "We take it as axiomatic," the study said, "that the best medium for teaching is the mother tongue of the pupil." Since that statement was made, arguments and counterarguments have been presented in a steady stream around the world.

Often attitudes toward language differences reflect implicit goals of the educational system itself. Although education has the larger universal function of storing and transmitting knowledge, it also has specific functions which differ from one society to the next. The implicit goals of bilingual education also vary from society to society; they often overlap within a given society and may or may not reflect the aims of the society as a whole. The following list of implicit goals, which is obviously not all-inclusive, is offered as a starting point for serious considerations of the implications of bilingual education (UNESCO 1953; Bull 1964).

To Assimilate Individuals or Groups Into the Mainstream of Society

The aim is to socialize people for full participation in the community.

Americans have assumed—and this has been more tacit than explicit—that immigrant and indigenous groups will be rapidly assimilated into American core society until they are culturally indistinguishable. De-ethnization and acculturation are central to American history and American national awareness. Writing in the mid-1950s, Einar Haugen noted that "Americans have tended to take it for granted that 'foreigners' should acquire English and that a failure to do so was evidence by implication of a kind of disloyalty to the basic principles of American life. . . ." (Fishman 1966). In most cases in the United States, bilingual education of any kind has had the implicit aim of assimilating the individuals into mainstream American life.

Assimilation has also been a major goal in Alsace and Brittany in France, where young speakers of the provincial vernaculars Alsacian and Breton have been constrained by the educational system to learn standard French for absorption into mainstream French society. There has been periodic resistance to this national goal, sometimes provoked by unpopular language requirements, in these and other provincial areas of Europe.

It is interesting to note that in Europe language deviations are often at the periphery of a nation's frontiers, as in Alsace, Brittany, the Basque areas of France and Spain, along the Pyrenees, the Südtirol in northern Italy, Catalonia in Spain, Upper Silesia in Prussian Germany, and Schleswig in Germany near the Danish border. Paradoxically, deviations at the borders of a country which defy assimilation at the same time reinforce the widespread notion of nations based on a common linguistic core (Petersen 1972; Minot 1970).

To Unify a Multilingual Society

> The aim is to bring unity to a multi-ethnic, multi-tribal, or multi-national linguistically diverse polity.

In Ghana there are estimated to be between 47 and 62 languages spoken. The major ones are the Akan dialects, particularly Fanti and Twi, and Dagbani. These operate to a limited extent as lingua francas in the regions where they are used. Other important languages are Ewe, Ga-Adangbe, and Kasem. The official language of the country is English, but nine indigeneous languages have been given the status of national languages, their selection having been based on their use in other neighboring countries as well as in Ghana. In the schools, the policy has been to use local vernaculars in the schools for the first few years of primary education, shifting to a lingua franca of African origin in the middle years of schooling, at least in areas of linguistic differentiation, and then using English at the upper levels and in university education.

There are textbooks in Fanti and Twi; and Fanti, Twi, Ewe, and Ga are all specified as curriculum and examination subjects. The use of vernaculars at the lower levels to assist the schoolchild in cultural adaptation was part of British colonial policy.

Policy in post-independence Ghana stressed linguistic unification, with even more time devoted to English. The political and economic needs of the country took precedence over any presumed psychological needs of the child (Spencer 1963; Armstrong 1968; Foster 1965; Graham 1971).

In the Soviet Union, Russian is the official language and the medium of communication between federal and constituent governments. Non-Russian peoples, however, comprise nearly half of the country's entire population and are steadily increasing in numbers. Fully one-third of the population, according to official records, speaks an indigenous language other than Russian as its mother tongue.

In contrast to Tsarist Russia, the Soviet government set out to stimulate the growth of national cultures, seeking to preserve the national languages of the republic and, where crucial to education, the minority languages as well. Mother tongues were seen as vehicles to communicate Soviet ideology. Of 169 "nationalities," 50 are national ethnic groups which have more than 20,000 members, with strong feelings of national consciousness expressed in a native language and native literature. There are 14 non-Russian republics, each of which represents a large ethnic group.

A Soviet aim has been to unify all these groups into one, with a predominantly Russian language and tradition through an educational policy designed to foster unity in diversity. The policy of the government is to educate the Soviet child in his mother tongue during the early years of his schooling. Thus thirty-five percent of the pupils are taught in a language other than Russian, and 59 languages are used as media of instruction throughout the U.S.S.R. (The Baltic languages use the Latin script, the Georgian and Armenian languages have their own alphabets, and the languages of other minorities use the Cyrillic alphabet which Russian uses.) Many of the schools use the major language of the republic in which a school is located as the language of instruction.

In the Russian Republic, however, not only is the major language Russian used in the schools, but 44 additional languages also serve as media for teaching, although pupils from the small minorities in that Republic who do not speak Russian as their mother tongue represent only 6% of the population. Smaller ethnic groups in other republics also enjoy political and cultural autonomy and their languages are used in schools and in local government and other institutions.

By requiring Russian as a subject in the schools and pushing its increased use for official and public purposes in the republics, the government has encouraged expansion of Russian culture and the uniting of Soviet peoples as a single people. Today, Russian-medium schools seem to be preferred over "native" schools in urban areas, and Russian is usually the language of instruction for the children of officials and army officers transferred around the country. Books written in Russian get published more rapidly than those written in other languages. Most higher education is now in the Russian language, except for some universities in the Ukraine, Georgia, and Armenia. Knowledge of Russian is a prerequisite for entrance into institutions of higher learning, and a Soviet citizen has to use Russian to get ahead in the party apparatus (Wohl 1973; Kreisler 1961; Kilarz 1952; Barghoorn 1956).

To Enable People to Communicate with the Outside World

The aim is to introduce language of wider communication in addition to the unifying national language so as to make it possible for nationals to interact with foreigners.

In a country like Holland, where the language is spoken by very few other than the Dutch, there is need for international languages. The educational system provides for this need by requiring all children in seventh grade and above to learn both English and German.

In Nigeria English was adopted as the national language, after its long pre-independence use, first as a European trade language and then as a colonial language. Other non-indigenous languages of wider communication, such as French and German, are also offered as foreign languages at the higher levels of education with the aim of training some Nigerians for professional, commercial, and diplomatic contact with other countries in Africa, Europe, and elsewhere.

In the Soviet Union the teaching of foreign languages has been a major concern of policy makers, particularly because of the need of scientists to profit from achievements in other countries, and the urgency for the government to expand its international trade and extend its participation in international affairs. In all the Soviet schools, a choice of language is offered. Foreign-language instruction is even included in the schooling of pupils with speech difficulties. There are special foreign-language-medium high schools in which certain subjects are taught through the medium of a single foreign language. These schools are highly selective and prestigious, but sometimes foreign languages are also used as the media of instruction for certain subjects in the "all age," or general education, schools (Lewis 1962).

To Gain an Economic Advantage for Individuals or Groups

The aim is to provide language skills which are salable in the job market and can put a person ahead on jobs and status.

Thailand and Japan are two examples of countries which need large numbers of trained personnel who have some proficiency in English or in another internationally useful language. Thai and Japanese are fully modernized languages serving the complex requirements of economic and scientific activities within their countries, but their usefulness falls off (abruptly in the case of Thai, to a lesser but critical degree in the case of Japanese) when this activity is carried on with other countries. Therefore, pupils who will be going on to jobs in business, government, or technology need bilingual schooling. The economic premium placed on language skills in both countries is reflected not only in the variety of bilingual education used in government and private schools but in the large numbers of commercial language schools and in the demand for, and good pay offered to, native-speaking English tutors.

To Preserve Ethnic or Religious Ties

> The preservation of ethnic or religious identity in an individual or group may or may not go against general national goals.

In the United States more than 2000 ethnic group schools offer language instruction, and often religious or other classes, after school hours or on weekends, for the purpose of maintaining ethnic identity. Although the implicit national goal of assimilating immigrant ethnic groups into the mainstream is not served by these schools, they do not greatly threaten the goal, since they have little effect on the speed with which their pupils acquire English and are ultimately absorbed into American life. However, these schools are the most active language-maintenance institutions in immigrant communities and they survive longer in the face of the formidable odds against them than other ethnic-group institutions which seek to promote linguistic conformity (Fishman 1966).

In Ethiopia, on the other hand, national goals of education for economic development are closely served by two traditional patterns of literacy acquisition: the Ethiopian Orthodox church-school, and the Muslim Quranic school. Both have long provided church education and basic competence for religious observances to the young in those communities. The child who learns to read and write Geez, the classical liturgical language of the Ethiopian church, will then also be able to read and write Amharic, the national language of Ethiopia, and Tigrinya, another major language, since these use the same alphabet. Moreover, the child is taught Geez in Amharic, so that if it is not his mother tongue he learns it in the process of his religious training.

The child who learns to read aloud, to recite from memory, and to write sections of the Koran in Arabic (ordinarily with little or no understanding of what he is reading or reciting) may be picking up skills in a language which is of limited use in broader Ethiopian society; but his training, like that of the child in the Orthodox church-school, prepares him to enter a government school or other institution, and thus serves as his basic primary education.

An increasing number of pupils are becoming literate in these two traditional systems, and the systems themselves are being modernized to incorporate new methods, materials, and subject matter. The Ethiopian government is allying itself more purposefully with the traditional schools and providing sponsorship, financing, and curriculum guidelines. At the same time, the traditional schools are feeding fewer graduates into religious higher schools and more of them into government higher institutions (Ferguson 1971).

> Preserving a child's ethnic heritage by arbitrarily tying him to it in school may be counterproductive if this policy has a retarding effect on his learning process.

In the Republic of Ireland children live in an overwhelmingly English-speaking environment and are exposed to the Irish language only in the schools, under the government's policy of promoting the restoration of Irish as the national language. Studies of the impact of using Irish instead of English as the medium of instruction in the schools suggest that Irish children will be educationally handicapped, at least for the period of time it will take Ireland to evolve its policy of national bilingualism in a monolingual national environment.

More specifically, the findings show that English-speaking Irish children who are learning arithmetic in the Irish medium do poorly in problem solving and are almost a year behind those who are learning arithmetic in the English medium (although their performance in mechanical arithmetic operations is not affected). The children's Irish language ability is not improved in the process, nor is their English language ability in any way weakened.

The facts indicate that incentive is a key to the success of education in other than the mother tongue. Contrast, for example, the immigrant youngster in the United States with the native Irish child. The immigrant youngster has enormous incentive to learn English because it is all he hears around him and he is rewarded with acceptance when he learns it. The Irish child has little incentive to learn Irish; his environment is English-speaking and he can acquire this second language only from his teachers. The motives for learning Irish are abstractly cultural and political, not urgently practical (Macnamara 1966).

> A child may have the incentive to learn through the medium of the language associated with his ethnic heritage (which may even be his mother tongue) and yet be hindered by the linguistic limitations of the particular language for teaching a certain subject.

Kpelle, a language of Liberia, has a decimal number system which is essentially like ours, and objects are counted. There is also a well-developed system of terminology for placing objects into sets, but the classification system implied by this is not normally used in everyday language. Moreover there are no abstract arithmetical operations; the Kpelle do not work with pure numerals nor can they speak of them. All arithmetic is tied to concrete situations, and multiplication and division exist only as repetitions of addition and subtraction. Operations are generally carried out on numbers up to 30 or 40. The fraction system is rudimentary: the term "half" is either used as a general term for any part of a whole (1/10, 9/10, etc.) or treated as a meaningless symbol in arithmetic operations. Kpelle terms for relations of equality, inequality, and comparison between objects and sets of objects are in graded series according to degree of sameness or similarity.

Mathematics education for the Kpelle must be adapted to the linguistic facts of the Kpelle language if it is to be carried out in Kpelle. If it is carried out in English, it must be adapted to the very real differences between the Liberian pidgin English spoken by many pupils and teachers, and the standard English used in mathematics textbooks (Gay and Cole 1967).

To Reconcile Different Political, or Socially Separate, Communities

Language can mediate between social or political groups. The implication may
be that the more fortunate have a responsibility to the less fortunate which can
be fulfilled partially by learning their language to communicate with them.

A notable example of this goal is the French-English project in St. Lambert,
Quebec, which has been reported extensively by W. E. Lambert and R. C. Gardner
(1959). (Lambert, Gardner, Olten, and Tunstall 1968; Lambert, Yackley, and
Heim 1971; Lambert and Tucker 1972). Briefly, parents of English-speaking
children volunteered to enroll their children in French-medium schools where the
youngsters received no formal education in English. At the end of the first year, a
battery of psychological, language, reading, and personality tests showed that the
children were all within the norms for their age and grade level. Four years later,
they were doing as well as their peers in both French and English.

A similar project has been attempted in Culver City, California, where
English-speaking children (primarily from well-to-do homes) are sent to a
Spanish-medium school, in an effort to enhance communication between the
Anglo and Chicano communities in this suburb of Los Angeles.

To Spread and Maintain the Use of a Colonial Language

This goal, which is similar to the mainstream goal, is to socialize an entire
population to a colonial existence and a colonial language.

The English language is a pervasive and dominant feature of Indian national life
today because it played a central role in pre-independence India as the language of
the colonial British government, and before that as the language of traders. In
1600, the East India Company was awarded a charter to develop trading interests
on the subcontinent. The British Parliament assumed more control after 1757,
and one hundred years later it took over from the East India Company and
governed India as a colony until 1947.

For approximately the first 80 years of India's colonial existence, English
was the de facto language of administration. In 1835, English was deliberately
chosen, over the Indian vernaculars, and Sanskrit and Arabic, as the language of
government and education as a result of a recommendation made by Thomas B.
Macaulay to the British Governor-General.

In his recommendation, Macaulay argued for the English language on the
grounds that it had the lexical resources needed to educate a class of Indians for
modern government, that it provided direct access to bodies of scientific and
other knowledge, and that it was an ideal medium for educating the elite class of
Indians who would be the link between the British rulers and the masses of
uneducated Indians. Thus English became the medium for primary and secondary
education.

Vernaculars began to replace English in the lower grades after 1921 and at the secondary level after 1937, and there were post-independence campaigns to replace English entirely with one of the indigenous languages. Nevertheless, English has remained the language of science and technology, big business, the courts, the legislative bodies, most state government transactions, and university instruction. It is widely used in the print and broadcast media, as a language of publication, and for communications and transportation. A command of English is a prerequisite for the better jobs everywhere in India.

Part of the reason for the maintenance of English as a unifying national language after its spread under colonial rule is that India's language situation is so complex. The most suitable alternative to English as a national language would seem to be a "Hindustani" variety of Hindi/Urdu, since it is the indigenous language spoken by the greatest number of people (over 150 million), but its use is almost exclusively limited to the northern states of India. Hence the stipulation in 1963 by India's Parliament that English might continue to be used for official purposes as long as was necessary, although Hindi had been constitutionally established as India's official language (Chatterji 1954; Le Page 1964; Ohannessian 1966a; Ohannessian 1966b; Spencer 1963).

The spread and maintenance of a colonial language was also a primary goal of bilingual education in Algeria under the French. Arabic and French were used as media of instruction in the schools, with the aim of socializing an Arabic-speaking Algerian population to the increasing use of French, and to support the French colonial economic and administrative system.

Still another example is the Ivory Coast, which to this day strikingly reflects the features of its French colonial past. Though the major vernacular languages have a place at the lower levels of trade, and in broadcasting, French is the language of government, communications, and commerce, and French is used as the medium of instruction from the child's first year of school. There is no provision for teaching indigenous languages even as school subjects (Mumford and Orde-Brown 1935).

To Embellish or Strengthen the Education of Elites

Much of bilingual education in the world is primarily for elites, and much of that which is now generally available to all began as education for elites.

Mexico is one of many countries in which there are alternative schools providing bilingual education to elites as well as government schools serving the majority. For example, a German-language-medium school in Mexico City serves not only the sons and daughters of German diplomats and businessmen living in Mexico, but also the child of Mexican or foreign families who want it and are able to pay for it.

In Europe, there are six multi-language international schools conducted under the jurisdiction of the European Economic Community (the Common Market). These schools, located in Karlsruhe, Germany; Luxembourg; Bergen,

Norway; Varese, Italy; Brussels; and Mol-Geel, Belgium, are open to the children of EEC officials and employees as well as to the children of parents unconnected with the organization, if there is room and they can pay the high tuition.

First graders are taught in their mother tongues in all subjects. In the second year, another language is added. In the third year, all children regularly attend "European classes" in which the four official EEC languages—French, German, Italian, and Dutch—are used interchangeably. By the secondary education level, many subjects, including biology and history, are taught in a language other than the pupil's native tongue. After he decides whether he will emphasize science or arts, the student is taught his chemistry or philosophy in one of the other languages. He also may elect to learn English, and Greek or Latin. By the time he graduates, the pupil can speak five languages and has learned in three or more of them.

The Common Market schools have been flooded with increasing numbers of applicants each year. School authorities express concern about attracting students for prestige reasons alone, but the schools undeniably fill an elitist function, and are an ambitious bilingual education experiment for a select group.

The European Atomic Energy Community (Euratom) has a similar international multilingual school in Italy, and the United Nations International School in New York City, for the children of UN officials as well as others not connected with the UN, offers bilingual instruction to the offspring of the elite.

Attempts have been made to spread the idea of European integration through schooling which would be pan-European in design and approach, and would be multilingual in practice. The Council of Europe and the European Coal and Steel Community have contributed to this aim. The College of Europe at Bruges, Belgium, founded in 1950, offers bilingual instruction in French and English; an applicant must use both languages to be admitted, and for his examinations, although he may do his thesis in just one language (Eicholz 1968).

To Give Equal Status to Languages of Unequal Prominence in the Society

As a democratic or egalitarian policy, two languages of unequal status in a nation may be treated as exactly equal under the law.

Finland has been bilingual Finnish-Swedish since prehistoric times, although only 9% of a present-day population of 4 million have Swedish as their mother tongue. For a period of 600 years, Finland was a part of Sweden, and historically, Swedish cultural and linguistic influences have been strong everywhere in Finland. Until the end of the 19th Century, the upper class in Finland was almost exclusively Swedish-speaking.

Unlike many other countries with two or more languages, the Finnish- and Swedish-speaking segments of Finland's population have always been integrated parts of the society. Nevertheless, an enormous effort has been required to ensure that Finland's educational system makes use of the Swedish language in rough balance with the now dominant Finnish language. Finnish-speaking communities use Finnish as the medium of instruction and are required to study Swedish; similarly, Swedish-speaking communities use Swedish as their medium and are required to study Finnish (Runeberg 1971).

To Deepen Understanding of Language and Culture

> Languages can be used in education to introduce cultures of other times and places, to open new views of reality, or to give insights into human nature.

One of the most familiar justifications of foreign language instruction in the liberal arts curriculum is that it teaches the student to "think in another language" and to appreciate values and ways of life different from his own. This may be through the history of a civilization, as when Europeans study the Greek and Latin classics or Indians study Sanskrit. It may be confronting an "exotic" literature or oral tradition, as when an American university offers undergraduate instruction in Chinese or Quechua. It may be parents who want their child to learn French, even if he may never have a chance to use it directly.

This goal may be seen in the linguist's desire to understand the workings of language, the historian's need to understand an ancient time through its language, or someone's simple wish to enjoy the use of another language for its own sake. This goal is put last, as being in many respects the most difficult to plan for, to implement, and to evaluate, but in a fundamental sense it may be the most important goal.

ATTITUDES AND EXPECTATIONS

Much of the controversy over bilingual education is due to the fact that the implicit goals have little to do with language per se but are concerned rather with the attitudes and expectations of people in the society.

For example, if a youngster's parents, teachers, neighbors, and above all, peers place a high value on a language or language variety and use it around him, the youngster will learn it. The schools can help, but they cannot do the whole job of adding a language or replacing one with another.

In the United States the immigrant child is under steady pressure from all sides in his new environment to learn English and to lose his immigrant language, although there may be counterinfluences at home to retain the language (Fishman 1966).

In Ethiopia, the memorization of the Koran by Muslim children, and of the Psalms of David by Ethiopian Orthodox Christian children, is accomplished without recourse to "modern" teaching methods and without understanding of what is being memorized. Yet the high value placed on a youth's having completed one of these tasks and the status he thereby achieves motivate him to accomplish it (Ferguson 1971).

In Schwaben, a state in southwestern Germany, the child's German dialect at home is very different from the standard German he encounters when he first enters school, yet he learns appropriate levels of the standard language relatively quickly. Schwäbisch children simply come to school expecting to learn school German and are expected by the community to achieve a useful command of it. Acquiring the additional register is part of the whole important process of attending school—and they do it (Fishman and Luders 1972).

By contrast, many American Black children who speak Black English at home have prolonged trouble with standard American school English. Speculation about their being "less verbal" than white children is unfounded, since these youngsters often show great verbal skill and creativity in their own variety of English when speaking with their peers off the school grounds. However, in many cases neither they nor the community expect them to acquire the school register, and they do not.

Although the educational system can be a major means of spreading a language, it is not always the most important means. Language may spread with the help of the educational system or independent of its influence, or even in spite of it—that is, counter to the language-policy aims of the system.

In Nepal, the Nepali language spread at first largely independent of education. It was widely spoken over the whole country long before a national policy of universal free primary education was adopted and schools began to appear in the remote hill areas where they had not been before. When the schools did increase in number and accessibility, they simply lent support to the use of the Nepali language, and its standardization in popular use, by Nepalese who spoke other mother tongues.

In East Bengal at the time of Pakistan's partition from India, Urdu was designated as the language to be used for official purposes, but it failed, in spite of its promotion by Pakistan's founder Mohammed Ali Jinnah and the Muslim League. Bengali, which was already present as the mother tongue of the overwhelming majority of East Pakistan's population, prevailed. Bengali's status as a national language on equal terms with Urdu was not secured until there had been prolonged protest, bloodshed, and civil instability which were intolerable to the national leadership. And even then the seeds of a nationalist movement which would grow beyond control 17 years later were already sown by the language issue. East Bengal was a case in which language policy for national life and for education ran so blatantly counter to the practical facts of language use and to popular emotions that it was doomed in advance to fail.

SUMMARY

The first evidence of bilingual education is on clay tablets from Mesopotamia during the third millennium B.C. Since then, the use of two or more languages in the formal education system of a society has continued down through the ages and around the globe.

In addition, bilingual education, in the sense that language variety used in the classroom either differs appreciably from that used in ordinary conversation or is even a different language altogether, is universal.

Throughout the world, the use of more than one language in education serves to further a variety of implicit as well as explicit educational goals. These goals are different at various educational levels and within various social frameworks, and they often overlap or are in conflict with one another.

Ultimately, the success of bilingual education can be measured only in terms of specific goals, and it depends more on people's attitudes and expectations than on pedagogical methods or on linguistic factors such as the degree of difference between languages or language varieties.

VII

Educational Perspectives on Bilingual Education

Vera P. John

and Ellen Souberman

A major step in support of bilingual education was taken by the UNESCO Conference in 1953 where experts from many parts of the world assembled. They concluded that the best medium for learning and teaching is the mother tongue of the student. The monograph summarizing this conference, *The Use of Vernacular Languages in Education*, has been an influential document, used by many to further the development of bilingual education in the United States and throughout the world. The authors of this chapter would have liked to speak with the authority and experience reflected in the international scope of that historic document, but their own knowledge limited them to a discussion of educational issues which have arisen in the United States over the past century. It is their hope that this chapter will touch on concerns which are important in bilingual programs beyond the American borders as well.

INTRODUCTION

For over a century, public schools in this country have been committed to a duality of functions: imparting educational skills, as well as socializing children in a manner which reflects national objectives. Through the schools, and to some extent in the army, a shared reality is created in a country of enormous physical and cultural differences—where children drawn from communities of varying cultural and linguistic backgrounds are taught to learn in a single language, to commit themselves to a similar set of values, to develop overlapping tastes, and to have hopes and dreams consistent with the "American way of life."

A thorough examination of this socializing role of schools has resulted in the view of educational institutions as both the cause and the solution to many serious societal tensions. Most observers agreed that the long-standing policy of schools which sought to implement the melting-pot ideology threatened the survival of native cultures and of languages other than the national language. This awareness resulted in increasing political demands for the creation of equal educational opportunities, by those groups in our society who have come to see the traditional school as the enemy of non-white and poor children.

These concerns were buttressed by the availability of statistics which showed that children from non-English-speaking communities have the least number of years of schooling and the most limited access to higher education and professional jobs, even lower than that of American Blacks.[1] These communities, too, have resorted to political action and legal solutions, akin to the *Brown* v. *Board of Education*, U.S. Supreme Court decision (1954), to establish a basis for a changed political and educational reality.

While the recognition that schools have traditionally failed children from non-English and poor communities is widespread, the solutions which have been offered for a different future vary considerably. The most frequently suggested approach is the development of transitional bilingual programs,[2] aimed at minimizing cultural and linguistic differences between the mainstream and the minority child, thus facilitating his/her integration and assimilation into the dominant culture in the fastest and most effective manner.

One way to document these differing educational policies concerning non-English-speaking children is to examine recent court decisions in this area. *Lau* v. *Nichols* (1974), a U.S. Supreme Court decision, dealing with the educational opportunities of Chinese children in San Francisco, calls for the implementation of a transitional bilingual model. That decision relied on Section 601 of the 1964 Civil Rights Act which "bans discrimination based 'on the ground of race, color, or national origin,' in 'any program . . . receiving federal assistance' "; and on a 1970 HEW regulation (35 Federal Register 11595) which stated: "where inability to speak and understand the English language excludes national origin—minority group children from effective participation in the educational program offered by a school district, the district must take affirmative steps to *rectify the language deficiency* in order to open its instructional program to these students." [Emphasis added] The Court also cites the California Education Code which establishes proficiency in English as the goal of the entire educational system and which authorizes bilingual instruction, only "to the extent that it does not interfere with the systematic, sequential, and regular instruction of *all* pupils in the English language." [Emphasis added]

Clearly, the Court's decision that 3000 Chinese children in the San Francisco public school system should receive instruction in their native language is merely a recognition on their part that these students need "remedial" help before they can become full participants in the standard educational programs offered. The Court states: "Basic English skills are at the very core of what these public schools teach. Imposition of a requirement that, before a child can effectively participate in the educational program he must already have acquired those basic skills is to make a mockery of public education. We know that those who do not understand English are certain to find their classroom experiences wholly incomprehensible and in no way meaningful."

The Court did not deal with the cultural characteristics and mores which are rooted in one's native language nor did it deal with the possibility that a people might very well desire to retain their cultural identity. This decision addressed itself only to the remedying of a "deficiency" among the Chinese children.[3]

A transitional program, then, does not require significant changes in the underlying assumptions governing school practices today. An alternative view of bilingual education, however, does imply more fundamental changes. This second approach is discussed by Seda (1970), who argues that:

> Cultural pluralism . . . implies: 1) The recognition of the fact that culture determines people's identity. 2) That the cultural diversity of our world ought to be encouraged in order to stimulate the diversification of answers to human problems, a diversity which might save humanity under changing environmental conditions. (It is known that homogeneity has been suicidal in the biological world for some species.) 3) The differences which different human groups contribute to cultural pluralism should be seen in their beauty. 4) Under conditions of racism the assimilation in the "melting pot" of groups classified in racial terms such as the Mexican, Puerto Rican, Native American and Blacks, has resulted in massive destruction of their creative potentialities. Internalization of the racist assumptions of this culture results among members of these "racial" groups in a stigmatized identity.

Some educational policies, as well as some court decisions, do take into account the destructive effects of past school practices, as described by Seda, upon children's self-concepts and sense of cultural dignity. However, it is still unclear how far the courts will go in *enforcing* a pluralistic view of education. A recent and very hopeful example of court action in this area is the *U.S.* v. *State of Texas et al.* decision (1971), which outlines an important direction for bilingual programs. In this decision, a U.S. District Court addressed the problem of Chicano education in the San Felipe Del Rio Consolidated Independent School District in three areas: bilingual and bicultural programs; faculty recruitment and training (including paraprofessionals); and curriculum design and content. In adopting a Comprehensive Educational Plan, the Court stated that it was "the responsibility of the educational agency to provide an individualized instructional program which is compatible with (the children's) cultural and learning characteristics . . . while *recognizing the cultural and linguistic pluralism* of the student body and providing equal opportunity for *reinforcement and expansion of that plural- ism* . . . (and providing) for the characteristics of the child's immediate environment and the characteristics of the larger environment in which he shall function in the future." [Emphasis added]

To ensure the furtherance of cultural pluralism as an educational goal, the court called as an example for the following actions on the part of the schools: "pluralistic instructional approaches"; affirmative recognition of the value of all cultural environments and language backgrounds; that neither Spanish nor English be presented "as a more valued language"; the "development of culturally relevant, fair and reinforcing instructional materials in social studies"; the "evaluation and subsequent modification of all instructional materials for the elimination of all stereotyping, historical misrepresentations and other negative cultural presentations"; and the "modification and expansion of home economics curriculum to respond to the life styles, family structures and needs of children in all cultures represented in the student body." The Court also recommended the creation of community councils to evaluate programs and formulate educational goals and objectives; and the increased participation of parents at all levels, "in the language they best understand." [Another decision recommending similar changes in the school system, *Serna* v. *Portales* (1972), has been appealed by the Portales Board of Education to the U.S. Ninth Circuit.]

This decision is impressive not only in its insistence that schools assume full responsibility for developing and maintaining diverse cultures and languages in America, but also in its detailed recommendations for enforcing such a policy.

The differing models implicit in these two court decisions can best be understood when linked to the sociological and historical literature concerning ethnic groups in America. Most scholarly writings of the past analyzed the relationship between the Anglo-Saxon, dominant groups and immigrant and native groups from the point of view of the immigrant's experience. Writers such as Glazer and Moynihan (1963) describe various patterns of assimilation—the ways in which a family from an ethnically and culturally different background becomes assimilated into the American mainstream. Though they do point out that the process is never quite complete and that ethnicity remains a critical aspect of city living, their focus, nonetheless, is upon assimilation.

In the last quarter of a century, social scientists and spokespeople of Third World communities in America have written on these matters from a different point of view. They have documented the extraordinary fact that in spite of the powerful pressures and influences of the politically dominant groups—both Anglo-American and Spanish—attendant to a three hundred-year period of colonization, the native peoples of this continent and island territories have managed to transmit and sustain their indigenous languages and cultures.

While the emphasis of scholarly writings up until and including World War II was upon the process and speed of assimilation, the more contemporary writings, particularly by those who are either members of or closely affiliated with native groups, document the mechanisms of *cultural survival*. One example of this process is described in a recently completed dissertation about the small island of Guam, a territory of the United States. Riley (1974) writes:

For the past three hundred years the island of Guam in the Western Pacific Ocean has been under the jurisdiction of three different powers: Spain, Japan, and the United States. Over the centuries there was a steady flow of edicts, decrees, and general orders issued by Spanish kings, Japanese generals, and American governors all stating basically the same idea: Chamorro is to be supplanted by the metropolitan colonial language, and the most efficient way of attaining this goal is through the establishment of schools. As the years passed, the native population dwindled either because of intentional political strategies of genocide or because of sickness and epidemics. In spite of this, Chamorro continued to exist as a vibrant, dynamic, and eminently useful mode of communication. Even today, fully three hundred and fifty-two years after Magellan sighted the island, Chamorro is still the first language of the vast majority of those Americans born in the Territory.

Increasingly, studies such as the one conducted by Riley are suggesting that before examining the particulars of a bilingual program within school walls, it is imperative to understand the magnitude of the impact of mass communication, travel, urbanization, and industrialization upon native, immigrant, and impoverished rural peoples in the latter half of the 20th Century. In the context, bilingual education emerges as a function of a multitude of forces; some of these are legal and political in nature; others are reflections of more general economic and social developments, characteristic of different communities. A full discussion of these complex interrelationships is beyond the scope of this chapter. A single example is offered to illustrate the nature of these interrelationships as they developed in one community.

The American Indians have traditionally resisted policies of assimilation. Nevertheless, in the 1950s the Bureau of Indian Affairs embarked on an energetic plan of relocating reservation Indians into the major urban centers of this country, within the context of systematically terminating the reservations.[4] These efforts were developed for the purpose of placing Indians into industrial jobs, with the long-range goal of permanently resettling large numbers of reservation Indians in the cities. An enormous emotional and cultural loss was suffered by those who were relocated. Collier (1969) documented some of the outcomes of this policy for the Navajos in California.

Indian organizations which emerged in the late fifties and early sixties gave high priority to developing alternatives to the government's policy of relocation. The Navajo Nation used the limited resources offered by the War on Poverty to strengthen the economic base of their people living on the reservation. While the earliest efforts in the use of the Navajo language as an instructive medium (70% of children entering public schools are monolingual speakers of Navajo) were transitional in nature, more recently a number of contract schools[5] have pioneered in placing the Navajo language and culture at the core of children's education. We see these efforts as reflective of increased economic development by and for Navajos on their reservation, along with the increased possibilities for their employment in industrial, service, and professional fields. Thus students schooled in Navajo and English throughout their entire education will be able to use their native language, in both its oral and written forms, in their daily work with their people.

The Navajos, a people who live on and control an expanse of land the size of West Virginia and who number 125,000, present an unusual setting for the development of bilingual education. For other indigenous and non-English-speaking people, the particular combination of economic, social, and political conditions results in more limited options for the development of native-language instruction.

A thorough analysis of the role of schools in non-white communities necessarily leads to an examination of more fundamental issues concerning the relationship between these communities and the greater body politic. (A fuller discussion of these issues can be found in other chapters of this volume, for instance, Chapters II and VIII.)

Thus the particulars of specific plans for the education of children are but the tip of the iceberg in the larger context of current national debates concerning pressing political choices on issues such as self-determination and cultural pluralism. In this introduction, we have posited a polarity of educational modes for bilingual-bicultural education—the transitional vs. the pluralistic. We will now examine the attempts of some communities to establish a genuinely pluralistic educational model, often without the extent of potential resources available to a group such as the Navajos.

ISSUES AND CONTROVERSIES

The development of bilingual programs is a demanding and complex endeavor. It requires the identification of children who would benefit from such an educational effort; the choice of effective models of learning and teaching; the choice of curriculum; the training and recruitment of educational personnel; and, most important, a joint effort on the part of the community and the school system in formulating educational goals and shaping the educational process. In all such aspects of planning and execution, the kinds of choices discussed in the Introduction loom large for the participants. Often, for example, when an examination is made of the curriculum chosen by a particular community for its bilingual program, it becomes apparent that no basic decision has been made as to whether to follow a transitional or pluralistic model. The tension created by the absence of such a choice is inevitably reflected in the nature of the planning.

Who Should Be Educated in Bilingual Classrooms?

During the academic year 1972-1973, bilingual programs were funded in 29 states of the United States, as well as in Guam, the Mariana Islands, Puerto Rico, and the Virgin Islands. The projects represent 24 languages and dialects, including English.[6] The range of efforts is enormous in terms of language varieties and geography, but only 5% of national-origin minority children—those who would be the logical beneficiaries of bilingual instruction—were participating in such programs (Casso 1973). It is clear, then, that the availability of bilingual education falls far below meeting the need. In addition, many have posed the question of how to assess the nature of the need.

In some non-English-speaking communities many parents are dubious about the value of native-language instruction for their children. In these situations, voluntary enrollment in bilingual classes has been the practice, particularly at the inception of such a program. Frequently, the success of such efforts has produced increasing parental confidence in the value of bilingual education, which in turn resulted in efforts to extend that schooling to a larger number of classrooms and to additional grade levels.

Parental concern regarding the introduction of bilingual education in low-income schools can in part be attributed to the fact that for generations now non-English-speaking children have been forced to use only English in the classroom.[7] That very practice has produced its own consequences; it has created negative attitudes among many people toward their own native language and an emphasis upon the importance of competence in English as a basic vehicle for economic success and security in this society.

An additional cause for uncertainty rests in parents' concern that bilingual classes may very well operate as a less blatant form of tracking for their children than the by now well-documented practice (particularly in the California schools) of placing large numbers of Spanish-speaking children in EMR (educable mentally retarded) classes (Casso 1973). Because of these practices, many parents are understandably doubtful about any programmatic effort to separate their children from those of more affluent communities, as potentially being one more practice which would continue to deny their children the right to a meaningful and intellectually rewarding education.

Black and Chicano psychologists and educators have written extensively about the issues of testing and in particular about the way in which I.Q. tests are used against children from Third World communities. Robert L. Williams has shown that when tests are administered to Black children with instructions that approximate their own styles of verbal interaction, as well as their idioms, these children perform better than when the same tests are given to them with standard instructions (Roberts 1974). It has also been shown that the placement of Chicano children in EMR classes by the California Public School System was a function of a particularly blatant misuse of intelligence and achievement tests. Children whose knowledge of English was limited were judged "subnormal" through evaluation instruments which did not tap their true intellectual and survival skills (Mercer 1971).

In addition, significant examiner effects on children's tested performances have been documented in a longitudinal study of Puerto Rican children. Stylistic differences between two examiners, both Spanish-speaking, well-trained members of the children's ethnic community, resulted in consistently higher performances by those children tested by the woman examiner who perceived them as friendly, capable, and cooperative. Also, verbally loaded tests revealed greater differences in achievement than did performance tests (Thomas, Hertzig, Dryman, and Fernandez 1972).

There is yet another issue relevant to the education of low-income and minority-group children which is more basic than the inappropriate use of tests to classify and categorize children, but which is more often completely ignored by educational scholars. This involves the impact upon children of environmental conditions in poor communities and their effects upon the full development of intellectual potential among these children. While bilingual education does offer educational and intellectual advantages to children drawn from non-English-speaking communities, these children are also confronted with extreme poverty and seriously deteriorated conditions of living.

A recent report of the National Academy of Sciences, entitled, "The Relationship of Nutrition to Brain Development and Behavior," is important and illuminating in this regard. The Academy states, that "the weight of evidence seems to indicate that early and severe malnutrition is an important factor in later intellectual development, above and beyond the effects of social-familial influence."[8] The percentage of children from non-English and poor communities who are indeed suffering from the sequella of malnutrition, birth injuries, and other medically untreated illnesses is unknown; but the relative proportion of children thus afflicted is unquestionably higher in poor communities than among those from more affluent communities.[9]

The lack of serious attention paid to environmentally caused (i.e., dilapidated housing, lack of medical care, poor nutrition) but biologically mediated damage to poor children has critical consequences. Comparisons between white and non-white or middle-class and lower-class children have been made and racist conclusions about the relative intellectual potential of each of these groups have been offered.[10] Men like Jensen, Shockley, and Ginsburg have attributed differences in test performances among culturally and/or linguistically distinct groups of children to fixed, racially linked genetic variables. Their theories have been disseminated among educators, some of whom accept these "explanations." In light of the increased popularity of such views, the recently completed and carefully controlled research of M. Smilansky in Israel (1974) is extremely relevant. Using intelligence tests, Smilansky compared 1600 children of European and non-European parentage, all of whom were raised in the *same* environment. He found that in contrast with control children who lived in communities of varying resources the kibbutz-raised children, although of various skin colors and from different cultural backgrounds, showed no significant differences on intelligence tests. The results of this study are important in terms of generating an increased understanding of the American situation, other than that offered by psychologists such as Jensen. In both Israel and the United States, the lower economic and social position of certain groups was said to be the result of a variety of causes, all of which were thought to be difficult to modify by environmental means. But Smilansky's study provides substantial support for the proposition that differences in test scores among ethnic groups are not determined by racial or cultural identity but rather are the product of specific environmental conditions concomitant with low- or high-income living.[11]

Because the impact of the physical environment upon the intellectual development of the children of the poor is so inadequately explored and understood, a widespread belief has been generated that views the great majority of children from low-income backgrounds as being less well suited to academic success than their peers from economically advantaged homes. This overriding belief governs most school practices, including bilingual programs. We propose an alternative strategy.

The educational needs of poor children are manifold. In some communities where native-language-dominant or bilingual children live, parents and others have chosen to support bilingual education as one means to ensure the survival of their culture and language, and as a more effective way of imparting knowledge to their children. In these communities, it is likely that bilingual instruction will benefit the children. However, an educational solution alone is not enough. In any *serious* effort aimed at minimizing differences in educational opportunities available to children from distinct communities, the improvement of conditions which support and nurture the capacity to learn is also essential. Lastly, a more careful evaluation of those children who have been damaged by causes described above is needed. These children may not benefit from large-group instruction, be it monolingual or bilingual. For them, other educational solutions are needed, including careful attention to supplementary nutrition, smaller classes, and innovative approaches to learning and teaching.

The overwhelming hope which is currently being placed upon bilingual education as an important solution for the implementation of equal educational opportunities cannot help but lead to disappointment and failure without a broader approach to learning. This approach would include the environmental and nutritional, as well as linguistic and cultural factors, which contribute to and shape the effective education of every child.

Models of Learning and Teaching in Bilingual Classrooms

In the contemporary literature on language acquisition, scholars are stressing the prevalence with which children generate their own syntactic rules based upon the input of the languages or language that they hear. Susan Ervin-Tripp's (1974) study of second-language learning in Switzerland is a good example. She describes how children, using their experiences as speakers of one language, develop powerful, heuristic strategies which they then apply to their acquisition of a second language. It is possible, in this context, that the immersion programs of St. Lambert in Canada have been effective, in part, because they provide Anglo-Canadian children learning French with a learning setting which is conducive to the development of such strategies.

However, the great majority of instructional programs for children attending bilingual schools in the United States consist of structured lessons in the national language and, in some instances, pattern-drill rehearsal and practice in the native language. This approach to bilingual education presents a paradox. The long-range goal of such efforts is to create, in a substantial percentage of the American people, the ability to speak, read, and write in two languages with ease and confidence. In addition, bilingualism may offer these individuals certain intellectual advantages; some psychological studies have shown that bilinguals have a greater flexibility of thought and a more differentiated sense of meaning and expression than monolinguals. However, these gains may very well be vitiated by the approaches which are now being used to move toward these goals; i.e., the methods of implementation may seriously interfere with the objectives of bilingual education.

An interpretation of this situation which seems reasonable to us is that the popularity of instructional methods contrary to those favored by most linguists and psycholinguists as being supportive of the process of language acquisition is an expression of a pervasive fear among those who work with non-English-speaking pupils. They find it necessary to prove by daily practice that the role of the national language (English) is and should be central to the educational experiences of these children. Their concern, we think, is then translated into a heavily emphasized method of structured instruction with lesson plans and extensive curriculum materials, all aimed at the proficient acquisition of English. This method is followed in spite of the fact that the very ways in which the language is being taught to low-income, non-English-speaking children contradict methods which have been found to be most effective in other countries and in middle-class communities.

In this regard, it is interesting to note that Susan Ervin-Tripp (1974) found that children between four and nine, the age period in which most bilingual programs are currently operating, learn a second language at different rates. The older children utilize more powerful strategies for the acquisition of a second language. In light of these results, the practice of introducing English to non-English-dominant children at the very beginning of their school careers may not be the most effective educational strategy. In fact, the prevalent educational practice of exposing younger children to prolonged instruction in English has often resulted in the children's failure to develop total competence in either their native language or English. The possible consequence of such a policy is that children fail to develop, in either their native or national language, the full range of language functions as described by Halliday (1974). John, Horner, and Berney's (1970) study on story retelling among Indian children illustrates the effects of "premature bilingualism" in this regard.

Educators working with children in a bilingual program seem to be struggling with a number of conflicts concerning the timing and focus upon English in the classroom. However, their approach to education may also have been influenced by the large literature on low-income children, in which it has been argued that children from poor communities lack skills in abstraction and therefore need to be taught by rote and drill methods. This type of approach has been implicit in the Distar program. It also forms the basis of the recommendations made by Jensen (1969). Jensen describes two types of intelligence and argues that it would be a disservice to Black children to teach them by principles of discovery and rule production, when their type of intelligence would benefit more by methods of associational learning.

A frequent comparison has been made between the acquisition of French by native speakers of English in Canada (as documented by Lambert and Tucker) and the acquisition of English by non-English-speaking poor children in the United States. It has been suggested that the greater ease with which the former group of children acquired competency in French as compared with the difficulties which many non-English-speaking poor children experience in acquiring skills in English in this country may be attributed to attitudinal factors. These authors concur. For example, the low status of Spanish in Texas or Papago in Arizona is undoubtedly a significant factor in forming children's attitudes toward their native language and in creating feelings about themselves as learners of languages other than their mother tongue.[12] However, this may be but part of the explanation.

An additional and related factor is the role of native and ethnic languages in the United States, outside the schools. Fishman, in Chapter III, suggests that "the more a language of instruction is ... dependent on the school (as a setting for acquisition) and lacks counterparts outside of the school, the less it is rated successful in achieving its goal (of developing competencies in that language among learners)." Most of the 24 languages currently used in bilingual classrooms have been maintained in the context of family interactions and in the midst of severe and continuous opposition to their survival on the part of the majority of this society. As a result, these languages were not, and are not today, part of the reality of all domains of living for children born into these speech communities. For example, these children rarely hear their native language on the radio or TV, nor do they see it printed in commercial publications. City children who are speakers of Portuguese, French, or Yiddish seldom see their languages used on billboards or street markings.

The above are but a few illustrations which indicate that support for language development for speakers of non-English tongues in America is very limited outside the school environment. This fact must influence the full development of these children's native language and their willingness and active participation in acquiring the national language. In this regard, the opportunities available to low-income, non-English-speaking children are more limited than those open to Canadian children or to middle-class American children living abroad.

Thus studies of language acquisition seem to support the proposition that the full, and hitherto impossible, development of native languages is necessary for the effective intellectual growth of coordinate or fluent bilinguals. It is our contention, then, that only if pluralism is practiced and adequate resources are made available to meet this goal will the individual child, born into a non-English-speaking community, be able to effectuate his/her potential for acquiring two languages.

In summary, some of the important issues related to the learning-teaching process in bilingual classrooms are as follows: (1) the choice of an effective model for learning, particularly in the acquisition of a second language; (2) the social parameters relied upon to develop native and second languages, i.e., school-only or a variety of interpersonal and societal settings; and (3) the mastery of English, its timing and importance, in the context of acquiring full competence in two languages, in their spoken and written forms.

The Cultural Dimensions of Bilingual Classrooms

As yet, relatively little progress has been made in developing bilingual programs effectively rooted in the cultures and the communities of the children they serve. To some extent, the duplication of an existing educational model which is based on mainstream society with a new bilingual format is unavoidable. The lack of large numbers of trained personnel and the lack of materials for native-language instruction are still serious handicaps for the development of bilingual programs.

In addition, the difficulty that adults in general, and teachers and parents in particular, have in creating methods of teaching and socializing different from those by which they were taught and socialized as children also contributes to a resistance to innovation in education. This conflict between the needs of generations now in the schools and the methods of teaching and socializing to which they are exposed has been documented over the past two decades by a large literature on alternative education and educational criticism. However, most of these works are based upon the educational needs of middle-class children and educational alternatives developed for them (Kozol 1972). A parallel literature dealing with effective, culturally rooted educational planning for the low-income child is still in the process of being formulated.

One significant aspect of the education of culturally distinct children is the role of educational personnel drawn from non-English-speaking poor communities. Since the inception of Headstart, aides have been recruited from poor communities to participate in the classrooms of their children and their neighbors' children. But their role, in most instances,[13] has been limited to offering physical services to the children; disciplining them in their native language; and occasionally providing individual instruction to a child who may be slower in acquiring the subject matter than are his/her peers. Seldom have the educational personnel drawn from these communities been equal participants with certified teachers in the development of new curriculum or in the development of culturally based learning experiences in music, art, or oral history. These fields of instruction are known only to the members of a particular community and are absolutely essential if a bilingual experience for children is to be a bicultural one as well.

The point is made in a recent issue of *The Rican, Journal of Contemporary Puerto Rican Thought*, which is devoted to education. It argues that bilingual programs have to go beyond the language aspect "and recognize that inherent in such programs is a true concern for culture. As such the type of teachers, materials and expected results will be different than if the cultural aspects were ignored. We do not want Puerto Ricans to assimilate into Anglo America. We certainly do not want Spanish to be the tool which accelerates the process of assimilation. Bilingual programs which are good for Puerto Ricans are those which keep us Puerto Ricans, which teach us to be happy with ourselves, keep us healthy and make it possible for us to survive in a hostile environment. Bilingual programs must also play a crucial role in helping to make the United States safe for diversity."[14]

A bilingual and bicultural program can be successful only if it has the full and energetic participation in the leadership of educational personnel drawn from the community which the program serves. This is of importance not only in the development of culturally relevant curriculum but also in questions concerning language policy. In the early stages of bilingual education, many teachers were recruited from Central and South America, and from Spain, to teach in Spanish in these classrooms. These early recruitment efforts have created friction in two ways. First, job opportunities sorely needed by members of poor, non-English-speaking communities were taken over by those brought from abroad. An alternative strategy would have been to train Chicanos, Puerto Ricans, Asian Americans, and American Indians to become bilingual teachers, concurrent with the development of these programs, thus avoiding the tensions created by importing educators from abroad.

Second, reliance upon Spanish-speaking teachers from abroad has raised the issue of local dialects vs. world Spanish. The recognition of the importance of mother-tongue instruction and instruction in the vernacular is based on the concept that children should first learn in the language of their homes and then at a later age, through developing competencies in reading and writing, they will acquire "world Spanish." But, if educational personnel are not recruited from a child's home community, then (s)he initially learns in a dialect other than his/her own. In this context, it is important to note that a child's self-confidence can be impaired not only when (s)he is told not to speak Spanish in school but also if the teachers convey to him/her that his/her particular vernacular is inferior or unacceptable. In each instance, a serious loss of self-esteem ensues.

Some efforts are currently underway in teacher-training institutions to remedy the situation described above. For example, the Navajo Office of Education, in collaboration with a number of Southwestern universities, is implementing a plan to train 1000 Navajo teachers in the near future, who would serve those classrooms which include primarily Navajo children. Such a massive effort requires modifications of traditional teacher-training practices; it relies heavily upon on-site education, and the accrediting of teaching experience on the part of aides and other classroom personnel. These kinds of innovative, teacher-training programs are becoming more prevalent. But they are being resisted by teachers who are not members of national-origin ethnic communities, because the success of such programs would have a serious effect upon the ethnic composition of teaching staffs. It is unlikely that many native speakers of English will become fluent bilinguals and thus be able to compete effectively with those who, by experience and upbringing, have all the preparation to provide critical resources to bilingual classrooms. Thus the issue of who shall be hired to teach is a current area of controversy in bilingual education.

One of the least explored parameters of culture relevant to bilingual education is the pace or rhythm with which a culturally and linguistically distinct people communicate with each other, and the need to develop corresponding instructional settings. The creation of such instructional environments would necessitate a profound study of the communities into which bilingual classrooms are placed, and a greater participation by bilingual individuals raised in those communities, who could determine the most meaningful context of learning, either classroom- or community-based.

The most eloquent spokespeople of bilingual communities have consistently argued that for each of the culturally relevant areas discussed above (curriculum, teaching and learning methods, teaching personnel, and instructional settings), it is important to have a community board which has major responsibility for deciding educational policy and evaluating ongoing bilingual programs. In the context of creating bilingual programs which are based on a pluralistic rather than a transitional model, a community board is one means by which a linguistically and culturally distinct, low-income community can ensure that its cultural, linguistic, and survival needs will be met through the education of its children.

The Role of Evaluation in Bilingual Education

The literature on the evaluation of bilingual programs suffers from most of the problems confronting educational research in general. Evaluative approaches to these programs consist of simple, unidimensional tests, which focus on a *product* of educational intervention, with little consistent regard for the learning processes. Thus partisans of one or another model of intervention can usually find some research documentation which supports their particular bias, out of a welter of often contradictory sets of findings.

Nevertheless, funded projects require that some effort at evaluation be included in the plans for innovative educational programs; and therefore, those charged with the introduction of bilingual education into public schools usually have no recourse but to include some evaluative aspect.

The time frame in which most of these efforts are carried out may result in misconceptions about the effectiveness of bilingual education. Because programs are frequently funded on a year-to-year basis, evaluation takes place during the early stages of a program's development and among children who themselves may be at a period of their own intellectual growth during which the potential gains of a bilingual program could not yet be demonstrated. In fact, the evaluation results obtained by the Sustained Primary Program for Bilingual Students in the Las Cruces, New Mexico, Public School System illustrate a distinctive performance curve among elementary students in bilingual classrooms.

The program in Las Cruces is well established; it was initiated in 1967 and was described by John and Horner (1971) as having the following characteristics: a pre- and in-service teacher-training program developed in cooperation with New Mexico State University and supervised by an imaginative and committed coordinator who knew how to utilize all possible resources available for this program. Enrollment, as in many other programs, is voluntary; parents can choose to enroll their children in English-only or bilingual classrooms in the same school. But perhaps the most critical feature of the program is that it ranges from kindergarten to sixth grade. These program characteristics distinguish this as one of the strongest Title VII programs initiated in the early days of bilingual education.

Some of the findings of the last published Las Cruces evaluation, carried out by Professor Douglas Muller from New Mexico State University, show that in the area of academic subjects, such as reading, language, and arithmetic, children in second and third grades who have been instructed in English progress better than bilingual children. However, by the sixth grade, bilingual children overtake those instructed in English only; children educated in bilingual classrooms do better in the academic disciplines, as measured by the California Achievement Test, *including their proficiency in the English language.* [15] The bilingually instructed children also maintain a consistent and impressive superiority in performance in Spanish throughout the elementary grades.

The conclusions of this study lend support to the position of those who are committed to major bilingual efforts, including that of the authors. However, many factors have contributed in the Las Cruces setting to create a situation in which children's gains could be effectively measured by standardized tests. Similar findings may not emerge in the absence of one or more of the particularly supportive conditions present in those programs. The significance of this evaluation lies in the warning that it offers against short-term evaluative efforts. These results, in conjunction with recent reports in the psycholinguistic literature, illustrate the lack of a straight-line development in children who are acquiring two languages (Lavallee 1973).

There have been few major efforts at evaluation of Title VII programs. This is no accident, as even those researchers who are deeply committed to an evaluation design find themselves in a situation where it is difficult to make comparisons between different classrooms in the same school, not to mention the difficulties inherent in comparing programs in more varied settings, as, for example, between two cities.

The methodological problems which confront the researcher in this field are summarized by Engle (1973). She states, "The difficulty of separating the effects of the language of initial reading, the language of instruction, the ethnicity of the teacher, and the political sociolinguistic settings of the experiments is evidenced by the fact that few have been successful in isolating any of the factors." She also points out that evaluation studies "differ tremendously in the length of time they allow children before final assessment. There is a serious lack of longitudinal evaluations covering more than a one or two year time span."

In addition to evaluation by means of standardized tests, observational methods are used at times by independent evaluators. These observers have frequently reported little correspondence between program objectives stated on paper and the changing realities of bilingual classrooms. A process-oriented evaluation is costly; it is considered "unscientific" by many. But, without it, it is difficult to discover whether an absence of gains in the performance of students in bilingual classrooms is the failure of bilingual education or the failure of the genuine implementation of bilingual education on the part of a particular program.[16]

The continued existence of bilingual programs may indeed be precarious if based solely upon federal funding and viewed from the narrow perspective of short-term evaluations. While these are very real problems confronting those committed to bilingual education, we have tried to point out some other contemporary developments. Among these is the increasing support for multicultural education from state and local governments, as well as from universities. Though some of these agencies limit their conception of bilingual education to a transitional model, there have also been some recent court decisions which have suggested a comprehensive and pluralistic approach to bilingual education.

The enactment of Title VII legislation which authorized the spending of federal funds for bilingual programs was significantly dependent upon the political activities generated by bilingual communities. Today, the question of whether these programs will become a stable and well-integrated part of the education of all children in states with a multilingual and multicultural heritage is even more dependent upon community-parental support and support from the academic community. The distant promise of a fully developed, pluralistic education contains the possibility of educational equality for all children without the loss of individual or cultural diversity and allows us to begin the exploration of human learning and growth whose dimensions are still unknown to us.

NOTES

1. These statistics are quite widely available. The most recent summary of them appears in Casso (1973).

2. Bilingual programs are those "in which two languages are used as media of instruction" (Mackey 1968).

3. Recent analyses of bilingual programs have shown that the majority of funded programs are transitional in nature. Some state legislatures have explicitly directed their public schools to adopt a transitional model (Massare 1973).

4. Legislation during the Eisenhower administration planned the termination of federal responsibility for eleven Indian tribes. This policy succeeded in two communities, the Clameth of Oregon and the Menominee of Wisconsin (Orfield 1970).

5. A contact school is one in which the school enters into a contractual relationship with the Bureau of Indian Affairs, Division of Education, whereby the BIA gives the school a lump-sum grant and then the school board and the principal make all decisions regarding hiring and firing, purchases, and curriculum.

6. *Guide to Title VII ESEA Bilingual Bicultural Projects in the United States, 1972-1973.* Austin, Tex.: Dissemination Center for Bilingual Bicultural Education.

7. Although the New Mexico State Constitution requires bilingual instruction in the public schools, this policy has never been enforced.

8. "The Relationship of Nutrition to Brain Development and Behavior." Prepared by the Subcommittee on Nutrition, Brain Development, and Behavior of the Committee on International Nutrition Programs. National Academy of Sciences, National Research Council. Washington, D.C. June 1973, p. 8.

9. The kind of brain damage we refer to is based on the research summarized by Birch and Gussow (1970). They found that inadequate nourishment may interfere with the full development of a neurophysiological base necessary for the normal growth of visual, auditory, and intellectual processes. This should not be confused with recent claims by some psychologists that poor and minority peoples are suffering from emotional "limbic brain disease" and their subsequent recommendations of psychosurgery as a remedy.

10. A recent analysis of Jensen's research methods and the political context of his work may be found in Gould (1974).

11. We refer to the Smilansky study to negate the genetic conclusions offered by researchers such as Jensen, Shockley, and Ginsburg. However, it should be clear from our discussion of pluralism that we are not suggesting a monocultural setting for all children. Rather, we are arguing that if each culturally distinct community has the available resources through which they can create a situation where education and individual development are of the highest priority, full emotional, physical, and intellectual growth will be a natural consequence.

12. Cruz Reynoso, School of Law, University of New Mexico, has communicated to us his observation that Mexican students entering American schools late in elementary school do better than indigenous Chicano students of the same age group, in spite of the fact that in each case the students' native language is Spanish. This, he believes, can be attributed to differing attitudes toward the native language and toward the children as learners.

13. An important exception to the limited role which aides have in most bilingual classrooms is the situation of aides in the Rio Grande Pueblos' classrooms. There aides have provided the necessary continuity and stability in schools where Anglo teachers come and go.

14. Editorial, *The Rican, Journal of Contemporary Puerto Rican Thought.* pp. 3-4.

15. "Evaluation of the Fifth Year (1972-1973) of the Sustained Primary Program for Bilingual Students in the Las Cruces, New Mexico Public School System." Title VII ESEA, Project 97-00232-0, Grant 410232. Professor Douglas G. Muller, Project Evaluator. New Mexico State University.

16. Personal communication from Mrs. Lucy Gutierrez, doctoral candidate in elementary education and Title VII evaluator, University of New Mexico.

VIII

Philosophical Perspectives on Bilingual Education

Theodore Andersson

DEFINITIONS

Each of the two topics which comprise our subject, philosophy and bilingual education, needs to be defined and circumscribed if we are to stay within reasonable limits.

Philosophy—Greek *philos*, loving + *sophia*, skill, knowledge, intelligence, wisdom—the synthesis of all learning, focuses attention on the human being as a conscious, thinking, feeling, acting, learning creature. We are particularly interested in the individual as a learner and shall concern ourselves primarily with the child, in whom we envision not only the already somewhat independent personality with certain rights and opportunities but also the potentially mature, fully developed man or woman who may in turn be viewed both as an individual and as a member of a family and of a variety of larger groups.

In seeking to develop philosophical perspectives on bilingual education we shall avoid the abstractions of philosophical specialists but shall rather let ourselves be guided by such non-technical definitions as the following: "the general principles or laws of a field of knowledge, activity, etc." (Webster); "a basic theory; a viewpoint" (The American Heritage Dictionary); "the critical study of the basic principles or concepts of a particular branch of knowledge, especially with a view to improving or reconstituting them" (Random House

Dictionary); and "the system of values by which one lives" (The American Heritage Dictionary).

Bilingual education does not lend itself easily to definition. As William F. Mackey points out (1972, 150-151), "Schools in the United Kingdom where half the subjects are taught in English are called bilingual schools. Schools in Canada in which all subjects are taught in English to French Canadian children are called bilingual schools. Schools in the Soviet Union in which all subjects except Russian are taught in English are bilingual schools, as are schools in which some of the subjects are taught in Georgian and the rest in Russian. Schools in the United States where English is taught as a second language are called bilingual schools, as are parochial schools and even weekend ethnic schools." As first Director of the International Center for Research on Bilingualism in Quebec, Mackey could observe the great variety of meanings evoked by the term "bilingual education." More definitions, he concluded, would only add to the confusion. "What is needed, therefore," he contended, "is not another definition of bilingual schooling or bilingual education but a classification of the field to account for all possible types—in other words, a typology." Mackey has elaborated such a typology, which he discusses in Chapter IX. We shall therefore leave to him the elaboration of the concepts of bilingualism and bilingual education.

Without pursuing the matter of definition, which Einar Haugen (1973) also surveys, let us adopt as a working definition of *bilingualism* and *a bilingual* "knowledge of two languages" and "one who has such knowledge." Such a definition obviously ranges all the way from mere (oral and reading) understanding of one of two known languages to equal mastery of two or more languages in all domains (equilingualism). In this we agree with Macnamara (1967b, 59-60).

We have seen that the apparently straightforward concept of bilingual education or bilingual schooling is susceptible of varied interpretation. However, there is in the United States—at least in official circles—an accepted working definition. This definition first appeared (see Andersson and Boyer 1970, vol. 2, appendix B) in the Draft Guidelines to the Bilingual Education Program under Title VII, Elementary and Secondary Education Act of 1965, as Amended in 1967 (P.L. 90-247). It reads as follows:

"Bilingual education is instruction in two languages and the use of those *two languages* as mediums of instruction for any part of or all of the school curriculum. Study of the history and culture associated with a student's mother tongue is considered an integral part of bilingual education." In revised Guidelines for Bilingual Education adopted by the Texas Education Agency and approved by the Texas State Board of Education (1974, 21) appears the following definition:

"Bilingual education is an authorized instructional program encompassing the total education process in which two languages (English and another language) shall be used for a portion of, or all of the curriculum. Bilingual instruction may be provided throughout all the grade levels in accordance with statutory provisions and the current Statewide Design for Bilingual Education."

Schooling Versus Education

In current usage *bilingual education* and *bilingual schooling* are usually synonymous and interchangeable, but *bilingual education* is sometimes understood to include bilingual instruction in school (bilingual schooling) as well as out-of-school bilingual learning, e.g., children from two language groups playing together or children watching a bilingual television program, such as Carrascolendas or Villa Alegre.

Transition Versus Maintenance

Does, and should, a given bilingual program aim to maintain the active use, and even cultivation, of a non-English language (x-language) in our society; or should it use the x-language as a teaching medium only to facilitate the x-speaker's learning of English and be abandoned as soon as he can carry his full burden of learning in English? This is a fundamental question, left unresolved in the Bilingual Education Act, which speaks only of meeting "the special educational needs of children of limited English-speaking ability. . . ." (Andersson and Boyer 1970, II, 2). It is touched on lightly in the *Draft Manual for Project Applicants and Grantees,* dated Mar. 20, 1970 (U.S. Government Printing Office, No. 51-877), which states that "Bilingual education is the use of two languages, one of which is English, as mediums of instruction for the same pupil population in a well-organized program which encompasses part or all of the curriculum and includes the study of the history and culture associated with the mother tongue. A complete program develops *and maintains* [our emphasis] the children's self-esteem and a legitimate pride in both cultures." This wording is far from being explicit; so we must conclude that bilingual program planners working under federal legislation are free to design either transitional or maintenance programs.

What about state legislation? "A recent survey shows that 11 states now have legislation dealing with bilingual-bicultural education" (Mazzone 1973; Geffert et al. 1975). In general, state legislation prescribes transitional bilingual education. The Massachusetts law includes the word "transitional" in its title. The Texas law, S.B. No. 121, provides for the establishment for "children whose native tongue is another language" of "a compensatory program of bilingual education [which] can meet the needs of these children and facilitate their integration into the regular school curriculum." Section 21.455 specifies that "Every school-age child of limited English-speaking ability residing within a school district required to provide a bilingual program for his classification shall be enrolled in the program for a period of three years or until he achieves a level of English language proficiency which will enable him to perform successfully in classes in which instruction is given only in English, whichever first occurs." "Why," asks Mazzone in his paper, "did the bilingual movement in Massachusetts opt for a transitional program? It is because maintenance schemes were unattainable." The same political constraint was and is felt in Texas.

It is clear from the foregoing that neither the United States Congress nor the state legislatures are politically ready to endorse maintenance programs. The closest approach to such an ideal has perhaps been made in Texas. Here Spanish, the most vital of the many non-English languages, is being constantly renewed and reinvigorated through direct contact with Mexico. A Mexican-American has been appointed Associate Commissioner of Education for Educational Programs for Special Populations in charge of well-staffed Offices of Bilingual and Migrant Education in the Texas Education Agency. A Statewide Design for Bilingual Education approved by the State Board of Education states that, "The primary goal of Bilingual Education is successful achievement by the student of the goals of the educational process, using two languages, developing proficiency in both, but acknowledging English as the basic language of instruction in all schools and assuring its mastery by all pupils in the schools." This basic document then delineates Complementary Goals, Coordinate Goals, Priorities, and Components of Bilingual Education. [1]

It now remains to examine the philosophy and practice of local school districts. Though the Bilingual Education Act was signed into law by President Lyndon B. Johnson on Jan. 2, 1968, it was not funded until Fiscal Year 1970. This first year 76 programs were launched, out of 315 proposals received. "Of the 76 programs, 68 involved Spanish, 58 of these programs benefiting Mexican-Americans, 7 Puerto Ricans, 2 Puerto Ricans and other language group, 2 mixed Spanish-speaking groups, one Spanish and Sioux, one Spanish and Pomo, one Spanish and Keresan and Navajo, and one Spanish and Chinese. There were 2 programs in Portuguese, 2 in Cherokee, and one in Chinese (Cantonese, plus the one noted above)" (Andersson 1971, 433).

Rolf Kjolseth (1970), a sociologist at the University of Colorado, analyzed some of these programs, identifying them with one of two typical models: "One, the Assimilation model, embodies an optimal selection of those program characteristics which tend to promote ethnic language shift. The other, the Pluralist model, comprises an optimal structure for promoting ethnic language maintenance." He found that "most bilingual education programs—quite contrary to the usual statements of program goals—highly approximate the Assimilation model. This means that the structure of 'typical' existing programs . . . can be expected to foster the accelerated demise of the ethnic mother tongue."

The most comprehensive evaluation of the first federally funded programs is that of Bruce Gaarder (1970). From a critical study of their plans of operation and of returns from a questionnaire sent to the project directors, Gaarder concludes that "in the large majority of these programs there is such inadequate attention—time, resources, and understanding—to the other tongue, as compared to the attention paid to English that, on the whole, the concept of bilingual education represented by these plans of operation seems to be something less than the legislation and its advocates intended." One weakness that Gaarder discovered from reading the plans of operation was that most of the teachers were not prepared for bilingual schooling, that "to a large extent the projects expect to depend on the teaching services of aides, sometimes called paraprofessionals, 'bilingual' individuals usually drawn from the community, rarely required to be literate in the non-English tongue, and paid disproportionately low wages." Gaarder observes pointedly that "the merely bilingual person is the product of the very kind of schooling which bilingual education aims to correct." Neither teachers nor aides are prepared for the kind of teaching expected: "They are expected to teach through the non-English tongue such subject fields as mathematics, science, the social studies, and language arts. There is a common belief that the person who speaks two languages can say anything in one that he can say in the other. That is simply not true. The most common situation finds such a speaker facile in one or more 'domains' of usage in one language, and in other domains in the other." Gaarder notes still another difficulty: "Teachers are expected to represent and present authentically, fully, fairly, two cultures: that of the United States and that of the non-English mother tongue child's forbears. In most cases they must somehow interpret a third culture, the amalgam, because the Puerto Ricans in continental United States, and Mexican-Americans, and Franco-Americans find that their cultural patterns are in essential ways different from either of the two parent cultures."

A third evaluation of current bilingual programs has been provided by Joshua Fishman and his collaborator John Lovas (1970), who have concluded that "bilingual education in the United States currently suffers from three serious lacks: a lack of funds (Title VII [of the Elementary and Secondary Education Act-Bilingual Education Act] is pitifully starved), a lack of personnel (there are almost no optimally trained personnel in this field), and a lack of evaluative programs (curricula, material, methods)." In considering bilingual projects in this country as a whole, Fishman, though conscious of Mackey's comprehensive typology, adopts a four-part typology of his own which he considers adequate to reflect the present situation: Type I, Transitional Bilingualism, is one in which the non-English language "is used in the early grades only to the extent necessary to permit children to 'adjust to school' and/or to master subject matter, until their skill in English is developed to the point that it can be used as the medium of instruction." Type II, Monoliterate Bilingualism, admits of "goals of development in both languages for aural-oral skills, but does not concern itself with literacy skills in the mother tongue." Type III, Partial Bilingualism, "seeks fluency and literacy in both languages, but literacy in the mother tongue is restricted to certain subject matter, most generally that related to the ethnic group and its cultural heritage." Type IV, Full Bilingualism, is the kind of program in which "students are to develop all skills in both languages in all domains. Typically, both languages are used as media of instruction for all subjects (except in teaching the languages themselves). Clearly this program is directed at language maintenance and development of the minority language." Fishman numbers himself "among those who value the maintenance and development of cultural and linguistic diversity in the United States." Like Kjolseth and Gaarder, he doubts that "most of the existing and proposed bilingual education programs have [this] as their goal."

We may conclude this section on transition versus maintenance with the observation that the maintenance programs envisioned by such educational leaders as Fishman, Gaarder, and Kjolseth will not be easily achieved. Many, perhaps most, communities are far from being convinced of the desirability of linguistic and cultural pluralism. Even those communities which do enthusiastically espouse the pluralistic ideal find themselves handicapped by a lack of adequately prepared personnel, a shortage of suitable materials, and insufficient sophistication in establishing these new educational patterns.

Having attempted to explain what bilingual education is and how variously it is viewed, let us now try to provide a rationale for it. Why should educators consider adopting this relatively new educational design—or one of the many possible designs—and why should parents and other taxpayers support bilingual schooling? In short, what are the values of bilingual education?

THE VALUES OF BILINGUAL EDUCATION

In writing this section we rely heavily on the following sources. The master work in this field is the encyclopedic *Language Loyalty in the United States*, by Joshua Fishman et al. (1966). Useful too are the brilliant report, "The Challenge of Bilingualism," by A. Bruce Gaarder et al. (1965); "A Prepared Statement," presented by Gaarder (1967b) to Senator Ralph Yarborough's Subcommittee on Labor and Public Welfare at a hearing on Bilingual Education; an excellent chapter on "Bilingualism," also by Gaarder (1969); and "A Rationale for Bilingual Schooling," Chapter IV, in Andersson and Boyer (1970).

Bilingual education is of course valued differently from country to country and indeed from community to community. We shall deal primarily with the United States but without focusing on individual states or communities.

Is Bilingualism Desirable or Undesirable for the Nation?

This is a fundamental question of values related to a particular time and set of circumstances in a specific nation.

William A. Stewart (1962, 15; 1968, 532) describes two fundamentally different policies:

1. The eventual elimination, by education and decree, of all but one language, which remains to serve for both official and general purposes.

2. The recognition and preservation of important languages within the national scene, supplemented by universal use of one or more languages to serve for official purposes and for communication across language boundaries.

In today's world as in the past the first of these policies is the more common. An historical example is the conquest of Southern France by Simon de Montfort in the thirteenth century, the suppression of the *langue d'oc* and of Provençal literature, and the consequent unification of France under one language, the *langue d'oïl*. The non-recognition of minority languages (Basque, Breton, Provençal) continues in France today, as it does in Spain (e.g., Basque, Catalan, and Galician), in Sri Lanka (Tamil), and in many other countries.

Stewart's second policy of societal bilingualism is exemplified by Canada with its two official languages, English and French; Finland, where both Finnish and Swedish are official; Paraguay, where a majority of the population uses Guaraní informally and Spanish formally—a linguistic phenomenon called *diglossia* (Ferguson 1959, Kloss 1966, Gaarder 1969); Switzerland with its four official languages, French, German, Italian, and Romansch in addition to the informal Swiss German; and the Republic of South Africa, where both Afrikaans and English are official but the indigenous black languages are unrecognized.

How to reconcile national unity, usually identified with unilingualism, with diversity, in the form of linguistic and cultural pluralism, is the philosophical problem. Ideally, both are desirable, and in some nations (e.g., Finland, Paraguay, Switzerland) they seem to be successfully realized. In other cases, as in Belgium, each language group, the Dutch-speaking Flemings and the French-speaking Walloons, feels such deep-seated antagonism toward the other that the ideal of national unity seems beyond reach. Nothing short of a mutual all-out declaration—of friendship—seems to give any hope of success.

> For the United States of America in this latter half of the twentieth century the question of desirability [of multilingualism] for the nation seems almost rhetorical. America's relations, official and unofficial, with almost every country in the world, involving diplomacy, trade, security, technical assistance, health, education, religion, and the arts, are steadily increasing. The success of these international relations often depends on the bilingual skills and cultural sensitiveness of American representatives both here and abroad. In our country, as in every important nation, educated bilingualism is an accepted mark of the elite, a key which opens doors of opportunity far and wide. [Andersson and Boyer 1970, I, 41]

Fishman et al (1966) estimates that in 1960 there were over nineteen million native speakers of languages other than English in the United States, and there is no reason to believe that the situation has changed significantly since then. "The languages most widely spoken are Spanish, Italian, German, Polish, French, and Yiddish, but there are substantial numbers of speakers of thirty or more tongues, including Portuguese, not to mention at least forty-five American Indian languages with over 1000 speakers" (Gaarder 1969, 168). Large enclaves, especially when reinforced by immigration, "can be remarkably language-tenacious" (Gaarder 1969, 166).

> The study of Fishman et al. [1966] of demographic data across three genera-tions shows four categories of numerical gain or loss and prospects for the future:

a. Sharp losses: Norwegian, Swedish, Czech, Slovak, Slovenian, Finnish, German, Danish, and Yiddish. Unusually large immigration and revitalization movements would seem required to stem further decline.

b. Moderate losses: French, Lithuanian, Rumanian, Polish, Hungarian, Russian, and Portuguese. Continued sizable immigration and/or language maintenance movements are needed if these are not to fall into the sharp-loss category.

c. Moderate gains: Dutch, Italian, Arabic, and Serbo-Croatian.

d. Sharp gains: Greek, Ukrainian, and Spanish.

All in all, the above languages lost approximately one sixth of their claimants between 1940 and 1960 [Gaarder 1969].

Is it a sentimental illusion [Gaarder asks (1969, 166)] that it would be in our national interest, and in the interest of every child concerned, for the United States, still culturally and linguistically pluralistic, to set the world an overt, acknowledged example of peoples living in full harmony together?

Of the many "foreign" languages spoken natively in the United States Spanish is by all odds the most vital, thanks to the continuing migration from Mexico, Puerto Rico, Cuba, Central and South America, and other Spanish-speaking countries. According to a recent Census Bureau survey, "the Spanish speaking numbered 10.6 million in March 1973, compared with 9.2 million the year before. . . . Included in the Census Bureau's latest estimate were 6.3 million persons of Mexican origin, 1.5 million of Puerto Rican origin, 700,000 of Cuban origin, and 2 million of Central or South American or other Spanish" (Cabinet Committee 1973). Gaarder's analysis (1969, 166-169) of the Mexican American case from the point of view of language maintenance is worth quoting:

The Spanish-surnamed in five states, Texas, New Mexico, Colorado, Arizona, and California, number over five million. Among them for over 400 years several factors have always strongly favored wide retention and dominance of the Spanish language for most intra-group (as opposed to inter-group) purposes. The chief factors are five: (1) proximity to Mexico and ethnic identity with the Mexican people; (2) the oral—as opposed to literate—orientation with the bulk of the people, immigrants from Mexico, and the resulting paucity of newspapers, magazines, books in Spanish; (3) the extreme scarcity of intellectuals among the immigrants; (4) marked social cleavage among the people themselves; and (5) the traditional discrimination by Anglo-Americans against any visible minority in respect to educational policy (thus limiting education and upward mobility) and in respect to social commingling (thus favoring isolation and linguistic solidarity). The first factor, which can always be expected to favor the retention of Spanish, is far less potent than it might be. The remaining ones have combined to leave Spanish today peculiarly exposed to an accelerated shift to and replacement by English.

The mid-20th-century movement in the United States toward egalitarianism finds Mexican Americans with an intelligentsia—developed through English, oriented toward the dominant English community, and increasingly vocal in English—demanding and likely to achieve an end to the discriminatory practices. That intelligentsia speaks Spanish too and is demanding a place and a role for Spanish, but no one has suggested what the place and role are to be. The answer—for the Mexican Americans and any other enclave of Americans who continue to speak a tongue other than English—seems to lie in the concept of diglossia. Instead of the prevailing confusion of views which find the two languages competing with each other for the speaker's loyalty and thus forcing his decision to choose between them, diglossia offers a pattern for coexistence of the two languages within the bilingual individual, for intra-group purposes and without competition.

There has always been diglossia of a sort in the Southwest. The difference between what has been and what must be if Spanish is to survive and flourish is a subtle but all-important one. Although in the past, as now, Spanish has always been used for some things and English for others in fixed and predictable ways, both the past and the current view has always been that English will inevitably replace Spanish. Each person must choose, they say, and education forces the choice of English. At best it has been either/or: either remain isolated and continue to speak Spanish, or cut all ties and anglicize. The key to diglossia, to stable co-existence of languages, [is] the socially recognized and approved (hence supported) use of the two tongues for compartmentalized, complementary (not competing) functions. The assignment of functions to each language can be made only by the speakers themselves. However, the fact that such assignments are usually reached by a social process outside of the speakers' awareness does not preclude conscious sociolinguistic planning. Nor does complementarity preclude a high degree of literacy in both tongues. As we have seen above, full exploitation of Spanish for technical and professional purposes demands such literacy.

Along with literacy in Spanish—achieved through bilingual schooling in a social context of diglossia—would come an unexpected revelation and reward: a realization of the excellence of the Spanish spoken in the Southwest. There are exceptions, to be sure, but I maintain that millions of Americans in the Southwest speak Spanish as good as the English spoken around them, group for group at any level, and all the children are capable of it. . . .

Is language planning in the United States an impossibility? The imperatives are three: to merge the foreign-language teacher's small academia of elitist bilingualism with the national reality of nineteen million claimants of a non-English mother tongue; to strengthen that resource in each child concerned by offering bilingual education in the schools; to assure the permanence of our precious enclaves of natural folk bilingualism by gaining social recognition, approval, and support for diglossia.

We return to Stewart's two mutually exclusive propositions with which we began this section on the desirability of bilingual education for the nation. For the person who knows only his native tongue and who has associated mostly with monolinguals like himself, it is natural to regard another language as a complication, a nuisance, something "foreign." Such a person is likely to prefer Stewart's first option and may represent the *transition* end of the maintenance-transition continuum. On the other end of the continuum are the language loyalists among the nineteen million native speakers of a non-English language together with most of the social scientists who have studied the question of bilingualism (Fishman 1964, 1965a, 1965b, 1966a, 1966b, 1967, 1968; Fishman et al. 1966; Fishman and Lovas 1970; Gumperz 1962, 1964; Labov 1966; Hymes 1967a, 1967b; Gaarder 1967a, 1967b, 1969, 1970; Gaarder et al. 1965). In between there will be persons with every possible admixture of cultural experience, social conditioning, and personal conviction. Let us imagine a referendum in which every American voter casts his ballot for one of two propositions: (1) Every newly naturalized American citizen should make all reasonable efforts to learn English well and to understand and participate in the American way of life, without expending his time and energy on maintaining and cultivating his mother tongue. (2) Every newly naturalized American citizen, while making all reasonable efforts to learn English well and to understand and participate in the American way of life, should make every effort to maintain and cultivate his mother tongue. What the result would be is pure guesswork. During the period of massive immigration, from 1880 to 1915, when the melting pot theory held sway, the overwhelming majority of Americans would surely have voted for proposition one (Zangwill 1909, 1914). Over the last half century the melting pot theory has begun to be discredited (Glazer and Moynihan 1963) and cultural pluralism has gained more adherents. For example, in a recent book, *Future without Shock*, Louis B. Lundborg, Chairman of the Board of the Bank of America and himself the son of immigrants from Sweden, expresses (p. 148) his view of the melting pot: "Granting the tremendous strengths that each of these blood- and culture-streams has added to American life; and granting that each of these new Americans had an obligation to assume his role as an American and not remain forever an alien visitor here, I never had thought it was necessary for these people all to be 'melted down' into one single common-denominator alloy. I have resisted the thought that all the richness of their ancestral history must be incinerated away. I have preferred to think of them as a great mosaic in which their differences of cultural heritage add color and beauty and variety to our American scene."

Straws in the wind indicate a slight shift away from the acculturalistic point of view and toward linguistic and cultural pluralism. We are still far from realizing that the mother tongue and the cultural heritage are integral parts of the character, the personality, and the self-concept of the individual as of the ethnic group, worth conserving for the good of our nation. As forty-nine Scandinavian professors, assembled in 1962, so eloquently said, "L'extermination d'une langue, d'une culture et d'un peuple sont une seule et même chose." (The extermination of a language, of a culture, and of a people are all one and the same thing.) (Naert, Halldórsson et al. 1962, 355).

The evidence seems clear. The vision of such a thoughtful layman as Lundborg and the conclusions reached by students of bilingualism coincide. Equally clear is the need of foreign-language skills on the part of the increasing numbers of Americans who are called upon to communicate with our foreign neighbors in all parts of the world. What better source for such communicators within our country than the native speakers of the languages of the world, provided only that their education is adequate for their prospective tasks? The case for societal bilingualism or diglossia, for bilingual education, and for linguistic and cultural pluralism is overwhelming. At the same time, opposition—or at least indifference—to these desirable social, political, and educational goals is also overwhelming. Why? The simplest answer is that the majority of American citizens are simply unaware of the values of bilingualism. If this is so, the remedy would seem to be better information, better education: education which includes *skill* in the use of languages other than English, *knowledge* of the nature of language and language acquisition and of the relation of language and culture, *intelligence* in the planning of education to meet national educational needs, and *wisdom* in dealing with intellectual and emotional factors in our American way of life, specifically, cross-cultural understanding. We shall return to this subject after considering bilingualism in the individual child.

Is Bilingualism Desirable or Undesirable for the Individual Child?

The Findings of Research

The pros and cons of this vexed question have been best analyzed by Working Committee II, under the chairmanship of Bruce Gaarder, for the 1965 Northeast Conference. Under the heading *Is Bilingualism a Handicap?* the Committee (Gaarder et al. 1965, 66-67) summarized the contradictory research findings and found that "The majority of investigators conclude that bilingualism has a detrimental effect on intelligence, although others found little or no relation between bilingualism and intelligence. A few studies have actually found evidence suggesting that bilingualism may have favorable intellectual consequences."

The Committee cites the following studies against bilingualism.

Darcy (1946) compared two groups—monolingual and bilingual—matched for age, sex, and social class, among 212 American preschool children of Italian parentage. She found that "In every age and sex division, the mental ages of monoglots surpassed those of the bilinguists on the Stanford-Binet Scale, while on the Atkins Test, the performance of the bilinguists was consistently superior to that of the monoglots."

Testing American-born Jewish preschool monolingual and bilingual children of similar socioeconomic level, Levinson (1959) found that the two groups performed similarly on the Goodenough test and on most subscales of the Wechsler Intelligence Scale for Children (WISC), but on the Stanford-Binet and the WISC Arithmetic, Vocabulary, and Picture Arrangement Subtests the monolinguals scored higher.

Johnson (1953) used a new technique for measuring objectively the linguistic balance of 30 Spanish-English bilingual boys by dividing the number of words produced in English in five minutes by the number produced in Spanish and also administered a performance (Goodenough Draw a Man) and a verbal (Otis) test to the subjects. The results showed that the more bilingual the subjects were the better they did on the performance test and the poorer on the verbal test.

Spoerl (1944) compared a group of monolingual college freshmen with a matched group of bilinguals (who had learned two languages before school entrance). There was no significant difference between the two groups on the 1937 Stanford-Binet or the Purdue Placement Test, but the bilingual group revealed a slight inferiority on five of the verbal items of the Stanford-Binet scale.

Gaarder's Committee summarizes these findings in these words: "Even though most of the studies in themselves cannot be considered conclusive, a general trend does emerge from their results. In the area of verbal intelligence, the majority of the studies examined (including these as well as others) found that bilinguals did not perform as well as monolinguals on standardized tests, some studies found no difference between the two groups, and about an equal number found that the bilinguals performed significantly better than the monolinguals. On the basis of results such as these, most investigators concluded that the bilinguals suffered from a language handicap which interfered with their functioning in the verbal area. They did not state that the bilinguals were intellectually inferior, that is, that they had less intelligence, but just that they gave evidence of a language deficiency." Only a few studies have considered the effect of bilingualism on academic achievement and almost none have dealt with the question of social adjustment.

In taking up "the case for bilingualism," the Gaarder Committee points out two procedural faults in some of the earlier studies: (1) Bilinguals were actually from lower-class homes and would therefore also be intellectually deficient (W. R. Jones 1960). (2) "Most of these considered bilingual for the purposes of educational and psychological studies of the sort considered here were not equally fluent in the two languages. . . . Therefore it is not at all surprising to find that bilinguals, when called upon to manipulate ideas rapidly or form concepts in their second language, do not fare as well as native speakers of that language. . . . An analogous case [they suggest, a little sardonically] would be to decide the intellectual fate of second language teachers on the basis of their ability to make inferences or form concepts in a second language under time pressure!"

Peal and Lambert (1962) corrected this procedural error in their comparison of two matched groups of French-Canadian children, one group clearly monolingual in French and the other clearly balanced bilinguals. "The results indicated that the bilinguals were significantly *superior* to the monolinguals on both verbal and non-verbal tests. This finding suggests that, under certain circumstances, bilingualism appears to have a favorable effect on intellectual development. . . ."

Gaarder and his colleagues raise the question whether the learning of two languages in early childhood can theoretically have a different effect on intellectual development from the learning of one language. Since the development of a child's intellectual potential is believed to depend on his environmental experiences, may we not view bilingualism as an enriching experience? "The bilingual child has two ways of perceiving and two ways of responding to things in his environment; he masters two linguistic systems; he is exposed to and must learn to adjust to two different sets of cultural experiences. If these experiences are considered to be enriching in any way, they might be expected to have some effect on the bilingual's developing intelligence."

We have noted the general conclusion that unequal bilinguals, when tested in English (their second language), do less well than monolinguals on verbal tests. How well do bilinguals compare with monolinguals on other verbal tasks involved in their general academic performance? Spoerl's study (1944) reveals that the bilinguals excelled the monolinguals in school work even though their I.Q.s did not differ significantly and their performance on verbal tests was somewhat poorer. A reanalysis of the Peal and Lambert data reveals that if monolingual and bilingual subgroups are selected in such a way that the overall mean I.Q. of the two groups is equal, the bilinguals are significantly superior in school grades. "A similar finding emerges from a . . . study by Anisfeld (1964) in which two groups of subjects—one monolingual and the other bilingual—equated on I.Q., SES, sex, etc., differed significantly on school marks . . . , the bilinguals being ahead." A study by Lerea and Kohut (1961) found that "a group of bilinguals took significantly fewer trials on a verbal learning task than did a group of monolinguals matched with them for age, sex, and SES, suggesting that part of the bilingual's precocity in school may be attributed to a superior skill in learning. . . . There is, then, both empirical evidence and theoretical support for the notion that some forms of bilingualism may not be a handicap but may be an important asset in some areas of development."

VALUES OF BILINGUAL EDUCATION FOR THE ENGLISH-SPEAKING CHILD IN THE UNITED STATES

There has never been any question about the value of knowing foreign languages for children who belong to a high socioeconomic class (Andersson and Boyer 1970, vol. 1, 41ff.). In our country, as in other countries, the elite considers such knowledge essential for participation in international affairs, and for the elite there is theoretically no constraint on international mobility. To argue that children of low socioeconomic status will never need to use other languages is in effect to reduce their opportunity for full participation in national life, and this is contrary to our democratic ideals. If knowledge of languages is good for some, access to such knowledge should be open to all. But equal educational opportunity, to which principle we eagerly pay lip service, is perhaps nowhere farther from being realized than in foreign-language education and in related bilingual education, conduct of which can be described by the phrases "too little, too late, and too badly."

The Foreign Language Program (FLP) of the Modern Language Association (MLA) undertook in the 1950s to spark a reform in foreign-language education. Longer sequences of study—four to six years instead of two—did slightly alleviate the problem of "too little." A cautious endorsement of foreign languages in the elementary school (FLES) helped to encourage at least experimental programs in every state, with a consequent partial—and unfortunately temporary—alleviation of the "too late" problem. The problem of quality proved to be the most refractory, although the efforts of the MLA-FLP did result in some improvement in the definition of goals and in the quality of instructional methods and materials, teacher training, and evaluation. Perhaps the most significant accomplishment of the MLA-FLP was helping to persuade Congress to include foreign languages with science and mathematics in the National Defense Education Act of 1958 (NDEA) as deserving of special support because of their direct relation to national defense. Truth forces us to state that the combined massive programs of the MLA-FLP and of the NDEA, though beneficial, failed to produce a truly significant and lasting improvement in the effectiveness of foreign-language learning, nor did they lead directly, as might have been expected, to bilingual education.

Can the new trend toward bilingual education be so conceived as to bring about such an improvement, for both English-speaking and non-English-speaking children? Considering for the present the case of English-speaking children only, there are at least five reasons for believing that bilingual education can indeed be so conceived and planned as to give English-speaking children new hope for acquiring proficiency in one or more other languages—while enjoying the experience.

First, most bilingual programs begin in kindergarten or grade one, giving English-speaking children contact with another language at age five or six, as compared with twelve, thirteen, or fourteen in the traditional high-school program or nine or ten in the usual FLES and high-school programs.

Second, to the extent that bilingual schooling is planned as a sequential and progressing program, through the elementary grades at least, for the benefit of both the English- and the x-language speaker, it gives promise of much greater effectiveness than the two- to four-year FLES and high-school programs.

Third, if, as the bilingual legislation prescribes, the English-speaking child's second language is used not only as a school subject but as a medium of instruction for one or more of the school subjects, and if the second language is used in a natural and functional way for approximately half of the time in the school day—as compared with fifteen to twenty minutes a day in FLES—the chances of learning the second language are considerably augmented.

Fourth, the contact with teachers and aides who are native speakers of the x-language and representatives of the x-culture provides the English-speaking learner with authentic models for his second-language learning.

And fifth, the mingling throughout of English-speaking children with children who speak the x-language authentically will provide a setting for informal learning, often the most effective kind. Gradually and without strain Anglo children will in this way become accustomed to representatives of another culture and tolerant, if not appreciative, of cultural differences. Since cross-cultural harmony depends on the sensitiveness of the Anglo majority, this acquisition at an early age of cultural awareness may indeed be the single most important value to be derived from bilingual education. What better preparation can one imagine for the future citizen and school board member?

VALUES OF BILINGUAL EDUCATION FOR THE
x-LANGUAGE-SPEAKING CHILD

Bilingual education is generally thought of as benefiting the non-English-speaking child primarily. It is perhaps true that the minority child is the most direct beneficiary; but, as we have suggested in the preceding paragraphs, it may well be the English speaker who derives the greatest—and essential—benefit from bilingual bicultural education. And ultimately everyone—society as a whole—will be the gainer if the minority individual and group are conscious of making a contribution to the pluralistic culture of the nation and the individuals of the English-speaking majority are aware of the values to the nation resulting from the contributions of the various minorities.

Let us first consider the five- or six-year-old child who has spent his preschool years in an x-language-speaking family and community and approaches that first day of school, the trauma of which has been so often described. The first school days are of course not traumatic for every minority child. He may come from a bilingual family in which two languages—the x-language and English—are used regularly. Or the child may have been exposed to enough English in the community or on radio and television to have been immunized against the shock of English in school. It is rather the child who has lived in a monolingual x-speaking family and community who presents the school with the real challenge. Can the school welcome him as he is and make him feel at ease from the first day?

The first value of a successful bilingual education program is just this: that both the child and his parents feel welcome from the outset by being greeted warmly in their own language by an x-speaking teacher with whom the school beginner and his parents can identify. This feeling of security by the minority child is always protected by the sensitive teacher, for only the secure child can develop the joy of learning, the second value of a sound bilingual program. Fostering an eagerness to learn and a joy in the process is the mark of a skillful teacher, but more than skillful teaching is required. The program must be so planned and implemented that it will challenge and not discourage the individual child. The teacher will use, and encourage the child to use, the child's best medium for learning, whether this be his home language or English. The teacher will also remember that a child's learning does not begin in school; it merely continues. The more opportunities a child has to demonstrate previous learning, the more eager will he be to add to it. The sensitive and observant teacher can pick up any number of cues to the child's interests and make use of them in planning the classwork. One of the most common mistakes made by the teacher who wants not to overtax the child is to underchallenge him. We are reminded of the kindergarten child who came home after the first day at school and remarked in response to a question from her mother, "School was no fun. The teacher didn't even teach us how to read." The teacher not only must have high expectations of the pupils—as we have been reminded by the *Pygmalion in the Classroom* experience (Rosenthal and Jacobson 1968)—but also must not forget that the pupils have high expectations of him/her.

Closely related to the feeling of security and eagerness to learn is a third value, namely, a good self-image, which may be expected to characterize the x-speaking child in a sound bilingual program. Whatever term is used to designate this characteristic—positive, self-concept, sense of identity, self-reliance, confidence, self-esteem—it is an essential feature of effective bilingual schooling, evidence not only of good teaching and learning but also of a supportive atmosphere in the school and the community.

The first three values have to do with the creation of satisfactory conditions for learning, to which we must now add actual satisfactory learning. This calls for a sequential and incremental program or curriculum suited to the needs of the x-speaking as well as of the English-speaking pupil. We have mentioned the fact that the x-speaker is encouraged to use his best medium for learning, usually his home language, which he should be emboldened to cultivate and perfect as a learning instrument and a means of self-expression. In the words of an international group of educators meeting in Paris in 1951, "It is axiomatic that the best medium for teaching a child is his mother tongue" (UNESCO 1953, 11).[2] The acquisition, without delay, of reading and writing skills is a mark of a successful bilingual program. At the same time the x-speaker should be gradually initiated into English, with emphasis at first on hearing in meaningful contexts, then on speaking, and finally on reading and writing. The ingenious teacher will find interesting ways of providing the necessary experience and will know how to pace the learning in such a way as to whet the learner's appetite and not discourage him. There is of course no fixed limit to what may be learned through the learner's first language (L1) and his second language (L2). The wider the horizons opened by the teacher the better, provided the child's eagerness to learn is stimulated, not blunted. Subject matter should presumably touch upon all areas of human development: physical and health, affective, cognitive, and aesthetic. We should perhaps make special mention of social studies, a natural vehicle for the learning of the history and the culture of both the English-speaking and x-speaking group. In the words of the Texas Statewide Design for Bilingual Education (see Appendix), "Both the conflict and the confluence of the two cultures are presented in the social development of the State and nation in order to create an understanding and appreciation of each in a positive rather than negative sense." Let us remind ourselves of Jerome Bruner's hypothesis (1961, p. 33) "that any subject can be taught effectively in some intellectually honest form to any child at any stage of development."

The values suggested in the preceding paragraphs are those which may be expected of a well-designed and well-conducted bilingual program. That many programs are not so designed or so conducted is evident from the assessments of Gaarder (1970), Kjolseth (1970), and Fishman and Lovas (1970) already alluded to. Susan Ervin-Tripp (1970, 313-314) calls attention to the arresting difference between Canadian Anglophones learning French in Wallace Lambert's experimental program in St. Lambert (Lambert and Tucker 1972) and California Chicanos learning English in school. As she points out, the differences are social rather than linguistic. "In the Montreal environment, English-speaking children have no sense of inferiority or disadvantage in school. Their teachers do not have low expectations for their achievements. Their social group has power in the community; their language is respected, is learned by Francophones, and becomes a medium of instruction later in the school. In the classrooms, the children are not expected to compete with native speakers of French in a milieu which both expects and blames them to excel in their own language." The difference between these two situations is a measure of the distance we have to go to make a success of bilingual schooling in our country. But the first step in acquiring a philosophical perspective is to take into account the various factors in any given situation—social, political, cultural, economic, educational—to analyze and synthesize them; to run some field experiments; and gradually to approach a fit between the real and the ideal.

To bring us one step closer to the ideal, we should explore the perspective of the preschool years. There is a common hypothesis that after a certain age or certain ages or stages of development a child learns language or languages less efficiently than before. Since the hypothesis is both interesting and relevant to our study, let us explore it.

THE FACTOR OF AGE

Recent research confirms what perceptive educators have long known, that the human infant is a surprising learner. "Psychologist Benjamin Bloom estimates that about 50 percent of mature intelligence is developed by age four and another 30 percent by age eight. Some psychologists doubt whether any amount of remedial work later on will enable a child to develop intellectually to his full potential if he does not receive the proper stimulation at the proper time—that is, very young" (Carnegie Corporation 1969, 1).

We cite this arresting quotation, for it underlines what is coming to be accepted more and more as a truism by educational theorists, namely, that formal schooling normally begins at an age when much of the learning potential of a child has already been lost. Burton White, Director of Harvard's Preschool Project (White 1971; White, Watts, et al. 1973) comes to a similar conclusion. The California State Superintendent of Schools and the State Department of Education have been sufficiently impressed by the mounting evidence of the young child's great learning potential to propose, in a soundly reasoned report, that the school-beginning age be lowered to four, on a voluntary basis (Riles 1971). Realizing that the early-learning movement is accelerating rapidly, New York City school officials are experimenting with two-year-olds. "The earlier we get youngsters," says one administrator, "the better the chances of their doing well in school later." (*Newsweek,* Jan. 29, 1968, p. 48.) The results of early investigation are so promising that bilingual program planners would do well to include infants and preschool children in their designs, thus bringing the home and the school into a closer working relationship.

EARLY LANGUAGE LEARNING

We are coming to realize the unsuspected capacity of infants and young children for learning in general, but their extraordinary capacity for the learning of languages, both the mother tongue and other languages, has long been common knowledge. In the words of Maria Montessori, "Only a child under three can construct a mechanism of language, and he can speak any number of languages if they are in his environment at birth" (1959a, 40).

We cannot explain how man developed language, thus setting himself apart from the other animals, and we never cease to wonder at the infant's skill in mastering his mother tongue. Less well known is the fact that the range of vocal noises which the infant enjoys producing far transcends the limits of the community language. After making a number of sample recordings of the vocalizations of a single infant in the first year of life, Charles Osgood observes that "within the data for the first two months of life may be found all of the speech sounds that the human vocal system can produce" (1953, 684). This observation has enormous implications for the proponents of bilingual education. Linguists are agreed that by the age of about five and one-half the average child has mastered most of the sound system and much of the basic structure of his language, as well as a sufficient vocabulary to participate fully in the activities of immediate concern to him.

Another indication of the child's fantastic learning power is the size of his vocabulary. Mary Katherine Smith (1941, 343-344), using the Seashore-Eckerson English Recognition Vocabulary Test, found that "for grade one, the average number of basic words known was 16,900, with a range from 5500 to 48,800." Henry D. Rinsland (1945, 12), using written sources supplemented by children's conversation, counted 5099 different words used by first graders as an active vocabulary out of 353,874 running words.

In learning languages, young children astonish adolescents and adults, who have so much difficulty acquiring a second language. A well-known example of children's plurilingualism in a multilingual societal setting is that cited by British psychologist J. W. Tomb (1925, 52): "It is a common experience in the district in Bengal in which the writer resided to hear English children three or four years old who have been born in the country conversing freely at different times with their parents in English, with their *ayahs* (nurses) in Bengali, with the garden coolies in Santali, and with the house-servants in Hindustani, while their parents have learned with the aid of a *munshi* (teacher) and much laborious effort just sufficient Hindustani to comprehend what the house-servants are saying (provided they do not speak too quickly) and to issue simple orders to them connected with domestic affairs. It is even not unusual to see English parents in India unable to understand what their servants are saying to them in Hindustani and being driven in consequence to bring along an English child of four or five years old, if available, to act as interpreter."

Missionary families are a particularly rich source of examples to illustrate children's language-learning ability. "One American missionary family in Vietnam tells this story: When they went out to Vietnam, they were three, father, mother, and four-year-old daughter. Shortly after their arrival a son was born. The parents' work took them on extended trips to the interior of the country, at which times they left their children in the care of a Vietnamese housekeeper and a nursemaid. When the time came for the young son to talk, he did in fact talk, but in Vietnamese. Suddenly, the parents realized that they could not even communicate with their son except by using their daughter as an interpreter" (Andersson 1969, 42).

According to Dr. Wilder Penfield, the distinguished former Director of the Montreal Neurological Institute, "A child who is exposed to two or three languages during the ideal period for language learning pronounces each with the accent of his teacher. If he hears one language at home, another at school, and a third perhaps from a governess in a nursery, he is not aware that he is learning three languages at all. He is aware of the fact that to get what he wants from the governess he must speak one way and with the teacher he must speak in another way. He has not reasoned it out at all" (Penfield and Roberts 1959, 253).

In his biography of the Canadian Prime Minister, Louis St. Laurent, Bruce Hutchison (1965, 288) quotes the former Prime Minister as follows: " 'I thought,' he used to say in later years, 'that everybody spoke to his father in French and his mother in English.' "

From these examples, and from many others that could be found, educators may safely conclude that the learning of two languages does not constitute an undue expectation of children, especially very young children.[3]

LANGUAGE AND CULTURE

"Study of the history and culture associated with a student's mother tongue is considered an integral part of bilingual education." This quotation from the Draft Guidelines to the Bilingual Education Program (Andersson and Boyer 1970, II, Appendix B) emphasizes the relation of language to culture.

> Language is only one of the important parts of the characteristic behavior of a people bound together in one culture. It is closely connected with a particular way of feeling, thinking, and acting, and it is rooted in and reflects a commonly accepted set of values. Educators need to remember that a child born into a Spanish-speaking family in the Southwest, a Navajo child born on the reservation in Arizona, a Franco-American child born into a French-speaking family in Northern Maine, and a Chinese child born into a Cantonese-speaking family in San Francisco all enter different worlds, worlds which are organized and presented through the grid of the particular language that they hear about them and that they acquire. There is, therefore, an intimate relatonship between the child, his family, his community, their language, and their view of the world. How to harmonize these with American English and with prevailing American culture patterns without damaging the self-image of a non-English-speaking child is the challenge. It is not a minor one.

Bilingualism, Biculturalism, and the Community. Bilingual education can provide one important means of building, out of varied elements, a harmonious and creative community. It is not enough for educators to understand the [instructional] principles on which a solid bilingual program must be built; they must also create understanding throughout the community concerning the important connection between one's mother tongue, one's self-image, and one's heritage (both individual and group-cultural). One can hardly depreciate any people's language without depreciating the people themselves. . . .

Wherever the vicious circle begins, it is the community as a whole or the nation as a whole that suffers the consequences. Both those responsible for the administration of the schools and those who exert leadership in the community must search their consciences before deciding what kind of education to provide. The non-English-speaking child who at the beginning of school is unable to acquire literacy in English in competition with his English-speaking classmates and who is not permitted to acquire it in his own languages makes a poor beginning, that he may never be able to overcome. Frustrated and discouraged, he seeks the first opportunity to drop out of school; and if he finds a job at all it will be the lowest paying job. He will be laid off first, will remain unemployed longest, and is least able to adapt to changing occupational requirements.

The Bilingual Education Act was conceived to rectify certain obvious educational defects of the past. But educational discrimination is but one aspect of the ills which characterize our still far from perfect society; and the building of a better education system, resting on a full recognition of many languages and cultures, can be expected to make only a modest start toward our full knowledge and acceptance of ourselves for the vast multifarious unhomogeneous nation that we are. [Andersson and Boyer 1970, I, 47-48]

IS CROSS-CULTURAL UNDERSTANDING POSSIBLE?

We shall quickly skip over the prior question: Is cross-cultural understanding worthwhile? We assume that for the segment of any given population that is satisfied to associate exclusively with its own kind or is unwilling to make an effort to cross cultural boundaries or is disinclined to think about the matter at all, the answer to this question is, by implication at least, negative.

What of the more thoughtful of our fellow citizens? Social studies teachers proclaim as one of their aims to teach understanding between individuals, groups, classes, and cultures. Language teachers point out the close connection between language and culture and allege that language learning is essential to cultural awareness. Frequently the relative importance of language and culture is assayed, as, for example, in the following quotation from Wilmarth H. Starr (1955, 81-82):

It is some 10 years now since, having sought a commission in our military services with a view to contributing my limited knowledge of European languages to the cause, I found myself in the far Pacific, a 90-day wonder as a military strategist and a 17-month wonder as a Chinese scholar. Soon after my arrival in Asia, I witnessed in a striking way the linguistic barriers existing between men of the same nation, for I found myself in the extraordinary position of translator between two Chinese generals, the one from the south speaking to me in broken English, which I in turn rendered in broken Mandarin to the general from the north. The academic question is, Who was the foreigner in that situation? On another occasion, units of the fleet were immobilized at a critical time for lack of certain information that could only come from Chinese sources. Having been given *carte blanche* to get this information and having learned about Chinese ways, I paid a quite unorthodox call on the distinguished and influential Chinese mayor of Shanghai. After greeting him with utmost courteousness and a liberal sprinkling of the admiral's compliments, I sat down to several leisurely cups of aromatic tea. Some 45 minutes of casual conversation later, I broached my subject by begging to take leave, mentioning casually that we were sailing in the morning and that the admiral would like the mayor to be the first to know this. The mayor, not to be outdone in courtesy, asked if I would convey his respect to the admiral and would there be, by chance, any information he might send by me to that worthy gentleman. As a matter of fact, there was a small matter that the admiral would very much appreciate knowing about. A few telephone calls were made, some Chinese admirals and generals joined us for another bout with the teacups, and some time later I rejoined the flagship armed with the specific information.

Not my inadequate Chinese, but about seven cups of tea and the exchange of courtesies in an ancient ritual provided the key. An understanding between men rests upon something more than linguistic interchange; its roots extend into the cultural earth in which the men in question have their origins. . . .

THE SAPIR-WHORF HYPOTHESIS

The fundamental differences in thinking, in perceiving reality, reflected in language, intrigued Benjamin Lee Whorf (1966, 252), who has written:

> Actually, thinking is most mysterious, and by far the greatest light upon it that we have is thrown by the study of language. This study shows that the forms of a person's thoughts are controlled by inexorable laws of pattern of which he is unconscious. These patterns are the unperceived intricate systematizations of his own language—shown readily enough by a candid comparison and contrast with other languages, especially those of a different linguistic family. His thinking itself is in a language—in English, in Sanskrit, in Chinese. And every language is a vast pattern-system, different from others, in which are culturally ordained the forms and categories by which the personality not only communicates, but also analyzes nature, notices or neglects types of relationship and phenomena, channels his reasoning, and builds the house of his consciousness.

Whorf's principle of linguistic relativity, which has come to be known as the Sapir-Whorf hypothesis, states "that the structure of a human being's language influences the manner in which he understands reality and behaves with respect to it" (Carroll 1966, 23). Carroll speculates on "what makes the notion of linguistic relativity so fascinating even to the nonspecialist. Perhaps it is the suggestion that all one's life one has been tricked, all unaware, by the structure of language into a certain way of perceiving reality, with the implication that awareness of this trickery will enable one to see the world with fresh insight." Carroll continues by observing that "it would have been farthest from Whorf's wishes to condone any easy appeal to linguistic relativity as a rationalization for a failure of communication between cultures or between nations. Rather, he would hope that a full awareness of linguistic relativity might lead to humbler attitudes about the supposed superiority of standard average European languages and a greater disposition to accept a 'brotherhood of thought' among men. . . ."

Whorf's learning of the Hopi language—and of other American Indian tongues—enabled him to sense cross-cultural differences if not fully to understand them. But Whorf had extraordinary insight, not shared by many. In this learning of other languages and sensing of other cultures Ernst Cassirer (1962, 133) recognized the advantage of the child over the adult, observing that:

> We can still when learning a foreign language subject ourselves to an experience similar to that of the child. . . . Linguists and psychologists have often raised the question as to how it is possible for a child by his own efforts to accomplish a task that no adult can ever perform in the same way or as well. . . . In a later and more advanced state of our conscious life we can never repeat the process which led to our first entrance into the world of human speech. In the freshness, in the agility and elasticity of early childhood this process had a quite different meaning. Paradoxically enough the real difficulty consists much less in the learning of the new language than in the forgetting of a former one. We are no longer in the mental condition of the child who for the first time approaches a conception of the objective world. To the adult the objective world already has a definite shape as a result of speech activity, which has in a sense molded all our other activities. Our perceptions, intuitions, and concepts have coalesced with the terms and speech forms of our mother tongue. . . . When penetrating into the "spirit" of a foreign tongue we invariably have the impression of approaching a new world, a world which has an intellectual structure of its own.

Chester Christian, comparing the relative advantages of monolingual and bilingual education of children, writes (in a personal communication dated Feb. 13, 1974):

> The advantage of monolingual education to the child is that it tends to make him feel secure in the belief that the world is structured in harmony with his language, and therefore belongs to him more than to anybody else. I think that children feel this in much the sense that they feel their mothers belong to them and, to a lesser degree, their fathers. Their language is, then, more important than other languages, just as their parents are more important than other people. Just as the parents' politics, religion, and way of life tend to become those of their children, and provide them with a tangible reality out of the many possible realities in the world, the language of the parents provides them with a tangible culturalinguistic reality, and relieves them of the responsibility of making what would be otherwise very difficult choices.

On the other hand, he thinks that "Education in and through one language only tends to develop absolutist concepts of social and cultural realities. . . ." He therefore states: "My principal reason for thinking it desirable to expose children to other languages at an early age, if not to teach them more than one language, is to enable them to develop early a concept of cultural relativity."

Questioned about his own point of view, Christian responded (personal communication dated Feb. 25, 1974): "Insofar as I have a goal or ideal, it is to become as fully conscious as is possible for the kind of animal I am of all that existence, Being-in-the-Universe, is and may imply. In terms of this, language is both an aid and a hindrance. One language only, however, is less an aid and more a hindrance than are two or more. This, perhaps, is a statement of faith." A statement of faith to which many of us can subscribe.

We have not yet answered the question whether or not it is possible to understand another culture. Some would answer with a simple negative. A Korean graduate student with whom I discussed this question felt that cultural understanding between an Oriental and a Westerner could never be complete. He therefore echoed the sentiment contained in Kipling's famous verses:

> East is East and West is West,
> And never the twain shall meet.

Asked why he found it profitable to study Western thought, he replied that Orientals had much to learn from the West, especially in technological fields. In this point of view he agrees with F. S. C. Northrop, whose great book *The Meeting of East and West* (1946) we must consider before concluding this section.

Northrop explains in his Chapter XII, "The Solution of the Basic Problem," that "The task of the contemporary world falls into four major parts: (1) the relating of the East and the West; (2) the similar merging of the Latin and Anglo-Saxon cultures; (3) the mutual reinforcement of democratic and communistic values; and (4) the reconciliation of the true and valuable portions of the Western medieval and modern worlds. Running through all of these special tasks is the more general one, made imperative with the advent of the atomic bomb, of harmonizing the sciences and the humanities."

According to Northrop, "Cultures with differing political, economic, aesthetic and religious ideals or values are grounded in differing philosophical conceptions of the nature of man and of the universe ... [and] the task of relating the differing cultures is, in considerable part, that of removing the notion of each people that *nothing but* its theory is correct, thereby permitting each party to add to its own traditional ideals the equally perfect values of the other culture" (437). Northrop states that "our philosophical principle prescribes that both the aesthetic and theoretic components are required. Thus the ideal society must return to the primitive intuition of the past with respect to its aesthetically grounded portion and advance to the sophisticated science of the present with respect to its theoretically based part ... but rare is the individual who can master both components. Thus every society needs those who cultivate intuition and contemplation with respect to things in their naïve aesthetic immediacy as well as those who pursue science to the philosophical articulation of the theoretically known factor in things. It is precisely at this point that the native Indians of the entire American continent and the Negroes in the United States can take their place immediately in the good society, with something of their own to offer, leading and teaching with respect to the things of intuition and feeling, just as the white people can lead and teach them with respect to those things which must be known by inference and by theoretically constructed, and scientifically verified, doctrine" (459). In the context of the 1970s we would of course include the very considerable Spanish-speaking segment of our population, the segment which contributes the greatest vitality to our bilingual education.

The whole thrust of Northrop's book, as one can infer from the brief excerpts we have cited, is that it *is* possible to understand another culture. Whether or not it is ever possible *fully* to understand a culture and a language into which one has not been born is perhaps subject to doubt. Indeed, how often can we say that any two individuals, with the best will in the world, fully understand each other? To carry the point a step further, how much better we know ourselves when we see ourselves through others' eyes! And how much does not our acquaintance of another culture illuminate our understanding of our own culture? Human understanding is surely not an absolute but suggests an ideal on a continuum along which we can also have tolerance, sympathy, and compassion. It seems evident that early contact with a second culture promotes better understanding, as does knowledge of a second language. That early culture contact and the learning of a second language in early childhood is not an absolute prerequisite is suggested by the biography of Benjamin Lee Whorf, for he was able in full maturity to penetrate American Indian languages and cultures, culminating in Hopi, to the point of apprehending vividly their cultural values. Both Whorf and Northrop suggest that while members of certain cultures tend to have an intimate apprehension of the aesthetic and members of other cultures have a more natural affinity for the theoretical or scientific, each individual has something of both and may therefore aspire, if he wills it, to develop both faculties and thus to acquire some awareness of and tolerance for cultures which he does not immediately and instinctively apprehend. To the extent that he as an individual is successful and the society in which he lives is successful in achieving such cross-cultural understanding will he and his fellow human beings be taking the first steps toward a peaceful and a richly satisfying coexistence with groups and nations initially separated by vast philosophical differences.

Our conclusion then is that it is not possible in any absolute sense for us to achieve cross-cultural understanding but that it is possible to become partially aware of the cultural values of other peoples and that such awareness is promoted by contact, especially in early childhood, and by the learning of the language of a given culture.

CONCLUSION

The philosopher, like the poet, stands in awe before the mysteries of life, and especially of human existence. The poet tries to express his sense of wonder in words, beginning with the infant's fun in babble, continuing with what the French poet André Spire (1949) calls "plaisir poétique, plaisir musculaire"—referring to the sensuous pleasure one gets from rolling sounds over one's tongue—and fulfilling himself by creating fanciful structures of sound and sense.[4] The philosopher tries to penetrate and understand the mysteries and to communicate his insights to his fellow human beings.

One of the still unexplained human puzzles is language. How and when is it learned? How does it happen that each individual has his own unique form of speech, or idiolect, distinguishable from that of anyone else, while at the same time his speech conforms so closely to that of others living in the same group as to be recognized as belonging to the same dialect? Why is it that speakers of one dialect sometimes regard speakers of other dialects of the same language in ways that range from mild amusement to downright hostility? What light do these various reactions shed on the attitudes that speakers of one *language* have toward speakers of another? And what is the role of education in enabling us to understand and control human response to differences of dialect, of language, and of culture? Can the learning of two or more languages and the experience of two or more cultures induce a tolerance, or possibly even an appreciation, of human differences, and lead to a cross-cultural understanding and to a philosophy of linguistic and cultural pluralism? Our inquiry should have provided us with at least some tentative answers to these and other questions. In drawing together the various strands of our study, let us begin with the human infant, who perhaps constitutes the greatest mystery of all but is happily coming to be the subject of the most intensive observation and research.

Bilingualism and Biculturalism in Infancy and Early Childhood

Researchers are gradually discovering language-related activities closer and closer to birth. For example, "bodily responses to human speech are apparent in babies twelve hours old, and may even exist in the womb. Such instinctive responses, the researchers suspect, represent vital steps in learning to talk." (*Newsweek*, Feb. 18, 1974, p. 79). Exactly what the relationship is between listening movements, called "interactional synchrony," and understanding and speaking is unknown, but "if the infant, from the beginning, moves in precise, shared rhythm with the organization of the speech structure of his culture, then he participates . . . in millions of repetitions of linguistic forms long before he uses them . . . in communicating. By the time he begins to speak, he may have already laid down within himself the form and structure of the language system" (Condon and Sander 1974, 99-101).

Two other scientists (Ostwald and Peltzman 1974) have found through sound spectrographic analysis of newborn infants' crying that there are clear-cut differences, mostly in pitch, between the crying of normal babies and that of abnormal ones. "Although cases of fetal vocalization *in utero* have been reported (we ourselves have never detected it), one usually considers the respiratory actions of an infant following birth to be the onset of human sound production."

These recent research findings tend to support and dramatize earlier findings: on language acquisition (Osgood, Ervin and Miller, Ervin-Tripp, Lenneberg, and Lange and Larsson); on early development of human intelligence (Bloom); on early bilingualism or multilingualism (Penfield, Penfield and Roberts, Tomb, Montessori, Leopold, Ronjat, Pavlovitch, Tits, Rūke-Draviņa, and Mackey and Andersson forthcoming); on early reading and writing (Doman, Hughes, Monstessori, Stevens and Orem, and Söderbergh); on early bilingual education (Engle, Fishman, Gaarder, Jones, Kjolseth, Lambert, Mackey, Macnamara, Modiano, Riles, Texas Education Agency, and UNESCO); and on early cross-cultural awareness (Sapir, Whorf, Hall, Fishman, Hymes, Kjolseth, and Lambert and Tucker). Still not understood are the exact nature of the young child's learning and the limits of his superiority over adolescents and adults in the acquisition of languages and in the sensing of behavioral and cultural differences. How long does the child's cortex remain "uncommitted" (Penfield 1964)? Assuming that under favorable circumstances the learning of more than one language is to be preferred to non-learning, just when and how should such learning take place? Should the school-entering age be lowered so that it can be provided in school (Riles 1971)? Should it be provided to the preschooler at home with the aid of the school (Andersson 1974, 1975)? Or should the decision be left in the hands of Lady Luck, with the result that only those children who have foreign contacts learn foreign languages?

The extent to which infants' and young children's extraordinary potential for learning languages and sensing cultures is realized depends in the first instance on the families into which children are born, on the information to which these families have access, and on their sense of values. But in the final analysis, since education is also a public concern, it is the sense of values, the philosophical view, of the community, of society, of the nation which will largely determine how many of our children and which ones are to have the benefits of bilingual education—and with what success.

One promising bilingual comes to mind, named Mario, on whom Lady Luck has smiled. His father, one of our former graduate students, is an American educator of Italian descent, a fluent speaker of American English, of American (mostly Mexican) Spanish, and of Italian—to which he has added some French and Portuguese, a little Greek, and Esperanto. Mario's mother, a daughter of a Bolivian diplomatic family, was born in Rome, where she spent the first three years of her life. Extended stays in Argentina, Peru, and Venezuela have given her a familiarity with Spanish dialectal differences. In addition to keeping her Italian alive, she has learned English and French in school and reinforced her English by residence in the United States. Mario has been raised in Spanish but has heard a good deal of Italian and English. Having spent most of his young life in this country, he has been able to bring his English nearly up to the level of his Spanish. He understands ordinary spoken Italian but has not yet had sufficient opportunity to learn to speak it.

His father, Alvino Fantini, summarizes the situation by saying that "Mario was bilingual and bicultural with full awareness of these facts. Behaviorally he was well adjusted, with a strong feeling about his own identity in spite of many environmental changes. [At age five years four months he traveled to La Paz by himself.] He had received much attention and affection, and he was himself overtly affectionate. He was curious and interested in many things. . . . Linguistically, he was fully bilingual in at least two languages with a passive knowledge of a third." And his latest kindergarten teacher states that "There is no need to be concerned about his English; he speaks amazingly well for his age. I am also surprised by the naturalness with which he came into our class and became part of the group. Often new children take some time to adjust, but he came in as though he had always been there" (Fantini 1974, 48).

By way of contrast we recall a visit to a first-grade classroom in a rural school near Austin, Tex. Most of the children were Mexican Americans unable to understand English. The teachers, in this and the other classroom, neither understood nor spoke Spanish. Trained to teach English-speaking children only, they were clearly frustrated not to be able to reach these children, who sat silent, uncomprehending, and bewildered by the teacher's exhortations. The reader is referred to an eloquent photograph of a first-grader entering "a foreign world" (Andersson and Boyer 1970, I, opposite p. 40) and another of an apprehensive Mexican American father delivering two small children to school on the first day and wondering, "How will they treat my children?" (Ibid., opposite p. 41).

The more one observes the human infant and preschool child the more impressive does his capacity for inventing and for learning seem to be. There is first of all his mysterious learning of language, that of his own group or those in his environment (Tomb 1925; Montessori 1959a). In learning the language of his group one would think that he learns by imitation, but it appears that invention is much more significant than imitation. "The mother helps, but the initiative comes from the growing child," writes Dr. Wilder Penfield (Penfield and Roberts 1959, 240). Werner Leopold goes so far as to assert that "pronunciation is the only part of language that is chiefly imitated."[5] Dorothy McCarthy expresses the consensus when she writes, "Most present-day psychologists seem to agree with the opinion of Taine (1876) that new sounds are not learned by imitation of the speech of others, but rather that they emerge in the child's spontaneous vocal play more or less as a result of modulation, and that the child imitates only those sounds which have already occurred in its spontaneous babblings" (1954, 494-495). In "tying in" to another language the young child reveals at the same time a remarkable ability at cultural adaptation, at feeling comfortable with speakers of other languages, as shown by the English children in Bengal, cited by Tomb, and by the case of Mario in joining the Austin kindergarten.

Then there are other forms of early learning, such as reading (Doman 1964, 1974; Hughes 1971; Söderbergh 1971, 1973). Doman and Melcher (in press) present a truly dramatic case in the following in these words.

When you are confronted with a brain-injured two-year-old who is no further advanced than a newborn babe—who gives no evidence of being able to see or hear, let alone crawl or raise his head—teaching him to read isn't the first thing you think about. What you think about is how to get through to him, by any method, on any level.

Young Tommy was such a child. His eyes couldn't follow you, or follow a light, or work together. A loud noise wouldn't make him start. You could pinch him and get no reaction. In fact, the first time we ever got a reaction out of Tommy was when we stuck pins in him: he smiled. It was a great moment, for us and for him. We had established contact.

That was when Tommy was two. By the time he was four he was reading. . . .

A friend who specialized in teaching music to three-year-olds by means of the piano once remarked that she had not had a single pupil from the age of three who had not developed absolute pitch (fine pitch discrimination). And Susuki's success in teaching three-year-olds to play the violin is well known. This leads us to hypothesize that young children have an acute sensitiveness for the learning of music similar to that which they have for learning languages. And how many other areas there may be in which children's "sensitive periods" (Montessori 1958, 221) can speed their learning we do not yet know.

Pointing in the same direction is the research of J. McV. Hunt (1961, 357), who stresses the importance of the "match" between the child's intellectual development and his environmental experiences: "This match is still poorly understood, but it is the appropriateness of the match between the circumstances that the child encounters as he develops and the nature of his own intellectual organization at the time of the encounters that appears to determine in very large part his rate of intellectual development."

The goal of Burton L. White and his fellow researchers in the Harvard Preschool Project is to optimize human development "by studying the *overall* competence in children who have gotten off to a superb start in their early years" (White et al. 1973, 3). Their findings are similar to Hunt's: "Our study, even though incomplete at this writing, has convinced us of the special importance of the 10- to 18-month age range for the development of general competence. At this time of life, for most children, several extremely important developments seem to coalesce and force a test of each family's capacity to rear children" (Ibid., 234). White's project started as a study of the first six years of life, but "Accumulating evidence suggested that, although most educators were concerning themselves with the educational process of children age six and older, much of the child's crucial development was over by the age of six. By that age, so it seemed, it might already be too late to prevent stunted development and to insure full growth" (Ibid., 3-4). White goes on to explain, "If most of the qualities that distinguish outstanding six-year-olds can be achieved in large measure by age three, the focus of the project could be narrowed dramatically. We rather abruptly found ourselves concentrating on the zero-to-three age range."

Bloom's research indicating that a child has developed half of his mature intellectual potential by age four and 80% by age eight also suggests the importance of early exposure to languages, cultures, and other worthwhile human experiences, while the cerebral cortex is still partially uncommitted.

Just as, according to White, the educational establishment by concerning itself primarily with children six years of age and older neglects the most educable period of human life, so language educators, especially before the advent of bilingual education, have been a party to a curricular neglect. In a statement made to the Special Subcommittee on Bilingual Education of the United States Senate Committee on Labor and Public Welfare on May 18, 1967, Bruce Gaarder (1967b) eloquently describes this neglect:

> There is an anomaly, an enormous anomaly, in all that we do in the teaching of foreign languages in our country. . . . The anomaly I refer to is the fact that we spend, and I believe I could document it rather easily, at least a billion dollars a year on foreign language instruction at all levels, yet virtually no part of it, no cent, ever goes to maintain or further develop the native language competence which already exists in American children. It is as if one said it is all right to learn a foreign language if you start so late that you cannot really master it. It is all right for headwaiters, professional performers, and the rich to know foreign languages, but any child in school who already knows one is suspect. It is more than an anomaly. It is an absurdity that, as they say, passeth understanding.

Let us conclude with a hope, a hope springing from a philosophical perspective and proof against the disillusionment of history. Let us use such *knowledge* as we have—while pursuing further knowledge—concerning the learning potential of the human being, especially the human infant, concerning the nature and process of language acquisition, concerning cross-cultural understanding. Let us strive to perfect our *skill* in mothering, fathering, and teaching our children, again using knowledge already gained while adding to our experience. Let us use such *intelligence* and *wisdom* as we have by trying to understand the uniqueness of each human being and the infinite diversity of humanity, and let us therefore make every effort not to hobble children in our care by imposing on them our own limitations but rather to respect the sanctity of each human soul and the human dignity of every individual. Let us seek to understand better the interplay of individual with individual, of individual with diverse groups, and of group with group, all the way from family to nation. Let us not condemn the unfamiliar or the unknown, for by endeavoring to penetrate it we may find new stimulation. And in seeking to enlarge our philosophical perspective we could do worse than to lean on such a language loyalist as Joshua Fishman, on such a linguistic ethnographer as Dell Hymes, on such a linguistic analyst as William Mackey, on such an educational idealist as Bruce Gaarder, on such a visionary statesman as Ralph Yarborough, and on such a philosopher of cultures as F. S. C. Northrop.

Above all, we need to sustain our ideal of the bilingual or plurilingual child—like Mario—growing confidently and joyfully into maturity and ready to use his linguistic and cultural pluralism in any creative way he chooses. But we need to conceive the kind of communities and society that will guarantee children of the humblest families opportunities approximating those of Mario to grow into secure, imaginative future citizens capable of transforming today's social, economic, and political tensions into a more harmonious society of tomorrow. Already we are witnessing the birth of a spontaneous group expression in the form of Chicano literature. Similar artistic and musical folk expressions by other groups could with encouragement contribute to the "cultural mosaic" envisioned by Lundborg.

Our hope, then, is for a nation of bilinguals or multilinguals in settings of diglossia or polyglossia, a nation in which individuals and groups will gradually shift their effort from contention to mutual support.

NOTES

1. The full text of the *Statewide Design* is reproduced in the Appendix.

2. Patricia Lee Engle (*The Use of Vernacular Languages in Education: Language Medium in Early School Years for Minority Language Groups*, Arlington, Va.: Center for Applied Linguistics, 1975) contends that the best medium for teaching a child is not axiomatically his mother tongue. For example, there is the striking case of the St. Lambert Experiment, in which English-speaking children are taught altogether through French in kindergarten and the first grade and compare favorably with both English-speaking children in English and French-speaking children in French. She explores both sides of the question but comes to no firm conclusion.

3. For similar findings in school settings see Mildred R. Donoghue, "Foreign Languages in the Elementary School: Effects and Instructional Arrangements According to Research," *ERIC Focus Reports on the Teaching of Foreign Languages*, No. 3, 1969 MLA/ACTFL Materials Center, 62 Fifth Avenue, New York, N.Y. 10011.

4. A delightful display of children's imaginative creations in words and drawings is contained in the little book by the Soviet poet of childhood, Kornei Chukovsky, titled *From Two to Five*, translated and edited by Miriam Morton, with a foreword by Frances Clarke Sayers (Berkeley and Los Angeles: Univ. of California Press, 1966).

5. The Modern Language Association of America, "Childhood and Second Language Learning," *FL Bulletin* 49 (August 1956), 3; see also Leopold 1939, I, 22.

APPENDIX

A Statewide Design for Bilingual Education

Texas Education Agency
Goals of Bilingual Education
For Texas Public Schools

Primary Goal

The primary goal of Bilingual Education is successful achievement by the student of the goals of the educational process, using two languages, developing proficiency in both, but acknowledging English as the basic language of instruction in all schools and assuring its mastery by all pupils in the schools.

Complementary Goals

In order to make progress toward this primary goal, the following complementary goals should be sought:

1. Educational success on the part of the non-English-speaking student, through permitting him to learn in his first language while he is learning to function successfully in English.

2. Continued development by the non-English-speaking student of his first language as he is learning to function successfully in English.

3. Continued development on the part of the English-speaking student of proficiency in a second language.

4. Increased recognition by the total community (parents, teachers, administrators, students) of the importance of bilingualism and its contributions to better understandings among the peoples of our society.

Coordinate Goals

The above goals refer to the end products to be sought in terms of the development of students. In order for these goals to be reached, coordinate goals in Bilingual Education are that the local school districts:

1. Provide an environment conducive to learning.

2. Develop an effective program that will give each student an opportunity to make progress toward these goals.

3. Appraise the student's level of development of language, concepts, and experiences (exercising care to avoid testing the student in his second language until he has sufficient control of the language so that his true verbal abilities can be measured).

4. Have available sufficient numbers of personnel qualified to conduct the program.

Texas Education Agency
Priorities for Bilingual Education
In Texas Public Schools

Texas is made up of 26 ethnic and national groups which have contributed to its development. Among these, the largest number of non-English speakers are the speakers of Spanish. Therefore, it is appropriate that the initial focus of the bilingual education program be upon Spanish and English. In the future, bilingual programs may be developed in ethnic and national areas other than Spanish as they are needed and desired.

This initial priority focus on Spanish and English is not intended to apply to programs of instruction in foreign languages. Bilingual Education programs should not be regarded as replacements of these types of programs of instruction in foreign languages. Both of these types of programs should continue to be emphasized, each having related but distinguishable objectives.

The following are priorities for the implementation of effective Bilingual Education programs in the schools of Texas, in order of their urgency.

First Priority: A Bilingual Education program should be provided for all children entering school for the first time who speak little or no English.

Second Priority: A Bilingual Education program should be provided for all children in the primary grades who have not been able to master the English language.

Third Priority: For those children in the middle and upper elementary grades who have not been able to master the English language and attain success in learning curriculum content, bilingual instruction should be given.

Fourth Priority: For those students in secondary schools who have not been able to master the English language and attain success in learning curriculum content, bilingual instruction should be given.

Fifth Priority: Instruction for students at all levels who do not have difficulty with English, whether they are native speakers of English or native speakers of Spanish, should include the following components:

language development in English and Spanish
the concept of the confluence of cultures

The language development in this priority goes beyond the customary foreign languages programs.

Bilingual Education

Bilingual Education is a program developed to meet the individual needs of each child and is characterized by the following components:

I. *The basic concepts initiating the child into the school environment are taught in the language he brings from home.*
    Orientation to the classroom code of behavior and patterns of social interaction with his peers are developed by drawing from the child's resource of experiences and concepts and language which he has already learned in his home environment.

II. *Language development is provided in the child's dominant language.*
    The sequential development of the four language skills, i.e., listening, speaking, reading, and writing, is continued in the language for which the

child has already learned the sound system, structure, and vocabulary. This is exactly the same approach which has been used in the past. The only difference is the use of the dominant language of the child whose first language is not English. With this one change the child begins developing the skills with the use of his first language without having to wait until he learns his second language.

III.   *Language development is provided in the child's second language.*
By utilizing second language teaching methodology, i.e., teaching the listening and speaking skills by use of audio-lingual instructional techniques prior to teaching the reading and writing skills, the child immediately begins to *learn* a second language. For the English-speaking child this instruction is in the language of the other linguistic group involved in the program and, of course, English is taught to the child who comes from a non-English-speaking environment. Unique about this component of the program is the fact that the child does not have to re-learn language skills. He has only to transfer these skills learned in his first language to the second language.

IV.   *Subject matter and concepts are taught in the child's dominant language.*
Content areas which are considered to be critical to the intellectual and emotional development of the child and to his success in the school environment are initially taught through the use of the child's first language, thereby permitting and encouraging the child to enter immediately into the classroom activities, drawing from all his previous experiences as a basis for developing new ideas and concepts.

V.   *Subject matter and concepts are taught in the second language of the child.*
Since no language can be taught in a vacuum, content areas are also taught in the second language, providing the vocabulary and concepts which are needed for communication while the second language is being learned. Initially the number of ideas and concepts are necessarily few due to the limitations imposed by the amount of language the child controls. The teaching techniques are audiolingual in order to insure the development of listening and speaking skills. As the child's second language ability develops, more and more content is included and the other skills, reading and writing, are incorporated.

VI.   *Specific attention is given to develop in the child a positive identity with his cultural heritage, self-assurance, and confidence.*
The historical contributions and cultural characteristics identified with the people of both languages involved are an integral part of the program. Both the conflict and the confluence of the two cultures are presented in the social development of the State and nation in order to create an understanding and appreciation of each in a positive rather than negative sense.
　　By providing the opportunities for successful participation and

achievement, the child is encouraged to develop acceptance of himself and of others through social interaction.

This is a Revised Statewide Design for Bilingual Education approved by the State Board of Education on June 5, 1971. This revised design takes the place of the one approved by the Board November 11, 1968.

This design will constitute a uniform basis for all bilingual activities of the Texas Education Agency. Such activities include:

Bilingual programs based on State Statutes Articles 2654-1d and 2893, Vernon Civil Statutes.

Bilingual activities in Title I, Title I Migrant, and Title III, ESEA programs.

Projects under Title VII, ESEA.
State Accreditation Standards.

Multicultural curriculum guidelines required by Court Order.

If you need more information or assistance, please write or call

Dr. Severo Gómez
Association Commissioner for Educational Programs for Special Populations
Texas Education Agency
Austin, Texas 78701
Telephone: Area Code 512, 475-6663
M. L. Brockette
Commissioner of Education

IX

The Evaluation of Bilingual Education

William Francis Mackey

INTRODUCTION

Ever since the inclusion in public education of the use of two languages as media of instruction, there has been a growing demand for information on the effects of bilingual schooling and the use in education of languages other than that of the home. The problem was treated in international conferences as early as 1911 (HMSO 1923: 256ff.) and at several international conferences since that date, notably at Luxembourg in 1928 (BIE 1928), Aberystwyth in 1960 (UNESCO 1965), Moncton in 1967 (Kelly 1969a), Chicago in 1971 (Mackey and Andersson, eds., to appear), d'Aoste in 1972 (FMVJ 1973), San Diego in 1973 (San Diego 1973), Suresnes in 1973, and New York in 1974 (Proceedings to appear). Bilingual education itself is of great antiquity (Kelly 1969b); until modern times schooling in another language may have been more usual than schooling in the home language (Lewis 1965). Communities for whom schooling in two languages is an innovation have been concerned about the quality of the education provided to their children. Those who have had to pay for such education have wanted to know what they were getting for their investment. And since bilingual education has so often set off policy conflicts between parents and educators, both have called for evaluations to settle their controversies (Afendras and Pianarosa 1975).

Such controversies have motivated researchers to undertake a number of evaluative studies like those completed by Hughes, Saer, and Smith (1924) in Wales, by Arsenian (1937) in the United States, by Malherbe (1943) in South Africa, by Wieczerkowski (1963) in Finland, by Macnamara (1966) in Ireland, by Lambert and Tucker (1972) in Canada, and by Bustamente (1973) in Belgium—to name only these (Mackey, ed., 1972 and in press (d)).

There have also been periodical reviews of the literature on such experiments, particularly as they affect the measurement of intelligence (Darcy 1953, 1963), the education of young children (Rūķe-Dravina 1967), and mental development (Gulutsan in press).

A review of the published literature reveals that up to the beginning of the Second World War most of the studies were narrow in scope and lacking in experimental rigor; many of them, on the basis of a few local experiments in a few classrooms, elaborated sweeping generalizations on the effects of bilingualism and the value of bilingual education (Mackey 1952).

A general evaluation of bilingual education is as meaningless as the question of whether bilingualism is good or bad. Bilingualism is not something one does or does not possess (Mackey 1958). It is a relative trait that can be described and measured (Mackey 1962).

Bilingual schooling can be judged only for a specific population in a particular place and at a given time. And even after the who, where, and when are known, bilingual education can be evaluated only in terms of the alternatives. These may range all the way from a completely unilingual education to no education at all.

Within such a specific place-time-population context, it is indispensable to understand exactly what we are evaluating. It cannot be something called "bilingual education" or "bilingual schooling," since these vague terms embrace a universe of differences, ranging from the bilingual education of unilingual children to the unilingual education of bilingual children (Mackey 1970a).

We can only evaluate specific types of bilingual schooling one at a time for a particular group in an attempt to answer such specific questions as: to what extent do the modifications in the language behavior of this school population as it is produced in these classes enable this group of learners to achieve this particular linguistic or educational objective? If the objectives are either unknown or too vague, it may be impossible to make any evaluation at all. One may have to be satisfied for the time being with a description of what has been taking place (Mackey 1972; Cohen 1975; Mackey and Beebe).

Since so many people have little idea of what they want, such descriptions, if detailed enough, may help determine the objectives. For it is admittedly difficult for a community to decide what it wants if it has no idea what is possible. If we know what products are available, it is easier to select the ones which best fill our needs. In the case of bilingual education, our analysis of the realities of language contact may reveal that no formula can achieve exactly what is desired. Descriptive studies can at least show what one does not want, and they can enable one to aim at the best attainable objectives. They can also show that the numerous language-related variables within any group, affecting various types and degrees of bilingual behavior within the schools, will make it necessary to consider the evaluation of any one type of bilingual education as being essentially a problem of multivariate analysis.

As attempts to evaluate bilingual education have multiplied, people have indeed discovered more and more outside factors likely to affect the results. So many language-related factors have been identified that attempts have had to be made to put order into the whole area of bilingual education. One of the most notable has been that of Spolsky and his associates (1974). Spolsky has conceived the field of bilingual education in terms of a model composed of a basic hexagonal figure each side of which represents a set of factors which may have a bearing on the operation of a bilingual program. These sides are labeled respectively "psychological, sociological, economic, political, religio-cultural, and linguistic," the center of the figure being labeled "educational." The model comprises three of these six-sided figures, representing three levels of analysis. First is the situational level in which such factors as availability of educational resources, strength of religion and culture and of pressure groups, and the like, are considered. Second is the operational level, at which are considered such factors as curriculum, its cultural-religious content, and the control of the school. Third is the outcome level, which includes such things as scholastic achievement, effects on religion and culture, and the promotion of political awareness.
on religion and culture, and the promotion of political awareness.

As Spolsky points out, such factors have rarely been considered in the evaluation of bilingual programs because suitable means of measuring noneducational variables are simply not available. Even the educational factors have not been measured effectively, and the terms used have been vague. What, for example, does one mean by the quality of bilingual education? Does it mean that children feel happy and secure, that the education fits the capacities of each individual, or that it conforms to traditional styles of learning (Spolsky et al. 1974: 9)? How would one evaluate the relative success of a bilingual program for French-Canadian children in Calgary as compared with a similar program for Anglo-Canadian children in Quebec City, or with the one for French-Canadian children in Winnipeg, or compare an immersion course in Ottawa with the one in Halifax? Long-term and large-scale evaluations are rare indeed; in most countries they are nonexistent (Mackey 1974c).

Since language permeates all of man's activities, the value of any given type of bilingual education depends not only on what is being evaluated and why but on who is being so educated, where and when the program takes place, and how it has been executed. In other words, it depends on the aims and objectives of the program, the people for whom it was intended, their community and language, the changes to which they are subjected, and the ways and means at their disposal.

A successful bilingual education program would be one which attains its stated objectives with optimum results, within the limitations imposed upon the people involved and the situation in which they have to perform. Whether to try to modify the situation or to change the program can be decided only on the basis of an understanding of the above dimensions of the problem—the *what, why, who, where, when,* and *how* of the bilingual-education program. Let us therefore examine what this involves as regards aims; objectives; type of learner; the community; the languages, schools, and teachers at the disposal of the program; and the way all these means are used to achieve the objective.

AIMS OF THE EVALUATION

An evaluation of a bilingual-education program depends on the feature of it which we wish to examine. Are we interested, for example, in the effects of a certain formula of bilingual education on the solution of a particular educational problem or in how this formula compares with a certain type of unilingual schooling? How the evaluation is done will depend on what is being evaluated. Is it the bilinguality of the program or its effects?

Bilinguality of the Program

The main interest may be in the distribution of national languages in an educational system or in the capacity of the system to produce bilinguals. Is each language given its fair share as far as time and subjects are concerned? Or does the use and distribution of two or more languages in the educational system promote the sort of demographic equity desired? The one does not necessarily lead to the other (Gaarder 1970). The use of the same home language in education may be considered an honor in some areas and a stigma in others. For example, Bantus in some of the new African republics struggle for the educational use in their elementary education of their home language instead of English—or some other colonial language; whereas Bantus in the Republic of South Africa can resent the fact that they are educated in the home language instead of in English, a command of which would give them access to better jobs.

In considering the linguistic and demographic equity of a bilingual education program, one may wish to evaluate one type of schooling against another type (Mackey 1970a).

Effects of the Program

The aim of the evaluation may be to discover the effects of a given type of bilingual schooling on the languages themselves, on the community, or on the individuals taking the programs.

Effects on the Language

Government or ethnic-group representatives may wish to evaluate the long-term effects of a bilingual-education program on the languages themselves. Is the program likely to replace the use of one language by that of another? Is it likely to maintain the use of both languages at a certain level? Is it likely to restore the use of an all but dead language in some areas? The distinction between maintenance and restoration may be an important one, even for speech islands that may seem comparable. The fact, for example, that in Western Canada we have a number of isolated French-speaking communities does not mean that we can use the same criteria of evaluation for them—even though they may have the same type of bilingual schooling. In some of the French-speaking speech islands scattered throughout North America, just as in some of the Spanish-speaking speech islands and the many immigrant and aboriginal speech groups, one can indeed evaluate a bilingual education in terms of language maintenance; that does not mean, however, that one can evaluate all speech islands in the same terms. Some of the language difficulties of the Irish Republic could be traced to the use of criteria of language maintenance on problems of language restoration.

In other areas, however, maintenance is not enough. The government may wish to go beyond; it may have to evaluate a bilingual-education program as it contributes to the standardization of an official language. This is especially true when national and international languages are involved. A government may be interested in assuring that the national languages are mastered in a form acceptable to all. Leaders of a speech community may wish to know the extent to which the language learned in school conforms to the international standards of that language—especially if it is a language of wide culture and extra-national communication—such as English, French, and Spanish—with national speech communities located in all quarters of the globe (Mackey 1973).

Effects on the Community

A bilingual-education program is bound to have some effect on the community in which it takes place. The effect may be minimal, or it may be enough to unite the competing factions or contrariwise to split the community apart.

At the national level the government may wish to evaluate bilingual-education programs, not so much for language use, but mainly as they contribute to forging bonds of national unity. This may be based on a knowledge of the national languages or on the formation of attitudes likely to promote interethnic harmony or simply to avoid ethnic unrest. These attitudes may vary considerably from one community to the next. In some communities the national groups involved may view bilingual education only in terms of ethnic equity—evaluating a program, for example, only insofar as it provides equal job opportunities.

Effects on the Individual

Since educators and educational psychologists have long been involved in the evaluation of the effects on the individual of variations in educational procedures, it is not surprising that most evaluations of bilingual-education programs have been of this type. Many have been undertaken by psychologists at the request of parents or local education authorities concerned about the intellectual, emotional, cultural, and language development of children doing all or part of their schooling in a language little used in the home and the effects of such instruction on their scholastic achievement.

Early evaluations of bilingual schooling had propagated the notion that instruction in two languages inhibited the development of creativity and other intellectual abilities (Epstein 1915). Later studies demonstrated that such was not always the case (Peal and Lambert 1962). Some psychologists have argued that studying a second language actually enriches the conceptual development of the child (Vygotsky 1935, 1962).

Psychologists have also evaluated bilingual education in terms of the emotional stability of children forced to do their schooling in more than one language or in one they have not yet mastered. Bilingual education has thus been associated with such traits as stuttering (Pichon and Borel-Maisonny 1964), squinting and left-handedness (Henns 1928), and moral ambivalence (Schmidt-Rohr 1934). Some of these conclusions, however, have been contested.

One may wish to evaluate a program of bilingual education as it affects changes in the attitudes of the children and their cultural stereotypes (Gardner and Lambert 1972).

The evaluation of the scholastic achievement of children in bilingual schools as compared with that of children in unilingual schools has been the occasion for the greatest number and variety of studies. Some studies have concluded that certain bilingual-education programs may result in a relative loss of two years in levels of achievement in some of the basic subjects (Macnamara 1966). Studies of other programs, however, have suggested no such loss (Lambert and Tucker 1972).

While educational psychologists have evaluated bilingual-education programs as they affect scholastic achievement, linguists, language planners, and specialists in language teaching have been interested in measuring the effects of the program on language proficiency (Thévenin 1969). Such evaluation can apply both to the mother tongue and to the second language, to primary and to secondary language skills.

OBJECTIVES OF THE PROGRAM

One of the reasons why so much research in bilingual education has yielded apparently contradictory results is that it comprises evaluations of bilingual-education programs having different objectives. The fact, for example, that children in some bilingual schools have not mastered the national language as well as have children for whom it is the mother tongue may result in an unfavorable evaluation of such schools while in similar bilingual schools the fact that the mother tongue of the children has not been affected adversely may result in a favorable evaluation, although in both cases language knowledge of mother tongue and second language may indeed be comparable. In the United States, where ethnic integration has been a national policy, bilingual education has been evaluated in a different light than it has in Canada, where ethnic diversity, sometimes referred to as the Canadian mosaic, has been accepted as a national objective (Mackey 1974a). For example, as Macnamara (1973: 3) has pointed out, what depresses California educators is the lasting difficulties which their Mexican-American children are having with the mastery of English; what encourages Quebec educators is that the English of Anglo-Canadian children in the Montreal-type "immersion" programs has not been adversely affected by schooling in French.

What is being evaluated in a program of bilingual education will depend on why the program was instituted in the first place: the aims depend on the sort of objectives to be attained. Evaluation should begin with the question "What did the program set out to accomplish?" (Macnamara 1972). Results of evaluation will depend on the possibility of achieving the objectives, their relative importance, and the facilities at the disposal of those responsible for implementing them. In other words, results depend on the sort of objectives, their feasibility, their value level, and their organizational status.

The sort of objective to be evaluated must first be identified and distinguished from the possible objectives. If, for example, the objective is language maintenance, the evaluation cannot be based on scholastic achievement.

Second, the evaluation has to be based on attainable objectives. It is of no use simply to make a list of achievements that one would like to see people attain. One has to know the extent to which certain persons are able to attain them. In other words, the attainment of the objective can be evaluated only in terms of its feasibility. To establish such levels may require preliminary feasibility studies. If the feasibility is low, the objective may have to be dropped.

Third, the relative level of attainment depends on the value of the objectives in relation to other objectives. A nation may be willing to sacrifice a year's retardation in achievement in problem arithmetic in return for a certain degree of literacy in the national tongue; but it may be unwilling to reach this end at the price of the mental development of its children. Evaluation of results depends on cost as related to level of feasibility. Some governments have wasted a good percentage of their nation's budget trying to achieve objectives which are attained by only a small fraction of those attempting them. Large sums could have been saved through a cost-benefit analysis based on feasibility studies.

Finally, the evaluation depends on whose objectives are being studied—those of the parents, those of the central government, those of the regional government, those of the local community, or those of a certain ethnic organization responsible for the evaluation. A rationale for bilingual schooling in the United States, for example, has been suggested by Theodore Andersson and also by Bruce Gaarder (Andersson and Boyer 1970: 41-55).

Before the attainment of objectives is evaluated, the objectives themselves should be analyzed in relation to the dominant national ideologies, the areas of jurisdiction, policy convergence, national and regional priorities, language policy, educational policy, and the levels at which such policies are implemented.

Political Ideologies in Language Policies

It is important to determine at the outset the extent to which the objectives of a particular bilingual-education program agree with the dominant ideology. A program whose objective is the maintenance of a minority language will have little status in a nation dominated by the ideal of achieving unity through uniformity and of integrating all its citizens into the mainstream. On the other hand, a nation whose ideal is unity in diversity might well foster objectives of language maintenance and accord some status to programs with such limited cultural objectives as the appreciation of one's cultural heritage and that of the other national groups.

The long-term ideal may be the creation of nationhood and cultural independence through education in a national tongue after a period of transitional bilingualism. This, for example, was the ideal which India had set for herself after independence, the rationale having been laid out by Gandhi (1909), who believed that "To give millions a knowledge of English is to enslave them," because a foreign language as a mass medium is bound to remain foreign; "We write to one another in faulty English. . . . Our best thoughts are expressed in English. . . . Our best newspapers are printed in English" (Gandhi 1909).

Since human environments differ so much, it is not surprising that language-education policies should also differ (Rubin 1969). The language-education problems of Europe are not those of Africa, and those of Asia are not those of America. There are a number of reasons why this is so. It is that different areas of the globe differ in the number of languages they harbor, the number of people speaking them, what they do and who they are, and where they live, the status and standardization of their language, and its degree of resemblance to neighboring languages. Superimposed upon a pattern distribution of some 3000 languages are the national boundaries of some 200 countries fashioned by the desire of man to expand or consolidate the communities in which he lives. Within these few hundred boundaries are housed all the languages of the world. In most of the countries, however, only one language is considered to be the language of the country—the number of officially multilingual nations is very few, and even these do not recognize all the native languages of all their citizens. It is inevitable that most countries should be faced with problems of language education. But these problems and their solutions will differ from country to country, since in addition to the number, similarity, status, and standardization of the languages concerned, they are determined by the nature of the population speaking them, their degree of literacy, and local educational facilities (Mackey 1976d).

It is in relation to the limitations imposed by available educational facilities, the social structure and literacy of the population, the status, standardization, similarity, number, and distribution of the languages within its territory that a nation must determine the language objectives attainable through its educational and political institutions. These may include such aims as the political, economic, or cultural autonomy of the country, national unity, interethnic harmony, the control of interethnic tensions, the influx of technical knowledge from the outside, and integration into some supranational organization.

Language Education as a National Priority

Attainable language objectives depend on the pressures of other national priorities and their relation to language. In the multilingual societies, national priorities are often language-related (Khubchandani 1967). A need for technicians may be more urgent than is secondary education in the vernacular. Or a lingua franca may be widespread enough to risk its implementation as a national tongue, with the highest educational priority. In Tanzania, for example, Swahili has been chosen as a national language, and a new culture is being developed around it. In other countries, the highest priority may be that of national unity. In India, in the quarter century following independence, concession after concession had to be made to regional languages in order to stop or prevent secession; in other countries, education of whole generations may have to be sacrificed; planning for future generations at the expense of the present one has been a common trait of reformers, and this tendency must be taken into account in the evaluation of national linguistic objectives.

In countries where the primary national values are material ones, the vast majority of the population in any and all of the language groups may be more interested in economic questions than in linguistic policies. In countries where economic development has priority over language maintenance, people will tend to use one language—often that of the economically dominant group—at the expense of the other. This, however, may lead to the complete domination of a single language. In language-education policy, four different types of educational bilingualism have been considered: teaching the national language just long enough to permit its use as a medium of instruction; monoliterate bilingualism, where both languages are used orally but only one in writing; biliterate bilingualism, literacy in both languages, with one language limited to certain subjects; and complete bicultural bilingualism, with all subjects in both languages (Fishman and Lovas 1970).

Areas of Jurisdiction

Objectives are inevitably affected by those who impose them. Some or all of the objectives may be national, regional, provincial, or municipal. This will depend on the various areas of jurisdiction in education, language, and culture (Mackey 1976d).

The choice of objectives may be dominated by the political structure of the country. In loosely centralized national states, the preservation of ethnic languages and cultures may be the aim, and bilingual maintenance the educational policy in regions where ethnic minorities dominate. In Italy, such bilingualism affects only the populations of Trieste, Bolzano, and Gorizia. In Great Britain, it affects schools in parts of Wales and Scotland. In the Netherlands, it is confined to Friesland; whereas in Norway, it is limited to the Finns and the Lapps. A political structure of segmented pluralism as found in certain Central European states will also favor language maintenance through bilingual education. A bilingual-education program may become part of the politics of accommodation (Boelens 1976).

Contrariwise, in highly centralized nation-states, the objective may be the forging of a strong unified nation with a mobile superstructure of trained cadres. Here the educational policy may be one of transfer from one home language to the national tongue. France has given a remarkable example of an educational policy of language integration, and many of her former African colonies have followed suit, without however, adapting the policy to an indigenous language. For them, bilingual education, especially in primary education, is only a concession to their unsurmounted problems—the desire and ultimate objective being to make French the national vernacular. Some former British colonies have similar objectives. In Canada and the United States, it has long been the aim to transfer the community language of Amerindian and immigrant populations, through the schools, from the mother tongue to English. A transfer policy may start abruptly and fully in the first grade, as it has in France and her colonies, or it may extend through primary and secondary school years. As a national policy, it may cover one or more generations. Some countries may have a monolingual nation as a long-term objective but be obliged to settle for a bilingual policy for a generation or so. In such countries—Israel, for example—a long-term transfer policy is not to be confused with one of bilingualization (Rabin 1976).

A policy of bilingualization is characteristic mainly of bilingual or multinational federations. It generally arises out of the twofold objective of cultural autonomy of federated states on the one hand and the sharing of national responsibility on the other. Such a policy has been applied in Yugoslavia and in the Soviet Union, where Russian has been adopted as the second language of the autonomous Soviet republics and used as the all-union language.

Countries with bilingual-education policies differ greatly in the degree and amount of control which they exercise, the flexibility allowed at each level, and the extent and effects of interaction between various levels of society. The control from the central government may be one of executive edicts or one of advice and persuasion. In some federated states there is little central control of language policy. The overall principles are simply states in the federal constitution, as they are in Yugloslavia, and the constituent states are required in their own constitutions to elaborate the application of these principles in their own language and educational policies (Mackey and Verdoodt 1975).

Degrees of Policy Convergence

In highly centralized nation-states, the central government may determine the extent to which education will be bilingual. In nations practicing a certain degree of political pluralism, however, political entities in different regions may have different policies and different objectives. In Canada the policies of the Prairie Provinces have differed from those of Quebec. The extent to which such divergence may be tolerated depends on the degree of autonomy of the constituent political entities. If it is as complete as the autonomy of a Swiss canton, the objectives of a public bilingual-education program may not be questioned. Divergence between the policy of any of the regional entities and that of the central government, however, is another matter; a lack of convergence of central government policies with those of the regions may lead to conflict, pitting the periphery against the center, as it were.

Multinational societies attempt to avoid such policy conflicts, and some have established constitutional provisions for their resolution; others have relied on the application of some overriding principle—assumed or overt (Mackey and Verdoodt 1975). Since it is a tendency of all establishments to maintain the status quo and that of minorities to lend themselves to emotional exploitation of their national sentiments, it has seemed wise to base national language policies on certain overtly stated principles. The two main ones are the principle of territoriality and the principle of personality. According to the principle of territoriality a language belongs to a certain territory. The personality principle, on the other hand, gives the individual the language of his choice.

In practice, these principles may generate contradictions. On the one hand, the state may not be able to give all individuals an open choice of language in education, the courts, and government administration; on the other hand, the application of the territoriality principle may infringe on basic rights. Both principles may have to be applied under certain restrictions (Mackey in press (c)).

Policy Implementation

Success in the application of such principles and other language objectives also depends on how they are implemented and at which level. Imposition of language policies by force may arouse stronger opposition than the implementation of economic ones, especially if the former threaten the employability of a group. Implementation of language-education objectives may take place at the national, regional, or local level. If language distribution throughout any country or area is not homogeneous, the success or failure of a bilingual-education policy may depend largely on its implementation at the community level. The type of adaptation necessary and the ability to implement the policy depend on the social structure of the community, its language-distribution pattern, the nature and degree of contact between language groups, the political and educational criteria of the administrators, the attitude of the population, and the motivation of the parents.

In the last analysis, it will be the motives of parents with children in the bilingual program that may be decisive. Parents who have already lost their ethnic language may simply desire that their children learn enough of it to talk to their grandparents or with other relatives. Or the motives may be economic, in the sense that a better-known language means better education means better jobs. In Canada, this had long meant English.

Although a small minority of English-speaking Catholics in small Quebec towns had in the past sent their children to French (Catholic) rather than English (Protestant) schools, this was only for a few years, that is, "long enough to learn some French." As religious importance decreased, however, ethnic identity dominated. But during the period following the Quiet Revolution in Quebec, French became more attractive to English-speaking parents. In the smaller cities, the law may have forced parents who wanted to be religiously right in their choice of schools to be at the same time ethnically wrong, or vice versa (Mackay 1961). As the effects of the Quiet Revolution in Quebec began to make the English minority feel like one, there was great pressure from the parents for bilingual education for their children. How they succeeded in the context of Modern Montreal could be an excellent case study in the educational ecology of language contact (Mackey 1974b).

The motives of the parents, however, may not always conform to the educational policies of the school system. Educators may indeed agree with the importance of the ethnic language as a vehicle of cultural integrity, and may permit its limited use as a means of improving the self-image of children whose ethnic origin is not that of the national majority. Parents may also look upon the introduction of another school language from a purely educational point of view—basing their policy on the usefulness of the language in the educational system and on its professional possibilities. They may well ask where the language leads in the future education of the children and the extent to which it can be used in secondary school, college, and university. They may also consider the extent to which the language may be useful in the student's future career. Educators in Europe used to consider German necessary for a scientific career, English for business, French for diplomacy, and Latin or Greek for medicine. The cultural status of these languages, however, has been continually changing (Mackey 1973, 1975).

Whether the educators, the parents, the local government, or the central government has the last say may seriously affect the implementation of the objectives. Whether these policies are centrally or regionally controlled, they are at the heart of an interaction network whereby the population (society) through its government may affect and be affected by language policy through its education agencies. But the implementation of curriculum through the teachers (T) and materials (M) may indirectly reach the individual language learner (L) and user, who comes to school from that same population whose language environment has shaped him (S), and determine what he does and learns (L) (Figure 1) (Mackey 1970b). The realities of the environment, however, may modify a policy as it is implemented at the community level and eventually in the school (Mackey 1976).

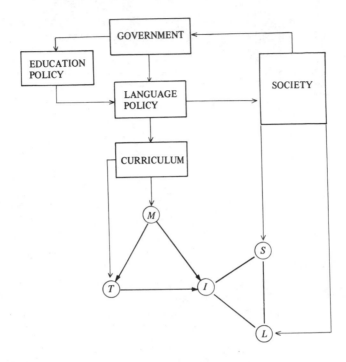

M = Method and material variables: texts, tapes, films
T = Teacher variables: what the teacher does
I = Instruction variables: what the learner gets
S = Sociocultural variables: what the environment does
L = Learner variables: what the learner does

Figure 1   Language Education and Language Policy: An Interaction Model
(Mackey 1970b)

TYPE OF STUDENT POPULATION

In evaluating a bilingual-education program, especially for its effects on the individual, one cannot ignore the influence of many of the individual character-istics—particularly of those which are obviously language-related. If some of the learners in one of the groups share a language- or subject-related advantage not found to the same extent in the other groups, one may have no means of telling whether a difference between the groups is due to this advantage or to the difference in the type of schooling, unless one identifies the advantage and takes into account the extent to which it has influenced the results.

One group may differ from the other in the following language-related and subject-related characteristics: basic demography, language demography, home-language behavior, home backgrounds, psychological profile, school behavior, and homogeneity.

Basic Demography

Basic demographic factors likely to influence the results of an evaluation include the size of the student population and its stability, its age range, the birthplace of the students, where they have lived, and the school they have attended.

While a large bilingual school population may promote a certain undesirable linguistic nucleation, a very small population, on the other hand, may not provide the sort of varied bilingual contact necessary to mastering and maintaining the other language. Communities a section of whose population is highly mobile are likely to produce a linguistically different type of school population than do more stable communities.

A class of pupils ranging in age from six to nine is obviously not comparable with a class of twelve-year-olds. If one of the groups to be evaluated contains a higher proportion of pupils born, raised, or schooled in a country where the national tongue is one of the languages being tested, the language-learning potential of this environmental difference would have to be taken into account.

Language Demography

Even more relevant to the comparability of groups is the particular language composition of each. If one group has a high proportion of pupils whose mother tongue is one of the languages being tested, the two groups may not be comparable. Proficiency in the mother tongue and degrees of extra-scholastic and school bilingualism must also be taken into account. Both languages may have been affected in ways that are not immediately obvious. High-coverage words, for example, may be used more frequently by students from bilingual homes (van Overbeke 1970). There may also be a tendency toward semantic generalization (Segalowitz and Lambert 1969).

Home-Language Behavior

In cases where a significant proportion of those taking the bilingual-education program have a home language other than that of the community, it may be necessary to take into account the home-language behavior of each pupil. The fact that two pupils in the same bilingual community speak the same home language does not mean that they are ipso facto linguistically comparable. They may vary widely in the dialect used, its degree of bilingual admixture, its stability as a home language, the extent to which it is used in the home, the language competence of those speaking it, the type and number of oral and written impressions it provides to the pupil through radio, television, magazines, books, and newspapers, and the extent to which the pupil himself uses it with members of his family. Some way may have to be found, therefore, of measuring the population's degree of bilingualism (Cooper 1969; Mackey 1976c).

The home language in bilingual communities may vary to the extent of supplying the school with a linguistically varied and heterogeneous population (Figure 2). Each student's entering language profile is determined by his own language behavior at home. This may be described in terms of input and output. Frequent and prolonged exposure to the oral forms of a language through radio and television and to its written forms through magazines and books in one language rather than in another may determine the type and extent of the pupil's lexical and collocational repertoire. His output in speaking to either or both his parents, and friends and relatives in one language rather than the other may have resulted in a greater fluency in that language (Figure 3). A quantifiable language behavior profile may have to be established for each student (Mackey 1966).

In a multiethnic community, the language competence of the school population cannot be taken for granted, since each language skill which a pupil may have in each of his languages may exist in any possible level of competence.

If, however, the school population is composed of two unilingual beginning groups to be made bilingual through the school, it may be possible to divide the school population into degrees of bilingualization, the highest degree being found presumably in the highest grade (Figure 4).

Home Backgrounds

Language behavior, however, is not the only relevant characteristic which the home imprints upon the child. It is now widely accepted that such areas as social status and economic status of the family must be taken into account in the evaluation of educational programs. In bilingual schooling such family variables as ethnocentricity, socioeconomic status, geographical and social mobility, social aspiration, and relation with the school and with the community may have to be taken into account.

In each of his languages, the entering language behavior of the pupil may have been fashioned by the stability of the home. In broken homes the child may have experienced a disturbing switch of home language. A pupil's language behavior will also be affected by the pattern of usage and language competence of his parents and their visitors, their literary background as seen in the books and periodicals in the home, their degree and type of mobility, which may have included foreign residence and travel abroad, their economic and educational level, which could result in a certain selectivity, and their educational aspirations for their children, which may give high priority to the learning of languages useful in higher education and in later life.

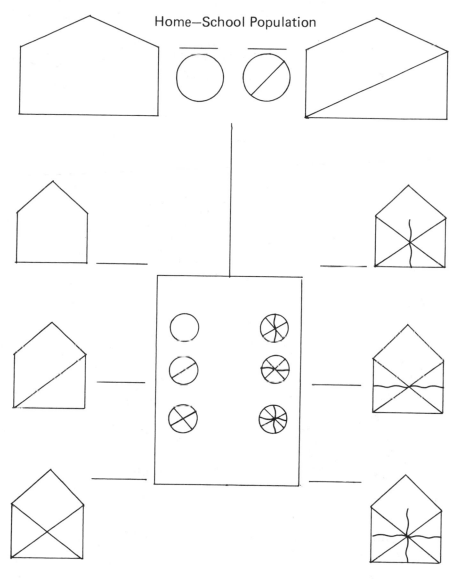

Figure 2   Home-Language Backgrounds

Psychological Profiles

As in any other school, the academic success of a bilingual school population may depend on the psychological profiles of the pupils. These include measurable traits—intellectual, emotional, scholastic, and attitudinal. In bilingual schools, however, emotions and attitudes may be closely related to language and

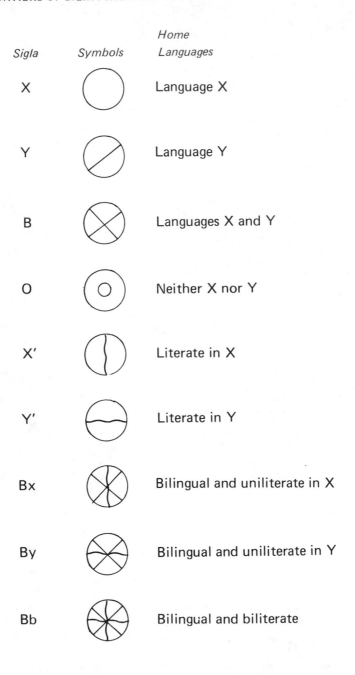

		Home
Sigla	Symbols	Languages
X	◯	Language X
Y	⊘	Language Y
B	⊗	Languages X and Y
O	◉	Neither X nor Y
X′		Literate in X
Y′		Literate in Y
Bx		Bilingual and uniliterate in X
By		Bilingual and uniliterate in Y
Bb		Bilingual and biliterate

Figure 3   Types of Entering Language Behavior

Population

Composition and Distribution

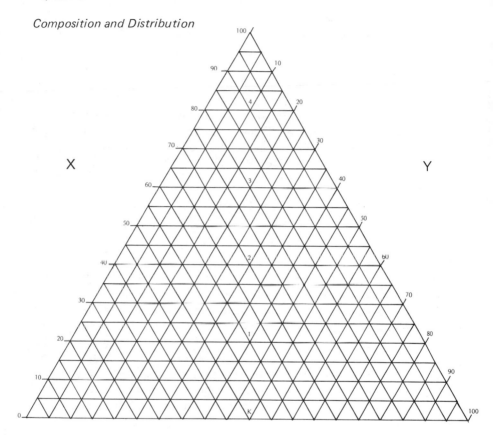

GRADE
$K = 50 X + 50 Y$
$1 = 40 X + 40 Y + 20 B (5Bb + 10Bx + 5By)$
$2 = 30 X + 30 Y + 40 B (10Bb + 20Bx + 10By)$
$3 = 20 X + 20 Y + 60 B (15Bb + 30Bx + 15By)$
$4 = 10 X + 10 Y + 80 B (20Bb + 40Bx + 20By)$

Figure 4   Grade Distribution by Degree of Bilinguality: An Example

intimately associated with past experiences in and outside the home. Within the home, a language may be emotionally associated with a parent or relative whom the child may like or dislike. And the child may come to school with language-related ethnic attitudes fashioned for him in the home. These may affect his attitudes toward his teachers and the school, toward his home language and his second language, and toward the very idea of study and learning. He may also respond more favorably to certain learning strategies (John 1970). The personality, beliefs, and motivation of the students involved in a program of bilingual education may well affect its outcome. So can the student's concept of himself as a member of an ethnic group. Accounts of ethnic heroes and the playing of ethnic music may be brought into the program to enhance this self-image; but if the learner believes that he is a member of a group with no future he may reject its language and culture as a waste of time. This and other factors can produce motivational and attitudinal factors which affect the pupils' success in mastering the language of the program (Gardner and Lambert 1972).

School Behavior

The actual behavior of a student in school is likely to affect the outcome of a bilingual-education program. If he makes little use of either of the languages—or of both—he is unlikely to improve his speaking skill in those languages. A small group of children of migrant workers may be lost in the atmosphere of a large bilingual school and become too timid to speak, in either language, with the teacher, with other pupils, or among themselves. In uniethnic schools, occasion to use one of the languages may be provided only by the teachers, whereas in biethnic schools it may also be provided by the entire student body. Since the actual behavior is relevant intergroup, interpupil and pupil-teacher relations have to be studied.

Homogeneity

Since there are several ways in which one group undergoing a program of bilingual education may differ from another group undergoing the same program, the problem of a group's homogeneity may itself become significant. A group of learners with a high degree of demographic and behavioral homogeneity may create fewer problems than would a large heterogeneous group. On the other hand, if the homogeneity is linguistic, the group itself may provide little opportunity for the use of the other language.

TYPE OF COMMUNITY

The success or failure of one program of bilingual education as opposed to another may be due as much to the community in which it takes place as it is to the nature of the student population for whom the program was intended. If one community opposes the program and another community supports it, results are likely to differ. The program will also be affected by the nature of the community, its size and location, its political status, its socioeconomic character, its ethnic structure, the literacy of each of its ethnic groups, and their cultural and educational facilities and interethnic attitudes (Mackey and Beebe).

Size and Location

A bilingual-education program in a small hamlet may not be comparable with one conducted in a large metropolitan center. If the hamlet is isolated, it may or may not contribute to language maintenance. If, however, it is located close to a population mass speaking one of the languages in question, that language may be reinforced both in the community and in the school.

Political Status

The political status of the community may well determine the administrative conditions under which the program must operate. Is the community a village, a town, a city, a canton, a county, a rural region, a suburb, or a ghetto in a larger urban area? How much political autonomy does the community possess and in what fields? How much control does the community exercise over the bilingual-education program? Answers to such questions may well explain why some programs obtain the crucial community support they need and others do not.

Socioeconomic Character

The economic and social character of a community can well affect the outcome of a bilingual-education program, especially in a biethnic community, since economic and social activity may be culturally determined. It may be significant to know whether the economic function of the community is mainly agricultural or industrial, the extent to which its social character is hierarchical, the effects of class rivalry, the vertical or social mobility of each group, its stability, birth rate, and geographic mobility, its employment level, and its language requirements for obtaining employment.

The problems are made more complex by the presence in multilingual societies of concurrent characteristics such as occupation, race, and religion. In Malaysia, for example, language has been associated with both race and occupation, reinforcing the group loyalty and linguistic nucleation of the urban Chinese on the one hand and the rural Malay on the other. In Quebec education, language has traditionally been associated with religion—so much so that the entire educational system was originally designed as if the population were made up exclusively of English Protestant and French Catholics, so that, except in private schools or in big cities, French-speaking Protestants and English-speaking Catholics sometimes had to choose between their language and their religion. Many of the other ethnic groups, Italian in particular, wishing to educate their children in the language of their choice had to give up both, that is, as far as public education was concerned. With the rise of ecumenism in the Christian religions, however, and the great decline in the influence of the church in the secular life of contemporary Quebec, divisions along language lines began to overshadow those of religion.

Ethnic Structure

What is also likely to affect the language-related results of a bilingual-education program is the ethnic structure of the community in which it takes place—the number and size of the language groups, their linguistic nucleation and ethnicity as reflected in the customs, beliefs, religion, and occupation held in common, and the intensity with which they are practiced and maintained, the political, social, and economic status of each of the ethnic groups, its ethnic organization as reflected in its own schools, churches, and service groups and their importance in the community, and the bilinguality of each group as indicated by the percentage of bilingual homes and interethnic marriages.

The type and number of possible bilingual schools in a community will depend on whether and to what extent the language groups are segregated or unsegregated. In Montreal, for example, the degree of segregation of the population has been reflected in two systems of unilingual schools. When language segmentation is congruent with segmentation upon religious and socioeconomic lines, it encourages the creation of a system of segregated schools as, for example, has existed in Montreal, where there has been one segregated public city school system for English-speaking Protestants and another for French-speaking Catholics. The latter school system maintains English-speaking Catholic schools in which may be found the bulk of European immigrant children, all supported by public funds. Another segregation factor is one of status—most of the managerial posts in business, industry, and finance being held by English-speaking Protestants and by some bilinguals. The English-speaking commercial elite of Montreal who have done business with half a continent have regarded not Quebec or Canada but rather North America as their domain. Having come from and moved to a variety of Canadian and American cities, and being connected with large firms and corporations, they have found it easier to move than have their French professional counterparts. In this context it is not surprising that such people have insisted on a North American education for their children—and not a bilingual one, where much of the time would be devoted to instruction in a language they may never use.

Closer to the base of the socioeconomic pyramid was another group equally averse to a certain type of bilingual education and for similar reasons. These were the immigrants, who had regarded Montreal as a North American city and have not wanted to be hindered from moving to other Canadian cities for better jobs. Like their cousins in Toronto, they found it only natural to send their children to English-speaking schools, thereby integrating them into Montreal's Anglo community and eventually sharing its privileges and prestige. In this way they achieved both vertical and horizontal mobility. For the French-speaking elite, especially in the less anonymous small cities of Quebec, these two highly mobile sociolinguistic classes represented a threat both to the stability of the community and to the survival of its language. This French-speaking elite of professional and local entrepreneurs has been much more stable, not only because of the restricted area covered by its language but also because of the nature of its professions, the success of which depended on personal relationship with local clients and regional clientele. Their mobile English-speaking social counterpart was a different species. The typical one had been a hired manager, an executive of someone's policy, and if a newcomer, a person whose social antecedents were unknown. In a community where independence of income and family tradition were held in such high esteem, such persons could not aspire to the highest status. In fact, the English-speaking managerial class in Quebec has not entered the social circles of the French-Canadian traditional elite. And the Quebec professional elite had little in common with the English-speaking managerial class, and rarely sent its children to English schools. Yet most members of this elite have usually been quite at ease in English, for second-language ability in Montreal has been directly proportional to the number of years of schooling for Francophones; for the English-speaking population it seems to have been inversely proportional. The lower the education level of the families, however, the less the mobility and the longer the contact with French-speaking workers, giving a type of French which has not been the same as that taught in the English high schools.

Literacy

The extent to which an ethnic group is literate in its own language may determine the ease or difficulty with which that language may be used in a bilingual-education program.

The choice, proportion, and use of two or more languages in an educational system may depend on the type and amount of literacy of the population. If the educated have been traditionally literate in a classical or regional language, this literacy may have to be continued, along with a reading program, to make a more useful international language available to the population. This may be more difficult in some areas than it is in others. In countries with ancient civilizations embodying traditional scripts, as exist, for example, in Asia, a primary school pupil may have to master three entirely different scripts, one of which may not even be alphabetic (Kloss and McConnell in press).

Differences in script make different languages seem more distant in their written forms and make biliteracy for the masses difficult to achieve. Because of this, some nations have done away with the traditional script, by adapting a Roman alphabet to the national tongue. The phenomenal creation of modern Turkey is associated with such a move. Here, in the space of a few years in the mid-twenties, Mustafa Kemal Atatürk succeeded in transforming written Turkish from an Arabic to a Roman alphabet and in giving it permanence through a mass literacy campaign. This was accompanied by the elimination from the language of Arabic and Persian forms so prevalent in Ottoman Turkish. As a result, for most Turks reading their language in the 1970s, everything printed before 1928 has become unintelligible. And even when transliterated into modern Turkish, much of it was still unintelligible in context—replete as it was with Ottoman idioms, ideas, and values. The maintenance of an old literary tradition can thus become a new educational burden. In balance, however, this may have seemed a small price to pay for a modernization designed to meet the needs for new social structures.

Cultural and Educational Facilities

In evaluating a bilingual-education program, what may be most crucial is the presence or absence of educational facilities—schools, books, and teachers. If they are not available in one language, the system may have to function in another. Since raising the standard of living may depend on a more educated work force which in turn depends on schooling and eventually on a sufficient number of teachers trained in a world language, some communities may have to put teacher training on the top of their list of national priorities.

The mass media at the disposal of each ethnic group—radio, television, and the press—and the way they are used may well affect the survival of the language as well as its quality. The same can be said for ethnic libraries and the extent to which they are used.

Interethnic Contact

The type and extent of any interpersonal or intergroup contact between two ethnic communities are factors in determining what sort of bilingual education is possible. The fact that two ethnic groups live in the same city does not mean that they are socially any nearer than if they lived in separate towns. In the towns and cities of Quebec—especially in the smaller ones—contact between English and French has been either professional or perfunctory. Even in the sociable atmosphere of sports the different attitudes toward games have discouraged contact—the English seemed to take them seriously; the French regarded them as mere amusements or pastimes—with the possible exception of organized and professional spectator sport which, from time to time, would act as an inflated symbol of civic solidarity.

This segregation of the English and French communities has not, however, prevented a certain number of intermarriages from taking place. The mobile Anglo-Canadian and American bachelor has discovered that he could improve his economic standing by accepting a transfer to Quebec towns and cities. Since the sons of the town's French-speaking elite were away for professional training, the stay-at-home daughters found fewer marriageable men who were equally educated. A number of resulting French-English marriages supplied the schools with bilingual children whose language dominance, it was seen, depended on the socioeconomic level of their parents. It was likely to be French if the income was low and English if the income was high, since the latter, having fathers of the mobile managerial class, were committed to English.

One cannot assume that the closeness of two ethnic groups leads to interaction between them, for population mobility and segregation attenuate the effects of nearness. In Montreal the mobile English have been segregated from the more elite French majority—educationally, socially, professionally, economically, and even geographically. So much so that the bilingual schools that were created had an entirely English-speaking school population, the only French-speaking person in the class being perhaps the teacher. This resulted in the type of school dubbed "immersion" in Montreal—a type which had been the norm in most colonies of Asia and Africa. It is a monoethnic type of bilingual school whereby one language is used as a medium of instruction and a different language as the home language of the pupils. How this type of instruction fares in practice may depend on educational criteria and interethnic attitude.

Interethnic Attitudes

Interethnic attitudes may act as forces which prevent language-related changes from taking place in the educational system. The intensity of ethnic aspiration and the priorities accorded to the objectives of a community, however, may prevail over the effects of group prejudice. But systematic prejudice of employers and the community's attitude toward bilinguals may discourage students in a bilingual-education program from maintaining their home language. As a dominated ethnic group gains economic and social advantage, however, it may begin to pose a threat to the other ethnic groups. The resulting interethnic rivalry may create tension in the school community. The irredentism of a speech community may reach a point where the formerly dominant language is rejected as an instructional medium.

In such cases, the issue may well split the population. Although a majority of people may favor the retention of a national language, they may oppose its being forced upon their children, as the appearance of the Language Freedom Movement has testifed in Ireland, where parents insisted on the right of the individual to choose between Gaelic and English as the language of instruction.

On the other hand, the population may strongly oppose the granting of such freedom. Witness, for example, the demonstration in 1968 of the *Mouvement pour l'intégration scolaire* in Montreal and the vigorous opposition of the French-speaking population of Quebec to a bill (Bill 63) granting parents the freedom to choose the language in which their children should be instructed. In both cases it has been the force of attraction of a powerful language (English) which could only be diverted, both in Ireland and in Quebec, by government edict.

Even the threat of bilingualism may split an otherwise peaceful and congenial town where ethnic relations may have been ideal. The trilingual town of Bonnyville in Alberta in 1971, for example, split into opposing factions after the large French minority of about 50% discovered that they might be given official recognition as a federal bilingual district.

The success or failure of a program of bilingual education depends enormously on community enthusiasm and support. In Texas, for example, the presence of this feature in Laredo and the lack of it in San Antonio may have been the cause of the success of the former and the failure of the latter in launching successful bilingual-education programs (Andersson 1972).

In estimating the effects of public attitudes on the creation of bilingual schools, one must know whether the event is likely to split or to unite the community along ethnic or national lines, or to divide one generation against the other, whether the support is total, partial, or conditional, being the result of general consensus or of ethnic concession.

Since such motives and attitudes vary from one community to the next, the rate at which a community may adapt to change also varies (Mackey and Beebe).

THE LANGUAGES

The success of a bilingual-education program depends not only on who takes it and where it takes place but also on the languages themselves. The problems of teaching in two international languages like English and French are not the same as those of maintaining instruction in a local language spoken by a few hundred people. The fate of the program also depends on the number of competing languages in the community and on which of them have been chosen as school languages (Mackey in press a). The school languages which are used in the bilingual-education program may differ in degree of similarity, status, standardization, and dialect type—all of which will have some effect on the outcome of the program (Mackey 1973).

Number of Languages

Some communities are blessed—or cursed—with more languages than others. In planning for the progress of a country as a whole in power, prestige, or prosperity, the pressure of different groups each clinging to their own language may become an embarrassment (Kloss and McConnell).

Some national leaders may wonder whether linguistic heterogeneity is really necessary, or whether it is a luxury they can ill afford.

Many of the new nations have even found it expedient to adopt the language of their former colonial overlords. A few have even adopted two such languages. The only official languages in Cameroon, for example, are English and French, although neither is among the fifty or so native languages spoken in the country. Yet all public schooling is done in one or both of these two foreign tongues, as it was in the past. These languages, in their local variety, may even be regarded as African languages in countries where they have become media of mass communication, very much in the way local varieties of Latin came to be accepted as national languages.

It is not so much the number of languages in a country, however, which causes the problems—it is their demographic and geographic distribution. We could argue that more languages are spoken in the United States than in most countries. In addition to English, at least a hundred languages are spoken within the frontiers of the United States by populations ranging from one thousand to more than three million, if we count the colonial, immigrant, and native Amerindian languages. But not one of these languages is the mother tongue of more than 3% of the population. The overwhelming numerical majority of English speakers has made it possible to impose English, until recent years, as the sole language of education in the United States. If, however, the number of English speakers had been comparable with that of the other languages, the history of bilingual education in the United States would undoubtedly have been quite different (Kloss in press).

As a case in point, take the Soviet Union, whose population is comparable with that of the United States but whose language demography has a different distribution pattern. Here, despite state control and the predominance of Russian, more than seventy other languages had to be recognized as media of education in the schools. The Soviet Union is a large and populous country and some of the language minorities are represented by large populations. In smaller and less populous areas, language diversity can create problems of a different order. Take, for example, the Netherlands West Indies. In the Netherlands Antilles (Curaçao Group), more than 75% of the population speak Papiamentu and less than 25% Dutch or English, less than 10% Spanish. In other parts of the Netherlands Antilles (the Leeward Islands), Papiamentu is less than 25%, as is Dutch, whereas English accounts for more than 75%. In Surinam, however, some 18 different languages are used, 12 of them by less than 5% of the population, two by about 5%, and two each by about 10%, one (Hindustani) by about 25%, and only one (Taki-Taki) by more than 50% of the population (Stewart 1968). In the planning of its educational policy for this area, where Dutch is not understood by more than a quarter of the population, it was obviously necessary for the Dutch government in The Hague to take these language facts into consideration. As a matter of fact, the Netherlands government in the 1960s appointed an executive director in The Hague responsible for education in Papiamentu.

Numerical distribution, however, is not all; there are also the differences in geographic repartition. If nearly all the speakers of a language live in one part of the country, it makes it easier for the state to recognize a local language as a medium of instruction. This is a factor which distinguishes the colonial from the immigrant languages in America. For example, although the number of native speakers of Spanish, German, and Italian in the United States is comparable—

between three and four million each—Spanish, the first colonial language, is historically associated with a certain region, whereas German and Italian, the main immigrant languages are not (Fishman 1966). In some countries, like Belgium, Canada, Switzerland, and Yugoslavia, the geographical repartition of languages has been so marked as to permit the division of the country into linguistically autonomous regions each with its own language of schooling. Language division along geographic lines is not always territorial in the sense that part of the country is inhabited by people speaking another tongue. It may also be a division between town and country, producing comparable effects. When Malaysia achieved its independence in 1957, some 80% of the population was almost equally divided among Chinese speakers (39%) and Malay (41%), but the Chinese speakers were concentrated in the cities, with their progressive Chinese schools and colleges, besides a large Indian minority, whereas the Malay speakers chose to remain on their luscious and fertile land.

Interlingual Distance

The two languages chosen for the bilingual-education program may be highly similar or extremely different. If they are highly similar, the students will have less difficulty in understanding lessons given in the other language, although in speaking it, they may have a greater tendency to confuse one language with the other. Similarity, of course, is a matter of degree and is therefore susceptible to measurement (Mackey 1976).

In some countries, adjacent languages are so similar as to be mutually comprehensible. In such cases, the more useful one may have been selected as a language of education, with the assurance that all the pupils will be able to understand it. This is the case in areas where dialects are spoken at home and corresponding standardized languages used in the school. It is also the case for certain closely related languages, like Frisian and Dutch. Since there is no structural line of demarcation between different languages and different dialects, interlingual distance is a matter of degree, and this is measurable: some languages are closer than others. There are different types of interlingual distance, however, and different types of interintelligibility (Mackey 1974). This is reflected in the observation that attitudes toward intelligibility are not always reciprocal. For example, although 87% of Swedes think they are understood by Danes, only 40% of the latter agree that they in fact understand Swedish; 76% of the Danes say they are understood by Norwegians, while only 50% of these admit understanding Danish (Haugen 1966). English-speaking tourists, however, have always acted as if everyone could understand them, even though they themselves could understand no other language.

Interethnic attitudes, however, may inhibit interintelligibility of similar languages. In highly bilingualized areas, speakers will admit to understanding the language of highest status and not to understanding an inferior although closely related dialect of their mother tongue. Few Angas speakers admit to understanding the highly similar and nearby Sura language, but they will claim to understand Hausa, the great lingua franca of a vast area in the northern region of Nigeria (Wolff 1959). These attitudes, however, may be conditioned by the relative status of the languages in contact (Mackey in press (b)).

Language Status and Language Attraction

The fact that a language is easy to understand as a medium of instruction or that it is spoken by a good proportion of the population does not mean that it will be accepted by all. People are interested in the value of the language as expressed in its status; but they do not want to invest part of their lives learning what they might consider unimportant languages. It makes a difference whether the language of instruction—especially if it is not the language of the home—happens to have international status, whether it is an official or national language, or only a language of an ethnic minority (Lobelle 1972 and Mackey 1976b).

It is not only the political, economic, and cultural status of the language that has to be considered, but also its linguistic independence as measured in the extent to which it fills the needs of those who use it (Mackey 1973). A language of high international status, even though it is that of a minority, may be preferred as a medium of instruction—especially at the secondary level—to a national majority language. In the past, the French population of Belgium has been averse to having their children do their schooling in Flemish. Language status is a reflection of economic and cultural power (Mackey 1973). A powerful language may be preferred by the educated elite of a nation because it has so much to offer. If an ex-colonial language is chosen as an official language in a country where only a small fraction of the population has completed secondary school, only the elite is then able to enjoy the fruits of independence through control of the nation and the perpetuation of their class through schooling, the born leaders remaining at the local level using only local languages. Some of the first fruits of independence may include mass communication and the consequent acculturation of the country through its bilingual elite. For only they can afford such media as libraries and television, providing books and entertainment in their dominant second language, such facilities being entirely unavailable in the local vernacular. Since it may cost more than a thousand dollars a minute to make a commercial videotape or a television film, but only four dollars a minute to broadcast it, it may be far more economical for a country to buy the package, than to roll its own. In this way, rich countries propagate their culture, their cultural values, and their information through local elites who understand their language. Many of these same languages happen to be instructional media, not only because they have so much available, but also because they are so standardized. The attraction of one of the languages may also be due to its special religious or commercial importances (Ferguson 1970).

Language Standardization

Language skills are a fundamental prerequisite to education at any level. The teaching of reading and writing in school supposes not only the alphabetization but also a certain degree of standardization of the language to be read and written; it also supposes the existence of things in print. The extent of standardization and publication necessary to operate a worthwhile education program in a given language is not known; facts of standardization for the languages of the world have not been available (Kloss and McConnell in press). Some useful typologies, however, have been developed. In a bilingual community, the use of the languages in school may depend on whether one or both of the languages are standard, classical, vernacular, dialectical, creole, pidgin—in a descending order based on presence or absence of four characteristics: standardization, autonomy (e.g., dialect acting as a language), historicity (e.g., association with a national tradition), and vitality (e.g., use as the mother tongue of an isolated community) (Stewart 1968). A highly standardized language like Spanish, English, or Dutch may be more attractive to parents and local educators than a semi-creole like Papiamentu, even though the latter might be the home language of the majority. For a standardized language, with its written code of correct usage, enshrined in its grammars, dictionaries, pronunciation, and style manuals, can be handled in the sort of curriculum planning which public education requires, in a more orderly and less ambiguous fashion, than can a language where the difference between what is correct and what is unacceptable has not been established.

Dialect Type

The fact that a language has been standardized does not mean that the children who claim that language as their mother tongue will come to school speaking the standard form, nor that their parents have any knowledge of such a standard. Some regional dialects like the French of the Swiss Canton of Geneva may be close enough to the standardized language to permit one to ignore the differences. Others like the German of the Canton of Bern may diverge so much from the literary standard as to restrict their usefulness as the sole medium of schooling. That does not mean, however, that their dialectal status is low. On the contrary, they may have a high local status. Contrariwise, the local status of some of the dialects may be so low as to make their use in education doubtful. Or the dialect may be a social one associated with a socioeconomic class (Troike 1968).

The speech situation of the children may also be one of dialectal diglossia whereby they have been conditioned to use one dialect at home and with their friends and another dialect in other contexts (Chantefort 1971). Some children may come to school speaking a home language containing a high degree of admixture, and it may be difficult to tell whether they are mixing two languages or whether their language is already mixed (Mackey 1970c). The distinction is important in evaluating the language component of a bilingual-education program. One must know whether the program has been designed to help the children keep their two languages apart or whether it is intended to enrich the children's home language, and to what extent.

The dialect of the community, however, may be shifting toward or away from a national or international standard. Willingness of one language group in a community to have its children adopt the language of the other group will depend on its estimate, not only of the national or international status of their language, but also of how close the local dialect comes to the parents' idea of the standard. If the local dialect of a language—even one of great international prestige—is considered to be dialectal or impure, it may be rejected. Many English-speaking communities in Canada rejected the teaching of Canadian French because of a belief that it was dialectal. Since they had been acquainted with only a single language, Canadian English—one of unusual regional and social uniformity—they failed to realize that French, like most of the world's standardized languages, was really an abstract of several regional and social dialects, and that Canadian French contained ranges from the professional accents of radio announcers to the dynamic *joual* of unskilled workers. It is not the linguistic facts, but rather the language attitudes of the parents, which comprise the critical attitudinal criteria. The attitudes may be affected by the availability in bilingual communities of different radio and television channels using different languages (Mackey and Cartwright).

Languages of Instruction

The choice of dialects as teaching media may cause as many problems as the choice of the languages themselves. In communities whose dialects are far removed from their relevant standardized languages there is always the problem of whether the dialects themselves should be used in education. Parents who themselves use the dialect at home may object to its use in school.

Even the standard form of a language, however, may not have enough future to justify the investment of time needed to master it. Its use may be limited to oral communication within the class, while all reading and writing might be done exclusively in the standardized form of the second language. Since either language, or both of them, may be used for reading and writing, the educator, in each year of the program, is faced with a number of choices (Figure 5).

THE SCHOOL

After having analyzed the variables in the local and linguistic conditions under which the objectives of the program are to be attained, one must consider the ways and means used to attain them.

The means which may be used in different ways to implement various types of bilingual-education programs include both the school and its teachers. The schools in which bilingual education takes place may impose certain limitations on the program. What a school is, what it has, and how it operates may be crucial

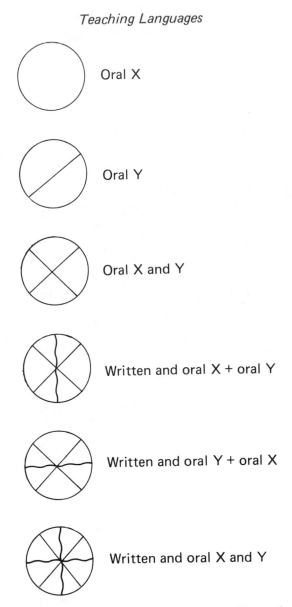

Teaching Languages

Oral X

Oral Y

Oral X and Y

Written and oral X + oral Y

Written and oral Y + oral X

Written and oral X and Y

Figure 5   Options in the Languages of Instruction

factors in determining the extent to which the program can succeed. This includes even its physical environment, as well as its policy and curriculum, its organization and its grouping of students, its type of scheduling and articulation of courses, the teaching materials it uses, and of course, its personnel.

Physical Environment

The location of a school, its available workspace, the accommodation provided, and its accessibility to the pupils may all affect the outcome of a bilingual-education program.

The location of a school and the area from which its student population comes can have some effect on the learning and interethnic attitudes in the school. Multiethnic bilingual schools located in areas of ethnic strife may have to operate at a handicap as far as their program of bilingualization is concerned.

The workspace which the school puts at the disposal of a bilingual-education program may or may not favor its outcome. Workspace may be limited to a small classroom in poor repair or it may include entire buildings containing a special materials room, a language laboratory, and a library.

Accommodations outside the classroom can also be important—recreational and sports facilities promoting interethnic contact, lunchrooms, project rooms, and common rooms where students can meet and discuss, and the provision of transportation facilities for students must also be considered.

Policy and Curriculum Implementation

Schools vary in the educational, social, political, or ethnic ideology on which they are based. Their very existence may be due to an effort to preserve the ethnicity of a group. The school may maintain close relations with the ethnic community, the parents, or the ethnic church. Its continued existence may sometimes depend on a public relations effort. The administrators of the school, however, being professional educators, may be less interested in promoting ethnic policies than in applying their basic educational philosophy. At all events, the support and cooperation of the school board may be a deciding factor just as much as an educational philosophy, such as that of Dalton, Dewey, or Montessori, on which the educational program of the school may have been based.

Such schools will also differ in the way they implement the government policy on bilingualization and the curriculum patterns imposed by the community.

In implementing a bilingual-education policy, local school administrators may not use the same criteria as did the policy makers. The latter may have acted on a criterion of national survival of the language or some other nationwide objective. The administrators, however, being more interested in the fate of the child than in the future of the language, may have to limit themselves to the use of educational criteria. This has led to conflict between the government and the educators.

Application of language policy in a school will depend on the importance given to the language component. The policy may be interpreted as just another language-teaching program, or it may be seen as an occasion to provide an equal educational status for each language.

The big organizational problem of bilingual schools is to fit the language patterns in the curriculum agreed upon by the community to patterns of language usage and language distribution within the classroom. Curricula may be patterned on a single- or dual-medium type, on a language-transfer or language-maintenance program, or as one of complementary or overlapping distribution of languages, as discussed below.

Organization and Administration

Organization is important in a bilingual school, since it may involve the cooperation of two or more school boards, different types of school organization, more and different types of articulation, special bilingual personnel, new types of grouping, curriculum, and policy implementation, and problems of scheduling.

The way the school is organized will to some extent determine the degree and type of bilingualism produced. If classes are segregated or divided along linguistic lines, there may be less interaction and less language learning. The school may be reorganized for bilingual team teaching, individualized instruction in the weaker language, intensive make-up language training, bilingual pairing systems, with additional extracurricular activities designed to prevent or break up language cliques.

The life and death of a bilingual-education program may depend on who controls the school, how the program is funded, and who determines the choice of languages and language standards. The type of school direction and contact with the bilingual program is most important.

Materials

Materials are important to the success of a bilingual program, since the lack of them may put all the teaching burden on the teacher and very little of the learning burden on the learner. The materials may vary in type, access, suitability, and language.

Types

Although one would expect to find as much printed matter (including workbooks and readers) in bilingual schools as one finds in unilingual ones, the same is not true for supporting visual and auditory aids. Since one is never sure of the degree of comprehension of a bilingual class in both languages or in either, semantically functional pictures can help get the subject-matter meaning across, while important language knowledge through the semantic interanimation of words and pictures (Mackey 1965).

Access

As important as having teaching materials in both languages is the ability of the school to distribute them. Some schools have a materials room for the teachers,

Teaching Materials

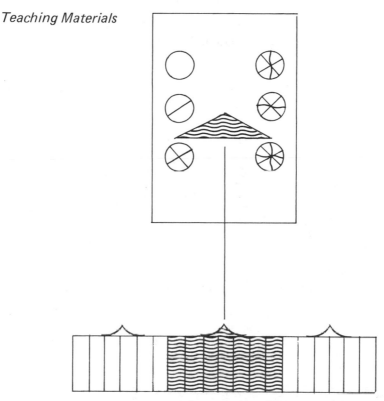

Figure 6   Teaching Materials in the Biethnic Classroom

and in the classroom, an alcove containing materials at the disposal of the pupils, but used at the discretion of the class teacher (Figure 6).

In addition to teaching materials, there are those most important auxiliaries to learning that are the library, the language laboratory, and the audiovisual services. Each can have facilities whose purpose is to promote the bilingualism of the school.

Suitability

It is not sufficient for a bilingual school to have abundant materials; the difficulty may really be that of getting the right kind. The materials may be unilingual in either language, general and bilingual, or specific and bilingual for use in the bilingual area only. Although authentic unilingual materials are of utmost importance, those prepared for use by ethnic groups elsewhere are not always suitable since they may not reflect the pupils' conceptual universe. And again, if they are designed for the sons of an educated elite, they may not be suitable for universal mass education. Cost to the individual and to the group may also decide the choice of materials.

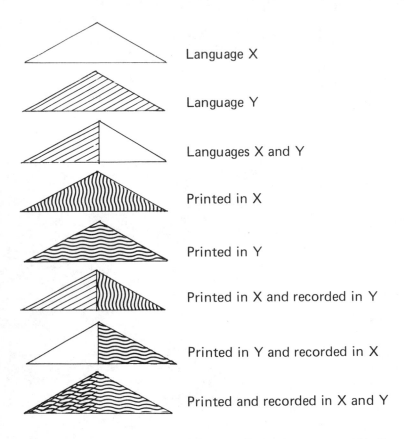

Language X

Language Y

Languages X and Y

Printed in X

Printed in Y

Printed in X and recorded in Y

Printed in Y and recorded in X

Printed and recorded in X and Y

Figure 7   Types of Materials According to Language and Media

Proportion by Language and Subject

If the bilingual learner is going to learn to read by reading, it is important that there be sufficient reading opportunity in both languages. An inventory can from time to time be made of the proportion of the materials devoted to each language and to each subject (Figure 7).

Personnel

It is obvious that one of the determining characteristics of a school is the quality of its personnel, including those specially involved in the bilingual-education program.

In addition to a principal, a librarian, a guidance counselor, a language-laboratory director, and a secretarial staff, a bilingual school may profit by the presence of other personnel whose concern is to maintain the bilingual character of the school. These may include a bilingual coordinator, bilingual teaching assistants, a visual-aids specialist, part-time advisers, master teachers, and resource persons—including volunteer parents. The administrative personnel may promote the bilingual character of the school without necessarily themselves being bilingual. A unilingual principal who is enthusiastic about bilingual education can do more for it than may an indifferent or blasé bilingual.

The staff-student ratio is bound to be an important factor in the evaluation of special educational programs—particularly the ratio of pupils to teachers.

THE TEACHERS

Of all forces that may determine the outcome of an educational program teachers and the quality of their teaching are the most crucial. More perhaps than in unilingual institutions, the success or failure of a bilingual school depends on the competence of its teachers—language competence, language behavior, professional competence, morale, and teaching methods.

Language Competence

In a bilingual school, language is far more than a subject; language competence is expected to be of a high order, since it provides for both models and media.

A great deal of language learning can take place in bilingual schools simply from the fact that pupils may be continually exposed to good models. The very presence of French expatriate teachers in colonial Africa, for example, was undoubtedly a fact in creating an African French of literary quality.

Although a bilingual school can function as such without a single bilingual teacher, some teachers are indeed bilingual, or eventually become so, and may even teach alternately in their two languages. Much depends on the home language or languages of the teachers.

Language Behavior

The language behavior of the teacher in class is a crucial element in the success of bilingual education. It may make a difference if the teacher uses his home language exclusively in his teaching, uses his second language, or uses both languages alternatively.

Professional Competence

Teachers may also be classified by professional competence according to their years of schooling, years of experience, time spent in retraining and in special courses, including courses in bilingual teaching, professional diplomas, teaching versatility, and experience in bilingual education and in teaching the relevant age groups.

The quality of teaching in a bilingual school depends largely upon the training and experience of the teacher, not only the usual, general professional training, but also training for bilingual teaching. In all, it includes general education (in years of schooling, degrees, and diplomas), subject-matter specialization, special education, including specialized teaching and special techniques—like team teaching and language training—including special training in teaching within the language limitations of the group (Mackey 1969). Indeed the way the teachers and textbook remain within the limited language range of the class and expand this range at the same rate as the learners may well become the deciding factor in the success of the program (Mackey and Noonan 1951).

A teacher's experience is valuable not only in the number of years of teaching school but in those spent in teaching a particular age group or a certain subject. Its value also depends on his experience in teaching in a bilingual school.

Teaching Methods

More important than a teacher's training and experience is the way he teaches. Unlike most unilingual schools any subject may have its language components.

The teacher in a bilingual school, whatever he may be teaching, may have to be constantly aware of his own and his pupil's language usage. There may be a language component in each of his courses, and this may include the type and degree of correction, the amount of pupil interaction, and the strategies used in teaching various language skills. When communication is not effective enough— when words fail—the success of the teaching may well depend on the teacher's ability to convey meaning through pictures and other materials. Language-teaching techniques in the language-arts classes may pose special problems in bilingual schools and should therefore by analyzed separately (Mackey 1965). Some skills like reading may pose special problems (Kellaghan and Macnamara 1966).

It is important, therefore, to examine the individual teaching and team teaching skills of the teachers, the level of classroom interaction, the types and extent of language correction outside the language classes, the use of pictorial media, and the techniques used in presenting new material—whether it be in one language only, with or without systematic repetition in the other language, or in both languages by controlled or free alternation (Mackey in press (a)).

Status

What may determine the type of teachers operating in a bilingual-education program is the status they have been accorded. This may depend on the availability of such teachers, how they are selected, their salary level, and the accommodations provided for them.

Morale

The success of bilingual education, especially that of a new program, owes a great deal to the morale of the teachers involved. This in turn depends on whether the program is free or compulsory, whether the teacher is conscious of its aims and objectives, and whether it has the support of the school board and the school administration and the backing of parents and of the population of the community. It will also be affected by the teacher's relationship with the students and their parents.

It is no exaggeration to say that some bilingual programs owe their success to the determination and inspiration of devoted teachers favorable to both language groups, entirely committed to the bilingual-education program and working in a team under an enthusiastic leader who enjoys a good relationship with the parents and the public.

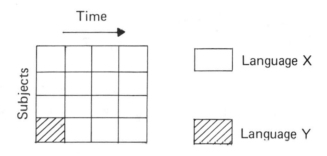

Figure 8   Grid for Classifying Language Distribution in the Program

THE PROCEDURES: CURRICULUM, NORMS, AND ASSESSMENT

Given these means (schools and teachers) to make a particular group of learners in a given community achieve a specific objective, what ways of achieving it were available? What were the options? Which were chosen? Were they the best choices? What patterns of language distribution were adopted for the time range of the program; which types of classes, what achievement norms, and what methods of assessment were used?

Language-Distribution Patterns

Within the national and regional language context, what basic types of bilingual schooling were possible through time-subject distribution within the limits of possible curriculum patterns?

Within this national and regional language context one can see the options according to language distribution by subject over the time range of the program. The time range is expressed horizontally and the various subjects or periods vertically (Figure 8).

The unit of variation along the time scale may be predetermined alternating the teaching language by the month, the week, or the day (Tucker, Otanes, and Sibayan 1970). Or the time variation for switching languages may be completely undetermined (Mackey 1972).

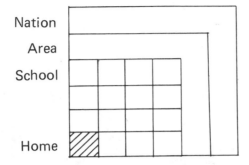

Figure 9   Grid for Classifying Language Distribution in the Community

There is a limited number of area and national language contexts in which a bilingual-education program can take place. If we place the school within the context of the area and the nation, we obtain nine possibilities, depending on whether or not the school program takes place in an area where the language of the home is dominant and in a nation where the language or languages of the area are the same as or different from those of the national language or languages (Mackey 1970a). The possibilities may be visualized in the form of a figure (Figure 9).

The distribution of languages by subject through the program results in a limited number of curriculum language patterns, each tending in a direction which produces a different long-term effect. The program may make use only of a language which is not that of the home, as in the so-called complete-immersion program. These single-medium (S) programs, are opposed to dual-medium (D) programs, in which two languages are used. The program may use less and less of one language, resulting in an eventual transfer (T) of the medium of instruction either completely (C) or gradually (G); or it may continue to use both languages; resulting in their maintenance (M) as school languages. The maintenance may consist of equal (E) and identical treatment of both languages; or it may consist of a different (D) treatment, using one language for some subjects and another language for others. Some of these programs may result in cultural change, that is, in acculturation (A); others in cultural revival, that is, in irredentism (I). The interplay of these basic distinctions generates a limited number of possible patterns (Figure 10).

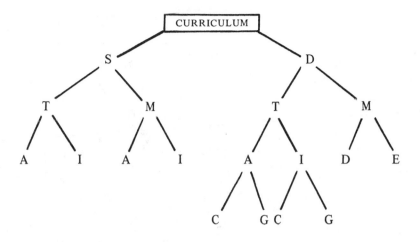

Figure 10   Types of Bilingual Curriculum Patterns

Distinctions between single-(S) and dual-(D) medium programs, accultural (A) and irridental (I), transfer (T) and maintenance (M), complete (C) and gradual (G) change generate ten possible types: SAT, SAM, SIT, SIM, DAT (C) DAT (G), DIT (C) DIT (G), DDM, and DEM.

Each of these types placed within each of the language-distribution contexts yields the full range of basic types of programs (Figure 11). To which of these types does the program belong? Do parts of the program belong to different types, and which ones are they? Is the type of program consistent with its objectives? Some schools having language maintenance as their stated objective may unwittingly be saddled with a language-transfer type of program. In such cases it is not surprising if they do not achieve their objective; and this must be explained in any evaluation which may be made of the program.

Types of Bilingual Classes

To achieve its objectives through a certain type of bilingual-education program the school may organize the teachers and teaching materials at its disposal in certain ways, and group its learners so as to achieve optimum results. How well is this done? How well does the school construct its class types with the people and materials at its disposal? How well do these types fit the type of program presumably based on the achievement of specific objectives (Figure 12)?

Class types depend on the distribution of languages used in teaching and in the materials as related to the home languages of pupils in the class. This can be tabulated as shown at the top of page 267.

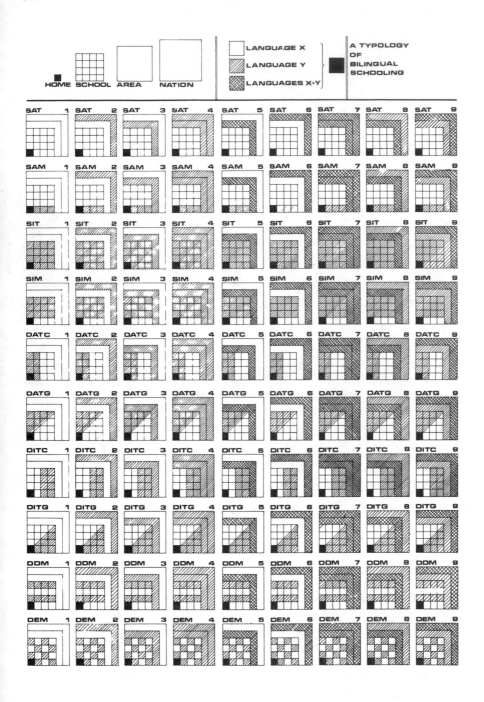

Figure 11   Types of Bilingual Schooling (Mackey 1970a)

Language used in teaching	Language of the materials	Home language of class
X	X	X
Y	Y	Y
M	M	M
		B
		H

X: Language X
Y: Language Y
M: Mixed (both X and Y used)
B: Bilingual home
H: Heterogeneous: composed of unilinguals and bilinguals

Various combinations of these three components can be expressed in such sigla as XYM, MYX, and MXH and arranged in such a way as to reveal the possible

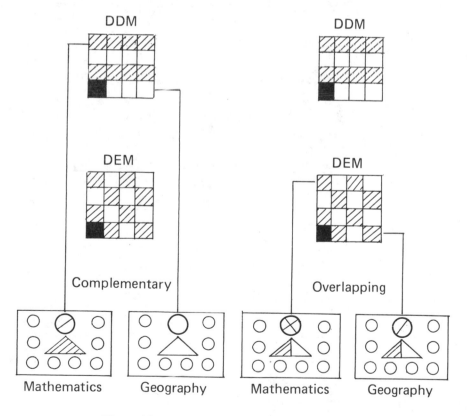

Figure 12   From School Type to Class Type

Figure 13   Types of Bilingual Classes

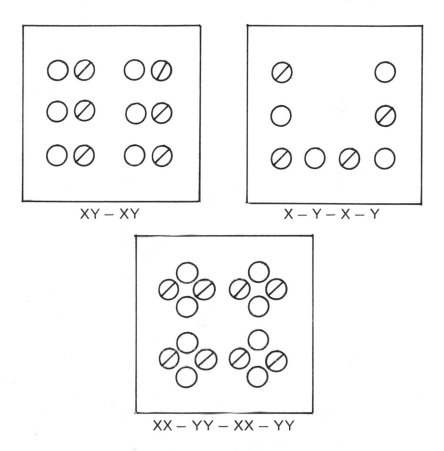

XY – XY   X – Y – X – Y

XX – YY – XX – YY

Figure 14   Seating Arrangements Promoting Bilingual Interaction

class types through which a given bilingual-education program can be implemented (Figure 13).

Within each class the learners may be arranged in order to promote bilingual discussion, bilingual group work, or bilingual learning (Figure 14).

Grouping

If bilingualization with high academic standards is the policy of the school, it may be necessary to group learners along several different lines—not only by age, grade, and academic achievement but also by home-language and second-language competence in comprehension, on the one hand, and expression on the other (Valencia 1972). One criterion may generate more groups than another, so that bilingual schools will differ in the number of such groups, their population per group (class size), the number of teachers by group according to function, and success norms by group.

Mixed School Population

Scheduling

	First period Language	Second period Language	Third period Unilingual Presentation Subject 1	Fourth period Unilingual Reinforcement Subject 1	Fifth period Bilingual Presentation Subject 2	Sixth period Unilingual Presentation Subject 3	Seventh period Bilingual Reinforcement Subject 3
			Grade 1	Grade 1	Grade 1	Grade 1	Grade 1
Room 1	X X X / X X B	Y Y Y / Y Y B	X X X / X X Bx	X X Y / X X By	M M H	X X Y / X X Bx	M M H
Room 2	X X Y	Y Y X	Y Y Y / Y Y By	Y Y Y / Y Y Bx	M M H	Y Y X / Y Y By	M M H
			Grade 2	Grade 2	Grade 2	Grade 2	Grade 2
Room 3	X X X' / X X Bx	Y Y X' / Y Y Bx	X X X / X X Bx	X X Y / X X By	M M H	X X Y / X X Bx	M M H
Room 4	X X Y' / X X By	Y Y Y' / Y Y By	Y Y Y / Y Y By	Y Y X / Y Y Bx	M M H	Y Y X / Y Y By	M M H

Figure 15   Scheduling the Bilingual Program: An Example

Grouping by mother tongue, home language, level of comprehension, or scholastic attainment is bound to affect the size and number of groups and the language distribution within each of them. This may determine the dosage of instructional languages and the number of teachers with whom each group has contact.

Success norms may vary from group to group. In return for the mastery of the other language a year of retardation in the basis subjects may be considered normal for some of the groups. Some schools may operate more efficiently on a system of multiple grouping.

Scheduling and Articulation

The price of this multiple grouping according to both the bilingual curriculum and the home-language and second-language ability of the pupils—effective as it may be—is a scheduling problem much more complex than that of unilingual schools. Classes may be organized at one time of the day across grades, by first- and second-language achievement levels, at another time of the day by subject and grade, and at still another time to permit language alternation in teaching. For an example of such a multiple schedule see Figure 15.

Articulation between language-related courses is one of the biggest problems of bilingual schools, especially if there are several subgroups or special classes based on degrees of language competence. There are the problems of articulation not only between the years and between the language courses themselves, but also between these and the subject courses. In cases where classes are split along language lines time may have to be scheduled to permit daily language alternation in the same subject, and daily articulation sessions for the teachers.

Achievement Norms

Results achieved through the implementation of the bilingual-education program will have to be evaluated according to the norms stated in the objectives to be achieved.

These may be the same as those of comparable unilingual schools, they may be uniformly lower or higher, or they may vary according to whether they are linguistic or scholastic.

Linguistic norms in bilingual education may be those of the mother tongue of unilinguals, so that the learner is evaluated as if he had two mother tongues. These may be set at the same age level as for unilinguals, or one of the language norms may be set at an age level a few years below that of the unilingual so that, for example, the second language of the twelve-year-old learners would be judged by achievement norms of nine-year-old unilinguals. On the other hand, the language achievement of the learners may be judged by second-language norms, for both languages or for either so that, for example, one or both of the languages of the elementary school graduates of the bilingual program might be judged by second-language norms for high school graduates specializing in the relevant foreign language.

The bilingual program may of course have established its own norms so as to take into account the particular types of home-language use of the learners. These may show a certain tolerance for the use of non-standard forms, permissible word borrowings, and dialectal variants.

Scholastic norms other than language may also be identical to those of the age group of comparable unilinguals. Or they may be different for certain subjects—depending on the objectives of the program. These, for example, may include a sacrifice of a year of achievement in subjects like history, geography, or problem arithmetic in return for the achievement of the language norms.

Assessment Methods

How these norms are assessed may vary considerably from one program to another. Some may make use of tests, examinations, or exhaustive inventories—or of all these methods.

In addition to description of the program and its objectives, most evaluations have included some sort of pretesting to discover the state of the pupil's knowledge before the program begins and some sort of posttesting after the program has been under way for a certain period of time. In longitudinal evaluations—which have been very few in number—this process may have to be repeated year after year.

Certain types of pretests may be used as a basis for comparing learners in the bilingual-education program with those in other programs. Such instruments, which may include readiness tests, non-veral I.Q. tests, and picture-vocabulary tests, are used to select groups of learners whose intelligence and attainment may be comparable with those of the bilingual education group.

The tests may include norms which have been standardized on unilingual learners. Some may have been designed for objective machine correction and mass administration. It is important to analyze such tests to discover exactly what they have measured and at what level (Savard 1969).

In order to obtain a better sample of the learners' performance, especially in the language skills, written and oral examinations may have been used in an attempt to obtain larger samples of the students' language performance.

Finally, since such samples do not give a complete picture, inventories may have been made to establish levels of vocabulary attainment in both languages. These may involve availability and familiarity texts (Mackey, Savard, and Ardouin 1971). Published studies on bilingual education by Wieczerkowski (1963), Macnamara (1966), Lambert and Tucker (1972), and others provide examples of the use of various assessment methods in studying the results of a bilingual-education program.

Objective tests, however, do have limitations, and because of this, it would be foolish to ignore the considered judgments of those closest to the program who have observed it with interest and concern over the longest period. The teachers and administrators most committed to the program are also most capable of throwing light on the interpretation of the results of tests and examinations. In addition to tests, examinations, and inventories, a battery of questionnaires will have to be developed in order to gather and quantify information about the community, the school, the learners' home background and language behavior, and the languages themselves. These questionnaires will have to be adequately pretested and standardized for the particular community (Mackey 1972). This battery of questionnaires, which may include a sociolinguistic survey of the community, is best administered before the program begins, since the inauguration and very existence of the new program may have some effect upon the replies. For the returns will have to be used to establish the comparability of various groups and the degree of influence of extrascholastic factors on the results achieved.

Since these factors are varied and numerous, the appended checklist may be of some help in the work of designing such questionnaires. The design of survey questionnaires, however, their testing, administration, and evaluation of returns, is a technical skill and it may be best to undertake this work in collaboration with specialists in the field.

CONCLUSION

In taking all the above factors into consideration one must not forget that they are not static; they are continually evolving but at different rates (Mackey 1970a).

The type and formula of a multilingual educational system may, for example, depend on the social structure of the population as control passes from the hands of an educated elite to those of the people and their elected representatives; and the educational system may be forced to change as well, especially if the elite has been educated extensively through a foreign language. This is the educational dilemma of several African countries. Their colonial educational systems, operated exclusively in the colonial language, were designed to produce a small number of well-educated persons capable of specialization in the home country. These comprised not only administrators but professionals as well, including some highly trained teachers. Their number after independence, however, was insufficient to meet the popular demand for schools. The unilingual curricula of such schools was suited to an elite, not to the needs of the masses for universal and fundamental education. To adapt the schools to these needs of a multilingual population, without sacrificing the continued and growing needs of the nation for well-educated professional people, presented schooling problems which were vaster, more complex, and more urgent than those of most other countries.

The choice, use, and effectiveness of languages in education may therefore depend on the degree of change in the immediate and distant social environment of the school. The immediate environment includes the school population and the distribution and status of each of its home languages. It also includes the related parent populations and the way they are categorized according to language use, education, and socioeconomical level.

The demographic characteristic of the surrounding community and its political power structure affect the language attitudes and educational decision of the parent population and eventually have an effect on the function of two or more languages within the school population. So do the demographic characteristics of the area and the nation and the implementation of official language policy.

It is only after studying these immediate and distant sociolinguistic forces in a particular environment, and their variables, that we can estimate the effects of a bilingual-education policy. Because these include so many variables, the evaluation of a bilingual-education program may depend on the discovery of correlated factors through the use of techniques of miltivariate analysis. In any objective evaluation of an educational program we must always consider the scientific assumptions on which any such study is based and its epistemological conception of human behavior as the result of environmental factors triggering an inner mechanism whose elements and operations are supposedly known. One must, however, keep in mind the limitation of these assumptions and the fact that we are really dealing, not with a mechanism, but with the behavior of self-motivated and often unpredictable human beings (Winch 1958). The evaluation of bilingual-education programs may help us understand what is happening and why it is happening; but it cannot provide us with a total guarantee that if such programs are repeated the results will always be the same.

A Checklist of Variables
EVALUATING BILINGUAL EDUCATION
Some Relevant Questions

I.   *What* is being evaluated?
    A.   The bilinguality of the program
        1.   Language distribution
        2.   Demographic equity
    B.   Its effects
        1.   On the languages
            a.   Replacement
            b.   Maintenance
            c.   Restoration
            d.   Standardization
        2.   On the community
            a.   National unity
            b.   Interethnic harmony
            c.   Ethnic equity

        3.   On the individual
              a.   Intellectual development
              b.   Emotional stability
              c.   Cultural development
              d.   Scholastic achievement
              e.   Language development
                    (1)   In the home language
                    (2)   In the second language
 II.   *Why* does the program exist?
        A.   Objectives
              1.   Type of objectives
              2.   Their feasibility
              3.   Their relative value
              4.   Who was responsible for them?
        B.   Relation to priorities of language policy
              1.   Integration
              2.   Diversity
        C.   Relation to priorities of education policy
              1.   Literacy in the home language
              2.   Literacy in the national languages
              3.   Equality of educational opportunity
        D.   Areas of policy jurisdiction
              1.   Over language and culture
              2.   Over education
        E.   Policy convergence
              1.   Between regions
              2.   With national policy
              3.   Resolution of policy conflicts
        F.   Policy implementation
              1.   Who implements the policy?
                    a.   A national body
                    b.   A regional authority
                    c.   A local authority
              2.   Using what priorities?
                    a.   National
                    b.   Regional
                    c.   Local
                          (1)   Community priorities
                          (2)   The parents' priorities
                          (3)   The educators' priorities
III.   *Who* is being evaluated (the students)?
        A.   Who are they?
              1.   How many?
              2.   How old?

        3.   Where were they born?
        4.   Where have they lived?
        5.   Where were they educated?
        6.   How stable is the group?

B.   What languages do they speak?
        1.   At home?
        2.   Among themselves?
        3.   How well do they know their home language?
        4.   How well do they know the second language?
        5.   How much do they use each language out of school?

C.   What do they use their languages for?
        1.   At home (dialect used)?
        2.   How often?
        3.   How consistently?
        4.   How well?
        5.   What languages do they hear and read?
            a.   On television and radio?
            b.   In magazines and newspapers?
            c.   From parents and relatives?
        6.   What languages do they speak and write?
            a.   To parents?
            b.   To other relatives and friends?

D.   What sort of homes do they come from?
        1.   Do the parents intend to preserve a language?
        2.   What is their social and income level?
        3.   How long have they been at that level?
        4.   How long have they been in the area?
        5.   How much education do they have?
        6.   How much do they want their children to get?
        7.   How active are they in the community?
        8.   Do they attend school activities?

E.   How do they feel?
        1.   About their home language?
        2.   About the second language?
        3.   About the school?
        4.   About learning in general?
        5.   About their ethnic group?
        6.   About their future?

F.   How do they behave?
        1.   With their teachers?
        2.   With other students?
        3.   With their own group?

G.   How alike are they?
  1.   Linguistically
  2.   Socially
  3.   Economically
  4.   Ethnically
  5.   Psychologically

IV.   *Where* are they (the community)?

A.   Where is the program located?
  1.   Size of community
  2.   Density and isolation

B.   How independent is it?
  1.   What sort of political unit is it?
  2.   What does it control itself?
  3.   What is controlled from elsewhere?

C.   How do the people live?
  1.   How do they make a living?
  2.   Are they divided into social classes?
  3.   How rigid and stable are the classes?
  4.   Is there any class rivalry?
  5.   Are many leaving or settling in?
  6.   How many are out of work?
  7.   How many need to learn another language to get a job?

D.   What sort of people are they?
  1.   How many languages are used and by how many people?
  2.   How many ethnic organizations are there and of what strength?
  3.   Are some of the jobs in the hands of certain ethnic groups?
  4.   What sort of ethnic organizations are there: church, school, social, political?
  5.   Do some have special political or social status?
  6.   Are some more bilingual than others?
  7.   How much contact is there between the ethnic groups?

E.   How many in each ethnic group can read and write?
  1.   In one language?
  2.   In more than one language?

F.   What facilities do they have?
  1.   How many public and ethnic libraries?
  2.   How many radio and television programs in each of the languages?
  3.   How many newspapers and magazines?

G.   How do the ethnic groups get along?
  1.   Who is prejudiced against whom and to what extent?
  2.   Do members of some ethnic groups have difficulty getting certain jobs?

        3.   What are the priorities of each ethnic group?

        4.   Is there rivalry between groups, and how is it expressed?

        5.   What is the attitude toward bilinguals and mixed marriages?

V.   *Which languages* are involved?

    A.   How many languages are involved?

    B.   How different are they?

    C.   How important are they?

        1.   Economically?

        2.   Politically?

        3.   Socially?

        4.   What can be done with them?

    D.   How standardized are they?

    E.   What dialects are used and in what way?

        1.   How close are they to the standard?

        2.   How are they considered in the community?

        3.   How are they used in education?

        4.   Is one dialect used for one thing and another for something else?

        5.   How intermixed are the languages?

        6.   Do more and more people tend to use one language rather than the other?

VI.   *Which schools* are used?

    A.   Where are the buildings and what are they like?

        1.   In what sort of area are they located?

        2.   How much workspace is there for the program?

            a.   How many classrooms and what are they like?

            b.   What per capita library facilities?

            c.   Is there a materials room?

            d.   Is there a language lab?

        3.   What sort of accommodation is there?

            a.   For recreational activities and sports?

            b.   For eating and drinking: cafeterias, canteens, and dining rooms?

            c.   For social activities: common rooms and project rooms?

        4.   How accessible is the school?

            a.   Distance traveled to school

            b.   Public transportation

            c.   School transportation

    B.   What are the aims of each school?

        1.   Does it have a religious, social, or political ideology and which sort?

        2.   Does it operate under a particular educational ideology (Montessori, école active, etc.)?

        3.   Is it operated for any ethnic group?

      4.   How does it relate to the community, the parents' organization, or the church group?

      5.   Do its aims have the cooperation of the school board?

      6.   Does it operate under certain administrative criteria?

      7.   What is its policy on extracurricular activities?

C.   How is it organized and administered?

      1.   Who has the authority?

      2.   Who pays for the school and its programs?

      3.   Who determines choice of language to be used?

      4.   What sort of director does it have and what are his contacts with the program, with its teachers, and with the community?

D.   How are the students grouped?

      1.   By which criteria?

          a.   By age?

          b.   By level?

          c.   By language comprehension?

          d.   By home language?

      2.   How many groups are there?

      3.   How many students per class?

      4.   What is the home-language distribution in each?

      5.   What teaching languages are used in each?

      6.   How many teachers per class?

      7.   How are the students seated?

          a.   In home-language blocks?

          b.   Alternatively by languages?

          c.   By which seating pattern?

E.   How is the school day divided?

      1.   How are the groups scheduled?

      2.   How do students advance from one level to the next?

F.   What sort of teaching materials are there?

      1.   What is available in each of the languages?

          a.   Textbooks

          b.   Visuals (including films)

          c.   Audio (including tape)

      2.   How accessible are these?

          a.   Are they easily available?

          b.   How are they distributed?

      3.   How suitable are they?

          a.   For whom were they first published?

          b.   How much do they cost?

              (1)   Individual students

              (2)   The school

          c.   How much of the teaching can they do?

      4.   How much of the teaching material is there for each of the subjects and in what language is it?

   G.   How many people have jobs at the school and what do they do?

      1.   How many program coordinators?

      2.   How many curriculum-development persons?

      3.   How many librarians—bilingual and unilingual?

      4.   How many language advisers?

      5.   How many language assistants (adult and pupil)?

      6.   How many volunteer parent aides?

      7.   How many office staff—bilingual and unilingual?

      8.   How many specialists and master teachers?

VII.   *Which teachers* participate?

   A.   How well do they know the languages they use?

      1.   Their second language?

      2.   Their home language?

   B.   How do they use them in their teaching?

      1.   How many teach in their home language?

      2.   How many teach in their second language?

      3.   How many teach in two languages?

   C.   How competent are they as teachers?

      1.   How many years of schooling do they have?

      2.   Which profressional diplomas do they hold?

      3.   How many years of experience?

      4.   How much experience in bilingual teaching?

      5.   How many specialist courses?

      6.   How much training in bilingual education?

      7.   How much experience with certain age groups?

      8.   How versatile are the teachers?

      9.   Did they volunteer for the program?

   D.   How do they teach languages and other subjects?

      1.   How do they stage the primary language skills: listening, speaking, reading, and writing?

      2.   How do they correct errors and how often?

      3.   How do they present and exercise new language forms?

      4.   How do they use the materials, including the visuals, and how often?

      5.   How do they present new concepts in various subjects?

         a.   In one language only?

         b.   In both languages—alternatively, consecutively?

      6.   How much interaction is there in the classes?

   E.   How do they feel about the program?

      1.   How committed are they to it?

      2.   Do they understand its objectives?

      3.   What do they think about bilingual education?

      4.   Do they work as a team?

      5.   What sort of support do they have?

          a.   From the administration?

          b.   From the parents?

          c.   From the community?

  F.   How do they rate in their profession?

      1.   How are they chosen?

      2.   What is their salary range?

      3.   What workspace are they given?

      4.   How competitive is their job?

VIII. How does the program operate?

  A.   How are the languages distributed?

      1.   In relation to the national and area language?

      2.   By time and subject?

      3.   According to the curriculum objectives?

      4.   What basic type of bilingual education predominates?

  B.   What sort of classes have been organized?

      1.   How do they relate to the type of program?

      2.   Is the instruction unilingual or bilingual?

      3.   Are the materials unilingual or bilingual?

      4.   Are the students unilingual or bilingual and to what extent?

      5.   What type of classes are treated by the grouping of students, materials, and teaching methods according to language?

  C.   What level of attainment is to be reached?

      1.   In each language?

      2.   In each subject?

  D.   How is the attainment determined?

      1.   Unilaterally or comparatively?

      2.   By which methods?

          a.   Examinations

          b.   Special tests

          c.   Special inventories

      3.   What have been the results and how are they judged?

X

Bilingual Education and Language Planning *

Joan Rubin

In recent years, interest in both language planning and bilingual education has grown, each independently of the other. In this paper I would like to explore how a language-planning approach may enhance planning for bilingual education. The discussion will first elaborate on the field of language planning and then consider the contribution language planning can make to bilingual education, especially in the American context.

LANGUAGE PLANNING

Language planning is *deliberate* language change, that is, changes in the systems of a language code or speaking or both that are planned by organizations established for such purposes or given a mandate to fulfill such purposes. Language planning begins with the identification of a problem, in particular with the identification of concrete areas of society that demand planned action regarding language resources. Language planning is thus focused on problem solving and tries to find the best (or optimal, most efficient, most valuable) alternative to solve a problem (Rubin and Jernudd 1971).

What might a language problem be? On the one hand, it is often defined in terms of language choice—the need to decide which variety/language will be used

*Originally presented in Albuquerque, N.M., Nov. 25, 1974. I wish to acknowledge the gracious help of Shirley Heath on an earlier draft of this paper.

by certain sectors of the polity. An example of such problems might be what language to use as a medium of instruction in education, or what language to use in mass communication, or what language to use in the legislature. It might also be defined as the modification of a language code to certain preferred specifications, namely, the modernization and standardization of the lexicon, grammar, pronunciation, or discourse. On the other hand, language problems could and have been defined in terms of societal needs, in terms of broader socioeconomic goals. Such goals might be the need for more ready access to information in industry or the need to reach a particular group to spread the message of family planning or agricultural improvements. Jernudd and Das Gupta (1971) have suggested that the definition of language problems should focus not merely on linguistic phenomena but rather on the sociopolitical motivation or rationale behind the isolation of language problems. These should be included in the classification and understanding of what language problems are. It seems that unless we understand how changes in language code or speaking relate to and are motivated by social concerns, we cannot do proper planning; in fact we are doomed to great frustration and waste of funds.

A couple of examples here, of the need to consider language problems in their social context, might clarify this point. About 5 years ago in the United States, a few linguists hit upon the idea that by writing readers in Black English they would enhance the black students' performance in school. This idea met with strong opposition. The black parents and teachers objected on the grounds that this would put black students in a disadvantageous position vis à vis the white student. Others noted that the difficulties did not lie in the language sphere but rather in the teacher's expectation of the student's incompetence. Changing the primer would not necessarily change the teacher's expectations (whether the teacher was black or white). Instead, it seemed important to focus on the teacher's attitudes. It might be said that using these Black English primers would call the teacher's attention to the student's need for greater understanding but it would not necessarily improve the teacher's expectations of the student. More important, a program which changes the school language without changing the society is directed only at the symptom and not at the cause of the problem. Indeed many remedial-education programs are ineffectual because of their isolation from real-life situations.

Another example of the need to relate language planning to real-life situations is the requirement for foreign-language study in American universities. The problem identified by many was the lack of knowledge about foreign languages typical of many Americans. As a result, a great deal of value was given to the requirement that each college student take two years of language. As a consequence of the limited view of language, a great deal of money was spent on teachers, materials, and students' time with little success. This problem was confounded by the lack of clarification of which language skills the student was indeed supposed to acquire. Still, it seems the problem was put backward. Instead of identifying a real need in the community for this skill, such as regular communication with non-English speakers in business or social interaction, the need was seen as an academic deficiency. Naturally, the necessary motivation or goals were not present and the entire venture was doomed to fail. A language problem must arise from the social setting; the need must somehow be felt by the target/client group; advantages must be perceived by them or else the problem is not really a problem and no amount of planning can change the situation.

Another characteristic of language planning is that it is future-oriented. That is, the outcomes of policies and strategies must be specified in detail in advance of action taken. In any forecasting there is uncertainty or risk, and therefore planning must allow for reformulations as new situations develop and as demands change. One of the useful contributions of the planning approach is that some sort of measure is established in advance by means of which one can assess whether what was set out was achieved and/used and whether the strategies have indeed been effective.

In an earlier paper (Rubin 1971) I outlined several steps to the planning process: fact finding; establishing goals, strategies, and outcomes; implementation; and feedback. Although planning may include these steps in different orders and degrees, consideration of all of them makes success more likely.

In the first step, the planner must have a certain amount of information about the situation in which the plan is to be effected. Probably, the more information the better. He should know something about the needs of the target or client which he intends to serve. He should know something about the sociolinguistic setting in which the plan is to be effected: what the patterns of usage are. He should recognize how his plan relates to other ongoing socio-economic and political processes. He should have some idea about the value of already functioning related models—in the case of bilingual education this would include knowledge of alternative bilingual models, of alternative effects of these models, of acceptance of these models. An example of where detailed information was gathered before making policy is the Bilingual/Bicultural Commission in Canada which did extensive studies before making its recommendations to the legislature.

In the second step, several levels of decision making and different personnel are involved. A policy maker may identify certain problems as requiring attention. He will then decide on the degree of priority he and his cohorts want to assign these problems, the decision depending in large part on the amount of money allocated to a particular piece of legislation. Sometimes the policy maker decides on policy based on knowledge of prior studies and a thorough assessment of the values and attitudes involved, but more often such decisions are made without prior studies. As a result, the problem of working out strategies, assessing available materials and human resources, and coming up with proper strategies to meet the stated goals of a piece of legislation is often difficult if not impossible. In the case of U.S. bilingual education, similar problems arose. The legislation came first, and only now are they beginning to get some training programs and materials development going so that they can begin to accomplish what was set out as goals.

The setting of goals seems to take place at several levels. First, a legislature may establish some general goals and assign responsibility for the implementation of a piece of legislation. Then the agency or institution which receives the mandate may define these goals more specifically, taking into account the amount of funding received and the capabilities of the staff. Finally, the implementors may define the goals in terms of the local situation. Often, in actual planning, outcomes are not established in advance even though it would be helpful if they were. Then, one could have some sort of evaluation of the strategies used.

The next step in planning is implementation. This process could involve (1) mobilization of resources and general financial and personnel management, (2) motivation and supervision of those concerned with both the management of the program and its targets, (3) the sequencing and coordination of related aspects of the policy, such as the preparation of texts in languages not formerly used as media of instruction. Needless to say, proper implementation is a critical variable in the success of any plan.

The fourth step in the planning process is evaluation. This includes analysis of trends and a general monitoring system as well as evaluation of specific aspects of a particular program. The planner needs to know whether the plan has in fact worked. He must assess whether the actual outcome matches his predicted outcome, and if not, why not. He must know this to modify his strategies in order to achieve his predicted outcome. Again, evaluation while critical at all states of planning is often the least attended to.

This completes the list and definition of the four steps or parts of planning, that is, fact finding; policy setting with goals specification, consideration of strategies and resources and predicted outcomes; implementation; and feedback. It is clear that planning in fact never quite matches this model. Not all planning includes the necessary evaluation or has the appropriate prior fact finding. Goals are often multiple, hidden, and not well ordered. Outcomes are not clearly specified in advance. But the model is there to help us when we need it. In addition, it is probably not a good thing to think of planning as a series of steps but rather to recognize that these steps may come into play at different points in the planning process. For example, goals may be set at a very high level in response to some general feeling that a problem exists. Then before proceeding with the establishment of strategies it might be necessary to gather further facts. Or evaluation might be included as a regular part of the implementation process.

There are several things to notice about language planning. First, policy making is not planning. Often, when evaluating the process of language planning, people say that language planning has failed. Upon closer examination, it turns out that there was little clear indication of the means of implementing the policy and little consideration of alternative means to achieve the goals. If the policy maker does not have proper background information and does not recognize that the plan must be coordinated with other sociocultural processes, it is more than likely to remain just a policy. A simple example will indicate what I mean. A Russian scholar tried to show the failure of Russian planning by pointing to the fact that a plan to substitute one particular word for another failed. Yet upon further consideration of what the government did do to try to change usage, it became clear that all the government had done was to make a pronouncement without offering incentives for use or sanctions for misusage, without specifying when this usage must be in effect. This is *not* planning, just policy setting. Another example of a lack of planning is the foreign-language requirement in U.S. universities. The language requirement was established without specifying what the skills to be attained were, without considering the student's need for this skill, and without considering social opportunities to use this skill. How could one be expected to relate goals to outcomes? No real planning was carried out.

In evaluating language planning, it should be clear what the goals really are. Is the policy meant to contribute to changes in language usage or is it meant to serve some other, sometimes hidden goals? A case in point is the Irish language situation. For years people have evaluated the attempt to make Irish the language of Ireland as unsuccessful. Indeed, many Irish scholars have told us that it was a failure. But if we look at the situation with a little more care, I think that we can say that the Irish planning might be considered successful. Even though the stated goal was to make Irish a household language, it seems that a major real goal was to achieve Irish liberation and nationalism. This they have done with consummate success. The point is that it is important to distinguish between real and stated goals. Quite often the policy makers mask what their real goals are for quite obvious political reasons. Evaluation of language planning must take this practice into account in assessing success.

In order to make a proper evaluation of the goals and their outcome, I have divided intended aims into three general areas: linguistic aims, semilinguistic aims, and extralinguistic aims.

Under linguistic aims, changes in the language code or usage are directly related to information needs. For example, when standardization is said to achieve greater precision, clarity, understanding, and efficiency in and of itself, one may argue that linguistic aims are being served and have been so identified by policy makers. Or when bilingual education is said to enhance a student's understanding of what is going on in the classroom, one may state that the purpose serves linguistic aims.

Under the rubric of semilinguistic aims are included instances where changes in the language serve not only linguistic aims but also social or political aims. The aims might be related to political control as well as to language benefits. In the most recent Russian decision that ethnic languages be written in Cyrillic rather than in Roman script which they previously had been, it can be seen that there are distinct linguistic advantages because speakers of the ethnic languages will not have to learn two systems. However, the decision clearly has political aims in that since Russian is written in Cyrillic, learning to read through Cyrillic script will facilitate learning to read in Russian rather than in those languages written in Roman script. Another example of semilinguistic aims is the U.S. Bilingual Education Act and the rationale behind its passage. Bilingual education came right on the heels of the civil rights movement and relates as much to demands for sociopolitical and economic rights as it does to concerns for pedagogical improvement.

In some cases, no real language problem exists yet nonlinguistic goals are aided by focusing on language problems. These I call extralinguistic aims. An interesting case turns up in West Africa, where language differences were exaggerated in order to express national differences. Two different spellings were created for the Hausa language in order to emphasize national differences, although no real linguistic needs would seem to be served. A more striking case occurred in Russia for some of its Turkic languages. Stephan Wurm (1960) has documented the practice of deliberately writing orthographic representations of the same sound in different languages in a distinct manner in order to present recognition of strong cultural affinities among some Turkic peoples.

The point of this three-way division is to note that in evaluating language planning it is necessary to be clear about what the goals of the policy makers really were, even though they might not make their goals explicit. Otherwise our conclusions about the success or failure of language planning will be incorrect. In any event, it is important to note that language planning involves many steps and many people and multiple goals. The process of translation of these goals may often distort the original goals of the policy makers.

One final point before looking at language planning and bilingual education: it is important to see language planning within the framework of ongoing sociocultural interaction patterns and needs. If this is not taken into account, the chances for success are predictably quite low. This is because language is more than an instrument to impart referential meaning. Language is a *social activity* which serves to identify the speaker and to place him in a particular relationship with the addressee. In acquiring language, which is done in a social setting, we learn how to communicate our intent, how to effect social control, and how to achieve effectiveness regarding some communicative task. Surely language planning must take account of these functions if its purpose is to change human behavior. It must have the cooperation of the target or client population if the policy is to be effective. Good planning must recognize that language serves important social functions.

An illustration is the Hawaiian setting. In Hawaii, many speakers of Pidgin English are thought not to know Standard English. It has been observed that in fact many of them do know Standard English but are unwilling to demonstrate this knowledge on tests (Day 1974). The point here is that language knowledge is related very directly to feelings of social identity and social mobility. Those individuals who identify more with the local culture and who do not aspire to a more mainland style of culture are the ones who demonstrate little knowledge of Standard English. That is, their behavior is not related so much to efforts to teach them English as to their own social goals. In contrast, the Russians have often been quite successful in their attempts to teach Russian because other planning strategies enhanced the need for Russian. In particular, Russian migration patterns led to intermarriage with the other ethnic groups and to greater use by the other ethnic groups of the Russian language. The planning worked because it went hand in hand with ongoing sociocultural changes. There are many other examples, but the point seems self-evident.

LANGUAGE PLANNING AND BILINGUAL EDUCATION

Let us consider next what light language planning can shed on bilingual education. It should help clarify and make more specific goals, strategies, and outcomes. It seems necessary that those interested in bilingual education should be clear about the goals, settings, values, and attitudes, and the functions of languages involved as well as concerning themselves with the universal strategies for teaching reading and subject matter in mother tongue and in a second language.

A first consideration policy makers should take into account is what the *real* goal of bilingual education is. Bilingual education is usually not merely a pedagogical strategy to improve learning. More often it is connected to other social goals. In a widely reprinted article, Kjolseth (1970) pointed to two divergent goals within bilingual education. On the one hand, there is the pluralistic model which is characterized by the goal of *stable* bilingualism and biculturalism. On the other hand, Kjolseth (1970) described an assimilation model in which bilingualism and biculturalism are seen as a transition to unilingualism and uniculturalism. Kjolseth notes that the latter seems to be the predominant model in the United States. Most of our bilingual-education planning will depend on which model we choose. If the plurilingual model is preferred, bilingual education will be continued throughout the school system. It will be promoted among the major language speakers as well as among those from the minority languages. However, if assimilation is the model we choose, only minority-language members will be "subjected" to bilingual education and only for the minimum amount of time necessary.

Some would question the expenditure of any money for bilingual education even if one holds the assimilation model. A recent article by Stephen Rosenfeld, journalist, in the *Washington Post,* challenges the wisdom of the increase in funds for bilingual education. The article illustrates a common fear that bilingual education will somehow destroy the national unity of the United States. Rosenfeld expressed concern for the validity of using bilingual education to achieve even the assimilation model. He emphasizes his concern by citing Nathan Glazer, a noted scholar of ethnicity, who he says raised the question: "Is the current wave of ethnic feeling which now seems to be sweeping over America—the wave which carried bilingualism into public policy—weakening this common American glue and aggravating ethnic tensions and differences?" Rosenfeld challenges the idea that bilingual education can serve as a means of achieving eventual assimilation.

It seems clear that before deciding on bilingual policy, the policy makers need to be clear that their vision of the country is one that fits with the reality of the country and with the desires of the population. Granted there is a large part of "silent America" that sees the need for a monolithic cultural and linguistic model for common national purposes, does this mean that the glue of the country will come apart if the facts of multilingualism and pluriculturalism are recognized by school policies and if the school policies, where appropriate, allow the child to become acquainted with the reality of his community? That is, if the child lives in a plurilingual community where several languages are spoken in everyday communication, should not the school try to reflect these facts as well as providing education in the language used for shared public purposes? Often there is a lack of congruence between the sociolinguistic realities of the country and bilingual policy goals.[1]

If language policies are to serve both individual and national needs, the policies should try to address the following issues which Herbert Kelman, social psychologist (1971), described: (1) how to establish and facilitate patterns of communication (both internally and internationally) that would enable its socioeconomic institutions to function most effectively and equitably in meeting the needs and interests of the population; and (2) how to assure that different groups within the society, varying in their linguistic repertoires (for either ethnic or social class reasons), have equal access to the system and opportunities to participate in it. It seems that bilingual education can serve an important function by addressing these needs, especially if the planners have their goals more clearly in mind.

Let us now look at how planning strategies raise many questions for consideration. These must be seriously considered before a plan is made. One of the first questions is whether bilingual education is considered a disadvantage or an asset. A prevalent view is that learning through two languages is detrimental to the child and that bilingual education at best ought to be transitional. That is, it is all right to teach the student through two languages but only as long as is necessary. One should discontinue instruction in one as soon as possible.

A dissertation by Ben-Zeev (1972) considered the influence of bilingualism on cognitive development and cognitive strategy. Ben-Zeev studied children between the ages of five and a half and eight and a half who were bilingual in Hebrew and English, in the United States and in Israel. The U.S. bilinguals were the children of Israelis attending the Hebrew Day School. The children all came from educated homes. Ben-Zeev found that bilingualism leads to an increase in cognitive flexibility, even though *initially* there is some vocabulary deficit and some difficulty in forming associations. She predicts that the more lasting characteristic is likely to be a strategy of flexibility. She suggests that bilinguals do seek out the underlying dimensions in the patterns they confront and demonstrate a trait of readiness for reorganization. The bilingual seems to be able to change interpretations freely and experimentally, at least on the perceptual level. Ben-Zeev has used a variety of tests which illustrate more concretely than we have been shown before that being bilingual can have positive intellectual advantages.

Further research is needed to document the particular circumstances under which such cognitive advantages can be expected to accrue to the bilingual. We should note that Ben-Zeev's subjects were middle-class individuals whose parents wanted them to acquire a second language and who inculcated the children with the importance of that second language.

We may conclude that bilingualism per se is not a disadvantage but may in fact encourage certain kinds of cognitive growth and flexibility as the child attempts to attend to the distinct settings he is exposed to.

With the passing of the U.S. Bilingual Education Act, the recent Canadian promotion of more widespread bilingualism, and the decisions of several developing nations regarding the languages of education, there has been a considerable increase in the number of studies on the appropriate relationship between the mother tongue and whatever is designated as the second language. As the studies mount, it seems that confusion mounts as well. There are so many opposing views on the advantages and disadvantages of particular bilingual models that it is not at all clear what the hierarchy of priorities should be.

Two papers have attempted to assess the appropriate balance between the use of native language and a second language in teaching subject matter and language arts: one by Paulston (1973) and another by Engle (1975). Both scholars surveyed the major experiments which tested the effects of different strategies on reading and subject-matter achievement. Both found considerable contradictory evidence, even when comparing the most similar cases.[2] Both these scholars found that there are many complex interrelated variables that affect successful acquisition of reading and second-language skills.

Paulston points out the conflicting results from two widely recognized studies, one by Modiano who worked in Chiapas, Mexico, and another by Lambert, who worked in French Canada. Modiano found conclusive evidence in support of mother-tongue reading; whereas Lambert found that learning to read first in a second language, French, did not handicap native English speakers. The only reasonable conclusion to be drawn from the comparison is that language is not the major causal variable in successful school achievement. Other social factors seem more important.

One of the variables which appears critical in explaining these contradictory linguistic findings is relative social class. If we look at the French-Canadian situation, we see that the demand for instruction through a second language came from a group of middle-class English-speaking parents, living in the French-speaking part of Canada. These parents felt that learning French would enable their children to relate to their peers more effectively. There was no problem with the children's self-image; they came from a highly respected minority within the area. In the case of the Indians in Mexico studied by Modiano, the students who learned through Spanish all came from a socially subordinate group whose self-image was already quite negative. Learning the dominant group's language merely reinforced their negative views of themselves. Social class will also affect the teacher's expectation of student performance. Engle also found much evidence that the teacher's expectations of the student have a significant effect on his learning.

A second variable in considering strategies is the perceived usefulness of learning to read and speak a second language, as well as the opportunities to do so. Engle (1973) notes that Lambert has provided convincing evidence that learning a second language depends in part on the desire to identify with that ethnic group. At the least, learning must relate to a felt need to communicate with another group. Macnamara's work (1966) in Ireland, which showed a loss of skills in problem arithmetic when taught through Irish to native English speakers, may well relate to a misfit between school usage and outside functions. In my own studies in Paraguay (1968) I found that the less need for Spanish one had, the greater the failure rate in monolingual Spanish schools by students whose first language was Guarani. Engle (1973) recommends that before making policy on mother tongue versus second language, we need a description of the functions of the two languages in the broader community.

A third variable that seems quite important is the teachers' preparation for the job they are to do. In Paraguay, I found that in the normal schools no instruction was given in how to teach Spanish as a second language; rather teachers explained the students' failure as due to the students' laziness. The high retention rate among non-Spanish speakers definitely pointed to the need for training in teaching Spanish as a second language. Engle also found that the teacher's effectiveness and training play a tremendous role in the success of a program. She found that this factor is frequently ignored and the teacher's knowledge of the second language is not even assessed.

All the evidence that these scholars have looked at point to the fact that we cannot ask the question: "all other things being equal, should we teach a student through his native language or through a second/foreign language?" It seems that "all other things are never equal" and planners need to take into consideration many more of the social factors such as social identity, social aspirations, opportunity and desire for use, and available resources in both languages when deciding on language policy and planning strategies.

There is no simple answer to this question. In the planning process, knowledge about second-language learning and about the processes of reading and their universal qualities are important, but this information must always be considered within the local setting if the planner is to be effective and if the planners want to identify the best way of teaching through a second language.

In planning strategies, we need to think of the social setting and consider when and where each language is used and by whom. In this way, the school model can reflect more readily natural social interaction patterns. If the child's language is seen as appropriate for many situations with a second language or variety as appropriate for other situations, that is, if the classroom reflects the variety of language situations in which the child finds himself or could be expected to find himself, the acquisition of a second language or variety may not be so onerous; indeed, it may add to the child's repertoire instead of handicapping him. Such a strategy must be consonant with the existing patterns of social interaction and with the role of language in social life. If bilingualism were considered *adaptive* rather than *disadvantageous*, we might find that the plurilingual model might be more popular than it is today.

Khubchandani (1974), a scholar who has observed the plurilingual Indian society for many years, suggests that we should evolve "programs which widen the students' linguistic experience by *progressive differentiation* from local speech to supra-dialectal varieties, culminating in a sophisticated grasp of standard and literary styles for the community's motivated specialists." In other words, he suggests that we proceed from the known to the unknown as we make available to students the variety of speech which is found in most sociolinguistic settings. He suggests that work on languages in schools should correspond to the communication patterns among different speech communities prevailing in the region.

Thus far, our discussion has focused on the goals and strategies of bilingual education. One of the things which the planning model does is to place legislative and educational decisions in their proper framework, namely, in the sphere of social interaction and social values where these decisions must be implemented. To be good, planning must be part of other social changes and must relate to ongoing values and attitudes. To be more effective, bilingual education must take account of the many assumptions which sociolinguistic studies have brought to light.

Among these assumptions, the following are of direct importance:

1. Language is a social activity; the act of speaking takes place in a social setting between two or more persons who have particular messages to convey. In order to understand the message, it is not sufficient to pay attention to the grammar of a language. It is important to know a great deal more about communication. We need to know something about the context of the speech act, something about the relationship of the participants, something about the rules for conversing, something about the mood of the speech act, and something about the intentions of the speaker. To be effective, bilingual education must contain and convey something about the importance of the activity for which the language is being used. A bilingual program must convey something about the rules for usage.

2. The participants in a speech community share more than the rules for sentence construction or the same language; they share rules of speaking. In acquiring a language which is done in a social setting, we learn how to communicate our intent, how to identify ourselves, how to effect social control, and how to achieve effectiveness regarding some communicative task. What this means is learning how to be an effective communicator. Therefore, we must be cognizant of the rules for communicative competence and of the functions which people try to accomplish through language. Since there are differences between speakers of the same language, depending on their experience and the area where the language is spoken, and between speakers of different languages, bilingual

teachers cannot assume that if they merely teach the grammar and the lexicon of a language the student will be able to be an effective communicator. Nor should the teacher assume that because they have understood the grammar and lexicon of a child's statement they necessarily understand what the student's message is. In planning strategies for effective bilingual education, it is extremely important that textbook writers, curriculum specialists, and teachers make every effort to help the child become aware of the social variables which operate in every sentence we utter. Insofar as is possible the child should have the opportunity to learn the language in a natural setting so that the rules of speaking come to him/her with their full import.

In summary, we have been considering the contributions language planning can make to improve the implementation of bilingual education. We have pointed to the need to be clearer about the goals which the policy makers and executors have in order to avoid frustration in the implementation of the program. We noted that in examining the goals which planners, policy makers, and executors promote there may be a need to find the appropriate interface between these people. We stressed that planning must be part of a general social trend, that it must not ignore the target's goals and values. We have emphasized the need for planning in bilingual education to reflect the patterns of language use in the community at large. All this means that we shall probably require more information about language use and shall probably need to orient teachers to the significance of respecting that usage. In evaluating bilingual-education planning, it is necessary to see whether the goals set by the legislators and interpreted by a myriad of policy implementors are in fact serving communication needs, semilinguistic needs, or whether they are in fact serving only extralinguistic concerns.

SUMMARY

Thus far, we have looked at language planning as it relates to bilingual education. We have suggested that extensive planning is required if policies are to be adequately implemented. Planning requires that one set down clearly what the goals are, what strategies and means should be used to facilitate implementation, and what the projected outcomes will be. This is usually accomplished by successive stages of approximation as the responsibility is passed on for execution at lower levels. Without proper planning, the best of policies may poorly serve national interests.

Once good planning has been executed ("good" in the sense mentioned above) evaluation becomes easier to do because the necessary elements are all clearly set out and the evaluation can help clarify how successfully the plan has been executed—measuring actual outcome against strategies and against implementation. Good planning should permit us to evaluate whether the planning has been successful. In these days of greater accountability, this surely is something much to be desired. Bilingual education needs to be clear about what its real goals are, which strategies are the most helpful in achieving goals, and which implementation techniques were the most successful.

NOTES

1. However, just as the policy makers for bilingual education should recognize the need for bilingual training when the community is in fact bilingual, equally there should not be an unrealistic attempt to create a bilingualism where none exists unless the citizens are prepared to exert a fair amount of effort. An example of the attempt to promote a language when the need is not there is that of several Portuguese communities in California who long since had lost their skills in Portuguese but who were encouraged to appeal for bilingual monies. Such a school is doomed to failure just because it does not reflect the sociolinguistic patterns of the community or its felt needs.

2. We need not concern ourselves here with those instances of methodological difficulties or with those cases where important variables were not tested in an experiment.

REFERENCES

Chapter I

Abrahams, Roger D. 1972. "The training of the man of words in talking sweet," *Language in Society 1*, 1: 15-29.

Bernstein, Basil 1971-1975. *Class, Codes and Control,* 3 volumes. London: Routledge and Kegan Paul.

Bulu, Paul S. 1975. "The problems of multilingualism in Papua New Guinea." Report of the Sub-Regional Conference on Bilingual Education. Noumea South Pacific Commission. 47-53.

Bustamante, Van Overbeke, Verdoodt (in press) in (B. Spolsky and R. L. Cooper, eds.), *Case Studies in Bilingual Education,* Newbury House.

Cooper, Robert L. 1968. "An elaborated language testing model," *Language Learning,* Special Issue No. 3: 57-73.

Engle, Patricia Lee 1975. "The Use of Vernacular Languages in Education: Language Medium in Early School Years for Minority Language Groups," *Papers in Applied Linguistics,* Bilingual Education Series No. 3. Washington, D. C.: Center for Applied Linguistics.

Fishman, Joshua A. 1971. *Advances in the Sociology of Language.* The Hague: Mouton.

——— 1972a. *The Sociology of Language,* Rowley, Mass.: Newbury House.

——— 1972b. *Language and Nationalism: Two Integrative Essays,* Rowley, Mass.: Newbury House.

——— 1974. *Advances in Language Planning.* The Hague: Mouton.

——— 1976. *Bilingual Education: An International Sociological Perspective.* Rowley, Mass.: Newbury House.

Fishman, Joshua A., and Bernard Spolsky (in press). "The Whorfian Hypothesis in 1975: A Sociolinguistic Re-evaluation." To appear in *Language and Logic in Personality and Society,* edited by Harwood Fisher and Rogelio Diaz-Guerrero. New York: Academic Press.

Holm, Wayne 1972. "Some aspects of Navajo orthography." Unpublished Ph.D. Dissertation. Albuquerque: The Univ. of New Mexico.

Kruis, Sally 1975. "Language planning and Navajo education." Unpublished M.A. Thesis. Albuquerque: The Univ. of New Mexico.

Lambert, Wallace E. 1972. *Language, Psychology, and Culture.* Stanford, Cal.: Stanford Univ. Press.

Lewis, E. Glyn 1972. *Multilingualism in the Soviet Union.* The Hague: Mouton.

––– 1975. "The comparative study of bilingualism in education: a model and a prospectus of research." Paper read at the Bilingual Symposium, Annual Meeting of the Linguistic Society of America, December.

Mackey, William F. 1970. "A typology of bilingual education," *Foreign Language Annals* *3*: 596-608.

––– 1972. *Bilingual Education in a Binational School: A Study of Equal Language Maintenance through Free Alternation,* Rowley, Mass.: Newbury House.

Paulston, Christina Bratt 1974. "Implications of language learning theory for language planning: concerns in bilingual education." *Papers in Applied Linguistics,* Bilingual Education Series No. 1, Washington, D.C.: Center for Applied Linguistics.

Read, John, Bernard Spolsky, and Alice Neundorf (1976). "Socioeconomic implications of bilingual education on the Navajo Reservation." In *The Bilingual Child,* edited by Antonio Simoes, Jr. New York: Academic Press.

Spolsky, Bernard 1970. "Navajo language maintenance: six-year-olds in 1969," *Language Science 13*: 19-24.

––– 1971. "The language barrier to education," *Interdisciplinary Approaches to Language,* edited by G. E. Perren, CILT Reports and Papers, No. 6: 8-17.

––– 1973. "Advances in Navajo education," *Navajo Education 1,* 1: 2-3.

––– 1974. "Speech communities and schools," *TESOL Quarterly 8,* 1: 17-26.

––– 1975. "Prospects for the Survival of the Navajo Language," in *Linguistics and Anthropology: In Honor of C. F. Voegelin,* edited by M. Dale Kinkade, Kenneth L. Hale, and Oswald Werner. Lisse: The Petter de Ridder Press. 597-606.

Spolsky, Bernard, Joanna B. Green, and John Read 1974. "A model for the description, analysis, and perhaps evaluation of bilingual education," *Navajo Reading Study Progress Report, No. 23.*

Spolsky, Bernard, Penny Murphy, Wayne Holm, and Allen Ferrel 1972. "Three functional tests of oral proficiency," *TESOL Quarterly 6,* 3: 221-235.

Swain, Merrill 1974. "French immersion programs across Canada: Research findings," *Canadian Modern Language Review 31*: 117-129.

Chapter II

Adamesteanu, D. 1957. "Nouvelles fouilles à Gela et dans l'arriere pays." *Rev. Archell. 49*: 20-46 and 147-180.

Adams, E. 1940. In *Bulletin of the Ulster Place Names IV.*

Atkinson, B. F. C. 1952. *The Greek Language.* London: Faber and Faber.

Auerbach, E. 1965. *Literary Language and Its Public in Late Antiquity and in the Middle Ages.* London: Methuen.

Augustine 1954. *Confessions.* London: Dent (Everyman).

Aulus Gellius 1917. *Noctes Atticae XVII*: 17. Oxford: Clarendon Press.

Ausonius 1934. *Exhortations to His Grandson. Epistles XXII.* London: Oxford Univ. Press.

Baynes N., and H. Moss (eds.) 1952. *Byzantium–An Introduction.* London: Oxford Univ. Press.

Baron, S. W. 1967. *A Social and Religious History of the Jews,* 2d ed. New York: Columbia Univ. Press and Jewish Publication Society of America.

Baudel, M. 1973. *The Mediterranean and the Mediterranean World in the Age of Phillip II.* London: Collins.

Ben-Sassoon, H. H., and S. Ettinger (eds.) 1971. *Jewish Society through the Ages.* London: Weidenfeld.

Bloch, M. 1961. *Feudal Society* (trans. Manyon). London: Kegan Paul.

Bosch-Gimpera, P. 1940. "Two Celtic Waves in Spain." *Proceedings of the British Academy* 26.

——— 1949. "La formazione dei popoli Spagna." *Rivista di studi classici II:* 97-129.

Boardman, J. 1964. *The Greeks Overseas.* Middlesex: Pelican Books.

Bolgar, R. R. 1954. *The Classical World and Its Beneficiaries.* London: Cambridge Univ. Press.

Bozman, A. B. 1960. *Politics and Culture in International History.* Princeton, N.J.: Princeton Univ. Press.

Bryce, J. 1914. *The Ancient Roman Empire and the British Empire in India.* London: Oxford Univ. Press.

Buck, C. D. 1955. *Introduction to the Study of the Greek Dialects.* London: Clarendon Press.

Calder, W. M. 1911. "Corpus Inscriptionum Neo-Phrygiarum." *Journal of Hellenic Studies XXXI:* 160-168.

Carcopino, J. 1950. *Daily Life in Ancient Rome.* London: Routledge.

Cassano, P. V. 1973. "The Substrat Theory in Relation to the Bilingualism of Paraguay." *Anthropological Linguistics XV,* 9: 406-426.

Ceram, C. W. 1955. *The Secret of the Hittites.* New York: Knopf.

Cerny, J. 1971. "Language and Writing." In Harris (ed.), op. cit.

Chadwick, N. K. 1963. "The Celtic Parts of the Population of England." In H. Lewis (ed.), op. cit.

Chaytor, H. J. 1966. *From Script to Print.* London: Sidgwick and Jackson (reprint).

Chilver, C. E. F. 1941. *Cisalpine Gaul.* Oxford: Clarendon Press.

Chrysostom *Hom. Nab. in eccles. Pauli.* Migne. *Patrologiae Cursus Graeca LXIII.*

Cicero (Ed. Kayser) 1869. *Tusculanus.* Berlin: Tauchnitz.

——— 1958-65. *Letters to his Friends VII,* 3 volumes. Oxford: Clarendon Press.

——— 1901-03. *Rhetorica,* 2 volumes. Oxford: Clarendon Press.

Collingwood, R. G. and J. Myres 1931. *Roman Britain and the English Settlements.* London: Oxford Univ. Press.

Cook, J. M. 1961. "Greek Settlements in the Eastern Aegean and Asia Minor." Cambridge: *Cambridge Ancient History II:* XXXVIII. Cambridge: At the University Press.

Curtius, E. R. 1952. *European Literature and the Latin Middle Ages.* New York: Pantheon Books.

Davis, Thomas 1914. "Our National Language." *Selections from His Prose and Poetry.* London: Fisher Unwin.

Diehl, E. 1912. *Inscriptions Latinae Christianae Veteris.* Bonn: Weber.

Dill, F. 1926. *Roman Society in Gaul in the Merovignian Age.* London: Oxford Univ. Press.

Dostoevski, F. 1896. *Polnoe Sobranie sochinenii.* Leningrad: Akademyi Nauk SSSR.

Dunbabin, T. J. 1948. *The Western Greeks—The History of Sicily and South Italy.* Oxford: Clarendon Press.

Dupont-Sommer, E. 1940. *Les Aramaens.* Paris: Presses Universitaires de France.

Dvornik, F. 1949. *The Making of Eastern Europe.* London: Polish Research Centre.

——— 1970. *Byzantine Missions among the Slavs.* New Brunswick, N.J.: Rutgers Univ. Press.

Edwards, J. 1651. Preface to (Edward Fisher) *The Clarity of Divinity.* London: no pub.

Elcock, W. D. 1960. *The Romance Languages.* London: Faber and Faber.

Entwistle, W. J. 1936. *The Spanish Language.* London: Faber and Faber.

Evans, A. J. 1895. *Cretan Pictographs.* London: B. Quaritch.

Ewert, A. 1959. *The French Language.* London: Faber and Faber.

Falc'hun, F. 1968. "Gaulois et Gallo-Roman." *Onoma 13*: 371-378.
Fellman, J. 1973. "Concerning the 'Revival' of the Hebrew Language." *Anthropological Linguistics XV*, 5: 250-257.
Filip, J. 1956. *Keltvoe ve Stredni Europe* (The Celts in Central Europe). Prague: Czechoslovak Academy of Science and Arts.
––– 1960. *Keltska civilisace a jeji dedictivi.* Prague: Czechoslovak Academy of Science and Arts.
Firth 1935. "The Techniques of Semantics." *Transactions of the Philological Society.*
Francisci, P. de 1959. *Primordia Civitatis.* Rome: Studi Classici.
Glotz, G. and R. Cohen 1955. *Histoire Greque.* Vol. I. Paris: Presses Universitaires de France.
Gordon, C. H. 1962. *Before the Bible–The Common Background of Greek and Hebrew Civilisation.* London: Collins.
Gottein, S. O. 1971. "Jewish Society and Institutions under Islam." In Ben-Sassoon, op. cit.
Grenier, A. 1943. *La Gaule Celtique.* Paris: Didier.
Guldescu, S. 1964. *History of Medieval Croatia.* The Hague: Mouton.
Gwynn, A. 1926. *Roman Education from Cicero to Quintilian.* Oxford: Clarendon Press.
Haaroff, Th. 1920. *Schools of Gaul.* Oxford: Clarendon Press.
––– 1938. *Strangers at the Gate.* Oxford: Clarendon Press.
Hall, R. A. 1974. *External History of the Romance Languages.* New York: American Elsevier.
Hammond, N. G. L. 1962. "The End of Mycenean Civilisation and the Dark Age–The Literary Tradition." *Cambridge Ancient History II*: XXXVI. Cambridge: Cambridge Univ. Press.
Harris, J. R. (ed.) 1971. *The Legacy of Egypt.* Oxford: Clarendon Press.
Haussig, H. W. 1971. *A History of Byzantine Civilization* (trans. Hussey). London: Weidenfeld and Nicolson.
Heer, F. 1953. *The Intellectual History of Europe* (trans. Steinberg). London: Weidenfeld and Nicolson.
Hockett, C. F. 1958. *A Course in Modern Linguistics.* New York: Macmillan.
Honnyer, H. 1957. "Some Observations on Bilingualism and Language Shift in Italy from the 6th to the 3rd Centuries B.C." *Word 13*: 415-446.
Horace *Satires I*: x.
Heurgon, J. 1973. *The Rise of Rome* (trans. Willis). London: Batsford.
Isidore 1911. *Etymologus XI.* Oxford: Clarendon Press.
Jackson, K. 1953. *Language and History in Early Britain.* Edinburgh: Edinburgh Univ. Press.
Jakobson, R. 1969. *Selected Writings.* Vol. I: 144, 201. The Hague: Mouton.
James, J. C. 1920. *The Languages of Palestine and Adjacent Regions.* Edinburgh: Edinburgh Univ. Press.
Jensen, H. 1970. *Sign, Symbol and Script,* 3d Ed. London: Allen & Unwin.
Jerome 1929. *Epist. ad Galat.* Oxford: Clarendon Press.
Jones, A. H. M. 1937. *The Cities of the Eastern Province.* Oxford: Clarendon Press.
––– 1956. "Slavery in the Ancient Worlds." *Economic History Review 6.*
––– 1960a. *The Greek City.* Oxford: Clarendon Press.
––– 1960b. *The Later Roman Empire.* 3 volumes. Oxford: Blackwell.
Jungeman, F. H. 1959. "Structuralism in History." *Word XV*, 3: 460-475.
Keller, W. 1971. *Diaspora–The Post Biblical History of the Jews* (trans. Winston). London: Pitman.
Kluckhohn, C. 1954. "Culture and Behaviour" in (Lindzey, G., ed.) *Handbook of Social Psychology.* Cambridge: Addison-Wesley.
––– 1962. *Culture and Behavior.* New York: The Free Press.
Kramer, S. N. 1949. "Schooldays, a Sumerian Composition Relating to the Education of a Scribe," *JAOS 69*: 199-215.
Levy, P. 1950. *La Langue Allemande en France.* Paris: Didier.
Lewis, B. 1961. *The Emergence of Modern Turkey.* London: Oxford Univ. Press.

Lewis, H. (ed.) 1963. *Angles and Britons*. Cardiff: Univ. of Wales Press.

Lewis, E. Glyn 1972a. "Migration and Language in the USSR." *International Migration Review 5*: 147-159 and in (J. A. Fishman, ed.) *Advances in the Sociology of Language II*. The Hague: Mouton.

——— 1972b. *Multilingualism in the Soviet Union: Language Policy and Its Implementation*. The Hague: Mouton.

L'Isle, Williams *n.d. Divers Ancient Monuments in the Ancient Tongue*. London, no publisher.

Liversidge, Joan 1961. *Britain in the Roman Empire*. London: Cape.

Magie, O. 1950. *Roman Rule in Asia Minor–To the End of the Third Century after Christ*. Princeton, N.J.: Princeton Univ. Press.

Malmberg, B. 1961. "Linguistique Ibérique et Ibéro-Romane," *Studia Linguistica XV*, 2: 57-113.

Marrou, E. 1956. *A History of Education in Antiquity*. London: Sheed and Ward.

Meillet, A. 1951. *Linguistique Historique et Linguistique Générale II*. Paris: Société de Linguistique de Paris.

Miller, W. 1952. "The Byzantine Inheritance: In Baynes and Moss, op. cit.

Montet, P. 1964. *Eternal Egypt* (trans. Weightman). London: Weidenfeld and Nicolson.

Moscati, S. 1959. *The Semites in Ancient History*. Cardiff: Univ. of Wales Press.

——— 1960. *The Face of the Ancient Orient*. London: Kegan Paul.

——— 1968. *The World of the Phoenicians* (trans. Hamilton). London: Weidenfeld and Nicolson.

Murray, G. 1946. *Greek Studies*. Oxford: Clarendon Press.

Nesborough, U. R. de A. 1964. *The Last Myceneans and Their Successors*. London: Oxford Univ. Press.

Neuman, A. A. 1969. *The Jews in Spain*. New York: Octagon Books.

Obolensky, Dimitri 1971. *The Byzantine Commonwealth: Eastern Europe 500-1453*. London: Weidenfeld and Nicolson.

Oppenheim, A. L. 1972. *Ancient Mesopotamia*. London: Univ. of Chicago Press.

Orr, J. 1953. *Words and Sounds in English and French*. Oxford: Blackwell.

Pallatino, M. 1953. *The Etruscans* (trans. Cremona). London: Collins.

Palmer, D. R. 1954. *The Latin Language*. London: Faber and Faber.

Pirenne, H. 1937. *Mahomet et Charlemagne*. Paris: Librarie Félix Alcan.

Pliny 1904. *Naturalis Historia VI*. Oxford: Clarendon Press.

Polybius 1896. *Opera XXXI*. Oxford: Clarendon Press.

Pope, M. K. 1952. *From Latin to Modern French*. Manchester: Manchester Univ. Press.

Portal, R. 1969. *The Slavs* (trans. Evans). London: Weidenfeld and Nicolson.

Poultney, J. W. 1968. Review of Georgiev 1966. *Language 44*: 334-343.

Preaux, C. 1971. "Graeco-Roman Egypt." In Harris, op. cit.

Pulgram, E. 1959. *The Tongues of Italy*. Cambridge: Harvard Univ. Press.

Quintilian 1935. *Institutio Oratio*. Oxford: Clarendon Press.

Roberts, C. H. 1971. "The Greek Papyri." In Harris, op. cit.

Roberts, G. 1567. *Grammadeg Cymraeg* (Welsh Grammar). Milan: no publisher.

Rostovtzeff, M. 1941. *Social and Economic History of the Hellenistic World*. 3 volumes. Oxford: Clarendon Press.

——— 1959. *Social and Economic History of the Roman Empire*, 3d Ed. London: Oxford Univ. Press.

Roth, C. 1946. *The History of the Jews in Italy*. Philadelphia: Jewish Publication Society of America.

——— 1971. "Jewish Society and the Renaissance." In Ben-Sassoon, op. cit.

Safrai, S. 1971. "Elementary Education in the Talmudic Period." In Ben-Sassoon, op. cit.

Salesbury, J. 1547. *A Dictionary in English and Welsh*. Reprinted by Welsh Cymmrodorion Society, 1877. London.

Samarin, W. J. 1966. "Self Annulling Prestige Factors among the Speakers of Creole Language." In (W. Bright, ed.), *Sociolinguistics*. The Hague: Mouton.
Sapir, E. 1949. *Selected Writings*. Edited by Mandelbaum. Berkeley: Univ. of California Press.
Sarton, G. 1950. *A History of Science–Hellenic Science and Culture in the Last Three Centuries B.C.* 2 volumes. Cambridge: Harvard Univ. Press.
Shaffer, D. 1972. "The Hebrew Revival Myth." *Orbis 27*, 2: 315-326.
Smith, S. 1935. *Cambridge Ancient History III*: II. London: Cambridge Univ. Press.
Sommerfelt, Alf. 1954. *La Langue et La Societé: Caracteres Sociaux d'une Langage de type Archiaique*. Oslo and London: Kegan, Paul and Trench.
Sondages 1963. No. I: 41.
Spitzer, L. 1948. *Essays in Historical Semantics*. London: Blackwell.
Stern, M. 1971. "The Asmonean Revolt." In Ben-Sassoon, op. cit.
Sturtevant, E. H. and E. Hahn 1951. *A Comparative Grammar of the Hittite Language I*. New Haven: Yale Univ. Press, and London: Oxford Univ. Press.
Suetonius. *De Grammaticis*. Ch. 71.
Tarn, W. W. 1938. *The Greeks in Bactria and India*. London: Cambridge Univ. Press.
––– 1948-50. *Alexander the Great*. 2 volumes. London: Cambridge Univ. Press.
Tovar, A. 1954. "Linguistics and Psychology." In (Martinet, A. and U. Weinreich, eds.) *Linguistics Today*. Linguistic Circle of New York.
Toynbee, A. J. 1950. *A Study of History*. 12 volumes. 2d Ed. London: Oxford for Royal Institute for International Affairs.
––– 1953. *The World and the West*. London: Oxford Univ. Press.
Trubetskoy, N. 1927. *K. Problemi russkogo samopoznaniia*. Paris: Sobranie statei.
Twersky, I. 1971. "Aspects of the Society and Cultural History of Provencal Jewry." In Ben-Sassoon, op. cit.
Vasiliev, A. A. 1952. "Byzantium and Islam." In Baynes and Moss, op. cit.
von Humboldt, C. W. 1903-36. *Collected Works*. Edited by Leitzman. Berlin: Behr.
Wagner, M. L. 1909. "Die Sprache der Spanishen Juden." *Rev. de Dialectologie Romane I*: 487-502.
––– 1930. *Caracteres Generales del Judeo-Español de Oriente*. Madrid: Hernando.
Webster, T. B. 1958. *From Mycenae to Rome*. London: Methuen.
Whatmough, J. 1933. *Prae-Italic Dialects of Italy*. 2 volumes. Cambridge: Harvard Univ. Press.
Williams, G. 1967. *The Medieval Church in Wales*. Cardiff and London: Univ. of Wales Press/Oxford Univ. Press.
Woodhead, A. G. 1962. *The Greeks in the West*. London: Thames and Hudson.
Zachrisson, R. E. 1927. *Romans, Kelts and Saxons in Ancient Britain*. Uppsala Skrifter Utgivna av Kungel. Humanavistika Vetenskaps-Samfundet i Uppsala, 24.

Chapter III

Alatis, James E. (ed.) 1970. *Bilingualism and Language Contact: Anthropological, Linguistic, Psychological and Sociological Aspects. Georgetown Monograph Series on Languages and Linguistics, No. 23.* Washington, D.C.: Georgetown University Press.
Andersson, Theodore 1971. "Bilingual Education: The American Experience." *Modern Language Journal 55*: 427-440.
Andersson, Theodore, and Mildred Boyer (eds.) 1971. *Bilingual Schooling in the United States*, 2 volumes. Washington, D.C.: U.S. Government Printing Office.
Andersson, Theodore, and William F. Mackey (eds.). To be published. *Bilingualism in Early Childhood: Papers from a Conference on Child Language, November 1971*. Rowley, Mass.: Newbury House.

Anon. 1971a. *Bilingual Education for American Indians.* Washington, D.C.: Office of Education Programs, U.S. Bureau of Indian Affairs.

Anon. 1971b. *Razon de Ser of the Bilingual School.* Atlanta: Southeastern Educational Laboratory.

Armstrong, Robert G. 1968. "Language Policies and Language Practices in West Africa." In Fishman, Ferguson and Das Gupta (eds.), 1968: 227-236.

Balkan, Lewis 1970. *Les Effets du Bilingiusme Français-Anglais sur les Aptitudes Intellectuelles.* Brussels: AIMAV.

Burns, Donald H. 1968. "Bilingual Education in the Andes." In Fishman, Ferguson and Das Gupta (eds.), 1968: 403-414.

Cohen, Andrew D. 1975. *A Sociolinguistic Approach to Bilingual Education.* Rowley, Mass.: Newbury House.

Davis, Frederick B. 1967. *Philippine Language-Teaching Experiments.* Quezon City, Philippines: Alemar-Phoenix.

Dodson, C. J., Eurwen Price, and Ina Tudno Williams 1968. *Towards Bilingualism: Studies in Language Teaching Methods.* Cardiff: University of Wales Press. (See particularly Part II: Early Bilingualism: an experiment in the early presentation of a second language, pp. 17-77.)

Epstein, Erwin (ed.) 1970. *Politics and Education in Puerto Rico.* Metuchen, N.J.: Scarecrow.

Ferguson, Charles A. "The Role of Arabic in Ethiopia: A Sociolinguistic Perspective." In Alatis (ed.), 1970: 355-370.

Fishman, Joshua A. 1967. "Bilingualism with and without Diglossia; Diglossia with and without Bilingualism." *Journal of Social Issues 23* (2), 29-38.

Fishman, Joshua A., Charles A. Ferguson, and Jyotirindra Das Gupta (eds.) 1968. *Language Problems of Developing Nations.* New York: Wiley.

Fishman, Joshua A., and John Lovas 1970. "Bilingual Education in Sociolinguistic Perspective." *TESOL Quarterly 4*: 215-222.

Fishman, Joshua A., and Vladimir Nahirny 1964. "The Ethnic Group School and Mother Tongue Maintenance in the United States." *Sociology of Education 37*: 306-317.

Gaarder, A. Bruce 1970. "The First Seventy-six Bilingual Education Projects." In Alatis (ed.), 1970: 163-178.

John, Vera P. and Vivian M. Horner 1971. *Early Childhood Bilingual Education.* New York: Modern Language Association of America.

Kazshdan, Hayyim S. 1956. *Fun Kheyder un Shkoles biz Tsisho* (From the Traditional Elementary School and Russified School to Yiddish Secular Nationalist Schools). Mexico City: Kultur un Hilf.

Kelly, L. G. (ed.) 1969. *Description and Measurement of Bilingualism.* Toronto: Univ. of Toronto Press.

Kjolseth, Rolf 1972. "Bilingual Education Programs in the United States: For Assimilation or Pluralism?" In Spolsky (ed.), 1972: 94-121.

Kloss, Heinz 1966. "German-American Language Maintenance Efforts." In Joshua A. Fishman (ed.), 1966: 206-252. *Language Loyalty in the United States.* The Hague: Mouton.

Lambert, Wallace E. and G. Richard Tucker 1972. *Bilingual Education of Children: The St. Lambert Experiment.* Rowley, Mass.: Newbury House.

Lambert, Wallace E., G. Richard Tucker, and Alison d'Anglejan 1973. "Cognitive and Attitudinal Consequences of Bilingual Schooling: The St. Lambert Project Through Grade Five." *Journal of Educational Psychology 65*: 141-159.

Lange, D. L. (ed.) 1971. *Pluralism in Foreign Language Education.* (Britannica Review of Foreign Language Education, Vol. 3.) Chicago: Encyclopaedia Britannica.

Lewis, E. Glyn 1972. *Multilingualism in the Soviet Union.* The Hague: Mouton.

Mackey, William F. 1970. "A Typology of Bilingual Education." *Foreign Language Annals* *3*: 596-608. Also in Joshua A. Fishman (ed.) 1972: 413-432. *Advances in the Sociology of Language II.* The Hague: Mouton.

––– 1972. *Bilingual Education in a Binational School.* Rowley, Mass.: Newbury House.

Macnamara, John 1966. *Bilingualism and Primary Education: A Study of Irish Experience.* Edinburgh: University of Edinburgh Press.

––– 1973. The Generalizability of Studies of Bilingual Education. (Mimeo.) Montreal: McGill University.

Malherbe, E. G. 1946. *The Bilingual School.* London: Longmans.

––– 1966. *Demographic and Socio-Political Forces Determining the Position of English in the South African Republic: English as Mother Tongue.* Johannesburg: The English Academy.

Noss, Richard B. 1967. *Language Policy and Higher Education. (Higher Education and Development in South-East Asia,* Vol. 3, Part 2). Paris: UNESCO and the International Association of Universities.

Pietersen, L. 1969. *De Friezen en Hun Taal.* Drachten, Netherlands: Laverman.

Ramos, Maximo, José V. Aguilar and Bonifacio P. Sibayan 1967. *The Determination and Implementation of Language Policy.* (Philippine Center for Language Study Monograph No. 2.) Quezon City, Philippines: Alemar-Phoenix.

Rojas, Pauline 1966. "The Miami Experience in Bilingual Education." In Carol J. Freidler (ed.), 1966: 2, 43-45. *On Teaching English to Speakers of Other Languages.* Champaign, Ill.: National Council of Teachers of English.

Royal Commission on Bilingualism and Biculturalism 1965. *Preliminary Report*; 1967, *General Introduction, Book I: The Official Languages*; 1968, *Book II: Education.* Ottawa: The Queen's Printer.

Rubin, Joan 1968. "Language and Education in Paraguay." In Fishman, Ferguson and Das Gupta (eds.), 1968: 477-488.

Saville, Muriel R. and Rudolph C. Troike 1971. *A Handbook of Bilingual Education* (Rev. edition). Washington, D.C.: TESOL.

Sibayan, Bonifacio P. 1971. "Language Policy, Language Engineering and Literacy: The Philippines." In *Linguistics in Oceania. (Current Trends in Linguistics,* Vol. 8.) 1974, 1038-1062: The Hague: Mouton.

Special Subcommittee on Bilingual Education (U.S. Senate) 1967. *Bilingual Education: Hearings on S. 428,* 2 volumes. Washington, D.C.: U.S. Government Printing Office.

Spolsky, Bernard (ed.) 1972. *The Language Education of Minority Children.* Rowley, Mass.: Newbury House.

––– 1974. "Speech Communities and Schools." *TESOL Quarterly 8*, 17-26.

Swain, Merrill 1972. *Bilingual Schooling: Some Experiences in Canada and the United States.* Toronto: Ontario Institute for Studies in Education.

Tucker, G. Richard, Fe T. Otanes and Bonifacio P. Sibayan 1970. "An Alternate Days Approach to Bilingual Education." In Alatis (ed.), 1970: 281-299.

Vanek, Anthony L. and Regna Darnell 1971. "Canadian Doukhobar Russian in Grand Forks, B.C.: Some Social Aspects." In Regna Darnell (ed.), 1971: *Linguistic Diversity in Canadian Society.* Edmonton, Canada and Champaign, Ill.: Linguistic Research, Inc.

Weinreich, Uriel 1951. Research Problems in Bilingualism with Special Reference to Switzerland. Unpublished Ph.D. dissertation, Columbia Univ.

Chapter IV

Andersson, Theodore and Mildred Boyer (eds.) 1970. *Bilingual Schooling in the United States.* 2 volumes. Washington, D.C.: U.S. Government Printing Office.

Broadbent, Robert R. 1973. "Some Consequences of Following an Elementary School Curriculum in a Second Language." Unpublished M.A. Thesis, University of California, Los Angeles.

Bruck, Margaret and Sam Rabinovitch 1974. "The Effects of French Immersion Programs on Children with Language Learning Difficulties." Paper delivered at TESOL Convention, Denver, Colorado. March 9, 1974. (Quotes from printed abstract in convention program, p. 124)

Bull, William E. 1955. "The Use of Vernacular Languages in Education." *IJAL 21*: 289-294. (Reprinted in Dell Hymes, *Language in Culture and Society*, 1965: 527-533.)

Burns, Donald H. 1968. "Bilingual Education in the Andes of Perú." In (Joshua A. Fishman, Charles A. Ferguson, and Jyotirinda Das Gupta) *Language Problems of Developing Nations*, New York: Wiley. pp. 403-413.

Campbell, Russell N. 1972. "Bilingual Education in Culver City." *UCLA Workpapers in Teaching English as a Second Language 6* (June 1972): 87-92.

Campbell, Russell N. 1970. "English Curricula for Non-English Speakers." In (J. E. Alatis, ed.) Twenty-first Annual Roundtable: *Bilingualism and Language Contact: Anthropological, Linguistic, Psychological, and Sociological Aspects.* Washington, D.C.: Georgetown University Press. pp. 301-309.

Cathcart, Ruth L. 1972. "Report on a Group of Anglo Children After One Year of Immersion in Instruction in Spanish." Unpublished M.A. Thesis, University of California, Los Angeles.

Cohen, Andrew D. 1974. "The Culver City Spanish Immersion Program: The First Two Years." *Modern Language Journal 58* (March-April 1974): 3-4.

――― 1975. *A Sociolinguistic Approach to Bilingual Education: Experiments in the American Southwest.* Rowley, Mass.: Newbury House.

Cohen, Andrew D., Violet Fier, and Marco A. Flores 1973. "The Culver City Spanish Immersion Program—End of Year 1 and Year 2," *UCLA Workpapers in Teaching English as a Second Language 7* (June 1973): 65-74.

Davis, Frederick B. 1967. *Philippine Language-Teaching Experiments.* Quezon City: Alemar-Phoenix.

Engle, Patricia Lee 1973. "The Use of Vernacular Languages in Education: 1973" (A Literature Review prepared for the Ford Foundation Office of Mexico, Central America and The Caribbean). Instituto de Nutricíon de Centro América y Panamá (December 1973). 84 pp.

Fishman, Joshua A. 1973. "The Sociology of Bilingual Education." Unpublished report, supported by a grant from the Research Section, Division of Foreign Studies, Institute of International Studies, USOE-DHEW (Contract DFC-0-73 0588).

Flores, Marco A. 1973. "An Early Stage in the Acquisition of Spanish Morphology by a Group of English-Speaking Children." Unpublished M.A. Thesis, University of California, Los Angeles.

Gaarder, Bruce 1961. "Report of the Special Subcommittee on Bilingual Education of the Committee on Labor and Public Welfare, U.S. Senate, Ninetieth Congress.

Hymes, Dell 1965. *Language in Culture and Society: A Reader in Linguistics and Anthropology.* New York: Harper & Row.

John, Vera P. and Vivian M. Horner 1971. *Early Childhood Bilingual Education.* New York: The Modern Language Association.

Lambert, Wallace E. and G. Richard Tucker 1972. *Bilingual Education of Children: The St. Lambert Experiment.* Rowley, Mass.: Newbury House.

Lambert, Wallace E., G. Richard Tucker, and Alison d'Anglejan 1973. "Cognitive and Attitudinal Consequences of Bilingual Schooling: The St. Lambert Project Through Grade Five," *Journal of Educational Psychology 65*: 2 (1973): 141-159.

Macnamara, John 1966. *Bilingualism and Primary Education: A Study of Irish Experience.* Edinburgh: University of Edinburgh Press.

Modiano, Nancy 1968. "National or Mother Language in Beginning Reading: A Comparative Study." *Research in the Teaching of English 1*: 2 (Spring 1968): 32-43.

"Pattern Transmission in a Bicultural Community." 1967. Unpublished paper distributed by the Bureau of Intergroup Relations, State Department of Education, Sacramento, California. 8 pp. (ED 014 366)

Pozzi-Escot, Inés 1972. "Report on the Research Carried Out by the Linguistics Development Plan of the National University of San Marcos." Paper presented at Seminar on Bilingual Education, Lima, Perú. January 1972.

Prator, Clifford H. 1967. "Language Policy in the Primary Schools of Kenya." *On Teaching English to Speakers of Other Languages,* Series III. pp. 27-35.

Ramos, Maximo, José V. Aguilar, and Bonifacio P. Sibayan 1967. *The Determination and Implementation of Language Policy.* PCLS Monograph Number 2. Quezon City: Alemar-Phoenix.

Rist, Ray C. 1970. "Student Social Class and Teacher Expectations: The Self-Fulfilling Prophecy in Ghetto Education," *Harvard Educational Review 40*: 3 (August 1970): 411-451.

Rosenthal, Robert and Lenore F. Jacobson 1968. "Teacher Expectations for the Disadvantaged." *Scientific American 218*: 4 (April 1968): 19-23.

Saville, Muriel R. and Rudolph C. Troike 1971. *A Handbook of Bilingual Education.* Washington, D.C.: TESOL.

Teschner, Richard V. 1973. "Differing Approaches to the Study of Bilingual Schooling." *Modern Language Journal 57*: 8 (December 1973): 415-421.

Tucker, G. Richard 1974. "TEFL Research in the Middle East." Paper delivered at TESOL Convention, March 10, 1974. (Printed abstract in convention program, p. 58).

The Use of Vernacular Languages in Education. 1953. Monographs on Fundamental Education— VIII. Paris: UNESCO.

Wright, Lawrence 1973. "The Bilingual Education Movement at the Crossroads." *Phi Delta Kappan 55*: 3 (November 1973): 183-187.

Chapter V

Aellen, C. and W. E. Lambert 1969. "Ethnic Identification and Personality Adjustments of Canadian Adolescents of Mixed English-French Parentage." *Canadian Journal of Behavioral Science 1*: 123-128.

Alatis, J. E. (ed.) 1970. *Monograph Series on Languages and Linguistics.* No. 23. Washington, D.C.: Georgetown University Press.

Anastasi, A. 1968. *Psychological Testing.* 3d Edition. New York: Macmillan.

Anisfeld, M. and W. E. Lambert 1961. "Social and Psychological Variables in Learning Hebrew." *Journal of Abnormal and Social Psychology 63*: 524-529.

Argyle, M. and A. Kendon 1967. "The Experimental Analysis of Social Performance." In (L. Berkowitz, ed.) *Advances in Experimental and Social Psychology.* New York: Academic Press. Vol. 3: 55-98.

Arkwright, T. and A. Viau 1974. "Les Processus d'Association Chez les Bilingues." *Working Papers in Bilingualism* (2): 57-67. Toronto: Ontario Institute for Studies in Education.

Arsenian, Seth 1945. "Bilingualism in the Post-War World." *Psychological Bulletin 42*: 65-85.

Asher, J. and L. Garcia 1969. "The Optimal Age to Learn a Foreign Language." *Modern Language Journal 53*: 336-341.

Asher, J. J. and B. S. Price 1967. "The Learning Strategy of the Total Physical Response: Some Age Differences." *Child Development 38*: 1119-1227.

Bain, B. 1973. "Bilingualism and Cognition: Towards a General Theory." Paper read at Bilingualism Conference, Collège Universitaire Saint-Jean, l'Université de l'Alberta.

Balkan, L. 1970. *Les Effects du Bilinguisme Français-Anglais sur les Aptitudes Intellectuelles.* Bruxelles: Aimav.

Barik, H., M. Swain, and K. McTavish 1974. "Immersion Classes in an English Setting: One Way for Les Anglais to Learn French." *Working Papers in Bilingualism* (2) 38-56. Toronto: Ontario Institute for Studies in Education.

Bayley, N. 1970. "Development of Mental Abilities." In P. H. Mussen, ed. *Carmichael's Manual of Child Psychology.* Toronto: Wiley. pp. 1163-1209.

Belyaev, B. V. 1965. *Ocherki Po Psikhologii Obucheniya Inostrannym Yazykam.* 2d Edition. Moskva: Izdat. Prosveshcheniye. English Language edition 1964: *The Psychology of Teaching Foreign Languages.* New York: Macmillan.

Ben Zeev, S. 1972. The Influence of Bilingualism on Cognitive Development and Cognitive Strategy. Unpublished Ph.D. Dissertation. Chicago: The University of Chicago.

Blom, J. P. and J. J. Gumperz 1972. "Social Meaning in Linguistic Structures: Code Switching in Norway." In (J. J. Gumperz and D. Hymes, eds.) *Directions in Sociolinguistics: The Ethnography of Communication.* New York: Holt, Rinehart and Winston. pp. 407-434.

Bossard, A. 1945. "The Bilingual Individual as a Person." *American Sociological Review* 10: 699-709.

Bourhis, R. Y., H. Giles, and W. E. Lambert 1975. "Social Consequences of Accommodating One's Style of Speech: A Cross National Investigation." *International Journal of the Sociology of Language 6.* 55-72.

Brown, R. and E. H. Lenneberg 1954. "A Study in Language and Cognition." *Journal of Abnormal and Social Psychology 49*: 454-462.

Bruner, J. S. 1962. "Introduction." In (L. S. Vygotsky) *Thought and Language.* Cambridge, Mass.: M.I.T. Press.

Bruner, J. S. and H. Kenny 1966. "On Multiple Ordering." In (J. Bruner, R. Olver and P. Greenfield, eds.) *Studies in Cognitive Growth.* New York: Wiley.

Carmazza, A., G. Yeni-Komshian, and E. Zurif 1974. "Bilingual Switching: The Phonological Level." *Canadian Journal of Psychology 28*. 310-318.

Carroll, J. B. 1956. Summary of Validity Coefficients—Foreign Aptitude Battery. Unpublished manuscript. [Cited in R. Gardner and W. E. Lambert, 1972, *Attitudes and Motivation in Second Language Learning.* Rowley, Mass.: Newbury House.] Cambridge, Mass.: Harvard University.

––– 1963a. "Linguistic Relativity, Contrastive Linguistics and Language Learning." *International Review of Applied Linguistics 1*: 1-20.

––– 1963b. "Research on Teaching Foreign Languages." In (N. L. Gage, ed.) *Handbook of Research on Teaching.* Chicago: Rand McNally. pp. 1060-1100.

Carroll, J. B. and J. B. Casagrande 1958. "The Function of Language Classifications in Behavior." In (E. Maccoby, T. M. Newcomb, and E. L. Hartley, eds.) *Readings in Social Psychology.* 3d Edition. New York: Holt. pp. 18-31.

Cazden, C. B. 1970. "The Situation: A Neglected Source of Social Class Differences in Language Use." *Journal of Social Issues 26*: 35-60.

Cedergren, H. and D. Sankoff 1974. "Variable Rules: Performance as a Statistical Reflection of Competence." *Language 50*: 333-355.

Charlton, M. H. 1964. "Aphasia in Bilingual and Polyglot Patients—A Neurological and Psychological Study." *Journal of Speech and Hearing Disorders 29*: 307-311.

Chlenov, L. G. 1948. "Ob Afazii u Poliglotov." *Izvestiya akademii pedagogicheskikh nauk, RSFSR 15.* [Cited in B. Belyaev, 1965, *Ocherki po psikhologii obucheniya inostrannym yazykam.* (Moskva: Izdat. Prosveshcheniye).]

Chomsky, N. 1959. "A Review of B. F. Skinner's 'Verbal Behavior'." *Language 35*: 26-58.

Christophersen, P. 1973. Second-Language Learning: Myth & Reality. Harmondsworth, Middlesex, England: Penguin Books.

Cohen, S. P., G. R. Tucker, and W. E. Lambert 1967. "The Comparative Skills of Monolinguals and Bilinguals in Perceiving Phoneme Sequences." *Language and Speech 10*: 159-168.

Cummins, J. and M. Gulutsan 1974. Some Effects of Bilingualism on Cognitive Functioning. Unpublished research paper. University of Alberta.

Dalrymple-Alford, E. C. 1967. "Interlingual Transfer of Training." *Psychonomic Science 8*: 167-168.

––– 1968. "Interlingual Interference in a Color-Naming Task." *Psychonomic Science 10*: 215-216.

Dalrymple-Alford, E. C. and A. Aamiry 1969. "Language and Category Clustering in Bilingual Free Recall." *Journal of Verbal Learning and Verbal Behavior 8*: 762-768.

Dalrymple-Alford, E. C. and B. Budayr 1966. "Examination of Some Aspects of the Stroop Color-Word Test." *Perception and Motor Skills 23*: 1211-1214.

D'Anglejan, A. and G. R. Tucker 1973. "Communicating Across Cultures: An Empirical Investigation." *Journal of Cross Cultural Psychology 4*: 122-130.

Darcy, N. T. 1953. "A Review of the Literature on the Effects of Bilingualism upon the Measurement of Intelligence." *Journal of Genetic Psychology 82*: 21-57.

––– 1963. "Bilingualism and the Measurement of Intelligence: Review of a Decade of Research." *The Journal of Genetic Psychology 103*: 259-282.

Davine, M., G. R. Tucker, and W. E. Lambert 1971. "The Perception of Phoneme Sequences by Monolingual and Bilingual Elementary School Children." *Canadian Journal of Behavioural Science 3*: 72-76.

Diebold, R. A. 1968. "The Consequences of Early Bilingualism in Cognitive Development and Personality Formation." In (E. Norbeck, D. Price-Williams and W. M. McCord, eds.) *The Study of Personality: An Interdisciplinary Appraisal.* New York: Holt, Rinehart and Winston. pp. 218-245.

Diller, K. C. 1967. " 'Compound' and 'Coordinate' Bilingualism–A Conceptual Artifact." Paper presented to the Linguistic Society of America, Illinois.

Dillon, R. F., P. D. McCormack, W. M. Petrusic, M. Cook, and L. Lafleur 1973. "Release from Proactive Interference in Compound and Coordinate Bilinguals." *Bulletin of the Psychonomic Society 2*: 293-294.

Dyer, F. 1971. "Color-Naming Interference in Monolinguals and Bilinguals." *Journal of Verbal Learning and Verbal Behavior 10*: 297-302.

Edwards, H. P. and M. C. Casserly 1972. Research and Evaluation of Second Language Programs. Interim Report of the Ottawa Roman Catholic Separate School Board (mimeo).

Ervin, S. 1964. "Language and TAT Content in Bilinguals." *Journal of Abnormal and Social Psychology 68*: 500-507.

Ervin, S. and C. E. Osgood 1954. "Second Language Learning and Bilingualism." *Journal of Abnormal and Social Psychology* (Supplement) *49*: 139-146. [Also in (C. E. Osgood and T. A. Sebeok, eds.) *Psycholinguistics.*] Bloomington: Indiana University Press. pp. 139-146.

Ervin-Tripp, S. 1967. "An Issei Learns English." *Journal of Social Issues 23*: 78-90.

––– 1972. On Sociolinguistic Rules: Alternation and Co-occurrence. In (J. J. Gumperz and D. Hymes, eds.) *Directions in Sociolinguistics: The Ethnography of Communication.* New York: Holt, Rinehart and Winston. pp. 213-250.

Fishman, J. A. 1960. "A Systematization of the Whorfian Hypothesis." *Behavioral Science 5*: 323-339.

––– 1973. *Language and Nationalism: Two Integrative Essays.* Rowley, Mass.: Newbury House.

Fishman, J. A. (ed.) 1968. *Readings in the Sociology of Language.* The Hague: Mouton.

––– 1971. *Advances in the Sociology of Language 1.* The Hague: Mouton.

Fodor, J. 1965. "Could Meaning be an r_m?" *Journal of Verbal Learning and Verbal Behavior* 4: 73-81.

——— 1972. "Some Reflections on L. S. Vygotsky's *Thought and Language.*" *Cognition* 1: 83-96.

Frender, R. and W. E. Lambert 1972. "Speech Style and Scholastic Success: The Tentative Relationships and Possible Implications for Lower Social Class Children." In (R. Shuy, ed.) *Monograph Series on Languages and Linguistics.* No. 25. Washington, D.C.: Georgetown University Press. pp. 237-271.

Gardner, R. C. and W. E. Lambert 1959. "Language Aptitude, Intelligence and Second-Language Acquisition." *Canadian Journal of Psychology 13*: 266-272.

——— 1965. "Language Aptitude, Intelligence and Second Language Achievement." *Journal of Educational Psychology 56*: 191-199.

——— 1972. *Attitudes and Motivation in Second Language Learning.* Rowley, Mass.: Newbury House.

Gardner, R. C. and P. C. Smythe 1974. Second Language Acquisition: A Social Psychological Approach. Final report. Ontario Ministry of Education. London, Ontario: University of Western Ontario. Unpublished manuscript.

Gatbonton, E. 1975. Systematic Variation in Second Language Speech: A Sociolinguistic Study. Unpublished doctoral dissertation. Montreal: McGill University.

Gazzaniga, M. S. 1970. *The Bisected Brain.* New York: Appleton-Century-Crofts.

Genessee, F. 1974. Bilingual Education: Social-Perceptual Consequences. Doctoral dissertation. Montreal: McGill University.

Geschwind, N. 1965. "Disconnexion syndromes in animals and man." *Brain 88*: 237-294.

Giglioli, P. P. (ed.) 1972. *Language in Its Social Context.* Harmondsworth, Middlesex, England: Penguin Books.

Giles, H. 1970. "Evaluative Reactions to Accents." *Educational Review 22*: 211-227.

——— 1971. "Our Reactions to Accent." *New Society.* (October 14): 713-715.

Giles, H. and P. Powesland 1975. *Speech Style and Social Evaluation.* London: Academic Press.

Goffman, E. 1957. "Alienation from Interaction." *Human Relations 10*: 47-60.

——— 1967. *Interaction Ritual.* New York: Doubleday.

Goggin, J. and D. Wickens 1971. "Proactive Interference and Language Change in Short Term Memory." *Journal of Verbal Learning and Verbal Behavior 10*: 453-458.

Grinder, R. E., A. Otomo, and W. Toyota 1961. Comparisons Between 2nd, 3rd, and 4th Grade Children in the Audiolingual Learning of Japanese as a Second Language. Honolulu: University of Hawaii, Psychology Department. Unpublished manuscript. [Cited in J. Carroll 1963, "Research on Teaching Foreign Languages." In (N. L. Gage, ed.) *Handbook of Research on Teaching.* Chicago: Rand McNally. pp. 1060-1100.]

Guiora, A. Z. 1967. "Toward a Systematic Study of Empathy." *Comprehensive Psychiatry 8*: 375-385.

——— 1972. "Construct Validity and Transpositional Research, Toward an Empirical Study of Psychoanalytic Concepts." *Comprehensive Psychiatry 13*: 139-150.

Guiora, A. Z., R. C. Brannon, and C. Y. Dull 1972. "Empathy and Second Language Learning." *Language Learning 22*: 111-130.

Guiora, A. Z., H. L. Lane, and L. A. Bosworth 1968. "An Exploration of Some Personality Variable in Authentic Pronunciation of a Second Language." In (E. Zale, ed.) *Proceedings of the Conference on Language and Learning Behavior.* New York: Appleton-Century-Crofts. pp. 261-265.

Gumperz, J. J. and D. Hymes (eds.) 1972. *Directions in Sociolinguistics: The Ethnography of Communication.* New York: Holt, Rinehart and Winston.

Halliday, M. A. K. 1973. *Explorations in the Functions of Language.* London: Edward Arnold.

Hamers, J. F. 1973. Interdependent and Independent States of the Bilingual's Two Languages. Unpublished Ph.D. dissertation. Montreal: McGill University.

Hamers, J. F. and W. E. Lambert 1972. Bilingual Interdependences on Auditory Perception. *Journal of Verbal Learning and Verbal Behavior 11*: 303-310.

——— 1974. Visual Field and Cerebral Hemisphere in Bilinguals. Unpublished research report. Montreal: McGill University.

Haugen, E. 1956. *Bilingualism in the Americas: A Bibliography and Research Guide.* American Dialect Society. Publication No. 26. University of Alabama Press.

Hécaen, H. and R. Angelergues 1968. *Pathologie du Language, l'Aphasie.* Paris: Libraire Larousse.

Henmon, V. 1934. Recent Developments in the Construction, Evaluation and Use of Tests in the Modern Foreign Languages. [Cited in J. Carroll, 1963, "Research on Teaching Foreign Languages." In (N. L. Gage, ed.) *Handbook of Research on Teaching.* Chicago: Rand McNally. pp. 1060-1100.]

Herman, S. R. 1968. "Explorations in the Social Psychology of Language Choice." In (J. Fishman, ed.) *Readings in the Sociology of Language.* The Hague: Mouton. pp. 492-511.

Hill, J. H. 1970. "Foreign Accents, Language Acquisition and Cerebral Dominance Revisited." *Language Learning 20*: 237-248.

Hoijer, H. (ed.) 1954. *Language in Culture.* Chicago: University of Chicago Press.

Hymes, D. H. 1968. "The Ethnography of Speaking." In (J. A. Fishman, ed.) *Readings in the Sociology of Language.* The Hague: Mouton. pp. 99-138.

——— 1970. "Bilingual Education: Linguistic vs. Sociolinguistic Bases." In (J. Alatis, ed.) *Monograph Series on Languages and Linguistics,* No. 23. Washington, D.C.: Georgetown University Press. pp. 69-76.

——— 1971. On Communicative Competence. Philadelphia: University of Pennsylvania Press. [Reprinted in (J. Pride and J. Holmes, eds.) *Sociolinguistics.* Harmondsworth, Middlesex, England: Penguin Books. pp. 269-293.]

Ianco-Worrall, A. D. 1972. "Bilingualism and Cognitive Development." *Child Development 43*: 1390-1400.

Imedadze, N. V. 1967. "On the Psychological Nature of Child Speech Formation Under Condition of Exposure to Two Languages." *International Journal of Psychology 2*: 129-132.

Jacobs, J. F. and M. L. Pierce 1966. "Bilingualism and Creativity." *Elementary English 43*: 499-503.

Jakobovits, L. A. 1969. "Second Language Learning and Transfer Theory." *Language Learning 19*: 55-86.

——— 1970. *Foreign Language Learning.* Rowley, Mass.: Newbury House.

Jakobovits, L. A. and W. E. Lambert 1961. "Semantic Satiation Among Bilinguals." *Journal of Experimental Psychology 62*: 576-582.

Jensen, A. R. and W. D. Rohwer 1966. "The Stroop Color-Word Test: A Review." *Acta Psychologica 25*: 36-93.

Jespersen, O. 1922. *Language. Its nature, development and origin.* New York: Allen & Unwin.

John, V. 1970. Cognitive Development in the Bilingual Child. In (J. Alatis, ed.) *Monograph Series on Languages and Linguistics.* No. 23. Washington, D.C.: Georgetown University Press. pp. 59-67.

Jones, W. R. 1949. "Attitude Towards Welsh as a Second Language. A preliminary investigation." *British Journal of Educational Psychology 19*: 44-52.

——— 1950. "Attitude Towards Welsh as a Second Language. A further investigation." *British Journal of Educational Psychology 20*: 117-132.

——— 1959. *Bilingualism and Intelligence.* Cardiff: University of Wales Press.

——— 1966. *Bilingualism in Welsh Education.* Cardiff: University of Wales Press.

Jordan, D. 1941. "The Attitude of Central School Pupils to Certain Subjects, and the Correlation Between Attitude and Attainment." *British Journal of Educational Psychology 11*: 28-44.

Kamın, L. 1974. *The Science and Politics of I.Q.* Potomac, Md.: Lawrence Erlbaum Associates, Publishers.

Kelly, L. G. (ed.) 1969. *Description and Measurement of Bilingualism.* Toronto: University of Toronto Press.

Kintsch, W. 1970. "Recognition Memory in Bilingual Subjects." *Journal of Verbal Learning and Verbal Behavior 9*: 405-409.

Kintsch, W. and E. Kintsch 1969. "Interlingual Interference and Memory Processes." *Journal of Verbal Learning and Verbal Behavior 8*: 16-19.

Kohlberg, L., J. Yaeger, and E. Hjertholm 1968. "Private Speech: Four Studies and A Review of Theory." *Child Development 39*: 691-736.

Kolers, P. A. 1963. "Interlingual Word Associations." *Journal of Verbal Learning and Verbal Behavior 2*: 291-300.

――― 1964. "Specificity of a Cognitive Operation." *Journal of Verbal Learning and Verbal Behavior 3*: 244-248.

――― 1965. "Bilingualism and Bicodalism." *Language and Speech 8*: 122-126.

――― 1966a. "Interlingual Facilitation in Short-term Memory." *Journal of Verbal Learning and Verbal Behavior 5*: 314-317.

――― 1966b. "Reading and Talking Bilingually." *American Journal of Psychology 79*: 357-376.

Krashen, S. D. 1973. "Lateralization, Language Learning, and the Critical Period: Some New Evidence." *Language Learning 23*: 63-74.

Labov, W. 1969. "Contraction, Deletion and Inherent Variability of the English Copula." *Language 45*: 715-762.

――― 1970. "The Study of Language in Its Social Context." *Studium Generale 23*: 30-87.

――― 1971. Methodology. In (W. O. Dingwall, ed.) *A Survey of Linguistic Science.* Maryland: University of Maryland. pp. 412-497.

Lambert, W. E. 1955. "Measurement of the Linguistic Dominance of Bilinguals." *Journal of Abnormal and Social Psychology 50*: 197-200.

――― 1967. "A Social Psychology of Bilingualism." *Journal of Social Issues 23*: 91-109.

――― 1974. Culture and Language as Factors in Learning and Education. Paper presented at the annual TESOL meeting in Denver, Colorado.

Lambert, W. E. and S. Fillenbaum 1959. "A Pilot Study of Aphasia Among Bilinguals." *Canadian Journal of Psychology 13*: 28-34.

Lambert, W. E., R. C. Gardner, H. C. Barik, and K. Tunstall 1962. "Attitudinal and Cognitive Aspects of Intensive Study of a Second Language." *Journal of Abnormal and Social Psychology 66*: 358-368.

Lambert, W. E., J. Havelka, and C. Crosby 1958. "The Influence of Language Acquisition Contexts on Bilingualism." *Journal of Abnormal and Social Psychology 56*: 239-244.

Lambert, W. E., R. C. Hodgson, R. C. Gardner, and S. Fillenbaum 1960. "Evaluational Reactions to Spoken Languages." *Journal of Abnormal and Social Psychology 60*: 44-51.

Lambert, W. E., M. Ignatow, and M. Krauthamer 1968. "Bilingual Organization in Free Recall." *Journal of Verbal Learning and Verbal Behavior 7*: 207-214.

Lambert, W. E., M. Just, and N. Segalowitz 1970. "Some Cognitive Consequences of Following the Curricula of the Early School Grades in a Foreign Language." In (J. Alatis, ed.) *Monograph Series on Languages and Linguistics,* No. 23. Washington, D.C.: Georgetown University Press. pp. 229-262.

Lambert, W. E. and O. Klineberg 1967. *Children's Views of Foreign Peoples.* New York: Appleton-Century-Crofts.

Lambert, W. E. and N. Moore 1966. "Word-Association Responses: Comparisons of American and French Monolinguals and Bilinguals." *Journal of Personality and Social Psychology* 3: 313-320.

Lambert, W. E. and C. Rawlings 1969. "Bilingual Processing of Mixed-Language Associative Networks." *Journal of Verbal Learning and Verbal Behavior 8*: 604-609.

Lambert, W. E. and G. R. Tucker 1972. *Bilingual Education of Children*. Rowley, Mass.: Newbury House.

Landry, R. G. 1974. "A Comparison of Second Language Learners and Monolinguals on Divergent Thinking Tasks at the Elementary School Level." *Modern Language Journal 58*: 10-15.

Lantz, D. and V. Stefflre 1964. "Language and Cognition Revisited." *Journal of Abnormal and Social Psychology 69*: 472-481.

Leischner, A. 1948. "Ueber die Aphasie der Mehrsprachigen." *Archiv fur Psychiatrie 180*: 731-775. [Cited in Lambert, W. E. and S. Fillenbaum 1959. "A Pilot Study of Aphasia Among Bilinguals." *Canadian Journal of Psychology 13*: 28-34.]

Lenneberg, E. H. 1967. *Biological Foundations of Language*. New York: Wiley.

Leontiev, A. N. and A. R. Luria 1972. "Some Notes Concerning Dr. Fodor's Reflections on L. S. Vygotsky's *Thought and Language*." *Cognition 1*: 311-316.

Leopold, W. F. 1953-54. "Patterning in Children's Language Learning." *Language Learning 5*: 1-14.

Lindsay, P. H. and D. A. Norman 1972. *Human Information Processing*. New York: Academic Press.

Luria, A. R. 1959. "The Directive Function of Speech in Development and Dissolution, Part 1." *Word 15*: 341-352.

——— 1961. *The Role of Speech in the Regulation of Normal and Abnormal Behavior*. Oxford: Pergamon.

——— 1966. *Higher Cortical Functions in Man*. New York: Basic Books.

——— 1970. *Traumatic Aphasia*. The Hague: Mouton.

Macnamara, J. 1966. *Bilingualism and Primary Education*. Edinburgh: Edinburgh University Press.

——— 1967a. "The Bilingual's Linguistic Performance– A Psychological Overview." *Journal of Social Issues 23*: 58-77.

——— 1967b. "The Effects of Instruction in a Weaker Language." *Journal of Social Issues 23*: 121-135.

——— 1967c. "The Linguistic Independence of Bilinguals." *Journal of Verbal Learning and Verbal Behavior 6*: 729-736.

——— 1970. "Bilingualism and Thought." In (J. Alatis, ed.) *Monograph Series on Languages and Linguistics* No. 23. Washington, D.C.: Georgetown University Press. pp. 25-40.

——— 1972. "The Cognitive Basis of Language Learning in Infants." *Psychological Review 79*: 1-13.

——— 1973. The Cognitive Strategies of Language Learning. In (J. Oller, Jr. and J. Richards, eds.) *Focus on the Learner*. Rowley, Mass.: Newbury House. pp. 57-65.

Macnamara, J., M. Krauthamer, and M. Bolgar 1968. "Language Switching in Bilinguals as a Function of Stimulus and Response Uncertainty." *Journal of Experimental Psychology 78*: 208-215.

Macnamara, J. and S. L. Kushnir 1971. "Linguistic Independence of Bilinguals: The Input Switch." *Journal of Verbal Learning and Verbal Behavior 10*: 480-487.

Miller, S. A., J. Shelton, and J. Flavell 1970. "A Test of Luria's Hypotheses Concerning the Development of Verbal Self-Regulation." *Child Development 41*: 651-665.

Milner, B., C. Branch, and T. Rasmussen 1964. "Observations on Cerebral Dominance." In (A. V. S. De Reuck and M. O. O'Connor, eds.) *Disorders of Language: A CIBA Foundation Symposium*. London: Churchill. pp. 200-214.

Minkowski, M. 1928. "Sur un Cas d'Aphasie Chez un Polyglotte." *Revue Neurologique* *35*: 361-366.

Mittler, P. 1971. *The Study of Twins*. Harmondsworth, Middlesex, England: Penguin Books.

Neufeld, G. G. 1973. "The Bilingual's Lexical Store." *Working Papers in Bilingualism* (1): 35-65.

Nida, E. A. 1956. "Motivation in Second Language Learning." *Language Learning* 7: 11-16.

Nott, C. R. and W. E. Lambert 1968. "Free Recall of Bilinguals." *Journal of Verbal Learning and Verbal Behavior* 7: 1065-1071.

Paivio, A. 1971. *Imagery and Verbal Processes*. New York: Holt, Rinehart, and Winston.

Paradis, M. (in press). "Bilingualism and Aphasia." In (H. A. Whitaker and H. Whitaker, eds.) *Studies in Neurolinguistics*. New York: Academic Press.

Peal, E. and W. E. Lambert 1962. "The Relation of Bilingualism to Intelligence." *Psychological Monographs 76*.

Penfield, W. and L. Roberts 1959. *Speech and Brain Mechanisms*. Princeton: Princeton University Press.

Philips, S. 1970. Acquisition of rules for appropriate speech usage. In (J. Alatis, ed.) *Monograph Series on Languages and Linguistics,* No. 23. Washington, D.C.: Georgetown Univeristy Press. pp. 77-96.

Piaget, J. 1959. *The Language and Thought of the Child.* 3d Edition. London: Routledge and Kegan Paul.

——— 1970. "Piaget's Theory." In (P. H. Mussen, ed.) *Carmichael's Manual of Child Psychology*. New York: Wiley. pp. 703-732.

——— 1971. *Structuralism.* London: Routledge and Kegan Paul.

Pieris, R. 1951. "Bilingualism and Cultural Marginality." *British Journal of Sociology* 2: 328-339.

Pitres, A. 1895. "Etude sur l'aphasie chez les polyglottes." *Revue de médicine 15*: 873-879.

Politzer, R. L. 1965. "Some Reflections on Transfer of Training in Foreign Language Learning." *International Review of Applied Linguistics 3*: 171-177.

——— 1970. "On the Use of Aptitude Variables in Research in Foreign Language Teaching." *International Review of Applied Linguistics 8*: 333-340.

Preston, M. and W. E. Lambert 1969. "Interlingual Interference in a Bilingual Version of the Stroop Color-Word Task." *Journal of Verbal Learning and Verbal Behavior 8*: 295-301.

Pride, J. B. and J. Holmes (eds.) 1972. *Sociolinguistics*. Harmondsworth, Middlesex, England: Penguin Books.

Pritchard, R. A. 1935. "The Relative Popularity of Secondary School Subjects at Various Ages." *British Journal of Educational Psychology 5*: 157-179.

Randhawa, B. S. and S. M. Korpan 1973. "Assessment of Some Significant Affective Variables and the Prediction of Achievement in French." *Canadian Journal of Behavioral Science 5*: 24-33.

Richardson, K. and D. Spears (eds.) 1972. *Race, Culture and Intelligence*. Harmondsworth, Middlesex, England: Penguin Books.

Rubin, J. 1968. "Bilingual Usage in Paraguay." In (J. Fishman, ed.) *Readings in the Sociology of Language*. The Hague: Mouton. pp. 512-530.

Rumelhart, D. E., P. H. Lindsay, and D. A. Norman 1972. "A Process Model for Long Term Memory." In (E. Tulving and W. Donaldson eds.) *Organization of Memory*. New York: Academic Press.

Saegert, J., J. Obermeyer, and S. Kazarian 1973. "Organizational Factors in Free Recall of Bilingually Mixed Lists." *Journal of Experimental Psychology 97*: 397-399.

Saer, D. J., F. Smith, and J. Hughes 1924. *The Bilingual Problem*. Aberystwyth: University College of Wales. [Cited in S. Arsenian, 1945, "Bilingualism in the post-war world." *Psychological Bulletin 42*: 65-86.]

Sander, F. 1934. "Einfluss der Zweisprachigekeit auf die geistige Entwuicklung." *Bericht uber den 5. Kongress fur Heilpadagogik.* Cologne, 1930. [Cited in Weinreich, U. 1953. *Languages in Contact*. New York: Linguistic Circle of New York.]

Sankoff, G. 1972. "Language Use in Multilingual Societies: Some Alternative Approaches." In (J. Pride and J. Holmes, eds.) *Sociolinguistics*. Harmondsworth, Middlesex, England: Penguin Books. pp. 33-51.

——— 1974. "A Quantitative Paradigm for the Study of Communicative Competence." In (R. Bauman and J. Sherzer, eds.) *Explorations in the Ethnography of Speaking*. London: Cambridge University Press. pp. 18-49.

Savignon, S. J. 1972. *Communicative Competence*. Philadelphia: Center for Curriculum Development.

Schubert, J. 1969. "The V.R.B. Apparatus: An Experimental Procedure for the Investigation of the Development of Verbal Regulation of Behavior." *Journal of Genetic Psychology 114*: 237-252.

Schuell, H. and J. J. Jenkins 1959. "The Nature of Language Deficit in Aphasia." *Psychological Review 66*: 45-67.

Scovel, T. 1969. "Foreign Accents, Language Acquisition and Cerebral Dominance." *Language Learning 19*: 245-253.

Segalowitz, N. 1976. "Communicative Incompetence and the Nonfluent Bilingual." *Canadian Journal of Behavioural Science 8*: 122-131.

Segalowitz, N. and W. W. Lambert 1969. "Semantic Generalization in Bilinguals." *Journal of Verbal Learning and Verbal Behavior 8*: 559-566.

Sinclair, H. 1967. *Acquisition du Language et Developpement de la Pensée*. Paris: Dunod.

——— 1969. Developmental Psycholinguistics. In (D. Elkind and J. Flavell, eds.) *Studies in Cognitive Development*. London: Oxford University Press. pp. 315-336.

——— 1971. "Sensorimotor Action Patterns as a Condition of the Acquisition of Syntax." In (R. Huxley and E. Ingram, eds.) *Language Acquisition Models and Methods*. London: Academic Press.

——— 1972. "Some Comments on Fodor's 'Reflections on L. S. Vygotsky's *Thought and Language*'." *Cognition 1*: 317-318.

Soffietti, J. P. 1955. "Bilingualism and Biculturalism." *Journal of Educational Psychology 46*: 222-227.

Sokolov, A. 1969. "Studies of Speech Mechanisms in Thinking." In (M. Cole and I. Maltzman, eds.) *A Handbook of Contemporary Soviet Psychology*. London: Basic Books.

Spoerl, D. T. 1943. "Bilinguality and Emotional Adjustment." *Journal of Abnormal and Social Psychology 38*: 37-57.

Spolsky, B. 1969. "Attitudinal Aspects of Second Language Learning. *Language Learning 19*: 271-285.

Stonequist, E. V. 1937. *The Marginal Man*. New York: Russell & Russell.

Stroop, J. R. 1935. "Studies of Interference in Serial Verbal Reactions." *Journal of Experimental Psychology 18*: 643-661.

Taylor, L. L., J. C. Catford, A. Z. Guiora, and H. L. Lane 1971. "Psychological Variables and Ability to Pronounce a Second Language." *Language and Speech 14*: 146-157.

Taylor, M. 1974. "Speculations on Bilingualism and the Cognitive Network." *Working Papers in Bilingualism* (2): 68-124.

Treisman, A. M. 1964. "Verbal Cues, Language and Meaning in Selective Attention." *American Journal of Psychology 77*: 206-219.

Tucker, G. R. and A. d'Anglejan 1970. "Language Learning Processes." In (D. Lange, ed.) *Britannica Review of Foreign Language Education*. Vol. 3. Chicago: Encyclopaedia Britannica.

Tulving, E. and V. Colotla 1970. "Free Recall of Trilingual Lists." *Cognitive Psychology 1*: 86-98.

Vygotsky, L. S. 1962. *Thought and Language*. Cambridge, Mass.: M.I.T. Press.

Warren, R. M. and R. P. Warren 1966. "A Comparison of Speech Perception in Childhood, Maturity, and Old Age by Means of the Verbal Transformation Effect." *Journal of Verbal Learning and Verbal Behavior 5*: 142-146.

Weinreich, U. 1953. *Languages in Contact.* New York: Linguistic Circle of New York.

––– 1958. "Travels through Semantic Space." *Word 14*: 357-366.

Weinreich, U., W. Labov, and M. Herzog 1968. "Empirical Foundations for a Theory of Language Change." In (W. Lehmann and Y. Malkiel, eds.) *Directions for Historical Linguistics.* Austin: University of Texas Press.

Weisenburg, T. and K. E. McBride 1964. *Aphasia, a Clinical and Psychological Study.* New York: Hafner.

Whitaker, H. A. 1971. "Neurolinguistics." In (W. C. Dingwall, ed.) *A Survey of Linguistic Science.* Maryland: University of Maryland. pp. 136-251.

Whorf, B. 1956. *Language, Thought and Reality.* Cambridge, Mass.: Wiley.

Whyte, W. F. and A. R. Holmberg 1956. "Human Problems of U.S. Enterprise in Latin America." *Human Organization 15*: 1-40.

Wolff, P. H. 1967. "Cognitive Considerations for Psychoanalytical Theory of Language Acquisition." *Psychological Issues 5*: 299-343.

Yeni-Komshian, G. H. and W. E. Lambert 1969. "Concurrent and Consecutive Modes of Learning Two Vocabularies." *Journal of Educational Psychology 60*: 204-215.

Yeni-Komshian, G., D. A. Zubin, and E. Afendras 1968. "A Pilot Study on the Ability of Young Children and Adults to Identify and Reproduce Novel Speech Sounds." In *Annual Report of the Neurocommunications Laboratory of the Johns Hopkins University School of Medicine.* Baltimore, Md. pp. 288-305. [Cited in L. Jakobovits, 1970, *Foreign Language Learning.* Rowley, Mass.: Newbury House.]

Young, R. K. and M. I. Navar 1968. "Retroactive Inhibition with Bilinguals." *Journal of Experimental Psychology 77*: 109-115.

Young, R. K. and J. Saegert 1966. "Transfer with Bilinguals." *Psychonomic Science 6*: 161-162.

Chapter VI

Armstrong, Robert G. 1968. "Language Policies and Language Practices in West Africa." In (J. A. Fishman, C. A. Ferguson, and J. Das Gupta, eds.) *Language Problems of Developing Nations.* New York: Wiley. pp. 227-236.

Barghoorn, Frederick C. 1956. *Soviet Russian Nationalism.* New York: Oxford Univ. Press.

Bull, William E. 1964. "Review of *The Use of Vernacular Languages in Education (UNESCO).*" In (Dell Hymes, ed.) *Language in Culture and Society.* New York: Harper & Row. pp. 527-533.

Chatterji, Suniti K. 1954. "The Language Problem in Indian Education." Calcutta, India: *Bull. of the Ramakrishna Mission Institute of Culture* (January 1954).

Education for Europe: Reports, Proceedings, Recommendations, Europe Day 1959 of the International Union of Local Authorities. Vols. I, II, III. The Hague.

Eicholz, E. S. 1968. "Language Schooling." *The Christian Science Monitor* (Nov. 9, 1968).

Ellis, J., and J. N. Ure 1969. "Language Varieties: Registers." In (A. R. Meatham, ed.) *Encyclopaedia of Linguistics, Information and Control.* Oxford: Pergamon Press. pp. 251-259.

Ferguson, Charles A. 1971. "Contrasting Patterns of Literacy Acquisition in a Multilingual Nation." In (W. Whiteley, ed.) *Language Use and Social Change.* London: International African Institute. pp. 234-253.

––– 1973. "Language Problems of Variation and Repertoire." In *Daedalus* (Summer 1973). pp. 37-46.

Fishman, Joshua A. 1966. *Language Loyalty in the United States.* The Hague: Mouton. p. 10.

Fishman, Joshua A., and Erika Luders 1972. "What Has the Sociology of Language to Say to the Language Teacher?" In (Courtney Cazden, Vera John, and Dell Hymes, eds.) *Functions of Language in the Classroom.* New York: Teachers College Press.

Foster, Philip 1965. *Education and Social Changes in Ghana*. London: Routledge and Kegan Paul.

Gardner, R. C. 1960. "Motivational Variables in Second-Language Acquisition." Unpublished Ph.D. thesis. Montreal: McGill University.

Gay, John, and Michael Cole 1967. *The New Mathematics and an Old Culture: A Study of Learning Among the Kpelle of Liberia*. New York: Holt, Rinehart & Winston.

Graham, C. K. 1971. *The History of Education in Ghana*. London: Frank Cass.

Kilarz, Walter 1952. *Russia and Her Colonies*. New York: Praeger.

Kreisler, Abraham 1960. "Nationality and Language in the USSR, 1959." *Soviet Studies* (April 1960). *No. 4*: 445-451.

——— 1961. "Bilingualism in Soviet Non-Russian Schools." *Elementary School Journal 62* (November 1961). No. 2: 94-99.

Lambert, W. E., and R. C. Gardner 1959. "Motivational Variables in Second-Language Acquisition." *Canadian Journal of Psychology 13*: 266-272.

Lambert, W. E., R. C. Gardner, R. Olten, and K. Tunstoll 1968. "A Study of the Roles of Attitudes and Motivation in Second-Language Learning." In (Joshua A. Fishman, ed.) *Readings in the Sociology of Language*. The Hague: Mouton.

Lambert, W. E., and G. R. Tucker 1972. *The Bilingual Education of Children*. Rowley, Mass.: Newbury House.

Lambert, W. E., A. Yackley, and R. N. Heim 1971. "Child Training Values of English-Canadian and French-Canadian Parents." *Canadian Journal of Behavioral Science 3*: 217-236.

Le Page, R. B. 1964. *The National Language Question*. Oxford University Press. pp. 53-63.

Lewis, E. Glyn 1962. "Foreign and Second Language Teaching in the USSR." In *English Teaching Information Center Occasional Paper No. 1*. London: The British Council.

Macnamara, John 1966. *Bilingualism and Primary Education: A Study of Irish Experience*. University of Edinburgh Press.

Minot, Jacques 1970. *L'Entreprise Education Nationale*. Paris: Armand Colin.

Mumford, W. B., and G. St. J. Orde-Brown 1935. *Africans Seem to be French*. London: Evans Brothers, Ltd.

Ohannessian, Sirarpi 1966a. "Outline Report on the Position and Teaching of English in India." Washington, D.C.: Center for Applied Linguistics (August 1966).

——— 1966b. "A Study of the Problems of English Language Teaching in India: Report and Recommendations." Washington, D.C.: Center for Applied Linguistics (November and December 1966).

Oppenheim, A. Leo 1967. Translator; and Introduction to *Letters from Mesopotamia*. Chicago and London: Univ. of Chicago Press.

Petersen, William 1972. "Ethnic Structure in Western Europe." Paper read at Ethnicity Conference, American Academy of Arts and Sciences, Boston, Mass. Unpublished.

Runeberg, Arne 1971. "Some Observations on Linguistic Patterns in a Bilingual Society." Part 1. Helsinki: *Societas Scientiarum Fennica. Commentationes Humanarum Litterarum 17*: 4.

Spencer, John (ed.) 1963. *Language in Africa*. New York: Cambridge Univ. Press.

UNESCO 1953. *The Use of Vernacular Languages in Education*. Monographs on Fundamental Education: Paris: UNESCO.

Wilkins, Augustus S. 1905. *Roman Education*. New York: Cambridge Univ. Press. pp. 19-20.

Wohl, Paul 1973. "Minority Peoples Nag Russians." *The Christian Science Monitor* (Feb. 7, 1973).

Chapter VII

Birch, Herbert G., and Joan Dye Gussow 1970. *Disadvantaged Children, Health, Nutrition and School Failure.* New York: Harcourt, Brace.

Casso, Henry J. 1973. "Education of Children of the Poor—A Decade Ahead: 'A Chicano Perspective'." Speech delivered at the Invitational Conference on Educating Children of the Poor: 1975-1985, Chicago. April 1973.

Collier, John, Jr. 1969. Speech at Dilcon Boarding School, Dilcon, Ariz. July 1969.

Engle, Patricia Lee 1973. "The Use of the Vernacular Languages in Education: Revisited." A literature review prepared for the Ford Foundation Office of Mexico, Central America, and the Caribbean. University of Illinois at Chicago Circle. May 1973.

Ervin-Tripp, Susan M. 1974. "Is Second Language Learning Like the First?" *TESOL Quarterly 8,* 2: 111-136. June 1974.

Gaarder, A. Bruce 1970. "The First Seventy-Six Bilingual Education Projects." In (James E. Alatis, ed.) *Report of the Twenty-First Annual Round Table Meeting on Linguistics and Language Studies.* Washington, D.C.: Georgetown Univ. Press.

Glazer, Nathan, and Daniel Patrick Moynihan 1963. *Beyond the Melting Pot: The Negroes, Puerto Ricans, Jews, Italians, and Irish of New York City.* Cambridge, Mass.: The M.I.T. Press.

Gould, Stephen Jay 1974. "Racist Arguments and I.Q." *National History 83,* 5: 24-29. May 1974.

Halliday, M. A. K. 1974. *Explorations in the Development of Language.* London: Edward Arnold.

Jensen, Arthur R. 1969. "How Can We Boost IQ and Scholastic Achievement?" *Harvard Educational Review 39,* 1. Winter 1969.

John, Vera P., and Vivian M. Horner 1971. *Early Childhood Bilingual Education.* New York: The Modern Language Association of America.

John, Vera P., Vivian Horner, and Toni V. Berney 1970. "Story Retelling: A Study of Sequential Speech in Young Children." In (Harry Levin and Joanna Williams, eds.) *Basic Studies on Reading.* New York: Basic Books.

Kozol, Jonathan 1972. *Free Schools.* Boston: Bantam Books.

Lavallee, M. 1973. "Piagetian Stages and the Acquisition of a Second Language." Progress Report on a Doctoral Dissertation. March 1973.

Mackey, William F. 1968. "The Description of Bilingualism." In (Joshua A. Fishman, ed.) *Readings in the Sociology of Language.* The Netherlands: Mouton.

Massare, Ernest J. 1973. "Transitional vs. Maintenance Bilingual Education Programs: The Expediency of Compromise." ACTFL Workshop on Bilingual Education, Boston. Nov. 19, 1973.

Mercer, Jane 1971. "Sociocultural Factors in Labeling Mental Retardates." *Peabody Journal of Education 7,* 12: 188-203. April 1971.

Orfield, Gary 1970. "A Study of the Termination Policy." In *The Education of American Indians: The Organization Question.* Prepared for the Subcommittee on Indian Education of the Committee on Labor and Public Welfare of the U.S. Senate, 91st Congress, 1st Session, November 1969, *4:* 673-816.

Riley, George Alfred 1974. *A Sociolinguistic Study of Language Usage in the Territory of Guam.* Dissertation, University of New Mexico.

Seda, Eduardo 1974. "Bilingual Education in a Pluralistic Context." *The Rican, Journal of Contemporary Puerto Rican Thought 1,* 4: 19-27.

Smilansky, M. 1974. *Kibbutz Study.* Hartford, Conn.: Mediax.

Thomas, Alexander, Margaret E. Hertzig, Irving Dryman, and Paulina Fernandez 1972. "Examiner Effect in IQ Testing of Puerto Rican Working-Class Children." In (Stella

Chess and Alexander Thomas, eds.) *Annual Progress in Child Psychiatry and Child Development, 1972.* New York: Brunner/Mazel Publishers.

Williams, Robert L. 1974. "Stimulus/Response: Scientific Racism and IQ–The Silent Mugging of the Black Community." *Psychology Today* 7: 12. May 1974.

Chapter VIII

Andersson, Theodore 1969. *Foreign Languages in the Elementary School: A Struggle Against Mediocrity.* Austin, Tex.: The Univ. of Texas Press.

––– 1971. "Bilingual Education: The American Experience." *The Modern Language Journal* 55: 427-440.

––– 1974. "Bilingual Education and Early Childhood." *Hispania 57,* 77-78.

––– 1975. "Extending Bilingual Education into the Home." *FL Annals 8* (4): 302-305.

Andersson, Theodore, and Mildred Boyer 1970. *Bilingual Schooling in the United States.* 2 volumes. Austin, Tex.: Southwest Educational Development Laboratory.

Anisfeld, Elizabeth Peal 1964. "A Comparison of the Cognitive Functioning of Monolinguals and Bilinguals." Ph.D. Thesis, McGill University.

Bruner, Jerome S. 1961. *The Process of Education.* Cambridge: Harvard Univ. Press.

Cabinet Committee on Opportunities for Spanish Speaking People (1707 H Street N.W., Washington, D.C. 20506) 1973. "Cabinet Committee-Census Bureau Cooperation Results in More Accurate Count of Spanish Speaking Population." *Hoy 2,* 11: 3-4.

Carnegie Corporation of New York 1969. "Whether (and When) Little Children Should Be Helped to Learn." *Carnegie Quarterly 17:* 1ff.

Carroll, John B. 1966. *Introduction to Language, Thought, and Reality: Selected Writings of Benjamin Lee Whorf.* Cambridge, Mass.: The M.I.T. Press.

Cassirer, Ernst 1962. *An Essay on Man.* New Haven and London: Yale Univ. Press.

Christian, Chester C., Jr. Feb. 13, 1974, and Feb. 25, 1974, personal communications.

Chukovsky, Kornei 1966. *From Two to Five.* Translated and edited by Miriam Morton. Foreword by Frances Clarke Sayers. Berkeley and Los Angeles: Univ. of California Press.

Condon, William S., and Louis W. Sander 1974. "Neonate Movement Is Synchronized with Adult Speech: Interactional Participation and Language Acquisition." *Science 183* (4120): Jan. 11, 1974, 99-101.

Darcy, Natalie 1946. "The Effect of Bilingualism upon the Measurement of the Intelligence of Children of Preschool Age." *Journal of Educational Psychology 37:* 21-44.

Doman, Glenn 1964. *How to Teach Your Baby to Read: The Gentle Revolution.* New York: Random House.

––– 1974. *What to Do about Your Brain-Injured Child.* New York: Doubleday.

Doman, Glenn, and Daniel Melcher in press. "How Brain-Injured Children Learn to Read." In (William F. Mackey and Theodore Andersson, eds.) *Bilingualism in Early Childhood: Proceedings of a Conference on Child Language, November 1971.* Rowley, Mass.: Newbury House. In press.

Donoghue, Mildred R. 1969. "Foreign Languages in the Elementary School: Effects and Instructional Arrangements According to Reserach." *ERIC Focus Reports on the Teaching of Foreign Languages,* no. 3. MLA/ACTFL Materials Center, 62 Fifth Avenue, New York, N.Y. 10011.

Ervin-Tripp, Susan M. 1970. "Structure and Process in Language Acquisition." In (James E. Alatis, ed.) *Report of the Twenty-First Annual Round Table Meeting on Linguistics and Language Studies.* Washington, D.C.: Georgetown Univ. Press. pp. 313-344.

Ervin-Tripp, Susan, M., and Wick R. Miller 1963. "Language Development." In (Harold W. Stevenson et al., eds.) *Child Psychology: The Sixty-Second Yearbook of the National Society for the Study of Education.* Chicago: NSSE. pp. 108-143.

Fantini, Alvino E. 1974. *Language Acquisition of a Bilingual Child: A Sociolinguistic Perspective (to Age Five).* Ph.D. Dissertation. The University of Texas at Austin.

Ferguson, Charles A. 1959. "Diglossia." *Word 15,* 325-340.

Fishman, Joshua A. 1964. "Language Maintenance and Language Shift as a Field of Inquiry." *Linguistics 9,* 32-70.

――― 1965a. "Bilingualism, Intelligence and Language Learning." *The Modern Language Journal 49*: 227-337.

――― 1965b. "The Status and Prospects of Bilingualism in the United States." *The Modern Language Journal 49*: 143-155.

――― 1966a. "The Implications of Bilingualism for Language Teaching and Language Learning." In (Albert Valdman, ed.) *Trends in Language Teaching.* New York: McGraw-Hill. pp. 121-132.

――― 1966b. "Planned Reinforcement of Language Maintenance in the United States: Suggestions for the Conservation of a Neglected National Resource." In (Joshua A. Fishman et al., eds.) *Language Loyalty in the United States.* The Hague: Mouton. pp. 369-391.

――― 1967. "Bilingualism with and without Diglossia; Diglossia with and without Bilingualism." *The Journal of Social Issues 23,* 29-38.

――― 1968. "Sociolinguistic Perspective on the Study of Bilingualism." *Linguistics 39,* 21-49. Also in (Joshua A. Fishman, Robert L. Cooper, Roxana Ma, et al., eds.) *Bilingualism in the Barrio.* Language Science Monographs No. 7. Bloomington, Ind.: Indiana University, 1971. pp. 557-582.

Fishman, Joshua A., et al. 1966. *Language Loyalty in the United States.* The Hague: Mouton.

Fishman, Joshua A., and John Lovas 1970. "Bilingual Education in Sociolinguistic Perspective." *TESOL Quarterly 4,* 215-222.

Gaarder, A. Bruce 1967a. "Organization of the Bilingual School." *Journal of Social Issues 23,* 110-120.

――― 1967b. "A Prepared Statement." *Bilingual Education.* Hearings before the Special Subcommittee on Bilingual Education of the Committee on Labor and Public Welfare, United States Senate, Ninetieth Congress, First Session, on S. 428. Two parts. Washington, D.C.: U.S. Government Printing Office, I, 46-51.

――― 1969. "Bilingualism." In (Donald Devenish Walsh, ed.) *A Handbook for Teachers of Spanish and Portuguese.* Lexington, Mass.: D.C. Heath and Company, A Division of Raytheon Education Company, 149-172.

――― 1970. "The First Seventy-Six Bilingual Education Projects." In (James E. Alatis, ed.) *Report of the Twenty-First Annual Round Table Meeting on Linguistics and Language Studies.* Washington, D.C.: Georgetown Univ. Press. pp. 163-178.

Gaarder, A. Bruce (Chairman, Working Committee II), Joshua A. Fishman, Wallace E. Lambert, Elizabeth Anisfeld, Gerard J. Brault, Pauline M. Rojas, Louis L. Curcio, and Norman D. Kurland 1965. "The Challenge of Bilingualism." In (G. Reginald Bishop, Jr., ed.) *Foreign Language Teaching: Challenges to the Profession.* Report of the Working Committees, Northeast Conference on the Teaching of Foreign Languages. New York: The Modern Language Association Materials Center, 62 Fifth Avenue, New York, N.Y. 10011. 54-101.

Geffert, Hannah N., Robert J. Harper II, Salvador Sarmiento, and Daniel M. Schember 1975. *The Current Status of U.S. Bilingual Education Legislation.* Arlington, Va.: Center for Applied Linguistics.

Glazer, Nathan, and Daniel Patrick Moynihan 1963. *Beyond the Melting Pot: The Negroes, Puerto Ricans, Jews, Indians, and Irish of New York City.* Cambridge, Mass.: Harvard Univ. Press.

Gumperz, John J. 1962. "Types of Linguistic Communities." *Anthropological Linguistics* 4: 28-40.

――― 1964. "Linguistics and Social Interaction in Two Communities." In (John J. Gumperz and Dell Hymes, eds.) *The Ethnography of Communication.* Washington, D.C.: American Anthropological Association. 137-153.

Hall, Edward T. 1961. *The Silent Language.* Greenwich, Conn.: Fawcett Publications, Inc.

――― 1966. *The Hidden Dimension.* Garden City, N.Y.: Doubleday.

Haugen, Einar 1956. *Bilingualism in the Americas: A Bibliography and Research Guide.* University, Ala.: The Univ. of Alabama Press. Reprinted in 1964 and 1968.

――― 1973. "Bilingualism, Language Contact, and Immigrant Languages in the United States: A Research Report 1956-70." In (Thomas A. Sebeok, ed.) *Current Trends in Linguistics,* vol. 10, *Linguistics in North America.* The Hague: Mouton. pp. 505-591.

Hughes, Felicity 1971. *Reading and Writing before School.* New York: St. Martin's Press, Inc.

Hunt, J. McV. 1961. *Intelligence and Experience.* New York: The Ronald Press.

Hutchison, Bruce 1965. *Mr. Prime Minister, 1867-1964.* New York: Harcourt, Brace.

Hymes, Dell H. 1962. "The Ethnography of Speaking." *Anthropology and Human Behavior.* Washington, D.C.: The Anthropological Society of Washington. pp. 15-53.

――― 1964a. "Introduction: Toward Ethnographies of Communication." In (John Gumperz and Dell Hymes, eds.) *The Ethnography of Communication.* Washington, D.C.: American Anthropological Association. pp. 1-34.

――― 1964b. *Language in Culture and Society: A Reader in Linguistics and Anthropology.* New York: Harper & Row.

――― 1966. "Two Types of Linguistic Relativity." In (William Bright, ed.) *Sociolinguistics.* The Hague: Mouton. pp. 114-165.

――― 1967a. "Models of the Interaction of Language and Social Setting." *The Journal of Social Issues 23*: 8-28.

――― 1967b. *Studies in Southwestern Ethnolinguistics.* The Hague: Mouton.

――― 1974. "Sociolinguistics and the Ethnography of Speaking." In (Ben G. Blount, ed.) *Language, Culture, and Society: A Book of Readings.* Cambridge, Mass.: Winthrop Publishers.

Johnson, G. B. 1953. "Bilingualism as Measured by a Reaction-Time Technique and the Relationship between a Language and a Non-Language Intelligence Quotient." *Journal of Genetic Psychology 82*: 3-9.

Jones, William Richard 1960. "A Critical Study of Bilingualism and Non-Verbal Intelligence." *British Journal of Educational Psychology 30*: 71-76.

――― 1966. *Bilingualism in Welsh Education.* Cardiff, Wales: University of Wales Press.

Kjolseth, Rolf 1970. "Bilingual Education Programs in the United States: For Assimilation or Pluralism?" *Transactions* of the Seventh World Congress of Sociology, held in Varna, Bulgaria, Sept. 14-19, 1970. Also in (Bernard Spolsky, ed.) *The Language Education of Minority Children.* Rowley, Mass.: Newbury House. 1972. pp. 94-121.

Kloss, Heinz 1966. "Types of Multilingual Communities: A Discussion of Ten Variables." *Sociological Inquiry 36*: 135-145.

Labov, William 1966. *The Social Stratification of English in New York City.* Washington, D.C.: The Center for Applied Linguistics.

LaCrosse, E. R., P. C. Lee, Frances Litman, D. M. Ogilvie, Susan Stodalsky, and B. L. White 1970. "The First Six Years of Life: A Report on Current Research and Educational Practice." *Genetic Psychology Monographs 82*: 161-266.

Lambert, Wallace E., and Richard Tucker 1972. *Bilingual Education of Children: The St. Lambert Experiment.* Rowley, Mass.: Newbury House.

Lange, Sven, and Kenneth Larsson 1973. *Syntactical Development of a Swedish Girl Embla, between 20 and 42 Months of Age.* Part 1, Age 20-25 Months. Report no. 1. Stockholm: Stockholms Univ. Institutionen för Nordiska Sprak.

Lenneberg, Eric H. 1967. *Biological Foundations of Language.* With appendices by Noam Chomsky and Otto Marx. New York: Wiley.

Leopold, Werner F. 1939-1949. *Speech Development of a Bilingual Child,* 4 volumes. Evanston, Ill.: Northwestern Univ. Press.

Lerea, L., and S. M. Kohut 1961. "A Comparative Study of Monolinguals and Bilinguals in a Verbal Task Performance." *Journal of Clinical Psychology 27:* 49-52.

Levinson, B. M. 1959. "A Comparison of the Performance of Bilingual and Monolingual Native Born Jewish Preschool Children of Traditional Parentage on Four Intelligence Tests." *Journal of Clinical Psychology 15:* 74-76.

Lundborg, Louis B. 1974. *Future without Shock.* New York: W. W. Norton, Inc.

McCarthy, Dorothea 1954. "Language Development in Children." In (Leonard Carmichael, ed.) *Manual of Child Psychology,* 2d ed. New York: Wiley. pp. 492-630.

Mackey, William F. 1962. "The Description of Bilingualism." *Canadian Journal of Linguistics 7:* 84-85.

––– 1968. "The Description of Bilingualism." In (Joshua A. Fishman, ed.) *Readings in the Sociology of Language.* The Hague, Paris: Mouton. pp. 554 584.

––– 1970a. "A Typology of Bilingual Education." In Andersson and Boyer, *Bilingual Schooling in the United States,* vol. 2, appendix E, 63-82.

–– 1970b. "A Typology of Bilingual Education." *Foreign Language Annals 3:* 596-608.

––– 1972. *Bilingual Education in a Binational School: A Study of Equal Language Maintenance through Free Alternation.* Foreword by Joshua A. Fishman (Newbury House Series: Studies in Bilingual Education). Rowley, Mass.: Newbury House.

Mackey, William F. and Theodore Andersson (eds.) in press. *Bilingualism in Early Childhood: Proceedings of a Conference on Child Language, November 1971.* Rowley, Mass.: Newbury House.

Macnamara, John 1966. *Bilingualism and Primary Education.* Edinburgh: Edinburgh Univ. Press.

––– 1967a. "Bilingualism in the Modern World." *The Journal of Social Issues 23:* 1-7.

––– 1967b. "The Bilingual's Linguistic Performance–A Psychological Overview." *The Journal of Social Issues 23:* 58-77.

––– 1967c. "The Effects of Instruction in a Weaker Language." *The Journal of Social Issues 23:* 121-135.

––– 1973. "Nurseries, Streets and Classrooms." *The Modern Language Journal 57,* 250-254.

Mazzone, Ernest J. (Director, Bureau of Transitional Bilingual Education, Massachusetts Department of Education) 1973. "Transfer versus Maintenance Bilingual Education Programs: The Expediency of Compromise." A paper presented to the ACTFL Pre-Conference Workshop on Bilingual Education, Boston, Nov. 19, 1973.

The Modern Language Association of America (MLA) 1956. "Childhood and Second Language Learning." *FL Bulletin* 49. August 1956.

Modiano, Nancy 1968. "National or Mother Tongue in Beginning Reading: A Comparative Study." *Research in the Teaching of English 2:* 32-42.

Montessori, Maria 1958. *The Discovery of the Child.* Translated by Mary Johnstone. Reprinted. Adyar, Madras, India: Kalakshetra Publications.

––– 1959a. *Education for a New World,* third impression. Adyar, Madras, India: Kalakshetra Publications.

––– 1959b. *The Secret of Childhood.* Translated and edited by Barbara Carter. New impression. Bombay: Orient Longmans.

Naert, Pierre, Halldór Halldórsson, et al. 1962. "Appel d'un ensemble de professeurs des universités scandinaves en faveur de groupes ethniques et de langues menacées de disparition." *Revue de psychologie des peuples 17,* 355.

Newsweek 1968. "Listening Movements." *Newsweek,* Jan. 29, 1968, p. 48.

Northrop, F. S. C. 1946. *The Meeting of East and West: An Inquiry Concerning World Understanding.* New York: The Macmillan Company.

Osgood, Charles E. 1953. *Method and Theory in Experimental Psychology.* New York: Oxford Univ. Press.

Ostwald, Peter F., and Philip Peltzman 1974. "The Cry of the Human Infant." *Scientific American 230,* 3 (March 1974): 84-90.

Pavlovitch, Milivoïe 1920. *Le langage enfantin: Acquisition du serbe et du français par un enfant serbe.* Paris: Librairie Ancienne Honoré Champion.

Peal, Elizabeth, and Wallace E. Lambert 1962. "The Relation of Bilingualism to Intelligence." *Psychological Monographs, General and Applied 76,* no. 546.

Penfield, Wilder G. 1953. "A Consideration of the Neurophysiological Mechanisms of Speech and Some Educational Consequences." *Proceedings of the American Academy of Arts and Sciences 82:* 5.

――― 1964. "The Uncommitted Cortex: The Child's Changing Brain." *The Atlantic Monthly 214:* 77-81.

Penfield, Wilder G., and Lamar Roberts 1959. *Speech and Brain Mechanisms.* Princeton, N.J.: Princeton Univ. Press.

Piaget, Jean 1948. *Le langage et la pensée chez l'enfant.* Etudes sur la logique de l'enfant, I, 3e ed. revue et augmentée. Neuchâtel, Switzerland; Paris: Delachaux & Niestlé.

――― 1952. *The Origins of Intelligence in Children,* 2d ed. New York: International University Press.

――― 1955. *The Language and Thought of the Child.* Translated by Marjorie Gabain. Preface by Professor E. Claparède. New York: Meridian Books, Inc.

Riles, Wilson, and the California State Board of Education 1971. "Report of the Task Force on Early Childhood Education." Sacramento, Calif., Nov. 26, 1971.

Rinsland, Henry D. 1945. *A Basic Vocabulary of Elementary School Children.* New York: Macmillan.

Ronjat, Jules 1913. *Le développement du langage observé chez un enfant bilingue.* Paris: Librairie Ancienne Honoré Champion.

Rosenthal, Robert, and Lenore Jacobson 1968. *Pygmalion in the Classroom: Teacher Expectation and Pupils' Intellectual Development.* New York: Holt, Rinehart and Winston.

Rūķe-Draviņa, V. 1967. *Mehrsprachigkeit im Vorschulalter.* Lund: Gleerup.

Sapir, Edward 1949. In (David G. Mandelbaum, ed.) *Selected Writings in Language, Culture, and Personality.* Berkeley and Los Angeles: The Univ. of California Press.

Schmidt-Mackey, Ilonka. "Language Strategies of the Bilingual Family." In (William F. Mackey and Theodore Andersson, eds.) *Bilingualism in Early Childhood.* Rowley, Mass.: Newbury House. In press.

Smith, Mary Katherine 1941. "Measurement of the Size of General English Vocabulary through the Elementary Grades and High School." *Genetic Psychology Monographs 24:* 343-344.

Söderbergh, Ragnhild 1971. *Reading in Early Childhood: A Linguistic Study of a Swedish Preschool Child's Gradual Acquisition of Reading Ability.* Stockholm: Almqvist & Wiksell.

――― 1973. *Project Child Language and Project Early Reading: A Theoretical Investigation and Its Practical Application.* Report No. 2. Stockholm: Stockholms Univ. Institutionen för Nordiska Språk.

Spire, André 1949. *Plaisir poétique, plaisir musculaire; essai sur l'évolution des techniques poétiques.* New York: S. F. Vanni.

Spoerl, Dorothy T. 1944. "The Academic and Verbal Adjustment of College-Age Bilingual Students." *Journal of Genetic Psychology 64:* 139-157.

Starr, Wilmarth H. 1955. "Foreign-Language Teaching and Intercultural Understanding." *School and Society 81*, No. 2055.

Stevens, George L., and Reginald C. Orem 1968. *The Case for Early Reading.* With a prologue by R. Buckminster Fuller. St. Louis, Mo.: Warren H. Green, Inc.

Stewart, William A. 1962. "An Outline of Linguistic Typologies for Describing National Multilingualism." In (Frank A. Rice, ed.) *Study of the Role of Second Languages in Asia, Africa, and Latin America.* Washington, D.C.: Center for Applied Linguistics. pp. 15-25.

––– 1968. "An Outline of Linguistic Typologies for Describing National Multilingualism." In (Joshua A. Fishman, ed.) *Readings in the Sociology of Language.* The Hague: Mouton. pp. 531-545.

Texas Education Agency 1971. "A Statewide Design for Bilingual Education: Goals for Bilingual Education for Texas Public Schools." Austin, Tex.: Texas Education Agency.

Texas State Board of Education 1974. "Bilingual Education Policy Description." State Board Policy, No. 3251. *Official Agenda 21.* Austin, Tex.

Tits, Désiré 1948. *Le mécanisme de l'acquisition d'une langue se substituant à la langue maternelle chez une enfant espagnole âgée de six ans.* Bruxelles: Imprimerie Veldman.

Tomb, J. W. 1925. "On the Intuitive Capacity for Children to Understand Spoken Languages." *British Journal of Psychology 16*: 52.

UNESCO 1953. *The Use of Vernacular Languages in Education* (= Monographs on Fundamental Education, 8). Paris: UNESCO.

United Kingdom National Commission for UNESCO 1965. *Bilingualism in Education: Report of an International Seminar, Aberystwyth, Wales.* London: Her Majesty's Stationery Office.

United States Congress. Senate 1967. *Bilingual Education.* Hearings before the Special Subcommittee on Bilingual Education of the Committee on Labor and Public Welfare, United States Senate, Ninetieth Congress, First Session, on S. 428. Two parts. Washington, D.C.: U.S. Government Printing Office.

White, Burton L. 1971. *Human Infants: Experience and Psychological Development.* Englewood Cliffs, N.J.: Prentice-Hall.

White, Burton L., and Jean Carew Watts et al. 1973. *Experience and Environment: Major Influences on the Development of the Young Child.* Vol. 1. Englewood Cliffs, N.J.: Prentice-Hall.

Whorf, Benjamin Lee 1966. *Language, Thought, and Reality: Selected Writings of Benjamin Lee Whorf.* Edited and with an introduction by John B. Carroll. Foreword by Stuart Chase. Cambridge, Mass.: The M.I.T. Press.

Williams, Jac L. 1960. Bilingualism; A Bibliography with Special Reference to Wales. Aberystwyth: University College.

World Congress of Sociology, Seventh 1970. *Contemporary and Future Societies: Prediction and Social Planning; Abstracts. Sociétés contemporaines et sociétés futures: Prévisions et planification sociale; Résumes. (Varna, Bulgaria, Sept. 14-19, 1970) Sofia, Bulgaria:* Bulgarian Organizing Committee.

Zangwill, Israel 1909. *The Melting Pot.* New and rev. ed., 1914. New York: Macmillan.

Chapter IX

Afendras, E. A. and A. Pianarosa 1975. *Child Bilingualism and Second Language Learning: A Descriptive Bibliography.* (= CIRB Publication F-4). Quebec: Les Presses de l'Université Laval.

Andersson, Theodore 1972. "Bilingual Education: The American Experience." In (Merrill Swain, ed.) *Bilingual Schooling: Some Experiences in Canada and the United States*. Toronto: Ontario Institute for Studies in Education. pp. 55-72.

Andersson, Theodore and Mildred Boyer 1970. *Bilingual Schooling in the United States*, 2 volumes. Washington, D.C.: U.S. Government Printing Office.

Arsenian, Seth 1937. *Bilingualism and Mental Development: A Study of the Intelligence and Social Background of 3090 Bilingual Children aged 9-14 in Two Brooklyn Schools, Italian and Jewish*. New York: Teachers College Columbia Univ.

BIE 1928. *Le bilinguisme et l'éducation: travaux de la conférence international de Luxembourg, 1928*. Geneva: Bureau international de l'éducation.

Boelens, Kr. 1976. *Frisian-Dutch Bilingual Primary Schools*. The Hague: Ministry of Education and Science.

Bustamente, Hugo 1973. *Le bilinguisme en Belgique*. Louvain: Univ. Catholique de Louvain.

Chantefort, Pierre 1971. *La diglossie au Québec: limites et tendances actuelles* (Publication B-29). Quebec, Univ. Laval: Centre international de recherches sur le bilinguisme.

Cohen, Andrew 1975. *A Sociolinguistic Approach to Bilingual Education*. Rowley, Mass.: Newbury House.

Cooper, Robert L. 1969. "Two Contextualized Measures of Degree of Bilingualism." *Modern Language Journal 53*: 172-178.

Darcy, N. T. 1953. "A Review of the Literature on the Effects of Bilingualism upon the Measurement of Intelligence." *Journal of Genetic Psychology 82*: 51-87.

——— 1963. "Bilingualism and the Measurement of Intelligence. Review of a Decade of Research." *Journal of Genetic Psychology 103*: 259-282.

Epstein, Izhac 1915. *La pensée et la polyglossie: essai psychologique et didactique*. Paris: Payot.

Ferguson, Charles A. 1970. "The Role of Arabic in Ethiopia: A Sociolinguistic Perspective." In (James E. Alatis, ed.) *Monograph Series on Languages and Linguistics 23* (21st Annual Round Table). Washington, D.C.: Georgetown Univ. School of Languages and Linguistics. pp. 355-370.

Fishman, Joshua A., et al. 1966. *Language Loyalty in the United States: The Maintenance and Perpetuation of Non-English Mother Tongues by American Ethnic and Religious Groups*. The Hague: Mouton.

Fishman, Joshua A., and John Lovas 1970. "Bilingual Education in Sociolinguistic Perspective." *TESOL Quarterly 4*: 215-222.

FMVJ 1973. *Vocation nouvelle et rôle des villes et des régions en matière d'éducation bilingue*. Paris: Fédération mondiale des villes jumelées.

Gaarder, A. Bruce 1970. "The First Seventy-Six Bilingual Education Projects." In (James A. Alatis, ed.) *Monograph Series on Languages and Linguistics 23* (21st Annual Round Table). Washington, D.C.: Georgetown Univ. School of Languages and Linguistics. pp. 163-178.

Gandhi, Mohandas Karamchand 1909. *Hind Swaraj* (Indian Self-Government). Bombay.

Gardner, Robert C., and Wallace E. Lambert 1972. *Attitudes and Motivation in Second-Language Learning*. Rowley, Mass.: Newbury House.

Gulutsan, Metro in press. *Soviet Psychological Research on the Relation of Bilingualism to Mental Development*. Edmonton: Univ. of Alberta.

Haugen, Einar 1966. "Semicommunication: The Language Gap in Scandinavia." *Sociological Inquiry 36*: 280-297. (Reprinted in *The Ecology of Language: Essays by Einar Haugen*, selected and introduced by Anwar S. Dil, Stanford Univ. Press, 1972, pp. 215-236.)

Henns, Wilhelm 1928. "Erziehungsfragen der fremden Minderheiten, insbesondere das Problem der Zweisprachigkeit: Erfahrungen in deutschen Schulen im Ausland." *Le bilinguisme et l'éducation*. Geneva: Bureau international de l'éducation. pp. 69-86.

HMSO 1923. *Imperial Education Conference Report*. Whitehall, May 2, 1911. London: Her Majesty's Stationery Office.

Hughes, John, J. D. Saer, and F. Smith 1924. *The Bilingual Problem*. Wrexham: Hughes & Son.

John, Vera 1970. "Cognitive Development in the Bilingual Child." In (James E. Alatis, ed.) *Monograph Series on Languages and Linguistics 23*, (21st Annual Round Table). Washington, D.C.: Georgetown Univ. School of Languages and Linguistics. pp. 59-68.

Kellaghan, Thomas P. 1959. *A Study of the Verbal Ability of Bilingual Children*. Belfast: Queen's Univ. Thesis.

Kelly, Louis G. (ed.) 1969. *Description and Measurement of Bilingualism: An International Seminar, University of Moncton, June 6-14, 1967*. Toronto: Univ. of Toronto Press, published in association with Canadian National Commission for UNESCO.

Kelly, Louis G. 1969b. *Twenty-Five Centuries of Language Teaching*. Rowley, Mass.: Newbury House.

Khubchandani, L. M. 1967. "Language Planning in Multilingual Communication Networks: Comments on the Education Commission's Recommendations." *Proceedings of the Seminar on Linguistics and Language Planning in India, April 1967*. Poona: Centre of Advanced Study in Linguistics, Deccan College Research Institute.

Kloss, Heinz 1977. *The American Bilingual Tradition*. Rowley, Mass.: Newbury House.

Kloss, Heinz and Grant McConnell 1974. *Linguistic Composition of the Nations of the World. Vol. 1: Central and Western South Asia* (= CIRB Publication E-1). Quebec: Les Presses de l'Université Laval. *Vol. 2: North America* and *Vol. 3: Central and South America* (in press). *The Written Language of the World: A Survey and Analysis of the Degree and Modes of Use. Vol. 1: The Americas* (= CIRB Publication E-10) (in press).

Lambert, Wallace E., and G. Richard Tucker 1972. *Bilingual Education of Children: The St. Lambert Experiment*. Rowley, Mass.: Newbury House.

Lewis, E. Glyn 1965. "Bilingualism—Some Aspects of Its History." *Bilingualism in Education*. London: Her Majesty's Stationery Office. pp. 64-84.

Lobelle, Jan 1972. "Types of Bilingual Education." In (Merrill Swain, ed.) *Bilingual Schooling: Some Experiences in Canada and the United States. A Report on the Bilingual Education Conference, Toronto, March 11-13, 1971*. Toronto: Ontario Institute for Studies in Education. pp. 11-14.

Mackay, Jacques et al. 1961. *L'école laïque*. Montréal: Editions du Jour.

Mackey, William Francis 1952. "Bilingualism and Education." *Pédagogie Orientation* 6: 134-147.

——— 1958. "Bilingualism " *Encyclopaedia Britannica*. (Reprinted 1965 vol. 3, 610-611.)

——— 1962. "The Description of Bilingualism." *Canadian Journal of Linguistics* 7: 51-85. (Reprinted 1968 in (Joshua A. Fishman, ed.) *Readings in the Sociology of Language*. The Hague: Mouton. pp. 554-584.

——— 1965. *Language Teaching Analysis*. London: Longman. (Reprinted 1967. Bloomington: Indiana Univ. Press. New French edition 1972, *Principes de didactique analytique*. Paris: Didier. Revised and edited by Lorne Laforge.)

——— 1966. "The Measurement of Bilingual Behavior." *Canadian Psychologist 7*, 75-92.

——— 1969. "La rentabilité des minilangues." *Cahiers Ferdinand de Saussure 26*, 49-64.

——— 1970a. "A Typology of Bilingual Education." In Andersson and Boyer (1970), Vol. 2, pp. 63-82. (Reprinted in *Foreign Language Annals 3* (1970): 596-608; in Mackey (1972); and in (Joshua A. Fishman, ed.) *Advances in the Sociology of Language*, vol. 2. The Hague: Mouton. 1972.

——— 1970b. "Language Learning, Language Teaching and Language Policy." Foreword to Léon A. Jakobovits, *Foreign Language Learning: A Psycholinguistic Analysis of the Issues*. Rowley, Mass.: Newbury House.

——— 1970c. "Interference, Integration and the Synchronic Fallacy." In (James E. Alatis, ed.) *Monograph Series on Languages and Linguistics 23* (21st Annual Round Table). Washington, D.C.: Georgetown Univ. School of Languages and Linguistics. pp. 195-277.

Mackey, William Francis 1971. *La distance interlinguistique* (= Publication B-32). Quebec, Université Laval: Centre international de recherches sur le bilinguisme.

——— 1972. *Bilingual Education in a Binational School: A Study of Equal Language Maintenance through Free Alternation.* Rowley, Mass.: Newbury House.

——— 1973. *Three Concepts for Geolinguistics.* (= Publication B-42). Quebec: International Center for Research on Bilingualism. Reprinted in Vol. 2 (pp. 167-239) of *Sprachen und Staaten.* Hamburg: Stiftung Europa-Kolleg 1976.

——— 1974. "Les dimensions de la linguistique différentielle." *Le français dans le monde* 103: 25-31.

——— 1974a. "Géolinguistique et scolarisation bilingue." *Etudes de linguistique appliquée* 15: 10-33. Paris: Didier.

——— 1974b. *L'Ecologie éducationnelle du bilinguisme* (= Publication B-46). Quebec, Université Laval: CIRB (Centre international de recherches sur le bilinguisme).

——— 1974c. "Education bilingue et éducation biculturelle." *Collection CMIEB* 2: 1-20 (Paris: Centre mondial d'information sur l'éducation bilingue).

——— 1975. *Langue, dialecte et diglossie littéraire* (= Publication B-54). Québec: Centre international de recherches sur le bilinguisme. (Reprinted in *Diglossie et littérature.* Edited by Henri Giordan and Alain Richard, Bordeaux: Maison des Sciences de l'Homme, 1976, pp. 19-50.)

——— 1976. *Bilinguisme et contact des langues.* Paris: Klincksieck.

——— 1976a. "Polychronometry in Lesson Analysis." *System 4*: 48-68.

——— 1976b. "Las fuerzas lingüísticas y la factibilidad de las políticas del lenguaje." *Revista Mexicana de Sociología 38*: 279-309.

——— 1976c. "Niveaux et fonctions du bilinguisme." *Plurilinguisme et enseignement du français langue maternelle, langue seconde et langue étrangère* (Bulletin de la Fédération internationale des professeurs de français 12 (1975) et 13 (1976) = Actes du troisième congrès mondiale, tome 1) pp. 23-42.

——— 1976d. "Typologie des interventions dans le domaine de l'enseignement." In (J.-G. Savard and R. Vigneault, eds.) *Linguistic Minorities Symposium* (Pré-communications) Quebec: International Center for Research on Bilingualism. pp. 107-125.

——— in press (a). "Cost-Benefit Quantification of Language Teaching Behavior." To appear in *Die Neueren Sprachen.*

——— in press (b). "Identité culturelle, Francophonie et enseignement du français en milieu plurilingue. In (Hans Runte and Albert Valdmans, eds.) *Identité culturelle et Francophonie en Amérique II.* Bloomington: Research Center for the Language Sciences.

——— in press (c). "Prolegomena to Language Policy Analysis." To appear in *Language Problems and Language Planning.*

——— in press (d) *Le bilinguisme canadien: bibliographie analytique et guide du chercheur.* Quebec: Centre international de recherches sur le bilinguisme.

Mackey, W. F., and J. A. Noonan 1951. "An Experiment in Bilingual Education." *English Language Teaching 6*: 125-132.

Mackey, W. F., J.-G. Savard, and P. Ardouin 1971. *Le vocabulaire disponible du français,* 2 volumes. Paris: Didier International.

Mackey, W. F. and Von N. Beebe 1977. *Bilingual Schools for a Bicultural Community: Miami's Adapatation to the Cuban Refugees.* Rowley, Mass.: Newbury House.

Mackey, W. F. and R. Tousignant 1976. *Critical Analysis of Methods and Instruments for Evaluating Progress.* Vol. 2 of *Independent Study of Language Training Programmes in the Public Service* by G. Bibeau, W. F. Mackey, H. P. Edwards, R. LeBlanc, R. Tousignant (see also Vols. 3 and 5). 12 vols. Ottawa: Public Service Commission.

Mackey, W. F. and D. C. Cartwright in press (a). "Geocoding Language Loss from Census Data." To appear in the *Foncier Festschrift* edited by Bonifacio Sibayan, Manila, Philippines. Also in (W. F. Mackey and Jacob Ornstein, eds.) *Sociolinguistic Studies in Language Contact.* Quebec: Laval Univ. Press.

Mackey, W. F. (ed.) 1972. *International Bibliography on Bilingualism* (= CIRB Publication F-3). Quebec: Les Presses de l'Université Laval. (Vol. 2 in press.)

Mackey, W. F., and Theodore Andersson (eds.) in press. *Bilingualism in Early Childhood*. Rowley, Mass.: Newbury House.

Mackey, W. F., and Albert Verdoodt (eds..) 1975. *The Multinational Society*. Rowley, Mass.: Newbury House.

Macnamara, John 1966. *Bilingualism and Primary Education: A Study of Irish Experience*. Edinburgh: The Univ. Press.

——— 1972. "Prospectives on Bilingual Education in Canada." *Canadian Psychologist 13*: 341-349.

——— 1973. "The Generalizability of Results of Studies of Bilingual Education." Paper read at the Conference on Bilingualism in the West, September 1973, Edmonton: Collège St.-Jean of the University of Alberta.

Malherbe, E. G. 1943. *The Bilingual School: A Study of Bilingualism in South Africa*. Johannesburg: Central News Agency for the Bilingual School Association.

Peal, Elizabeth, and W. E. Lambert 1962. "The Relation of Bilingualism to Intelligence." *Psychological Monographs 76*: 1-23.

Pichon, E., and S. Borel-Maisonny 1964. "Begaiement des bilingues." *Le begaiement, sa nature et son traitement*. Paris: Masson. pp. 71-75.

Rabin, Chaim 1976. "Language Treatment in Israel." *Language Planning Newsletter 2* (4): 1-4.

Rubin, Joan 1969. "Evaluation and Language Planning: Some critical comments on the relationship." *Working Papers in Linguistics*. Honolulu: Univ. of Hawaii Department of Linguistics 5: 1-48.

Rūķe-Dravina, Velta 1967. *Mehrsprachigkeit im Vorschulalter*. Lund: Gleerup.

Savard, Jean-Guy 1969. *Analytical Bibliography of Language Tests* (= CIRB Publication F-1)(Vol. 2 in press). Quebec: Les Presses de l'Université Laval.

San Diego 1973. First Annual International Multilingual Multicultural Conference: Proceedings (San Diego, Apr. 1-5, 1973). Austin: Dissemination Center for Bilingual Bicultural Education.

Schmidt-Rohr, Georg 1934. "Stufen der Entfremdung: ein Beitrag zur Frage der Assimilation von Sprachgruppen." *Volksspiegel 1*: 75-82.

Segalowtiz, Norman, and W. E. Lambert 1969. "Semantic Generalization in Bilinguals." *Journal of Verbal Learning and Verbal Behavior 8*: 559-566.

Spolsky, Bernard, Joanna B. Green, and John Read 1974. *A Model for the Description, Analysis and Perhaps Evaluation of Bilingual Education* (= Navajo Reading Study Progress Report 23). Albuquerque: Univ. of New Mexico.

Stewart, William A. 1968. "A Sociolinguistic Typology for Describing National Multilingualism." In (Joshua A. Fishman, ed.) *Readings in the Sociology of Language*. The Hague: Mouton. pp. 531-546.

Thévenin, André 1969. "Accroissement du vocabulaire chez des enfants bilingues." *Le français dans le monde 64*: 18-25.

Troike, Rudolph C. 1968. "Social Dialects and Language Learning: Implications for TESOL." *TESOL Quarterly 2*: 176-180.

Tucker, G. Richard, F. E. Otanes, and B. P. Sibayan 1970. "An Alternate Days Approach to Bilingual Education." In (James E. Alatis ed.) *Monograph Series on Languages and Linguistics 23* (21st Annual Round Table). Washington, D.C.: Georgetown Univ. School of Languages and Linguistics. pp. 281-300.

UNESCO (U.K.) 1965. *Report on an International Seminar on Bilingualism in Education* (Aberystwyth, Wales, Aug. 20-Sept. 2, 1960). London: Her Majesty's Stationery Office.

Valencia, Atilano A. 1972. *Bilingual-Bicultural Education for the Spanish-English Bilingual*. Las Vegas: New Mexico Highlands Univ.

van Overbeke, Maurice 1970. "Entropie et valence de la parole bilingue." *Aspects socio-logiques du plurilinguisme: Actes du premier colloque AIMAV, Bruxelles, Sept. 23-25, 1970.* Paris: Didier.

Vygotsky, Lev S. 1935. *Umstvennoe Razvitie Detei v Protsesse Obucheniia* (Child Mental Development during Education) edited by L. V. Zankov et al. Moscow: Government Educational Publishers, p. 53-73. See also his *Thought and Language.* Translated from the Russian by Eugenia Hanfmann and Gertrude Vacar. Cambridge, Mass.: M.I.T. Press 1962.

Wieczerkowski, Wilhelm 1963. *Bilinguismus in frühen Schulalter: Gruppenprüfungen mit intelligenztests und mit dem Helsingforstest.* (= Commentationes Humanarum Litterarum 33: 2). Helsinki: Societas Scientiarum Fennica.

Winch, Peter 1958. *The Idea of a Social Science.* London: Routledge & Kegan Paul.

Wolff, Hans 1959. "Intelligibility and Inter-Ethnic Attitudes." *Anthropological Linguistics 3*: 34-41.

Chapter X

Ben-Zeev, Sandra 1972. "The Influence of Bilingualism on Cognitive Development and Cognitive Strategy." Unpublished doctoral dissertation. Univ. of Chicago, Comm. on Human Development.

Day, Richard 1974. "Can Standard English Be Taught or What Does It Mean to Know Standard English?" In *Florida FL Reporter, 12,* nos. 1, 2.

Engle, Patricia 1975. "The Use of the Vernacular Languages in Education." *Review of Educational Research 45*: 283-325.

Jernudd, B., and J. Das Gupta 1971. "Towards a Theory of Language Planning." In (J. Rubin and B. Jernudd, eds.) *Can Language Be Planned?* Honolulu: East-West Center, the University Press of Hawaii.

Kelman, Herbert C. 1971. "Language as an Aid and Barrier to Involvement in the National System." In (J. Rubin and B. Jernudd, eds.) *Can Language Be Planned?* The Hague: Mouton.

Khubchandani, Lachman in press. "Multilingual Education in India." In (B. Spolsky and R. Cooper, eds.) *Current Trends in Bilingual Education.*

Kjolseth, R. 1970. Bilingual Education Programs in the United States: For Assimilation or Pluralism? Sociolinguistics Program 7th World Congress of Sociology. Varnar, Bulgaria.

Macnamara, John 1966. *Bilingualism and Primary Education.* Edinburgh: Edinburgh Univ.

Paulston, Christina 1973. "Implications of Language Learning Theory for Language Planning." Unpublished paper presented at the AAAS/CONASYT symposium on "Sociolinguistics and Language Planning."

Rubin, J. 1968. *National Bilingualism in Paraguay.* The Hague: Mouton.

――― 1971. "Evaluation and Language Planning." In (J. Rubin and B. Jernudd, eds.) *Can Language Be Planned?* Honolulu: East-West Center.

Rubin, J., and B. Jernudd 1971. "Introduction: Language Planning as an Element in Modernization." In (J. Rubin and B. Jernudd, eds.) *Can Language Be Planned?* Honolulu: Univ. Press of Hawaii.

Wurm, Stephan 1960. "Comments on the Turkic Peoples of the USSR: The Development of Their Language and Writing," by M. A. Bashkakov. Oxford: Central Asian Research Center.